Silke Schmidt & Ed Galea (Eds.)

BeSeCu

Silke Schmidt & Ed Galea (Eds.)

Behaviour – Security – Culture

BeSeCu

Human behaviour in emergencies and disasters: A cross-cultural investigation

PABST SCIENCE PUBLISHERS
Lengerich · Berlin · Bremen · Miami · Riga
Viernheim · Wien · Zagreb

Bibliographic information published by Die Deutsche Nationalbibliothek
Die Deutsche Nationalbibliothek lists this publication in the Deutsche Nationalbibliografie; detailed bibliographic data is available in the Internet at <http://dnb.ddb.de>.

Acknowledgement

The book was written by the authors of the BeSeCu-group. The project BeSeCu (contract No. 218324) was funded under the European Union Framework programme 7 – Security. The authors acknowledge the collaboration of their project partners: Ernst-Moritz-Arndt University of Greifswald, Germany (Silke Schmidt – project coordinator, Daniela Knuth, Doris Kehl); Hamburg Fire and Emergency Service Academy, Germany (Frank Seidler and Eberhard Diebe); University of Greenwich UK (Ed Galea and Lynn Hulse); Institute of Public Security of Catalonia, Spain (Jordi Sans, Malin Roiha, and Lola Valles); Prague Psychiatric Centre, Czech Republic (Marek Preiss, Marie Sotolarova, and Marketa Holubova); MTO Säkerhet AB (MTO Safety AB), Sweden (Lena Kecklund, Sara Petterson, and Kristin Andrée); Main School of Fire Service, Poland (Jerzy Wolanin and Grzegorz Beltowski); Association of Emergency Ambulance Physicians, Turkey (Zeynep Baskaya Sofuoglu and Turhan Sofuoglu); University of Bologna, Italy (Luca Pietrantoni, Gabriele Prati and Elisa Saccinto); in undertaking this work and in allowing the project findings to be published. Special thanks go to Katharina Hegele and Katja Kallies for intensive work in formatting the book.

Internet: www.pabst-publishers.de · www.pabst-science-publishers.com
E-mail: pabst@pabst-publishers.de

ISBN: 978-3-89967-867-3

Formatting: μ
Cover photo: © Rouven Groß
Printed in Europe by booksfactory.de

Contents

Foreword

It is a great privilege to introduce "BeSeCu: Human Behaviour in Emergencies and Disasters: A Cross-Cultural Investigation", which makes a significant and timely contribution to our knowledge and understanding of human behaviour in a range of emergency events. The value of this work is further enhanced by the number and variety of people contributing to the project and its international perspective – a key consideration in what are increasingly multicultural and fluid communities.

This is a publication that will have a broad appeal and relevance to a range of audiences including academics, design engineers, regulatory bodies, emergency services and other agencies with a professional interest in fire safety and public health.

With a background in psychology, I naturally welcome the project's emphasis on survivor and first responder accounts along with the evacuation trials themselves. Equally, I recognise that there are many other specialist areas within the "fire and emergency" sector each developing its own methods, beliefs and approaches. What makes this project so valuable is that it brings a number of these together.

I feel there is much to be gained from greater collaboration between all the various disciplines and by adopting more mixed method approaches within projects. Indeed, these will be key features of the research that Kent Fire and Rescue Service are embarking upon with the University of Greenwich to look at human behaviour within accidental dwelling fires.

The rarity with which people experience emergencies mean it can be difficult for them to imagine and predict with any confidence what they would actually do during a life-threatening emergency. Consequently, this underscores the value of learning from survivors' real life experiences during such events and in turn designing effective tests based upon this.

Through projects such as BeSeCu we can empirically test, record and understand the strongest influences and behaviours present among those experiencing fires and other emergencies, all of which are unfamiliar situations for most people. It of course requires considerable effort and resources to achieve knowledge on the scale of this project, but the findings have such widespread application that the value and worth are immediately clear.

The focus on understanding cultural factors (both social and fire safety) is of particular interest. It is easy to make assumptions based on general cultural knowledge but appreciating their influence in emergency situations is of great relevance. The ability to use BeSeCu methodologies in future will further aid the ability to increasingly understand this important area. It moves forward our ability to ensure buildings and emergency responses incorporate features which work with general and specific cultural behaviours.

The knowledge obtained from the BeSeCu project means organisations can plan and develop prevention or response initatives with greater confidence and achieve more effective outcomes. They will also be better placed to influence inherent or instinctive human behaviours; rather than try and force desirable, but potentially counter-intuitive, ones during dynamic and unsettling events. Many have tried to "educate" the public without recognising the strength of their behaviours or the potential contribution individuals and groups can make to assisiting the responding bodies. The BeSeCu project will underpin the ability to use current approaches more effectively or, perhaps more importantly, develop new approaches.

As such, I welcome and applaud the contribution that this report makes to our knowledge and understanding of such an important topic. The authors, contributors and participants should be congratulated for providing us such rich material. It is now for us all to ensure we not only read this but fully consider and develop its findings together in our respective fields of work.

Ann Millington
Chief Executive
Kent Fire and Rescue Service

Introductory Notes

In recent years, we have witnessed a range of serious emergencies and disasters across Europe and the world, including terrorist incidents such as the World Trade Center attack in New York on 11 September 2001, the Madrid train bombings in March 2004, the London Underground and bus bombings of July 2005, the Turkish bombing campaign of August 2006, earthquakes in Turkey and Japan and devastating fires including the Dusseldorf airport fire of 1996, the Rhode Island disco fire of 2003, the Buenos Aires nightclub fire of 2005, the Paris hotel fire of 2005 and the Kamyshevatskaya (Russia) Nursing Home fire of 2007. Did culture play a role in determining how the people in these events responded? More significantly, could a better understanding of cultural responses to emergencies and disasters assist in developing better procedures for first responders, building designers and emergency management systems?

This book has evolved over 4 years from a multidisciplinary project funded under the 7th Framework Programme – Security. BeSeCu stands for BEHAVIOUR, SECURITY and CULTURE and the project has been a cross-cultural investigation of human behaviour in emergencies, disasters and evacuations, with the aim of better tailoring security-related communications, instructions and procedures. The BeSeCu consortium comprised an international group of nine partners and combines the work of researchers and end-users from eight different countries.

This book reveals the methodological developments and first findings from a cross-cultural study of evacuation trials as well as from a large cross-cultural field study of human behaviour in emergencies and disasters. This project is unique in terms of the cross-culturally simultaneous and interdisciplinary approach adopted in each step of the empirical research. The results are essential for the better planning of emergency/disaster management and evacuations as well as for informing future research.

Prof. Silke Schmidt
Department of Health and Prevention
Ernst-Moritz-Arndt-University Greifswald

Prof. Ed Galea
Fire Safety Engineering Group
University of Greenwich

1 Background

Silke Schmidt, Lynn Hulse & Ed Galea

The primary focus of this book is to demonstrate results of the international BeSeCu (BeSeCu stands for BEHAVIOUR, SECURITY and CULTURE) project on human responses to emergencies and disasters – a project that followed an interdisciplinary research approach, incorporating disciplines such as the social sciences, health sciences, mathematical and computer sciences. However, this book will also highlight collaboration beyond these disciplines, i.e. the scientific view on human responses is complemented by the perspectives of the fire and medical services since these are important groups of first responders involved in such incidents.

To date, "common knowledge" about people's behaviour in emergencies and disasters (referred to as "felt evidence") and evidence obtained from scientific studies have not always matched one another. There are several major research areas from which data about human responses to emergencies and disasters can be derived:

1. Psychological studies on the experiences of individuals in emergencies and disasters (e.g. regarding their evacuation response, their cognitions, emotions and actions)
2. Mathematical and engineering studies analysing evacuation responses by computer modelling
3. Psychological studies on the physical and mental consequences of emergencies and disasters
4. Sociological studies of the societal impact of major disasters, and those examining emergency management and prevention at an organisational level.

Each of these research areas has a different perspective. For example, psychological research focuses on testing or measuring mental and behavioural processes during an incident and the post-event impact of emergencies and disasters all at the individual or small group level. In contrast, engineers, mathematical and computer modellers are interested in the general or "normal" human response and try to simulate this response. Moreover, engineering sciences focus on hazard characteristics and official emergency responses, while the health sciences focus on optimising medical or mental health interventions in affected populations. In addition, there is the perspective of first responders and key political or organisational representatives. This chapter focuses on the first two research areas, examining the behaviour of people in emergencies and disasters with a particular focus on evacuating (mainly in cases of fire, but also in other types of events). The chapter summarises existing evidence on human responses related to evacuations in order to be able to compare the results of the BeSeCu group with that of previous studies.

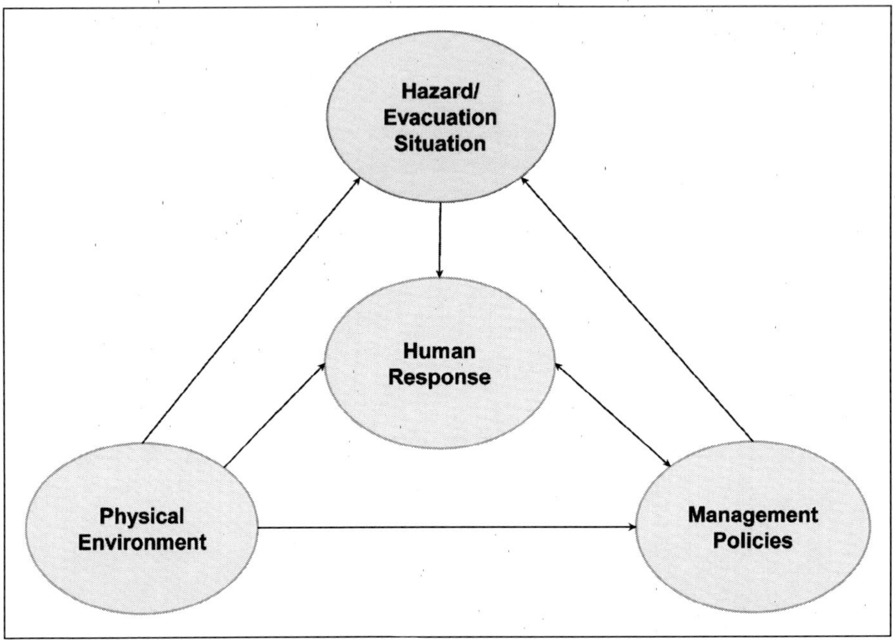

Fig. 1.1: Dimensions of Evacuation Behaviour – Four Analytical Dimensions, adapted from Fraser-Mitchell (2001)

Understanding has already been much advanced in one sense: it is now recognised that evacuees are thinking and feeling beings, which react according to factors associated with the past, present, and future, and can respond in a multitude of ways to the same incident, either independently or collectively with others. Therefore, their responses are deserving of much qualitative and quantitative analysis. Overall, responses to emergencies and disasters can be analysed by taking into account four distinct dimensions (see Fig. 1.1): characteristics of the hazard/ evacuation situation, the physical environment from which to evacuate, management policies and control implemented at evacuation and the human response including psychological and social characteristics (Fraser-Mitchell, 2001).

While the spatial and environmental characteristics of events such as fires received much scientific attention in the past, human behaviour factors (i.e. psychological, biological, sociological, and cultural characteristics), and their interactions with the spatial and environmental aspects, were relatively overlooked. It is much more common in the engineering literature to find consideration of the first three dimensions shown in Fig 1.1 (Fraser-Mitchell, 2001).

Researchers have since made steps to address this gap in knowledge, and there are some human behaviour factors which have become well documented and debated in the field of fire safety in the last two decades. For example, it has long been assumed that people automatically panic when faced with an emergency, and furthermore that such a reaction is a main cause of casualties or deaths in such situations. When a fire broke out in the Beverly Hills Supper Club in Kentucky in 1977, several British newspapers carried headlines along the lines of "Panic Kills 300" (The Sun). As well as mentions in the media, the word "panic" is often brought up by survivors of emergencies and disasters to describe the presence, or absence, of such a reaction in themselves and other survivors. Likewise, it has appeared in some emergency signage in the form of instructions, "DO NOT PANIC", and in safety manuals advising that information about the cause of the alarm be withheld in order to prevent panic from occurring. However, researchers such as Sime (e.g., 1990) and Quarantelli (e.g., 2002) have moved to debunk the idea that panic is a common, irrational, and contagious reaction in emergencies, noting that systematic studies and inquiries have found little evidence of this. Indeed, the National Fire Protection Association's report (cited in Sime, 1990) of the aforementioned Beverly Hills Supper Club fire found that, not only were the number of actual fatalities considerably fewer than that reported in the press, they were also due to smoke and carbon monoxide inhalation rather than panic. Moreover, the exposure to the smoke and carbon monoxide was attributed to the fact that club staff had been very slow to notify people of the fire, plus the fact they had allowed the number of people present in the cabaret room to far exceed the recommended maximum capacity thereby making it almost impossible for everyone to evacuate that space in time.

Other human behaviour factors that have received attention include: the tendency for people to evacuate not via the closest emergency exit but rather via the route by which they entered the building; and how a lack of training, experience, and preparedness in evacuees can negatively impact information processing and increase submission to leadership (see Shields & Proulx, 2006). Knowledge of such traits is useful in that some aspects can be represented in evacuation models to better simulate evacuation scenarios. Furthermore, this knowledge can lend to improved egress design (e.g., having emergency exit doors open automatically upon alarm thereby making them a more attractive route option; Benthorn & Frantzich, 2000) and evacuation training, such as the conductance of evacuation drills in commercial and public facilities and community fire safety programmes in residential areas.

However, safety research into human behaviour in emergencies and disasters is still in its infancy, with many studies looking at characteristics only in isolation or focusing on overt behaviour without probing the underlying rationale. Thus there is still much to explore.

Concerning the causes of events that prompt evacuations, in general three different types of disaster have been differentiated: (a) natural disasters, such as floods and earthquakes, (b) deliberate or man-made disasters, such as terrorist attacks and (c) technological disasters (e.g. the Chernobyl disaster, fires resulting from industrial accidents).

The classification of disasters raises fundamental questions about how to define disasters and how they can be differentiated from emergencies. The difference is conceived to be rather qualitative than quantitative (Tierney, 2009). There is no argument about whether earthquakes, the tsunami in 2004, the 9/11 terrorist attacks on New York, and a host of other natural, man-made and technological events that have occurred in the recent or more distant past were disasters, given the significant losses and disruption of life, property, social and economic functioning that these events caused. However, as well as posing greater impacts than emergencies, disasters involve a different official response, one that involves something other than just normal, local resources as an emergency would. Nevertheless, when looking at the behaviour of people (those directly involved) as an event unfolds, the question arises whether these types of disasters would have a different impact on individual evacuation responses than would emergencies such as domestic fires. Survivors of these incidents could feasibly go through a similar general process as survivors of disasters: e.g. encountering and interpreting cues to a hazard; experiencing emotions such as fear and thoughts surrounding risk to self, others and property; carrying out activities such as gathering items in advance of exiting their current location for a place of safety; etc. Also, individuals' preparedness for disasters and emergencies like fires could be similarly lacking, albeit for different reasons. Disasters are rarer events. Therefore, due to a lack of physical exposure, there will be a concomitant lack of experience and some of the general public might also underestimate the need to prepare for such events. In contrast, domestic fires are much more frequent events and therefore there is a greater chance of experiencing one. Yet, such emergencies receive less attention from the media than disasters. This could lead to lower saliency for domestic fires and similar smaller-scale emergencies, which in turn could lead members of the public to overlook such events and any need to prepare for them. It should be borne in mind that, as domestic fires occur far more frequently, the cumulative threat they pose to people/property, means they are no less deserving of serious attention than disasters. Such issues suggest the need to systematically investigate and compare human responses to different types of events involving evacuations to see whether there are similarities and/or differences – an approach adopted by the BeSeCu project.

Some types of event are more likely to occur in certain geographical regions and modern technology may offer the chance of early detection and warning of danger. However, other types of events can strike anywhere, at any time. The people at risk might be located in settings that are completely enclosed (e.g. buildings such as homes, public transport vehicles in stations) or in much less enclosed settings (e.g. stadia, open roads). Dealing with a threat or hazard when one is in an enclosed setting can involve different challenges to dealing with a threat or hazard when located in less enclosed settings; the former scenario is the focus of the BeSeCu group.

When disasters and emergencies do strike, there are two main types of action an individual can take to protect themself: evacuate or seek shelter. Evacuation is the term commonly used to describe the action of exiting a structure due to a threat or hazard (whether real or anticipated; Sorensen & Sorensen, 2007) and moving to a place of safety. Seeking shelter refers to withdrawing – again due to a threat or hazard – to another location within the structure where the individual would (they presume) face less risk. Sometimes self-evacuation is not possible (e.g. when a person is trapped or incapacitated by the hazard) and sometimes it is not advisable or necessary (e.g. when there is a greater risk of personal injury outside). In some cases, an individual may end up being evacuated or rescued by others, usually professionals such as trained staff or emergency services personnel. In this situation, the terms "evacuation" and "rescue" are used here to describe the individual leaving the structure under the command/supervision of others; "rescue" would additionally involve the individual requiring significant physical assistance (e.g. being carried out in someone's arms, being taken away by stretcher or boat, etc.).

Whether an individual self-evacuates or is evacuated/rescued by others, they tend not to be alone. However, when an individual leaves in the company of others that does not automatically mean they leave in a group – from a socio-psychological point of view (see for example Forsyth, 2010), there would also be a need for the individual to feel related in some socially meaningful way to the others with whom they are in close proximity (e.g. they are family members or close friends, or the event has fostered a sense of shared identity between strangers, e.g. Drury, Cocking & Reicher, 2009). The behaviour of an individual acting independently could possibly differ from one acting collectively in a group, e.g. with regards to risk perception, "appropriate" reactions, speed of movement, and so forth. Research has the potential to improve social scientific understanding of how people respond to the above kinds of factors involved in disasters and emergencies – i.e. to threat/hazard communications; to "unannounced" danger; to situations where the choice to leave/seek shelter is in the hands of the individual; to situations where the choice to leave/seek shelter is in the hands of professionals; to the influence of other survivors; and so on. Such research can also serve to inform practical disaster and emergency management at a community and national level.

1.1 Human behaviour and evacuation responses in emergencies and disasters: State and methods

How will people respond to a call to evacuate and behave during an evacuation? Most field study data and experiments conducted in this area have focused on subjects from the USA, Canada or Australia. It can be argued that these nations are quite similar with comparable cultures. If it is the case that a nation's culture – be it the social culture (i.e. shared system of values, beliefs and attitudes) and/or fire safety culture (i.e. the regulatory fire safety framework) – influences how people behave when responding to an unfolding event and how quickly they begin evacuating, then it could have a profound impact: (a) on the planning of procedures for evacuations and also (b) on the understanding and modelling of human behaviour. Furthermore it would raise questions about the applicability of existing models to different nations and cultures. The aim of the BeSeCu project was to conduct a cross-cultural investigation of behavioural reactions in situations requiring evacuation, examining the time taken to start evacuating and the evacuees' experiences throughout the event, in order to better tailor security-related communications, instructions and procedures and consequently improve safety. The two central research components of BeSeCu included collecting data from several different European countries and were run simultaneously: A social scientific study involving a range of target groups (survivors, first responders) and types of real event and an experimental study on human behaviour in building evacuations.

The empirical study of evacuations and human behaviour in fires began in the first part of the 1900s and has gained particular momentum since the 1970s (Bryan, 1999; Pauls & Jones, 1980). As this line of research has developed, studies have shown some long-held assumptions about peoples' behaviour during an emergency to be invalid. For example, as touched on earlier in this chapter, it used to be widely assumed that people would panic if given information regarding the hazard/threat that was necessitating the evacuation (Canter, 1990; Quarantelli, 2002). Now it is believed that such information can be imparted to people, and should be done so at as early an opportunity as is possible (Mileti & Sorensen, 1990). Research has also discredited the notion that people will exit immediately upon an alarm being sounded. For instance, Proulx (1994) found that it took people an average of three minutes to begin leaving their apartment buildings.

People's evacuation responses have been examined using a variety of methods, for example: post hoc analyses of first-hand accounts of real-life events (e.g., by interviewing the survivors); studies of real-life events relying on information from secondary sources such as public inquiries, the media, etc.; questionnaire surveys relating to real-life experiences; and experimental trials where a (usually unannounced) evacuation takes place in a building or other structure and the evacuees' behaviour and cognitions are explored through a mixture of on-site observations, video recordings, and questionnaires. All these methods have provided valuable data with which professionals with an interest in fire safety (e.g., engineers, modellers, architects, code writers) can work.

Canter (1990) summarised research findings obtained by several of the above methods and highlighted that evacuation responses to fires consist of several phases. The first relates to the activity a person is engaged in prior to becoming aware of the fire. This activity could be work-related (e.g., typing up a document on a computer), recreational (e.g., eating a meal, reading a newspaper, chatting on the telephone), or something less conscious (e.g., sleeping). Next is where people encounter cues which make them aware that something unusual is happening. These cues may be an alarm ringing or an official announcement to evacuate. Unfortunately, all too often the cues are ambiguous (e.g., simply a muted sound) which can lead to them being misinterpreted and/or ignored. However, the most common initial (and conscious) response is to investigate the cue(s) to establish the cause. Once the situation has been defined (either correctly or otherwise), the person may respond in several ways. Responses may revolve around information (e.g., moving position to find somewhere with a better view of the situation, seeking information/instruction via telephone, TV, radio, etc.) or withdrawing from the situation. Responses may also involve the person taking some course of action. This may be to actually evacuate the building/structure, combat the fire, warn others, or wait for further developments (e.g., for situation to improve, external help to arrive).

More recent investigations on the 9/11 World Trade Center (WTC) evacuations (e.g., Galea et al., 2010) have revealed that, in the face of that terrorist attack, evacuees similarly went through a set of distinct phases. They began with engagement in mainly work-related activities. Next was becoming aware that something unusual was happening through environmental or social cues. There then followed a response phase (including seeking further information or instruction; seeking refuge or actively dealing with fire or other hazardous environmental conditions; preparing to evacuate by collecting, removing, storing, or distributing items; devising an evacuation plan; searching floor(s) and instructing or helping others to evacuate; or, in some cases, continuing to work). The actual process of evacuating was also split into phases: horizontal evacuation (purposeful movement towards a floor exit; also movement through the horizontal transfer corridors in the emergency egress routes); vertical evacuation (in emergency exit stairwells or elevators); evacuation interruption (where the person purposefully interrupted their evacuation, e.g., to rest); and finally exit (once out of the stairs/elevators and making way out of the WTC complex to safety). Some of the activities in these phases are likely to be specific to the fact the building was a place of work (e.g., storing securities in vaults, shutting down computers), that it was a high-rise building (e.g., women collecting and changing into flat shoes to prepare for the long journey down the stairs), and would have been carried out by people whose role dictated such action (e.g., managers staying behind to liaise with other senior members of the company or to instruct employees to evacuate, fire wardens delaying their own evacuation to search areas). Moreover, previous experience might have impacted the number of phases a person went through (e.g., some WTC occupants who had been present during the 1993 bombing went straight from realising something was happening into the horizontal evacuation phase). Canter similarly states that occupancy, role, and earlier experience might alter the behaviour in the different phases with fires. Canter also highlights gender differences, for instance with females in domestic fire situations more likely to seek help from neighbours, and males more likely to combat the fire.

As well as looking at the nature of the responses to events such as fires and terrorist attacks, researchers have been collecting quantitative data, such as how long it took people to purposefully begin evacuating after receiving cues that something was happening (sometimes referred to as "Response Time"), the speed with which they travelled when evacuating ("Travel Speed"), and how long it took them to exit the building or other structure and reach a point of safety ("Evacuation Time"). A study of the published accounts of 9/11 WTC survivors (Galea, Lawrence, Blake, Dixon & Westeng, 2007) estimated that 60% of WTC1 occupants began evacuating within 5 minutes of the first plane hitting the building. Occupants in WTC2 in general responded more promptly, with over 90% estimated to have begun evacuating within 5 minutes of the first plane hitting WTC1 (N.B. A more fine-grained analysis of WTC response times was subsequently undertaken by the University of Greenwich using first-hand survivor accounts collected through interviews (Day, Hulse & Galea, 2012). This study confirmed that the majority of WTC occupants began evacuating within the first few minutes of WTC1 impact, with WTC2 occupants responding more promptly in general). Response time data was then incorporated into the buildingEXODUS evacuation model, developed by the Fire Safety Engineering Group at the University of Greenwich, to simulate the evacuation of WTC1 and explore different hypothetical scenarios. This work suggested that had at least one staircase remained intact from top to bottom in that tower, then it would have been possible that everyone who had survived the initial impact could have managed to safely evacuate the building. So human behaviour data can be used not only to increase the ecological validity of evacuation models, but also to aid their predictive capacity and consequently help inform building safety design.

Response time data can also help examine the effectiveness of evacuation systems such as fire alarms. Unannounced evacuation trials conducted in a low-rise building (university library) in the UK (Gwynne, Galea, Parke & Hickson, 2003; Gwynne, 2007) showed that a tone alarm went as far as to alert the students that something had happened but many delayed their evacuation until they received confirmation of the situation from staff, who were moving around the building vocally instructing people to evacuate. It was also not uncommon for students to collect their belongings and disengage from their previous activities (e.g., log off computers) before initiating evacuation. The response times (referred to as "pre-evacuation times" by the authors) for the samples ranged from a few seconds to over 200 seconds. People who did not receive prompts from the staff tended to have longer response time distributions than those who did (for instance, occupants in a private study area, isolated from others, continued to work after the alarm sounded and it was only after one person went out to investigate and saw people in other areas leave that they began their evacuation). Questionnaire data, collected once people had exited the building, revealed that while some students had experienced fire drills or evacuations from the building previously, others had not. Moreover, few had any knowledge of what an evacuation of the building would actually entail. In contrast, a trial involving the evacuation of a single enclosed laboratory inside the library using an unfamiliar, voice notification system which instructed people to immediately leave the lab by the nearest safe exit, produced significantly shorter response times (20-89 seconds); shorter than those of the aforementioned samples plus shorter than would normally be expected in such a scenario. While it was not possible to control all the variables across trials, these studies nonetheless provide suggestive evidence that evacuation will be much better aided when people are informed as well as alerted to an emergency situation (cf. earlier theories about panic).

The above findings have been gathered mainly from studies of fires but also occasionally from studies of some other kinds of incidents, thus it is possible that they could suggest a very general pattern of behaviour in emergencies and disasters. However, this is not a given. There could be behaviours unique to certain types of emergency or disaster. There could also be behaviours unique to certain types of population or subgroup, e.g. cultural group. Moreover, these findings might not be applicable across all other population subgroups, whether those categorised by socio-demographic factors such as age, gender, ethnicity, etc., or those categorised by their role in an emergency, e.g. civilian evacuees vs. fire and rescue personnel, medical personnel, other safety professionals.

1.2 Cross-cultural differences in human behaviour

Cross-cultural investigations into human behaviour have taken place in some fields of research. For example, a number of studies have provided evidence that when it comes to subjective responses regarding one's perceived health, there are generally more similarities than differences across cultures. In fact, there are a range of subjective concepts which seem to be universally valid and measurable across cultures, and which display only few differences between nations (Schmidt, 2003; Schmidt, 2007; Schmidt, Debensason, Petersen, Mühlan, Simeoni & Bullinger, 2006). Yet, evidence on the effects of culture on human behaviour in emergencies and disasters is limited. Where differences across cultures have been observed, e.g. concerning the amount of time taken to call the emergency services for help (Schmidt, 2003), these differences have been quite large. However, most of the findings on human behaviour in emergencies and disasters have been derived from national, mostly single or small-scale studies. The range of findings have been limited in their scope and so existing evidence needs to be confirmed in studies involving other target groups and other contexts (i.e. evacuations from structures other than just office/residential buildings), as well as being tested from a cross-cultural perspective.

To date, there have been several projects, particularly in the United States, e.g. those funded by the US Centers for Disease Control and Prevention as well as the National Institute of Standards and Technology, attempting to learn about human behaviour in emergencies and disasters. As mentioned earlier, the majority of readily available published evacuation data – data that is often used throughout the world for the creation of building regulations and for computer simulations to inform the design of buildings and also the development of emergency procedures – originates from a small number of countries such as the USA. In the field of fire safety engineering, it is common practice to assume that this data can be reliably applied more widely than the context from which it was collected. However, it cannot simply be taken for granted that people in different countries, or from different cultures, will respond in an identical fashion to e.g. Americans when faced with an emergency. Nor should it be automatically assumed that data collected in, say, the UK can be applied across the rest of Europe. While directives from the EU (or EEC) may have brought some safety regulations of its member countries more into line with one another, these directives only dictate the minimum standards required and do not necessarily provide detail on how these standards should be met. Therefore, the actual safety practices and procedures could vary greatly from one member country to another. Non-member countries could differ again. Moreover, each country could differ in their actual and/or perceived vulnerability to different types of emergencies and disasters based on their geography, population density, economic situation, technological resources, and so forth, and so behaviour could vary for this reason alone or in addition. Furthermore, behaviour could be influenced by the countries' social cultures.

A large, direct comparison of national (social) cultures was conducted by Hofstede and colleagues (2001; 2010). Survey data was collected in over 70 countries and scores were compared on several dimensions, i.e. clusters of values on which the countries could be distinguished. The four dimensions discussed here are: power distance (ranging from small to large, involving how people handle social inequalities and the relationship with authority); individualism vs. collectivism (relating to the relationship between the individual and the group); masculinity vs. femininity (being competitive vs. co-operative); and uncertainty avoidance (ranging from weak to strong and relating to ways of handling uncertainty or ambiguity). Though much of the data was collected in the 1960s and 1970s and from a particular population and setting (i.e. IBM employees, values in the workplace), Hofstede (2010) claims that replications and extensions of this work have found the countries' relative scores to be quite stable over time and demonstrated that the data can be applied more widely than its original context.

Hofstede's findings (2001; 2010) would suggest several socio-cultural differences amongst European countries. For example, the Czech Republic, Poland and Italy would be culturally similar nations in that they all have a larger power distance (i.e. accept a hierarchical order and thus subordinates expect leaders to tell them what to do), score higher on individualism (i.e. are centred on "me" rather than "us" with individuals only expected to take care of themselves and their immediate families) and masculinity (i.e. expect or admire assertiveness, achievement and heroism), and display a strong preference for avoiding uncertainty (i.e. desire rules, norms and procedures – even if they are not always followed, enforced or effective – and suffer greater stress because of attempts to avoid uncertainty, possibly leading to more obvious expressions/venting of emotion). However, Spain and Turkey could be grouped separately because although both also have larger power distances and are keen to avoid uncertainty, they are, in contrast, more collectivist nations (where teamwork is considered natural and there is a greater involvement with extended families and in-groups), and are more feminine (i.e. are more caring and modest and strive for consensus). Germany would be somewhat similar to the Czech Republic, Poland and Italy in that it is an individualistic, masculine, uncertainty avoidant nation but it differs by having a much smaller power distance and thus is a nation that would generally expect people on the lower levels to participate and be directly consulted in communications and decision making. The UK also has a smaller power distance and thus values greater social equality, and is further similar to Germany in the sense that it is individualistic and masculine, but it stands apart by being more comfortable with and accepting of ambiguous situations. Finally, Sweden would be the most different from all the other European countries mentioned above as it is an individualistic, extremely feminine nation with a smaller power distance and a very relaxed attitude towards uncertainty and any deviance from the norm. The people of this nation would generally be expected to display less stress and have a greater sense of well-being as a consequence.

Tab. 1.1: A comparison of national scores on Hofstede's (2001; 2010) dimensions of national (social) culture

Country	Power Distance	Individualism	Masculinity	Uncertainty Avoidance
Czech Republic	57	58	57	74
Poland	68	60	64	93
Italy	50	76	70	75
Spain	57	51	42	86
Turkey	66	37	45	85
Germany	35	67	66	65
UK	35	89	66	35
Sweden	31	71	5	29
USA	40	91	62	46
Canada	39	80	52	48
Australia	36	90	61	51

Table 1.1 displays the scores of the eight European countries on each of the four dimensions mentioned here. It also includes the scores of the USA, Canada and Australia, the countries from where a lot of the existing evacuation data derives. As can be seen, these latter three countries have a similar profile to one another: a smaller power distance, highly individualistic, masculine and more accepting of uncertainty. This makes them similar to the UK in terms of these socio-cultural traits but different to many of the other European countries. While Hofstede's (2001; 2010) data cannot be used to draw conclusions that different countries will likely behave differently to one another in an emergency or a disaster based on their social cultures, it certainly suggests a need to conduct a cross-cultural investigation given that issues surrounding relationships with authority, groups, competitiveness, co-operation and responses to uncertainty/ambiguity are all relevant to evacuation situations.

1.2.1 Previous studies on cultural evacuation responses

Forthergill, Maestas and Darlington's (1999) review of research into US disasters pointed to cultural differences in several aspects of the human responses to these events. For example, risk perception was shown to differ as a function of migrant status, with some studies suggesting that the differences were due to certain migrant groups having previous experience of the disasters in their country of origin, and consequently heightened perceptions of risk. However, other studies were reported as finding that migrant groups tended towards lower perceived risk than the White native populations. Fothergill et al.'s review also revealed that ethnic minorities may seek more information than Whites to try to confirm warnings received from authorities. As information seeking tends to increase response times in evacuations, it is important to try and establish why certain groups do not immediately accept warnings and consequently delay their evacuation. A further finding reported in the review, that evacuees and authority figures who share the same language can still experience communication problems due to words/phrases carrying different meanings for the different populations, shows that there might be subcultural differences which pose problems with language comprehension and subsequently evacuation responses to warnings.

Research conducted in eastern countries has also revealed cultural differences in behaviour concerning disasters. For example, Gaillard et al. (2008) examined the responses of several different ethnic groups to the 2004 tsunami in Indonesia. This work highlighted the difference in groups' immediate responses to the emergency: a quarter of one group, the Air Pinang inhabitants, chose to run to the hills while 18% of another group, the inhabitants of Kajhu, opted to stand still and pray. This suggests that how people view control over their destiny (either as being in their own hands or in the hands of someone/something else) might depend on one's cultural and religious beliefs. Once again, perceived risk or danger was found to be of interest with most respondents stating that their own perceptions spurred their response and 40% of the Air Pinang group reporting fear vs. only 11.1% and 26.3% of the Kajhu and J. Pahlawan respondents respectively. As in the aforementioned US studies, previous experience of threats played a part and differed across groups. The Air Pinang inhabitants felt culturally close to the sea and had generations of knowledge about the environment, past incidents, and were skilled in reading Nature's cues. As such, there were no deaths in this area as these inhabitants successfully removed themselves from the danger. In contrast, the inhabitants of Kajhu tended to lead more urban lives and the J. Pahlawan dwellers were mainly migrants and therefore both groups were less familiar with their environment. Their lack of experience was considered to be one of the reasons behind the higher rates of harm to these groups (cf. "disaster subcultures", see for example Granot, 1996). In all the above studies, the disasters tended to be natural ones. In more recent years, several large-scale man-made disasters have occurred across the world, and research into these might allow comparison of different cultures' responses to events that have a sudden, unexpected onset. For example, in 2003 an arson attack on a train in the Daegu subway system, South Korea, led to a fire spreading not only through the train carrying the arsonist, but also to a second train which had pulled alongside at the station. There were almost 200 fatalities, many being passengers in the second train that had been unable to evacuate as the train driver had fled the scene, inadvertently locking the train doors in the process. However, passengers in the first train were also likely to experience harm, due to their own behaviour. Photographs and accounts from the survivors of this event revealed that many of the train passengers remained seated, waiting for instruction, despite the obvious presence of smoke in the carriages. Only 7% of 146 survivors surveyed thought to immediately leave the train (Marlair, Lecoze, Woon-Hyung & Galea, 2004). Deliberate (terrorist) attacks on the transport systems in London, UK (in 2005) and in Madrid, Spain (in 2004) may provide a means of cross-cultural analysis of human behaviour in train incidents. Initial examination of photographs taken inside one of the underground trains in London suggest that some of the passengers may have responded in a similar way to those in Daegu, i.e. remaining seated in a smoke-filled carriage.

Evacuation trial data from a non-Western culture (Tavares, Gwynne & Galea, 2006) also suggests that there may be cross-cultural similarities, in this case with evacuations of low-rise buildings. Students in a Brazilian university library, where there was no formal fire safety systems or training (e.g., no fire alarms, no drills), were instructed by members of staff to evacuate. The recorded response times were reasonably quick, ranging from a few seconds to 70 seconds. The mean response time was similar to that found in UK evacuation trials, also conducted in a university library building, where the occupants had heard only a staff member's instruction to evacuate (Gwynne, 2007). These studies collectively imply that verbal notification systems which inform people, and not just alert them to the fact something unusual is occurring, are quite effective. Of course, this requires evacuees to understand the language used. Thus, it may be the case that notification systems targeting other sensory modalities (e.g., visual signs to evacuate) would be needed in addition to aid those who are not fluent in the native language.

References

Benthorn, L. & Frantzich, H. (2000). Fire alarm in a public building: How do people evaluate information and choose an evacuation exit? *Fire and Materials, 23 (6),* 311-315.

Bryan, J.L. (1999). Human behaviour in fire: The development and maturity of a scholarly study area. *Fire and Materials, 23,* 249-253.

Canter, D. (1990). An overview of human behaviour in fires. In: D. Canter (Ed.), *Fires and Human Behaviour,* 2nd ed., 205-234. London: David Fulton.

Day, R.C., Hulse, L.M. & Galea, E.R. (2012). Response phase behaviours and response time predictors of the 9/11 World Trade Center Evacuation. *Fire Technology.* Available via Online First.

Drury, J., Cocking, C. & Reicher, S. (2009). Everyone for themselves? A comparative study of crowd solidarity among emergency survivors. *British Journal of Social Psychology, 48 (3),* 487-506.

Forsyth, D.R. (2010). *Group Dynamics,* 5th ed. Belmont, CA: Wadsworth/Cengage.

Fothergill, A., Maestas, E.G.M. & Darlington, J.D. (1999). Race, ethnicity and disasters in the United States: A review of the literature. *Disasters, 23 (2),* 156-173.

Fraser-Mitchell (2001). Simulated Evacuations of an Airport Terminal Building, Using the CRISP Model. In: *2nd International Symposium in Human Behavior in Fire* (pp. 89-100). Boston, MA.

Gaillard, J-C., Clavé, E., Vibert, O., Azhari, D., Denain, J.-C. et al. (2008). Ethnic groups reponse to the 26 December 2004 earthquake and tsunami in Aceh, Indonesia. *Natural Hazards.* Available via Online First.

Galea, E.R., Lawrence, P., Blake, S., Dixon, A.J.P. & Westeng, H. (2007). The 2001 World Trade Centre Evacuation. In: N. Waldau, P. Gattermann, H. Knoflacher & M. Schreckenberg (Eds.), *Pedestrian and Evacuation Dynamics 2005,* Berlin: Springer, 225-238.

Galea, E.R., Hulse, L., Day, R., Siddiqui, A., Sharp, G., Shields, J. et al. (2010). The UK WTC 9/11 Evacuation Study: An overview of the methodologies employed and some preliminary analysis. *Pedestrian and Evacuation Dynamics 2008* (pp. 3-24). Berlin: Springer.

Granot, H. (1996). Disaster subcultures. *Disaster Prevention and Management, 5 (4),* 36-40.

Gwynne, S.M.V. (2007). *Notification effectiveness for large groups (Report).* Quincy, MA: The Fire Protection Research Foundation.

Gwynne, S., Galea, E.R., Parke, J. & Hickson, J. (2003). The collection and analysis of pre-evacuation times from evacuation trials and their application to evacuation modelling. *Fire Technology, 39 (2),* 173-195.

Hofstede, G. (2001). *Culture's Consequences: Comparing Values, Behaviors, Institutions, and Organizations Across Nations* (2nd ed.). Thousand Oaks, CA: Sage.

Hofstede, G., Hofstede, G.J. & Minkov, M. (2010). *Cultures and Organizations: Software of the Mind.* (revised 3rd edition). New York: McGraw-Hill.

Marlair, G., Lecoze, J.C., Woon-Hyung, K. & Galea, E.R. (2004). Human behaviour as a key factor in tunnel fire safety issues. *Proceedings of the Sixth Asia-Oceania Symposium on Fire Science and Technology,* pp. 658-668.

Mileti, D.S. & Sorensen, J.H. (1990). *Communication of Emergency Public Warnings: A Social Science Perspective and State-of-the-Art Assessment.* Oak Ridge, TN: Oak Ridge National Laboratory.

Pauls, J.L. & Jones, B.K. (1980). Research in Human Behavior. *Fire Journal, 74 (3),* 35-41.

Proulx, G. (1994). Time Delay To Start Evacuating Upon Hearing The Fire Alarm. *Proceedings Of Human Factors And Ergonomics Society, 38th Annual Meeting,* 811-815.

Quarantelli, E.L. (2002). Sociology of panic. In: N.J. Smelser & P.B. Baltes (Eds.), *International Encyclopedia of the Social and Behavioral Sciences* (pp. 11020-11023). Oxford: Elsevier.

Schmidt, S. (2003). *Cross-cultural analysis of health indicators across Europe: First results from the EUROHIS study. In Developing common instruments for health surveys.* In: A. Nosikov, C. Gudex (Eds.), Amsterdam, IOS Press.

Schmidt, S., Debensason, D., Petersen, C., Mühlan, H., Simeoni, M.C. & Bullinger, M. (2006). Cross-cultural performance of the DISABKIDS condition generic measure. *Journal of Clinical Epidemiology, 59,* 587-598.

Schmidt, S. (2007). *Cross-cultural analyses of components and determinants of health-related quality of life – Results from three European studies in children, adults and the elderly.* Lengerich (Germany), Pabst Science Publishers.

Shields, T.J. & Proulx, G. (2006). *The science of human behaviour: Past research endeavours, current developments and fashioning a research agenda* (Report NRCC-44520). Ottawa: National Research Council Canada.

Sime, J.D. (1990). The concept of panic. In: D. Canter (Ed.), *Fires and Human Behaviour,* 2nd ed., London: David Fulton, 63-81.

Sorensen, J.H. & Sorensen, B.V. (2007). Community Processes: Warning and Evacuation, pp. 183–199. In: H. Rodriguez, E.L. Quarantelli, and R.R. Dynes (eds.), *Handbook of Disaster Research.* New York: Springer.

Tavares, R.M., Gwynne, S. & Galea, E.R. (2006). Collection and analysis of pre-evacuation time data collected from evacuation trials conducted in library facilities in Brazil. *Applied Fire Science, 15 (1),* 23-40.

Tierney, K. (2009). Disaster response: Research findings and their implications for resilience measures. *CARRI Research Report 6.* Oak Ridge, TN: Community and Regional Resilience Initiative (CARRI). URL: www.resilientUS.org

2 Aims and approach of BeSeCu

Silke Schmidt & Ed Galea

General aims

The aim of the cross-cultural BeSeCu project is to investigate human behaviour in emergencies and disasters in order to better tailor security-related communications, instructions and procedures with a view to improving evacuations and, ultimately, safety. The project will provide evidence that will be useful to first responders, building designers and those involved in the development of emergency operating procedures for buildings.

An implicit assumption employed in emergency operating procedures is that people's responses will be independent of the cultural context in which the incident takes place. The project explores this assumption through the collection of objective and subjective data from several countries relating to the human response in emergencies and disasters.

Some of the main aims of the European security policy are: to develop knowledge for building capabilities that will help ensure the security of citizens from threats; to tailor security-related communications to the needs of the society to ensure optimal and concerted use of technologies to the benefit of civil European security; to stimulate the co-operation of providers and users; and to gain European citizens' acceptance of security interventions. However, in order to achieve these aims, evidence on differences in human behaviour in emergencies and disasters is needed, in particular in order to improve evacuation and protection strategies. Predicting human behaviour is one of the most complex areas of fire safety engineering.

Despite some recent advances with respect to knowledge of basic human reactions in emergencies and disasters, there is still an inherent lack of evidence and data on behavioural responses from a cross-cultural perspective. BeSeCu stands for BEHAVIOUR, SECURITY and CULTURE.

The objectives of BeSeCu are:

- To construct an evidence base on human behaviour in emergencies and disasters that integrates data from experimental trials and a field study of real experiences.
- To develop and test a sound survey methodology to investigate human reactions in emergencies and disasters that require evacuation or protection on a cross-cultural level from a broader perspective.
- To develop and test experimental approaches from a cross-cultural point of view.
- To investigate cultural differences in behavioural reactions to fires.

- To determine whether there are cultural differences in response times during evacuations
- To investigate cultural differences in the subjective experiences of emergencies and disasters, also taking sociodemographic factors into account. There will be a particular focus on differences determined by participants' nations as well as socio-economic determinants, since this has not been sufficiently addressed in previous research.
- To provide a list of components of human reactions – reactions that are either universal or subject to cultural differences – to first responders, to industry, and to policy makers.
- To provide an outline of a culturally-sensitive communication programme designed for first responders.
- To suggest types and areas of improvement in existing communications, instructions and interventions, as well as in security alerts.
- To disseminate survey and experimental findings as well as methodological tools to designers of buildings, designers of emergency operating procedures and first responders.
- To define important future steps for European security policy and research.

Each of these aims will be attained through a series of methodological steps. However, in order to be able to (A) conduct a comprehensive analysis of human behaviour in emergencies and disasters and (B) simultaneously assess objective data, the research agenda will incorporate two research arms and strategies: The first one will aim at a broad picture on cultural differences in people's reactions and will incorporate many centres as well as a wide range of events. This first strategy will employ a social science approach at gathering data and will integrate the vast knowledge that exists on cross-cultural instrument development. The second one is of equal importance and follows an experimental design where a few select structures, matched on several attributes including their functional purpose, occupancy, height, etc., will be targeted for evacuation and their data compared. This second scientific approach will employ a quantitative analysis and computer modelling. Both strategies will be adapted and harmonised with each other at specific stages of the projects, including the conceptual development of the project, instrument development, cross-cultural analyses of data and dissemination.

The main objective of the research activity is to assess cultural similarities and/or differences in objective measures of human responses as well as in subjective measures, and to develop evidence on human behaviour in emergencies and disasters. In order to address this objective, four international methodological instruments or procedures will be developed:

A cross-culturally developed and standardised instrument to assess the behaviour of survivors of security-relevant emergencies and disasters (BeSeCu-S)

- A cross-culturally developed instrument to assess the perception of observers of human responses to security-relevant emergencies and disasters (e.g. workers; BeSeCu-O)

- A cross-culturally developed and standardised instrument to assess first responders' attitudes and reactions concerning communication with survivors (BeSeCu-P)
- A standardised experimental procedure to assess objective reactions (BeSeCu-Evac with several sub-modules, e.g. observational scales, measurements, questionnaires, etc.)

These instruments will allow the analysis of the interrelationship and convergence of data from different sources. These instruments can be employed in further validation studies in other countries, and can be applied to other types of buildings and settings. BeSeCu will provide an evidence base and a tool box with the aim of dissemination. Another product is a recommendation of communication standards that are sensitive to cultural differences. Information should be provided in terms of all kinds of communication interventions: those that can be used in the design of a variety of structures, and those that allow better verbal communication for all sorts of first responders.

Methodology

The BeSeCu project will employ two research strategies. First a cross-cultural survey of individual experiences will be conducted with survivors of fires or other emergencies and disasters occurring in enclosed structures, first responders, and those affected in the community. This retrospective study will be carried out across eight European countries that vary in their cultural background. Second, experimental trials will be carried out in three countries simulating realistic evacuation scenarios. These will include objective measures (e.g. of response times) as outcomes as well as video-tape analysis.

Two types of research findings and products will be provided by the BeSeCu project: an evidence base that will enable designers of buildings to develop culturally-appropriate emergency operating procedures, and an evidence base that will help develop culturally-sensitive communication training to improve interventions.

To measure objective and subjective data on human responses, there are two common methodological approaches that can be adopted: (a) observing evacuation trials through hidden cameras to determine outcomes such as response times and (b) interviewing survivors and/or proxies (e.g. first responders) about their experiences in emergencies and disasters, capturing cognitive, emotional and behavioural components of people's reactions.

Although a range of studies were initiated in the late 1970s and early 1980s to investigate human behaviour in emergencies and disasters, these studies focused largely on the more obvious aspects of behaviour, i.e. visible actions; research into survivors' cognitive and emotional processes during the incident has been less common. Since computer modelling was introduced in the mid-1980s, this technique has been productive in generating a variety of simulations with which to investigate the capability to evacuate from a variety of environments. Evacuation models simulate the egress of large numbers of people, usually from enclosed structures such as buildings, trains, planes, and ships. The movement of individuals in such models can be determined by a fixed set of motion-rules. In the beginning, computer models represented little more than an automation of the calculation of regulatory formulations of the evacuation process, but more recently an array of evacuation models have evolved which go much further than this and aim to simulate the evacuation process as accurately as possible, e.g. EVACNET+ (Fahy, 1996), EXODUS (Galea, Blake, Lawrence, 2005) and EVARTSIM (Sharma & Turner, 2004). These models demonstrate good performance in predicting the evacuation performance and in realistically modelling human behaviour (Owen, Galea & Lawrence, 1996).

However, while such models' qualities include the ability to consider the human response as one factor among others (e.g. toxicity, hazards and the physical attributes of the structures), these programmes were not originally designed to increase professionals´ awareness of individuals' responses in emergencies and disasters but rather to predict mass responses. It has been suggested that the combination of evacuation modelling with broad analyses of in-depth interviews covering participants' subjective experiences and reflections on their internal processes (e.g. emotions, decision making) is one direction that future research should follow.

References

Fahy, R.F. (1996). EXIT89: High-rise evacuation model – recent enhancements and example applications. In: *Interflam.* Quincy, Massachusetts.

Galea, E., Blake, S. & Lawrence, P. (2005). *Report on Testing and Systematic Evaluation of the airEXODUS aircraft evacuation model.*

Owen, M., Galea, E. & Lawrence, P. (1996). The EXODUS Evacuation Model Applied to Building: Evacuation Scenarios. *J of Fire Protection Engineering, 8,* 65-84.

Sharma, S. & Turner, J. (2004). An object oriented approach to simulating agent-based behaviour. In: *SIGRADI conference.*

3 Results of focus groups and pretest data

3.1 Human behaviour and culture in emergency situations: Focus group analysis of first responders and key representatives

Zeynep Baskaya Sofuoglu, Turhan Sofuoglu, Elif Yildirim & Doris Kehl

Abstract

Natural and man-made disasters and emergencies, which are immense and traumatic events, influence human behaviours. Although, severity of disaster shape human responses; cultural features of the community have an important role on behaviours and responses during and after emergency. Therefore, it is aimed to determine if culture plays role in the communication of security relevant emergencies, crises or disaster situations between survivors/ victims and first responders / key representatives in this study. A interview guideline which mainly focused on response of responders and survivors is used for a sample of 61 first responders from Czech Republic, Germany, Poland, Sweden, Spain, Turkey and United Kingdom. It is found, that survivors' responses and behaviours are more positive and adaptive during the evacuation compared to the moment after the evacuation. Moreover, vulnerable groups behave different than general population. The participants from Turkey believed cultural features as important factors on human behaviours in emergency. It is also found, that cultural features have influence on communication and intervention process. In sum up, understanding human behaviours in disasters and emergencies and being aware of cultural influences on human responses are initial steps for crisis management.

Introduction

Disasters and emergencies usually cause social and spatial disorganisation of the territories a ected by these situations and specific human behaviour. Human behaviours in disasters and emergencies can be analyzed by individual or collectivist behaviours, which depend on the phases of emergency. However, these behaviours have common properties: they are essentially non-traditional and short-lived (Provitolo, 2009). Some behaviours, which include, confinement, flight, panic and deviant behaviours, correspond not to daily behaviours and are limited in time with a return to daily behaviours (Rodriguez et al., 2006).

"Culture" refers to integrated patterns of human behaviour that include the language, thoughts, communications, actions, customs, beliefs, values, and institutions of racial, ethnic, religious, or social groups (Cross et al., 1989). Culture and language may influence: health, healing, and wellness belief systems; how illness, disease, and their causes are perceived; the behaviours of patients/consumers who are seeking health care and their attitudes toward health care providers and the delivery of services by the provider who looks at the world through his or her limited set of values (Perry, 2006). Cultural differences may be important issues for people face emergency or disasters. Generally, causalities may not communicate properly due to their poor level of consciousness on the scene. In addition to this, first responders may not understand the needs of the causalities because of the physical environment conditions like; darkness, smoke, noise or other conditions like cultural differences.

For example, a Turkish woman who had suffered a heart attack reportedly died in Oslo on the 3rd of January 2010. Her daughter called ambulance dispatch centre 3 times, her son-in-law yelled at them when no ambulance was sent to the scene. Norwegian health dispatchers, dispatched police before sending an ambulance. The police arrested death woman's son-in-law. These types of incidents can happen all around the world, if the cultural and behavioural differences are not taken into account by the first responders.

Furthermore, because of emergencies and disasters generally cause chaotic environment, risk perception and response of survivors change according their cultural structure (Pidgeon, 1992). For instance, collectivist or fatalist cultural features of survivors can create difference in perception of disasters (Fothergill et al., 1999; Perilla et al., 2002). Due to different perception of the situation, some communication and intervention problems can occur during and after the evacuation between survivors and responders. Therefore, identifying and examining human behaviours and effects of culture on the behaviour are essential for every processes of evacuation.

BeSeCu (Behaviour, Security and Culture) is an investigation of cross-cultural and ethnic differences of human behaviour in crisis situation in order to better tailor security related communication, instructions and procedure founded in the 7th framework program of the European Commission. The BeSeCu consortium exists of an international group of eight partners and combines the work of researchers and end-users from eight different countries. Whilst witnessing in recent years a range of disasters across Europe, including terrorist inspired incidents such as the Madrid train bombings in 2004, the London Underground and bus bombings in 2005, floods such as the Elbeflut in Germany in 2002 or earthquakes such as the Marmara earthquake 1999 in Turkey, following questions about human behaviour in crisis situations gain importance: Did culture play a role in determining how the people in these disasters responded? More significantly, could a better understanding of cultural response to crisis situations assist in developing better emergency procedures? A cross-cultural survey of individual experiences conducted to identify determinants of inter-individual differences in people who have experienced evacuation situations, fire disaster survivors and survivors of similar crisis situations, but also workers and first responders as well as those affected in the community. This retrospective study carried out across eight European countries with diverse cultural background.

The aim of this study is to determine if culture plays role in the communication of security relevant emergencies, crises or disaster situations between survivors/ victims and first responders / key representatives. Furthermore this study will help exploring human behavioural responses in security relevant crisis situations across culture, nations and ethnic groups as well as attitudes and reactions of first responders/ key representatives on communication with disaster survivors.

Methodology

Face to face interviews were conducted with first responders and key representatives from Czech Republic, Germany, Poland, Sweden, Spain, Turkey and United Kingdom. Additionally, socio-demographic data and incident related information was gathered via questionnaire to verify that a wide range of profiles has been included in this phase of the study.

Interviews and participants

The interviews were divided into two parts. The first part consisted of open questions regarding participants' professional background. The topic of the second part was the kind of crisis situation that each centre has research on and comprised incident related questions. This part was divided into (a) a free narrative where the first responder/key representative told us (in his own words) about the crises situation they were involved in and (b) a semi-structured interview with more detailed questions about this situation.

Table 3.1: Distribution of Crisis Situation and Country

Type of crisis situation	Number of Interviews run at least for each group (first responder/ key representative)						
	DE	UK	SE	ES	TR	PL	CZ
Domestic fire	2	2	2	2	2	2	2
Terrorist Attack/ Fire in railway station	2	4	2	2	0	0	0
Earthquake	0	0	0	0	2	0	0
Flood	2	0	0	0	0	0	2
Collapse of a building	0	0	0	2	0	2	0
Evacuation in transport	0	0	2	0	2	2	2
TOTAL	6	6	6	6	6	6	6

All centres conducted at least 2 key representatives' and 2 first responders' interview s about a domestic fire situation. The distribution of type of crisis situation and country is shown in Table 3.1.

The professions (Fig. 3.1) and the study inclusion criteria (Fig. 3.2) of the key representatives and first responders were agreed before.

Profession of first responder	Profession of key representative
• medical/ psychological emergency support • armed forces • civil defence • staff responsible for evacuation • fire fighters • medical doctors, paramedics • police officers	• local administration officer • politician • mayor • town councillor • psychotherapist • journalist • working in NGOs dealing with crisis situations • working in survivor support networks

Fig. 3.1: Professions of First Responder and Key Representatives

Inclusion criteria
• experience in crisis situation • in contact with the victims immediately after the event or at the rescue operation • actively experienced a crisis situations, direct contact to victims, directly affected • involved in managing/ assisting an evacuation • responsibility for object safety • represent the people for whom they speak • consent to participate in the study

Fig. 3.2 Inclusion Criteria of First Responders and Key Representatives

Planning of interview process

The interviewers *(or moderators)* were part of the BeSeCu research team. The interviewer for the face to face interviews and focus groups should be the same in order to prevent bias and to benefit from the background information about special crisis situation.

The interviewees *(or participants)* were recruited according to the crisis situations. The ways of recruiting of participants is shown in Fig. 3.3.

Recruiting

- Health Protection Agency
- Federal Office of Civil Protection and Disaster Assistance
- Integrated Rescue System
- Emergency Medical Services
- Survivor Networks, associations of victims
- Media: internet, adverts in newspapers
- Direct contact with first responders and key representatives

Fig. 3.3 The Ways of Recruiting Participants

A standardized manual with guidelines for the face to face interview with first responder/key representative was developed and translated into the languages of the participating countries and followed by all project partners. The interview comprised four phases:

Introduction phase

The purpose of the interview was stated clearly and simply to the participant. The interview process was described and let the participant know about the time scheduled. Confidentiality assured. Before starting the interview consent sheet and socio-demographic questionnaire were given to the participant.

Warm up Phase

The most important aspect during the warm up phase was to build a rapport between the interviewer and the interviewee.

Key content phase

Moderators prepared well and read the instructions several times before carrying out the interview. The interview was leading from a more general part with a free narrative about the crisis situation to a more specific part. Moderators knew to encourage the interview partner to speak while using open questions and listen attentively to the interview partner. The language should reflect that of the participant, so the moderators reflected back words or phrases that interview partner used.

Closure phase (summarizing and closing)

Moderators summarized on important statements and insure that there are no misunderstandings. Furthermore the interview partner had the possibility to add statements on topics that seem important to him.

Analysis of the interview

Each project centre taped and then transcribed the interviews. Subsequently, English translations of the transcripts were made. The interviews were categorized consecutively by the moderator. Analysed categorizations and related questions were given in Fig. 3.4. All the categorization files were transferred to SPSS. It was a qualitative research with small quantitative parts also. Frequencies and rates of data were used to examine qualitative data. With respect to quantitative data Chi-squared test were used.

Categorization with subcategories	**Asked Question**
Cultural factors Cultural factors are important Cultural factors are unimportant	Given the setting and nature of the incident, were you expecting culture to be a significant/relevant factor?
Way of cultural factors Age Ethnicity Language Emotions Education Others	If culture is a significant/relevant factor, in what way?
Detection, perception, interpretation of the event Yes No	Did you notice any issues arising in people's detection, perception, interpretation of the event due to cultural differences?
Obstacles related to culture Yes, … No	Did you experience or notice any issues arising due to cultural differences and, if so, how were they dealt with?
Reactions of evacuees to intervention Cooperated Misunderstandings Incorporated Nor reactions	How did the evacuees react to your intervention?
Reaction of evacuees to communication Cooperated Misunderstandings Incorporated Nor reactions	How did you communicate with them and how effective was this?
Experiencing emotion during/after the emergency Satisfied Helplessness Stress Tired Fear Sadness	What kind of emotions did the people in this situation appear to be experiencing? As this?

Fig. 3.4: Categorization of the Interview *(cont. next page)*

Categorization with subcategories	Asked Question
Psychosocial/motivational components Cooperation Resistance Need of support Others No component...	Were there any psychosocial/motivational components that complicated the evacuation?
Behaviour pattern of general population/vulnerable groups Cooperated Calm Seeking information Trying to escape Aggressive Trying to save property Others No component	Were there any commonly occurring patterns of behaviour amongst the general population involved in the fire/situation/vulnerable groups of people?
Cultural differences affected emotions of evacuees Yes, ... No	Did you notice any issues arising due to cultural differences and, if so, how were they dealt with?

cont. Fig. 3.4: *Categorization of the Interview*

Results

General characteristics of participants

A convenience sample of 61 first responders and key representatives from eight European countries was drawn. The participant's distribution according to country was the following: 9 were from Czech Republic (14.8%), 8 from Spain (13.1%), 12 from Turkey (19.7%), 10 from Poland (16.4%), 7 from Germany (11.5%), 8 from Sweden (13.1%), and 7 from the United Kingdom (11.5%).

The average age of the 61 participants was 44.33 (SD = 1.09) years, and their ages ranged from 25 to 65 years. Educational level of the participants were generally high, only 2 (7.7%) of the participants were graduated from high school and 24 (92.3%) were graduated from a university.

Working characteristics of the participants are provided in Table 3.2. Among the participants 23 were key representatives (37.7%) and 38 (62.3%) were first responders. In respect to the participant's professional background, their specialization respectively their field of involvement in emergency situations differed in this study. The average of the years participants had been working in this field was 16.87 (SD = 9.08) years, with a range from 4 year to 41 years. Organisations which participants work with was as follows: 41 government (87.2%), 3 charity (6.4%), and 3 company (6.4%).

Features related to emergency situations

Among the first responders and key representatives 28 participants (45.9%) reported about a domestic fire, 4 (6.7%) about a flood, 4 (6.6%) about an earthquake, 7 (11.5%) about a traffic accident, 7 (11.5%) about a collapse of a building, 6 (9.8%) about a non-domestic fire, 1 (1.6%) about a terrorist attack, and 4 (6.6%) about complex emergencies such as bomb operation and chemical accident.

Of the emergency situations 27 occurred in cities (45%), 5 (8.3%) out of the city, 20 (33.3%) in a building, and 8 (13.3%) outdoors. Among the first responder's 12 of them (35.3%) were aware of the exits, only 1 first responder (2.9%) was aware that exits were damaged. Furthermore, there were no exists in 19 situations (55.9%) and in 2 (5.9%) of the cases exists were inaccessible because of the disaster. There is no statistically significant relationship between countries and first responder's and key representatives awareness of emergency exists (χ^2 [N = 37] = 27.778, ρ = .066; Cramér's V = .522, ρ = .066).

Table 3.2: Working characteristics of first responders and key representatives (N = 61)

	N	**(%)**
Professional background in emergency situations	**61**	**(100)**
Firefighter	20	(32.8)
Police officer	2	(3.3)
Health care personnel	10	(16.4)
Engineer	9	(14.8)
Manager	5	(8.2)
Other professional background	15	(24.6)
Specialization in emergency situations/Field of involvement	**55**	**(100)**
Civil defence	12	(21.8)
Fire service activities	8	(14.5)
Security activities	6	(10.9)
Management activities	16	(29.1)
Crises intervention	2	(3.6)
Trainer	3	(5.5)
Health specialist	3	(5.5)
Other emergency related fields	5	(9.1)
Responsibility/Role in emergency situations	**61**	**(100)**
Coordination	24	(39.3)
Rescue	24	(39.3)
Physiological support	5	(8.2)
Medical support	4	(6.6)
Communication	2	(3.3)
Material help	2	(3.3)

(cont. next page)

cont. Table 3.2: *Working characteristics of first responders and key representatives (N = 61)*

	N	(%)
Years on the job in emergency situations	**38**	**(100)**
0– 5 years	1	(2.6)
6–10 years	9	(23.7)
11–15 years	12	(31.6)
16–20 years	6	(15.8)
21–25 years	3	(7.9)
> 25 years	7	(18.4)

According to the data, 4.3% of experienced emotions during the emergency was frustration, 17.4% was confusion, 13% was cold bloodedness, 4.3% was sadness, 2.2% was helpfulness, 34.8% was stress. Experienced emotion after emergency differs from experienced emotion during the emergency. 7.1% of experienced emotions after emergency was tiredness, 42.9% was satisfied with rescue team, 32.1% was helplessness, 17.9% was stress, 23.9% numbness.

Cooperation (19.4%), unity (16.1%), presence (12.9), information seeking (9.7), trying to escape (32.3%) and complaining (6.5%) are common occurring behaviour pattern in general population according to 31 participants. On the other hand, in vulnerable groups behaviour pattern seems different. Participants indicated that need of more help (15.4%), resignation (15.4%), excitation (11.5%), aggressive behaviour (15.4%) and trying to save property (15.4%) are common occurring behaviour pattern in vulnerable groups.

Concerning general population 31.4% were families who formed groups, 8.6% neighbours, 2.9% friends, 20% evacuees, 8.6% leaders, 5.7% young people, 5.7% others and participants reported that 17.1% of the population did not form a group. With respect to vulnerable population 7.7% were families who formed groups, 7.7% people around the scene, 3.8% neighbours, 3.8% children, 11.5% elderly people, 7.7% people with disabilities, 7.7% young people, and 7.7% evacuees; furthermore participants reported that 42.3% of vulnerable population did not form a group.

Of the participants 18.2% evaluated resistance, 3% risk under estimation, 9.1% psychological problems and 21.2% need more support as psychosocial components which complicates the evacuation in vulnerable groups. On the other hand 48.5% did not specify any components. Civil organisations (2.6%), risk underestimation (5.3%), unity of group (7.9%), cooperation (10.5%) and resistance (23.7%) were the components which complicates the evacuation for general population. There were no statistically significant relationship between situation and psychosocial components that complicated evacuation for general population (χ^2 [N = 38] 29.70, ρ = .772; Cramér's V = .395, ρ = .722) and vulnerable population (χ^2 [N = 33] = 36.247, ρ = .052; Cramér's V = .524, ρ = .052). Of what were the aspects of cultural differences affected emotions of evacuees, 8% was village-town difference, 24% was family culture, 20% was being immigrant, 4% was trusting in fire fighters, 4% of time using differences, 8% was being wealthy, 8% was language differences, 4% was whining syndrome, 16% was related to being coldblooded and excitable, 12% was other.

Among the 44 participants 17 (38.6%) evaluated cultural factors as an important factor in emergency situations and 27 (61.4%) rated cultural factors as unimportant. Although there is no statistically significant relationship between centre and cultural factors (χ^2 [N = 44] = 11.569, ρ = .072; Cramér's V = .513, ρ < .05), some participants' opinions about cultural factors differ from each other. For instance, all of 7 participants of Spain assessed cultural factors as an unimportant factor. Similar to Spanish participants, 5 of 6 Polish participants labelled cultural factors as unimportant. On the other hand 8 of 12 participants from Turkey thought that cultural factors are important. Moreover, the way how culture affects the situation shows no statistically significant relationship with centre (χ^2 [N = 22] = 72.35, ρ = .051; Cramér's V = .74, ρ = .051).

Among the examination of the participants who believed that cultural factors are important, there are divergences between participants from different countries. Although 4 of 6 participants from Czech Republic (66.6%) emphasized on age and ethnicity, 1 participant (16.7%) emphasized emotional state. 5 of 7 Turkish participants (71.4%) gave a credit on education. 2 of them (26.6%) thought that ethnicity and emotional response are important. However 2 of 5 German participants (40%) emphasized the importance of language and ethnicity, 3 of 5 participants indicated that emotional responses and ethnicity is important as well.

Although 11 of the 43 participants (26.6%) claimed that culture is an important factor on attitudes while 28 (53%) did not. On the other hand, 2 participants (5%) claimed that it is not important but personal characteristics are important factors.

Countries' interpretation, detection and perception of the event was significantly different (χ^2 [N = 36] = 13.04, ρ < .05; Cramér's V = .74, ρ < .05). Spain, Czech Republic and Poland countries evaluated these as unimportant although Turkey and Germany evaluated it as important. Addition to this, age, education, stressors, gender and socioeconomic factors were determined as factors caused general differences with respect to detection, perception and interpretation of the event. There is a statistically significant relationship between cultural attitude differences and detection, perception, interpretation of the event (χ^2 [N = 36] = 13.03, ρ < .05; Cramér's V = .60, ρ < .05) 5 of the 6 participants (83.3%) who claimed that there are attitude differences such as beliefs and misunderstandings due to the culture also claims that detection, perception and interpretation of the event effected by it. 16 of 18 participants (88.9%) who claims that there are no attitude differences such as beliefs and misunderstandings due to the culture also claims that no detection, perception and interpretation of the event is not affected by it.

Evacuee's reactions to interventions are given in Table 3.3. Although evacuees responses towards interventions were not significantly affected by culture (χ^2 [N = 36] = 8.40, ρ = .078; Cramér's V = .483, ρ = .078), reactions of evacuees to communication showed statistically significant relationship with cultural factors (χ^2 [N = 27] = 7.703, ρ < .05; Cramér's V = .53, ρ < .05). 12 of 17 participants who thought cultural factors are unimportant, evaluated reactions of evacuees to intervention and communication as cooperated. On the other hand, 7 of 10 participants, who believed cultural factors are important, suggested that there are misunderstandings in reactions of evacuees.

Table 3.3: Reactions of Evacuees to Intervention and Communication

	Reactions of Evacuees to Intervention N = 46 (%)	**Reaction of Evacuees to Communication N = 37 (%)**
Cooperated	19 (51.4)	25 (54.3)
Misunderstandings	14 (23.0)	4 (8.7)
Uncooperated	0 (0.0)	13 (28.3)
No reactions	4 (10.8)	4 (8.7)

Cultural obstacles at emergency situation differed from centre to centre (χ^2 [N = 40] = 19.791, $\rho < .05$; Cramér's V = .70, $\rho < .05$). In general, centres did not report cultural obstacles besides all of German participants reported that culture is important obstacle. Way of dealing with obstacles did not differ according to scene (χ^2 [N = 26] = 25.56, $\rho = .181$; Cramér's V = .923, $\rho = .181$) or evacuees statistically (χ^2 [N = 15] = 2.577, $\rho = .462$; Cramér's V = .315, $\rho = .462$).

Table 3.4: Summary of associations with at least medium effect sizes

Independent Variable	**Dependent variable**	**$\chi 2$**	**df**	**ρ**	**Cramér's V**
Centre	Detection, perception, interpretation of the event	13.04	5	.023	.74
Cultural attitude differences	Detection, perception, interpretation of the event	13.03	2	.001	.60
Cultural factors	Reactions of evacuees to communication	13.41	2	.021	.64
Centre	Obstacles related to culture	19.79	6	.003	.70
Situation	Psychosocial components in general population	29.70	35	.722	.39
	Psychosocial components in vulnerable population	36.24	24	.052	.052
Centre	How culture effect	72.35	54	.051	.74
Cultural factors	Reactions of evacuees to intervention	8.40	4	.078	.48
Scene	Way of dealing with obstacles	25.56	3	.181	.92
Evacuees	Way of dealing with obstacles	2.57	20	.462	.32

Discussion and conclusion

This study has a different approach to survivors' behaviours and culture as it is investigating responding period of the disasters and emergencies.

Consistent with our findings, studies shows that, in emergency situations most people respond positively help others and deal with their circumstances adaptively (Mawson 2005). Except unity and collective behaviours, survivors of disasters identify their behaviour as "panic", when what they are experiencing or observing is rational behaviour based on fear (Clark, 2002). Due to experience fear in a crisis, fleeing from a disaster is often the most rational course of action (Quarantelli and Dynes, 1975). Accordingly, in our study survivors are tended to try to escape during the evacuation. On the other hand, Fothergill and her colleagues suggest in their review (1999), that social groups which encompass different ethnicity, religion, sexual orientation and age, disability people and poor socioeconomic status, are more vulnerable to disasters, due to factors such as language, housing patterns, building construction, community isolation and cultural insensitivities. Therefore, this finding can be related to our finding, which reported, that positive and adaptive behaviour patterns turn to negative and antisocial pattern in vulnerable groups. Low socioeconomic status and being minority can also influence stress coping mechanism and response to trauma (Allen, 1996).

We also found, that there are differences between experienced emotions during and after emergency. Survivors responded calmly as well as feeling of confusion during the emergency situation, but this feeling turn into helplessness and stress after the emergency situation. Generally, studies suggest that, survivors typically are rational and respond with logical and calm behaviour during the emergency. Moreover, they often aware of what to do to care for themselves and others, and they react accordingly while the processes of evacuation (Quarantelli 1986). Because of the immense, intense and traumatic nature of disasters, survivors' feelings change after the evacuation. Exposure to disasters is associated with increased survivors' risk for severe or prolonged psychological distress (Gleser et al., 1981), and also because of loss and mourning, survivors can feel negative feelings such as anxiety, stress and helplessness. Studies show that, Post Traumatic Stress Disorder (PTSD) rates range to 87% in earthquake cases (Başoğlu et al., 2002).

According to our results, there is a difference of opinions on the culture's effects between participants from Turkey and other countries. For instance, most of Turkish participants thought that cultural features are important factors in emergency situation. To the opposite, European countries such as Spain and Poland, evaluated cultural differences and features as unimportant factors. This result could be interpreted with that non-western cultures like Turkey emphasize collectivist values more than western culture (Sue & Sue, 2003). Collectivism is a sense of oneness with others and also the self is identified as part of a group which may have effects on every processes of evacuation (Hui and Triandis, 1986). Strength ties to family member are common in collectivist culture and this can cause difficulties in operations of responders. For example, this form of familism can cause implications in emergency-stricken setting, where family support may be decreased and insufficient to meet all needs (Perilla et al., 2002). Similarly to this, although European participants gave more credits on ethnicity and emotional state as cultural factors, Turkish participants evaluated education more important as a cultural factor. This difference could be thought as a sign of Turkey's development and civilization movement (Green, 1996).

As expected, the current result suggested that perceived cultural differences make harder the evacuation process. The participants declared that if there are different cultural features on the community, evacuees react less cooperative to communication and interventions. This situation may be a result of communication problems and attitude diversities between the ethnicities. Cultural and language barriers between disaster victims and emergency personnel can undermine relief efforts if not dealt with appropriately. For instance, cultural and language barriers between survivors and responders can delay the communication of critical information such as evacuation orders, vital health education and disease prevention information (Seidenberg, 2006).

The study had some limitations. Firstly, the sample size of this study is limited and a lot of participants did not respond all questions. There were a lot of unanswered items. This can be a result of our questionnaire, which contains open ended questions. Secondly, qualitative method does not allow conducting complex statistical analysis; however one special benefit of conducting interviews was to gain comprehensive background information about special crisis situation.

In sum of, consistent with our findings we could concluded, that the behaviours and attitudes differ in disaster and emergency situation. Especially, cultural features of the community and survivors perceptions of the natural and man-made disaster have a major role on behaviours on emergency situations. Therefore, investigation of human behaviours and responses can increase the success of crisis management. In addition to this, crisis management programs should consider cultural features' influences on survivors' behaviours.

References

Allen, I. (1996). PTSD among African Americans. In: A. Marsella, M. Friedman, E. Gerrity, R. Scurfield (Ed.), *Ethnocultural aspects of PTSD: Issues, research, and clinical applications.* Washington, DC: American Psychological Association.

Başoğlu, M., Şalcıoğlu, E. & Livanou, M. (2002). Traumatic stress responses in earthquake survivors in Turkey. *Journal of Traumatic Stress, 15 (4),* 269-276.

Clarke, L. (2002). *Panic – myth or reality? Contexts* (American Sociological Association). Fall 21-26.

Cross, T.L., Bazron, B., Dennis, K. & Isaacs, M. (1989). Towards a culturally competent system of care. Vol. I: *A monograph of effective services for children who are severely emotionally disturbed.* Washington, DC: Georgetown University Child Development Center.

Fothergill, A., Maestas, E. & Darlington, J. (1999). Race, ethnicity and disasters in the United States: A review of literature. *Disasters, 23 (2),* 156-173.

Gleser, G., Green, B. & Winget, C. (1981). *Prolonged psychosocial effects of disaster: A study of Buffalo Creek.* New York: Academic Press.

Green, B.L. (1996). Cross-national and ethocaltural issues in disaster studies. In: A. Marsella, M. Friedman, E. Gerrity, R. Scurfield (Eds.), *Ethnocultural aspects of PTSD: Issues, research, and clinical applications.* Washington, DC: American Psychological Association.

Hui, C. & Triandis, H. (1986). Individulam- collectivism: A study of cross-cultural researchers. *Journal of Cross- Cultural Psychology, 17,* 225-248.

Perilla, J.L., Norris, F.H. & Lavizzo, E.A. (2002). Ethnicity, culture, and disaster response: Identifying and explaining ethic differences in PTSD six months after. Hurricane Andrew. *Journal of Social and Clinical Psychology, 21 (1),* 20-45.

Perry, R. (2006). What is a disaster? In: H. Rodriguez, E.L. Quarantelli & R.R. Dynes (Eds.), *Handbook of disaster research.* New York: Springer, 1-15.

Pidgeon, N., Hood, C., Jones, D., Turner, B. & Gibson R. (1992). *Risk Perception, Risk, Analysis, Perception, Management.* London: Royal Society.

Provitolo, D. (2009). A new classification of catastrophes based on Complexity Criteria. In: M.A. Aziz Alaoui & C. Bertelle (Eds.), *From System Complexity to Emergent properties, Series Understanding complex systems.* Springer-Verlag, 179-194.

Rodriguez, H., Quarantelli, E.L. & Dynes, R.R. (2006). *Handbook of disaster research.* New York: Springer.

Seidenberg, J. (2006). *Cultural competence in disaster recovery: Lessons learned from the Hurricane Katrina experience for better serving marginalized communities.* Berkeley, CA: University of California at Berkeley Law School. Retrieved from http://www.law.berkeley.edu/library/disasters/Seidenberg.pdf.

Sue, W.D. & Sue, D. (2003). *Counseling the culturally diverse: Theory and practice* (4th ed.). New York: John Wiley and Sons, Inc.

Quarantelli, E.L. & Dynes, R.R. (1972). When disaster strikes (It isn't much like what you've heard or read about). *Psychology Today.* February, 67-70.

Quarantelli, E.L. (1986). What is disaster? The need for clarification in definition and conceptualization in research. In: B. Sowder & M. Lystad (Eds.), *Disasters and mental health: Selected contemporary perspectives.* Rockville, MD: National Institute of Mental Health, 41-73.

3.2 Results of focus groups and scenario pretest

Anna Grimm, Lynn Hulse & Silke Schmidt

The **BeSeCu-S,** an instrument to measure survivors' descriptions of an emergency or disaster they have experienced including a retrospective assessment of their cognitive, emotional and behavioural responses, was designed on the basis of focus groups and interviews with survivors of European emergencies and disasters. The analysis of focus group results was used in order to design and pre-test a pilot version of the BeSeCu-S in an international group of scenario participants and survivors of emergencies and disasters.

Focus groups were conducted to make a first qualitative step in analysing human behaviour in emergencies and disasters, and include both natives and migrants. Interviews and focus groups, including a questionnaire assessment of socio-demographic and event-related data and also posttraumatic stress measures were conducted with 125 survivors of fires, floods, terror attacks and collapses of buildings across eight European countries. A Q-sorting method was used for an in-depth analysis of the statements given in focus groups. The aim of the Q-sorting procedure was to group similar items into the same categories and to label these categories. With this approach a content analysis was conducted leading to a theoretical framework. A detailed description of the sample and research methods applied, as well as of the cross-cultural qualitative analysis revealing common behavioural, cognitive and emotional reactions in emergencies and disasters, can be found in Grimm, Hulse, Preiss and Schmidt (in press). Furthermore, an assessment of survivors' responses as a function of the different type of event they had experienced and the level of posttraumatic stress can be found in Grimm, Hulse, Preiss and Schmidt (2012). Examples of the survivors' narratives of their evacuation phase are given in Table 3.5 including information about the evacuation route, way finding, obstacles/ challenges and interaction with others.

Table 3.5: Survivor evacuation narratives with categories and citations from focus groups

Evacuation Process	Category	Citation from interview	n
Evacuation Route	Stairs/escalator/ exit door	There were stairs down to the platform.	16
	Balcony/window	It was the only exit, the staircase was blocked, the elevator was burning, so the only light spot was my balcony	12
	Emergency exit/ emergency lighting	It was the driver´s emergency exit. You know they (train staff) opened the front of the train and they put the step ladder down and you descend down onto the track.	11
	Elevator	The neighbour from upstairs fell through the elevator shaft and luckily he could get out that way.	2
	Other		3
Way finding	Following others	I can remember I was following in the foot path of another person who was ahead of me.	16
	Reverting to habit	Subconscious tells you to escape through the same door you have entered	8
	Led by light	I took the flashlight with me	7
	Mental map	I thought to myself "I still can't see any-thing" but I knew where I was. So I knew that if I went one, two (steps) and turned right, I'm now in between the seats.	5
	Using emergency knowledge	(...) If it's burning you should in no way go with the elevator because if the smoke gets in the elevator, the smoke detector releases the emergency brake.	3
Obstacles and challenges	Obstacles	The staircase was full of bricks, it was covered and we couldn't get out that way.	27
	Blocked exit	The front door to the other side, it was locked already. We couldn't get out there anymore.	12
	Accessible evacuation route	The stairwell wasn't full of smoke either so there was no breathing problem	9
	Congested	There was a fight to get out, people were hitting each other and jumping.	6
	Slow progression	He was operated (...) and unable to move.	5
	Other		2

(cont. next page)

cont. Table 3.5: *Survivor evacuation narratives with categories and citations from focus groups*

Evacuation Process	Category	Citation from interview	n
Evacuation interaction	Evacuation in a group	But we were lucky of course, that we didn't have to go through this alone, but in a group.	
	Family/friend		27
	First responder/ building staff		11
	Stranger		10
	Neighbour/colleague		9
	Alone		2

Additionally, various individual characteristics of survivors and situational characteristics of the event were assessed in order to investigate their influence on post- and peritraumatic stress. The descriptive analysis showed that situational characteristics were more often significantly related to post- and peritraumatic stress (s. table 3.6, table 3.7). Further analysis of the influence of individual and situational factors on post- and peritraumatic outcome variables using regression analysis, with consideration also of the influence of different types of events can be found in Grimm, Hulse, Preiss & Schmidt (2012).

Table 3.6: Descriptive analysis of the influence of individual characteristics on IES-R total plus subscale scores, and on peritraumatic emotional stress and risk perception (* p < .05; ** p < .01, *** p < .001)

Post & peritraumatic impact	Individual characteristics				
	Gender		Education		Age
	T	*d*	F	*f*	R
IES-R	– 1.81	.32	.27	1.50	– .12
Avoidance	– 2.31*	.67	1.16	1.46	– .07
Intrusion	– .87	.22	.04	.66	– .13
Hyperarousal	– 1.99*	.42	2.19	.58	– .11
Emotional stress	– 2.70**	.30	1.47	.23	– .05
Risk perception	– 1.22	.70	.84	.40	.03

Table 3.7: Descriptive analysis of the influence of event characteristics on IES-R total plus subscale scores, and on peritraumatic emotional stress and risk perception (* $p < .05$; ** $p < .01$, *** $p < .001$)

Post & peritraumatic impact	Time since event	Event characteristics				
		Duration	Fatalities		Injuries	
	r	*r*	T	*d*	T	*d*
IES-R	– .20*	– .35**	4.79***	.89	5.31***	1.13
Avoidance	– .18*	– .31**	3.11**	.71	4.96***	1.05
Intrusion	– .21*	– .33**	5.51***	1.00	4.99***	1.12
Hyperarousal	– .16	– .36**	4.48***	1.00	4.71***	1.00
Risk perception	– .33**	– .33*	2.73**	.66	2.40*	.60
Emotional stress	– .30*	– .38**	4.99***	1.31	3.13**	.71

The information extracted from the analysis of focus groups and interviews was used to design the pilot test of the instrument for survivors of emergencies and disasters (BeSeCu-S). The aim of this instrument was to assess behaviour, emotions and cognitions of people who had experienced one of the following events: a domestic fire, a fire in a public building, a terrorist attack, an earthquake, or a flood. Detailed descriptions of the pilot test can be found in Grimm, Hulse & Schmidt (2009) and Grimm, Hulse & Schmidt (2012) for details of the peritraumatic emotion and cognition scales.

3.3 Risk perception: Differences in perceived risk of emergencies and disasters across Europe – Data from the pilot study

Anna Grimm, Lynn Hulse & Silke Schmidt

Introduction

This chapter focuses on the analysis of risk perception in the pilot test data.

The estimation of the risk an emergency or disaster poses differs between laypersons and experts, possibly because laypersons may be more influenced by issues involving salience. For example, whereas natural catastrophes such as floods, storms and earthquakes are amongst the most common disasters in Europe (Preventionweb, 2011), public and media attention is mainly drawn to man-made disasters such as terror attacks (Grimm, Hulse & Schmidt, 2009). According to the "psychometric paradigm", sensational events are usually rated as more likely to happen (see Fischhoff, 1978; Slovic, 1987; Sjöberg, 2000). Also, the recent experience of an event in a country enhances the perceived risk: In 2006, 43% of a representative London sample believed their own lives were at risk from terrorism but when that same sample were surveyed in 2005, just less than two weeks after the 7 July London bombings, a significantly larger percentage (52%) believed their own lives were at risk (Rubin et al., 2005; Rubin et al., 2007). In both surveys by Rubin et al., 90% of the sample believed London was likely to experience another attack in the near future. In comparison to this, a Swedish sample (N.B. Sweden has, to date, not been a victim of terrorist attacks) rated the risk of a terror attack in their country as low, even significantly lower than other non-terrorist hazards (Sjöberg, 2005). Studies involving the estimation of the risk of natural hazards have also demonstrated differences in risk perception across countries and further indicate that this type of cognitive process is a complex one. For example, in Istanbul, the risk of an earthquake occurring was estimated at realistic levels in high-and low risk districts of the city. Yet the perceived risk of damage to property/the life of one's self and family was similar in both districts, with 70% of participants being more worried about daily life-threats such as traffic accidents, crimes, etc. (Tekili-Yesil et al., 2010). In contrast, in Bucharest, a country with a similar level of seismicity, 54% of participants reported being completely indifferent to the danger of an earthquake in comparison to only 10% who reported living in constant fear of this danger, despite each participant having experienced at least one earthquake already (Arma , 2006). When taking a look at the perceived risk of terror attacks, recent studies have revealed ambiguous findings. Shiloh, Guvenc and Onkal (2007) found no differences in samples of Israeli and Turkish students regarding perceived vulnerability to terrorism, whereas Steger, Frazier and Zacchanini (2008) found a significant difference in terrorism worries between Spanish and American students, which were not entirely explained by symptoms of posttraumatic stress or exposure to terror attacks. To our knowledge, a direct comparison between European countries on the perceived risk that different types of emergencies and disasters pose has not been conducted. Differences in risk perception could be due to differences in the nations' cultures (see Gierlach, Belsher & Beutler, 2010). Other factors often relevant to culture have been identified as predicting risk perception, such as age, female gender, migrant status and education (Arma , 2006; Eisenmann et al. 2009; Godwin, Willson & Gaines, 2005; Huddy, Feldmann, Capelos & Provost, 2002). However, one's views on the risk posed by emergencies and disasters is, as suggested by the aforementioned studies and other research, likely to be influenced also by one's previous experience of these kinds of event (Helweg-Larsen, 1999; Kellens et al., 2011) and the type of event (Ho, Shaw, Lin & Chiu, 2008).

Therefore we decided to assess the subjective risk posed by different types of emergencies and disasters and assess (1) whether the subjective risks differ across European countries, and (2) the influence of personal characteristics such as gender, age, education and previous experience on risk perception.

We were interested in the subjective perception of the risk posed (i.e. the concern about personally becoming the victim of an emergency or disaster) as there is evidence that this construct of risk perception especially is related to behavioural and psychological reactions (Godwin et al., 2005; Huddy et al., 2002).

Methods

The study described in this paper is part of a larger cross-cultural multi-centre research project called BeSeCu (Behaviour, Security, Culture) with the following centres participating: Greifswald, Germany; London, UK; Barcelona, Spain; Warsaw, Poland; Hamburg, Germany; Prague, Czech Republic; Stockholm, Sweden and Izmir, Turkey. The study was approved in all national institutional ethics committees and was part of a lager pre-test of a questionnaire for survivors of different European emergencies and disasters (see also Grimm, Hulse & Schmidt, 2012).

Participants

Recruitment was performed in each centre individually in November 2009. A total of 330 participants took part in the study with 53 participants from Germany, 20 from the UK, 53 from Spain, 50 from Sweden, 52 from Poland, 54 from the Czech Republic and 48 from Turkey. There was an almost even split of females (54.9%)

and males (45.1%). Mean age was 35.29 years (SD = 13.45). Three percent of participants had a migrant background; due to the small percentage of migrant participants, further analysis of this factor was omitted. On average participants reported about receiving formal education for 16.06 years (SD = 5.95). Thirteen percent of all participants had already experienced an emergency or disaster, mainly a fire, a flood or an earthquake. These events happened on average eleven years (SD = 9.5) ago.

Measures

Subjective risk was assessed on a 5-point Likert-scale from not at all (0) to strongly concerned (4) prompted by the following question: "Now, thinking about emergencies and disasters in general, how concerned are you personally about being the victim of the following events in the future?". Each question was translated and assessed in the national language. Data was assessed and questionnaires were filled in a standardised PASW/Excel data matrix in the respective countries. After assessment, the data matrix and original questionnaires were sent to the coordinating centre in Greifswald for final checking data analysis.

Statistical analysis

In order to detect whether there were any differences in risk perception, one-way ANOVAs plus post-hoc Scheffé tests were conducted and the effect size Cohen's f was calculated. For each type of event, an ordinal regression was run using subjective risk as the dependent variable, gender, previous experience and culture as factors and age and education as covariates. All statistical analysis was conducted with PASW, version 18.0.

Results

The subjective risk of becoming a victim was highest for fires (M = 1.38, SD = .98), then, in descending order, terror attacks (M = 1.12, SD = 1.14), floods (M = 1.10, SD = 1.10) and earthquakes (M = .83, SD = 1.19). Subjective risk perception was lowest in Sweden (M = .94, SD = .54), followed by the Czech Republic (M = 1.04, SD = .60), Germany (M = 1.04. SD = .54) and the UK (M = 1.14, SD = .56). These countries differed significantly from Spain (M = 1.86, SD = 1.02) and Turkey (M = 2.13, SD = .88). Poland (M = 1.47, SD = .74) differed significantly from Turkey and Sweden. Differences in the risk ratings across countries and types of event are shown in Table 3.8.

Table 3.8: Univariate F-Tests of subjective risk perception (including means, standard deviations and ES Cohen's f) for different types of emergencies and disasters across seven European countries

	F df (6,330)	f	SW	CZ	GER	UK	PL	ESP	TUR
Terror attack***	14.53	.58	.58 (.70)	.51 (.91)	1.02 (.96)	1.35 (1.04)	1.04 (1.07)	1.73 (1.33)	2.20 (.99)
Earthquake***	32.84	.78	.36 (.60)	.30 (.54)	.40 (.68)	.20 (.52)	.71 (1.22)	1.27 (1.33)	2.59 (1.14)
Flood***	8.45	.43	.50 (.68)	1.32 (1.03)	.69 (.95)	.65 (.81)	1.26 (1.23)	1.49 (1.19)	1.74 (1.15)
Fire***	9.87	.41	1,20 (.93)	.85 (.78)	1.03 (.67)	1.25 (.86)	1.72 (.94)	1.87 (1.07)	1.89 (1.05)

(*** = ρ < .001)

The ordinal regression showed that the nation the participants belonged to produced a higher, significant effect on risk perception than did the other socio-demographic variables (see Table 3.9). The model fitting statistic R2 (Nagelkerke) showed that the model explained most variance for earthquakes (.36), then explained less for terror attacks (.28), fires (.19) and floods (.17). The additional model fitting statistic indicated that the observed data were consistent with the estimated models for floods (χ^2 = 979.74, ρ = .41), fires (χ^2 = 1741.83, ρ = .99) and earthquakes (χ^2 = 878.22, ρ = .99), whereas this was not the case for terror attacks (χ^2 = 1093.29, ρ = .01).

Table 3.9: Regression coefficients of explanatory variables associated with the subjective risk perception of different emergencies and disasters

	Terror attack	Earthquake	Flood	Fire
Gender (male)	– .61*	– .07	– .10	– .38
Gender (female)	0	0	0	0
Previous experience (no)	.17	.20	– .49	– .92
Previous experience (yes)	0	0	0	0
Age	.01	.01	– .01	.01
Education	.01	-.02	.01	– .01
GER	– 2.28***	– 3.61***	– 2.10***	– 1.63***
UK	– 1.14*	– 4.38***	– 2.12***	– 1.55**
ESP	– 1.15*	– 1.93***	– .61	– .04
SW	– 2.85***	– 3.61***	– 2.40***	– 1.20**
PL	– 2.04***	– 3.22***	– 1.12*	– .24
CZ	– 3.60***	– 3.86***	– .87	– 2.26***
TUR	0	0	0	0

(* = ρ < .05; ** = ρ < .01; *** = ρ < .001)

Discussion

In general, the assessment of subjective risk perception showed participants across European countries perceived themselves to be at low risk from emergencies and disasters. First, it has to be considered that when the assessment was made, in November 2009, no major event struck the respective countries and none of them had a country-wide terrorism alert. Second, in comparison to other continents, Europe indeed can be considered a safe place considering the comparative occurrence of natural hazards and terrorism.

Table 3.10: Statistics for incident rates and fatalities associated with the emergencies and disasters terror attack, earthquake, flood and fire in seven European countries (Grimm, 2012)

		SW	CZ	GER	UK	PL	ESP	TUR
Terror attack[1] (2000-2006)	Incidents	8	3	15	25	–	732	477
	Fatalities	0	0	1	56	–	241	169
Earthquake[2] (2000-2009)	Incidents	0	0	1	1	0	0	15
	Fatalities	0	0	0	0	0	0	252
Flood[2] (2000-2009)	Incidents	0	6	6	15	5	8	18
	Fatalities	0	38	29	26	30	35	208
Fire[3]/ av. per year (2002-2006)	Incidents	26,772	19,369	184,485	489,942	179,815	–	59,618
	Fatalities	105	102	479	532	503	–	340

Statistics taken from [1] nationmaster.com; [2] EM-DAT; [3] CTFI; published in Grimm (2012)

When taking a closer look at the results, it becomes obvious that people's perception of the risk posed by emergencies and disasters is not a shared construct in Europe. Risk perception was influenced by nation, with Turkish and Spanish participants showing significantly higher rates of subjective risk for each type of event than participants from the UK, Sweden and Central European countries. Unlike Gierlach, Belsher and Beutler (2011), who found that significant differences in the level of perceived risk between Americans, Japanese and Argentineans was not influenced by actual exposure rates, we found that patterns of subjective risk perception in Europe do somewhat reflect the relative exposure to emergencies and disasters in respective countries (see table 3.10). For UK participants, becoming a victim of a terror attack was the risk they were most concerned about. Although not rated top, concerns about a terror attack were still high in Spain and Turkey as well. Accordingly, Spain, the UK and Turkey are the countries with the highest rates of terror attacks in Europe, with Spain even being among the five countries experiencing the most frequent terror attacks in the world (nationmaster.com, 2011).

Spain, the UK and Turkey have suffered from both external (e.g. Al Queda) and internal (separatist) terrorism. While the terror threat in Northern Ireland has diminished in recent years, 85 terror acts were committed in Spain in 2008 by separatist terrorists, mainly ETA, with four persons dying as a result (TESAT, 2009). In contrast to this, incidence rates of terror attacks and fatalities are low in the Czech Republic, Sweden and Germany (nationmaster.com, 2011). Accordingly, in these countries, and in Poland, the risk from terror attacks was rated as low. Nevertheless, it must be noted that in Sweden and Germany, becoming a victim of a terror attack was rated as the second highest risk, in Germany almost as high as the risk posed by fires. In fact, the risk of becoming a victim of a terror attack was, overall, the second highest risk for this European sample. Fires, the type of event with the highest incidence rates among all countries, was also the type of event rated as posing the highest risk overall. Nonetheless, only Polish, Swedish, Spanish and German participants rated fires as posing most risk. In 2006, the highest rate of fires per 1,000 inhabitants was in the UK with 7.2. In comparison to this, in Germany, Turkey, Sweden and the Czech Republic the rates were 2.3, 1.1, 3.0 and 1.0, respectively (Brushlinsky, Hall, Sokolov& Wagner, 2008). When taking a look at fire incidence rates in Europe, the comparatively high perceived risk for terror attacks is not a realistic one (see table 3.10). Although, nowadays, the explanatory power of risk perception models are discussed (Sjöberg, 2002), the sensation or, according to the psychometric model, the factor "dread risk" (Fischoff, 1978; Slovic, 1987) of an event such as a terror attack, has an influence on risk perception which is also reflected in the level of media coverage and political awareness. Also, in contrast to other types of event, terror attacks such as the World Trade Center attacks and the Madrid and London train bombings have produced psychological/health consequences such as evoking posttraumatic and depressive symptoms but also increased drug use, a phenomenon not limited to occurring in the direct victims of the attacks but also visible in people indirectly exposed (Galea et al., 2002; Miguel-Tobal, et al., 2006; Rubin et al., 2005; Rubin et al., 2007; Schuster et al., 2001; Silver,et al., 2002; Vlahov et al., 2002), which might also explain our findings. Regarding natural disasters, Turkish participants rated earthquakes as the type of event of which they were most likely to become a victim, differing significantly from the low ratings seen in other countries, the latter leading to the fact that earthquakes were the type of event with the lowest perceived subjective risk overall. This more accurately reflects the incidence and fatality rates of earthquakes in Europe (see table 3.10). It should be noted that Turkish recruitment was conducted in Izmir, a region with high seismicity. For floods, the findings are not as straightforward (see Table 3.8). Czech participants – all living in Prague, a city that was severely affected by the Vltava flood in 2002 – felt floods posed them the highest risk. Turkish, Spanish and Polish respondents also rated the risk of becoming a victim of a flood as high. Whereas in Germany and the UK, although the incident rates of floods there are comparable to that in the Czech Republic and Poland, the risk of becoming a victim of floods was rated significantly lower. We think that it should be taken into consideration that participants from these two western European countries were living in London and the North-East of Germany where major floods are not as likely to happen as in other parts of those countries. On the other hand, floods such as the Elbe flood 2002 in Germany and Central Europe or seasonal floods are continuously broadcast in the media so people should be aware of these events. However, one possible explanation could be that the appraisal of risk perception for floods differs from that for the other types of event. Floods have a longer onset, plus the possibility of early warning devices and the application of precautionary household damage prevention can evoke larger portions of control which might reduce perceived risk for floods (cf. Grothmann & Reusswig, 2006). Also the consequences of floods are more usually related to damage to property than to physical harm to one's family and one's self, so this aspect might lead to a perception of less risk.

Surprisingly, socio-demographic variables had little influence in this study on subjective risk perception. Although females reported higher risk perception than males for all event types, this finding was only significant in the case of terror attacks. Additionally, the variables age and education showed no influence on subjective risk perception. This result does not match the recent findings of others (cf. Arma , 2006; Ho, Shaw, Lin & Chiu, 2008, Kellens et al., 2011) and so we believe that socio-demographic variables may still be linked to risk perception. However, we suggest that our results might give reason to consider adjusting the relative influence of socio-demographic factors or testing their influence as part of an interaction with culture or other, more personal factors (Chauvin, Hermand & Mullet, 2006). Also striking is the fact that previous direct experiences of emergencies and disasters did not have an impact on the subjective risk of becoming a victim of an event, except for in the case of fires where there was a trend for previous experience to be a significant explanatory variable in the model. Helweg-Larsen (1999) showed that persons who were affected by an earthquake showed no optimistic bias (e.g. seeing oneself at being at less risk than others) regarding the risk of future earthquakes either immediately or at five months after the incident. It has to be considered that victims of emergencies and disasters in our study experienced their events quite a number of years ago. Thus we cannot rule out time since the event reducing the perceived risk here. Several other studies have found significant effects of previous experience. Kellens et al. (2011) showed that residents perceived the risk of floods at the Belgian coast to be higher when they had previous flood experience. In Fischhoff, Gonzalez, Small and Lerner's (2003) study, five terror-related events and three "routine risks" were rated. Only terror-related risks were judged higher among participants living within 100 miles of the World Trade Center. Ho et al. (2008) showed that people who have already experienced a flood or landslide rated the same incident as posing the highest risk, whereas people who had never experienced an emergency or disaster rated man-made hazardous events as posing most risk. Our study was methodologically different, investigating the influence of the experience of an emergency or disaster on subjective risk perception for different types of emergencies and disasters. Although participants with previous experience showed higher perceived risk for floods and fires than the average, this was not the case for earthquakes and terror attacks. As findings were not significant, it might be concluded that experiencing an emergency or disaster does not lead to higher general perceived risk but perhaps only to a more sensitive awareness for the event experienced. Regardless, these findings need to be treated with caution for several reasons. Our participants were only asked about their experiences of the types of event of interest (fires, floods, terror attacks and earthquakes), thus a conclusive comparison of survivors of each type of event with a no-experience group cannot be made. Also the limited sample size of survivors together with the aforementioned long period between assessment and event exposure means refraining from generalising these findings. A few further caveats concerning the study should be raised. The study was adequate concerning statistical power and overall sample size, but the observed effect sizes were small. Moreover, although efforts were made to control for age and gender across the different national subsamples, the overall sample was a convenience one. Furthermore, recruitment was mainly conducted in cities and so experiences in rural areas may be less well represented. However, we believe that, despite these limitations, a first step to assessing European risk perception of emergencies and disasters was made with this study. For future research, we suggest that it would be beneficial to explore the influence of socio-demographic variables and previous experience in Europe while including measures of the severity of the events and of emergency/disaster knowledge. In conclusion, the study was a first approach at analysing differences in risk perception across Europe. Fires and terror attacks were the types of event this European sample was most concerned about, followed by the natural disasters floods and earthquakes. Subjective risk perception differed significantly among countries. Although the concern about terror attacks was comparatively high in relation to the actual incidence rates of these events in Europe, the subjective risk ratings did nonetheless reflect somewhat the countries' histories of emergencies and disasters.

References

Arma, I. (2006). Earthquake Risk Perception in Bucharest, Romania. *Risk Analysis. 26, 5,* 1223-1234.

Brushlinsky, N.N., Hall, J.R., Sokolov, S.V. & Wagner, P. (2008). *World fire statistics.* CTIF: International association of fire and rescue services. p. 13.

Chauvin, B., Hermand, D. & Mullet, E. (2007). Risk perception and personality facets. *Risk Analysis, 27, 1,* 171-185.

Eisenman, D.P. et al. (2009). Terrorism-related fear and avoidance behavior in a multiethnic urban population. *American Journal of Public Health, 99, 1,* 168-174.

EM-DAT (2011). *The OFDA/CRED International Disaster Database.* www.emdat.be. Université Catholique de Louvain – Brussels – Belgium.

European Police Office (2009). *TE-SAT 2009: EU Terrorism Situation and Trend Report.* www.europol.europa.eu

Fischhoff, B., Gonzalez, R.M., Small, D.A. & Lerner, J.S. (2003). Judged terror risk and proximity to the World Trade Center. *Journal of Risk and Uncertainty, 26 (2),* 137-151

Fischhoff, B., Slovic, P., Lichtenstein, S., Read, S. & Combs, B. (1978.). How safe is enough? A psychometric study of attitudes towards technological risks. *Policy Science, 9,* 127-152.

Galea, S. et al. (2002). Psychological sequelae of the September 11 terrorist attacks in New York City. *New England Journal of Medicine, 346, 13,* 982-7.

Gierlach, E., Belsher, B.E. & Beutler L.E. (2010). Cross-Cultural Differences in Risk Perceptions of Disasters. *Risk Analysis, 30, 10,* 1539-1549.

Goodwin, R., Willson, M. & Gaines, S. (2005). Terror threat perception and its consequences in contemporary Britain. *British Journal of Psychology, 96,* 389-406.

Grimm, A. (2012). *Menschliche Reaktionen in Naturkatastrophen und technologischen Krisensituationen: Ergebnisse der explorativen Befragung von Überlebenden zur konzeptuellen Entwicklung eines standardisierten Instruments für das retrospektive Assessment* (Doctoral dissertation). Greifswald: Ernst-Moritz-Arndt Universität.

Grimm, A., Hulse, L. & Schmidt, S. (2009). Risk perception and psychological reactions in public crisis situations using the example of terror attacks. *Bundesgesundheitsblatt, 52, 12,* 1129-1140.

Grimm, A., Hulse, L., Preiss, M. & Schmidt, S., (in press). Post and peritraumatic stress in survivors of European disasters: An explorative study about the influence of individual and event characteristics across different types of disasters. *European Journal of Psychotraumatology, 3 (7382),* 1-9.

Grimm, A., Hulse, L., Preiss, M. & Schmidt, S., (in press). Behavioural, cognitive and emotional responses in European disasters: Results of survivor interviews. *Disasters: The Journal of Disaster Studies, Policy and Management.*

Grothmann, T. & Reusswig, F. (2006). People at risk of flooding: Why some residents take precautionary action while others do not. *Natural Hazards, 38,* 101-120.

Helweg-Larsen, M. (1999). (The Lack of) Optimistic Biases in Response to the 1994 Northridge Earthquake: The Role of Personal Experience. *Basic and Applied Social Psychology. 21, 2,* 119-129.

Ho, M.-C., Shaw, D., Lin, S. & Yao-Chu, C. (2008). How Do Disaster Characteristics Influence Risk Perception? *Risk Analysis, 28, 3,* 635-643.

Huddy, L., Feldmann, S., Capelos, T. & Provost, C. (2002). The consequences of terrorism: Disentangling the effects of personal and national threat. *Political Psychology, 23,* 3, 485-509.

Kellens, W., Zaalberg, R., Vanneville, W. & de Maeyer, P. (2011). An Analysis of the Public Perception of Flood Risk on the Belgian Coast. *Risk Analysis 31: no.* doi:10.1111/j.1539-6924.2010.01571.x.

Miguel-Tobal, J.J. et al. (2006). PTSD and depression after the Madrid March 11 Train Bombings. *Journal of Traumatic Stress, 19,* 1, 69-80.

Nationmaster (2011). *http://www.nationmaster.com/cat/ter-terrorism*

Preventionweb.net (2011) *http://www.preventionweb.net/english/countries/statistics/index_region.php?rid = 3.*

Rubin, G.J. et al. (2007). Enduring consequences of terrorism: 7-month follow-up survey of reactions to the bombings in London on 7 July 2005. *British Journal of Psychiatry, 190,* 350-356.

Rubin, G.J. et al. (2005). Psychological and behavioural reactions to the bombings in London on 7 July 2005: cross sectional survey of a representative sample of Londoners. *British Medical Journal, 331, 7517,* 606-611.

Schuster, M.A. et al. (2001). A national survey of stress reactions after the September 11, 2001, terrorist attacks. *New England Journal of Medicine, 345, 20,* 1507-12.

Shiloh S., Guvenc G., Onkal D. (2007). Cognitive and emotional representations of terror attacks: A cross-cultural exploration. *Risk Analysis, 27, 2,* 397-409.

Silver, R.C., Holman, A., McIntosh, D.N., Poulin, M. & Gil-Rivas, V. (2002) Nationwide longitudinal study of psychological responses to September 11. *Journal of the American Medical Association, 288, 10,* 1235-1244.

Sjöberg, L. (2005). The perceived risk of terrorism. *Risk Management, 7, 1,* 43-61.

Sjöberg, L. (2002). Are risk perception models well and alive? *Risk analysis, 22, 4,* 665-669.

Sjöberg, L. (2000). Factors in risk perception. *Risk Analysis, 20,* 1-20.

Slovic, P. (1987). Perception of risk. *Science, 236, 4799,* 280-285.

Steger, M.F., Frazier P.A. & Zacchanini J.L. (2008). Terrorism in two cultures: Stress and growth following September 11 and the Madrid Bombings. *Journal of Loss and Trauma, 13,* 511-527.

Tekeli-Yesil, S., Dedeoglu, N., Braun-Fahrlaender, C. & Tanner M. (2010). Factors Motivating Individuals to Take Precautionary Action for an Expected Earthquake in Istanbul. *Risk Analysis. 30, 8,* 1181-1195.

Vlahov, D. et al. (2002). Increased use of cigarettes, alcohol, and marijuana among Manhattan, New York, residents after September 11th terrorist attacks. *American Journal of Epidemiology, 155, 11,* 988-996.

Weiss, D.S. & Marmar, C.R. (1997). The Impact of Event Scale – Revised. In: J.P. Wilson & T.M. Keanne (Eds.), *Assessing psychological trauma and PTSD* (pp. 399-411). New York: Guilord Press.

4 Development of field study instruments BeSeCu-S and BeSeCu-FR

Daniela Knuth, Doris Kehl & Silke Schmidt

In this section the process of developing the Field Study Instrument for Survivors (BeSeCu-S) and First Responders (BeSeCu-FR) is described. The study was carried out in eight European countries (i.e. Czech Republic, Germany, Italy, Poland., Sweden, Spain, Turkey and the UK) between May 2008 and April 2011. The field study instruments were developed in consecutive steps including qualitative and quantitative data approaches (see Fig. 4.1).

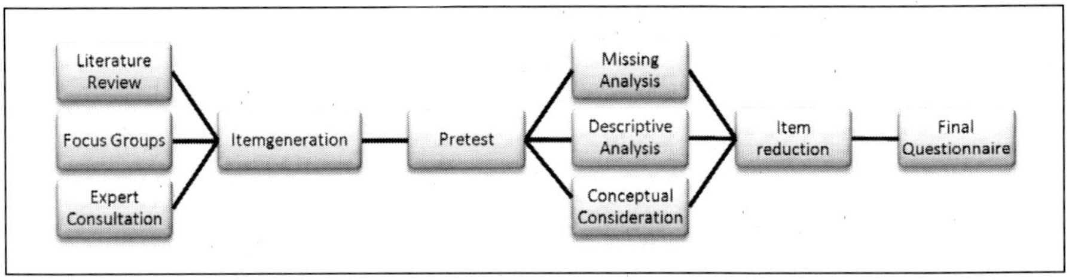

Fig. 4.1: Process of questionnaire development

Literature review

The literature review focused on (a) existing national and international scientific evidence on security research and human behaviour and (b) the state of the art of how cross-cultural communication issues have been implemented into security-related interventions from end-users' perspective. Key topics of the literature reviewed were the different factors which might have an impact on emergency and evacuation procedures as well as on firefighters' professional performance such as human response, evacuation behaviour with its human, fire and building features, emergency communication, emergency information and emergency warning, victims' threat assessment, compliance and willingness to evacuate etc.

Consultation

In addition to the interdisciplinary BeSeCu team of researches and end-users (e.g. firefighters, emergency medical services), national and international experts from fields of security research as well as national accident investigation boards supported the project as members of an international advisory group. The collaboration between researchers and end-users enabled a better distribution of the newly gained knowledge (Fisher, 2010).

Focus groups and interviews

In order to learn about more people´s reactions in different emergency situations, focus groups were executed. A benefit of using the focus group technique in which a small group of people is interviewed regarding a topic which they all have in common, is the possibility that all participants have the opportunity to interact with each other and respond to diverse views (Plummer-D'Amato, 2008). The main purpose is to elevate specific perceptions, thinking patterns and vocabulary of the target group which can be used to generate questions for a survey (Morgan, 1997; Plummer-D'Amato, 2008).

Cross-cultural focus groups and interviews were conducted with 144 survivors who had experienced one of the following crisis situations: a domestic fire, a terroristic attack, an earthquake, a flood, a collapse of a building, a bus accident or a fire in a public building (32 focus groups and 14 interviews). Information of 132 participants (out of the 144) could be used for further analysis (Freitag, Grimm & Schmidt, 2011). Furthermore, cross-cultural focus groups and interviews were conducted with 54 emergency personnel (paramedics, firefighter, physicians etc.) and key representatives (counsellors, journalists, NGOs, politicians etc.).

In the focus groups and interviews of survivors, relevant topics regarding human behaviour, experiences and reactions in emergencies and disasters were explored. Each participating centre included the following topics in their focus groups: Setting of the emergency situation, recognition, reaction, evacuation, professional intervention, communication, emotions and risk perceptions, cultural differences in behaviour in crisis situations.

In the focus groups and interviews of first responders and key representatives, questions regarding professional background and experience with large scale emergencies were explored. Furthermore, participants were asked to report about their experiences in a typical domestic fire or another emergency situation in which they were involved. Questions were asked with respect to setting/characteristics of the emergency situation, recognition of the emergency, decision making and risk perception, interventions and interactions, emotion, and behavioural reactions.

All focus group participants provided demographic and core incident-related information via questionnaire. Face-to-face interviews were only conducted if a participant didn´t wish to take part in a group setting. A focus group manual summarized the basic information regarding procedure and training of interviewers. Furthermore information in terms of counselling and support for traumatized people was identified prior to the interviews.

Each centre transcribed their focus groups according to the transcribing guidelines determined in the manual. Subsequently, transcripts were translated into English. Q-sort technique was used in order to categorize statements and develop a glossary. Based on this glossary the transcripts of the focus groups and interviews were re-rated and the frequencies of each category were analyzed. Subsequently, a set of items with corresponding answer categories were derived.

Pretest

Based on the list of categories from the focus groups, the literature review and the expert consultations, a pilot form of BeSeCu-S and BeSeCu-FR was generated and translated into all respective languages. The pilot forms were then tested in the eight European countries via paper-pencil questionnaires. A standardized pre-test manual was distributed to and followed by all project partners. The pretest was conducted in order to test feasibility, practicability as well as the difficulty of items and scales in the questionnaire (Rubin, Pronovost & Diette, 2001).

Pretest of BeSeCu-S

In the pretest of BeSeCu-S principles of the Cognitive Interview Technique were used to enhance the capacity for remembering the critical situations. In a Cognitive Interview the interviewee is asked to reminisce about the experienced situation. Typically the interviewer reconstructs the context of the event and then goes through the event in different orders, beginning with the chronological order. According to the cognitive interview technique, which can enhance the accuracy of remembering the event in detail (Kohnken, Milne, Memon & Bull, 1999), the questions of the BeSeCu-S were arranged in the chronological order of the event with the four main stages:

1. Beginning/Initial perception of unusual cues,
2. Understanding of what's going on,
3. Evacuation, and
4. Time after the event.

At each stage, setting information, behaviours, emotions and cognition were obtained. The subdivision into stages was used since survivors in the focus groups stated that it is very hard for them to indicate how they felt during the incident, since their feelings as well as behaviours changed throughout these stages. Especially the literature concerning human behaviour in fire supports this approach (Kuligowski, 2008, 2009; Sime, Creed, Kimura & Powell, 1992). Five different emergency scenarios (domestic fire, fire in a public building, terrorist attack, earthquake and flood) were developed to expand the target population and consequently include participants who did not experience an emergency before. Furthermore a cognitive debriefing task was performed with the target population. This method was used to ensure an understanding of the questions in the way it was intended (Eremenco, Cella & Arnold, 2005). Cognitive debriefing is an important technique to learn more about the way a question is understood, the ability and willingness to retrieve the information in question and the quality of the given response options (e.g. response format) (Collins, 2003).

The pilot form of the BeSeCu-S questionnaire included 106 questions. The first 84 questions refer to the emergency situation and were subdivided into the above mentioned four main stages. In the end, 22 socio-demographic questions were interrogated.

Pilot data were collected from 336 participants from whom 25 experienced one of the events in question. In order to further test the questionnaire in the target population, 11 participants took part in a cognitive debriefing which consisted of reading the questionnaire aloud to the participant and incorporating comments regarding the understanding, interpretation and usefulness of a question and its response format. Participants had to be at least 18 years old in order to be eligible for the study. The mean age of all participants was 35.48 (SD = 13.51) with a range from 18 to 85 years. 55.1% of the participants were female and 44.9% male. The sample of the pretest was highly educated since the mean time of education was 16.00 years (SD = 5.93) and 48.4% of all participants had completed an university degree and 21.4% did at least start university. 23.3% finished a higher secondary qualification, 4% stated intermediary secondary qualification as their highest completed qualification and only 2.8% had either no formal qualification (0.6%) or the lowest formal qualification attainable in their country (2.2%). 74% of all participants were either employed (66.6%) or self-employed (7.4%). 18.9% were students or unpaid volunteers, 2.8% were unemployed, 0.6% were permanently disabled or on long-term sick leave and the final 3.7% were already retired. With 55.1% most participants were Single, 37.0% were married, 6.6% were divorced or separated and 1.3% were widowed. Regarding the different countries involved in the pretest 16.1% of the participants came from the Czech Republic, 15.8% from Germany another 15.8% from Spain, 15.5% from Poland, 14.9% from Sweden, 14.3% from Turkey, 6.0% from the U.K. and the final 1.8% from Italy. Within the sample of real survivors 44.0% had experienced a domestic fire, 24.0% an earthquake, 16.0% a flood, 8% a terroristic attack and further 8% a fire in a public building. All participants that did not experience one of these incidents answered the questionnaire with respect to the scenario they were given. 26.0% of the 311 participants got a domestic fire-scenario, 21.2% a terroristic attack scenario, 19.3% read a scenario involving an earthquake, 17.0% answered with reference to a flood-scenario and the final 16.4% got a scenario of a fire in a public building before answering the questionnaire.

Pretest of BeSeCu-FR

The pilot tested BeSeCu-FR instrument, which was constructed for emergency personnel in general, comprised 10 domains with a sum of 171 main items. In the beginning were questions about socio demographic information including migrant status (18 main items), working characteristics (7 main items), and about theoretical knowledge and practical experience regarding different emergencies and disasters: domestic fire, fire in a public building, flood, earthquake, terrorist attack, and traffic accident (21 main items). These domains were followed by questions regarding personal experience of threat and distress in working life (2 main items) and questions regarding general risk perception in respect to the six above mentioned emergency situations (18 main items). The next domains contained questions about a specific emergency situation with non-migrant (29 main items) and migrant (25 main items) victims. Furthermore, the intercultural environment of the emergency personnel was assessed with another domain. The questionnaire concluded with assumptions and experiences of how population groups react in emergency situations (18 items) and evacuation issues with specific vulnerable groups e.g. children and elderly (4 main items).

For the pre-test a convenience sample of 260 was drawn. Participants could be included in the pre-test if (a) they work professionally in emergency situations (as fire fighters, paramedics, emergency physician, police officer, pastoral caregiver etc.) and if (b) they have had direct contact to victims of an emergency situation in the past.

The average age of the 260 study participants was 36.1 (SD = 9.6) years, and their ages ranged from 18 to 67 years. Among the participants 79.1% were males. The lowest formal qualification had 3.9% of the participants, 12.8% an intermediary secondary qualification, 44.2% a higher secondary qualification, and 39.1% a university degree. Among the participants 45.5% were firefighters, 13.2% paramedics, 9.3% emergency physicians, 12.8% police officer, 8.6% other first responder (e.g. mental health professionals, pastoral caregiver), 8.7% were both firefighter and paramedic, and 1.9% had two other professions. Overall, 67.3% worked as operational personnel and 32.7% were considered as leading personnel. On average, participants worked as first responders 12.1 (SD = 8.5) years with a range from 1 to 36 years. Most first responders (88.1%) described their current status as employed and 6.3% were honorary members. The remaining 5.6% described themselves with other categories (e.g. student).

Item reduction

To identify possible items for deletion and as indicator for acceptance and feasibility a detailed missing and descriptive analysis was conducted. Latest research results regarding item construction, wording and structure of a questionnaire were taken into consideration, to ensure the effectiveness of the questionnaire

(Faulmann, Prüfer & Rexroth, 2009; Handa, et al., 2008; Martin, et al., 2007). Furthermore comments from the cognitive debriefing task were integrated and the finalization of the questionnaire was the result of a last workshop with members of all participating project centres. All decisions to delete, keep or revise a certain item were based on consensus i.e. decided unanimously after a discussion of the group. Instructions, contact information as well as a number of items were revised and modified. Some important design choices were made to ensure the quality and cross cultural comparability of the questionnaire and its response scales. Additionally the number of open questions was reduced, since this type of question is considered especially tiring and therefore increases the risk of drop outs and missing data (Griffith, Cook, Guyatt & Charles, 1999).

Field study

In the following sections the field study will be described in detail in order to display the integration of the cross cultural focus groups and the pretest results into the final questionnaires. Furthermore some results of the field study are presented.

Translation process

Based on focus group and pre-test results final questionnaire drafts were developed in English, therefore a translation into all corresponding languages (i.e. German, Czech, Polish, Spanish, Italian, Swedish and Turkish) was necessary. The translation process focused on conceptual equivalence rather than literal equivalence, since previous research has shown that literal translation alone does not ensure the equality of the measured constructs (Lin, Chen & Chiu, 2005). The guidelines of the WHO were followed by using the translation method forward-backward-forward translation to achieve the best possible cross-cultural harmonisation. At least one translator of each participating country translated the final English questionnaire into the respective target language. In case of two independent translations a reconciled forward translation was created, meeting all demands of conceptual equivalence with the original English pilot draft. The (reconciled) forward translation was then back translated into English by a third translator unfamiliar with the original English version to avoid biases. The backward translation was either made by a translation agency or a native English speaking person. All backward translations were sent to the coordinating centre and subsequently checked for conceptual equivalence with the original English version. Possible meaning-diversities of individual items detected in the backward translation were discussed between the project partners and modified if necessary. After final revisions for each target language, the coordinating centre finalized the layout of all translated questionnaires to ensure comparability in respect to design and layout.

Recruitment

Each partner was responsible for recruiting a nationwide sample in their own country and therefore applying the appropriate recruitment strategies. Since eight countries were involved in this study, there is a great variety of approaches to contact the target population. A manual with recruitment instructions was given to each project partner. Various possible strategies such as top down recruitment via fire brigades, radio interviews etc. Additionally, the following possible contact partners were recommended: Health Protection Agency, Federal Office of Civil Protection and Disaster Assistance, Integrated Rescue System, emergency medical services, Survivor networks, associations of victims, Media (i.e. Internet, adverts in newspapers). The most commonly used strategies in this project are described below. Participants were given the opportunity to order a paper pencil questionnaire without any costs as well as filling it out online.

The BeSeCu project as well as the questionnaires were advertised in various internet portals (e.g. for fire fighter, fire survivors, psychologists, general public) and social networks like Facebook, Twitter or StudiVZ. A BeSeCu Facebook page was created on which updated information regarding the study was available as well as a direct link to the questionnaire. Furthermore the BeSeCu homepage was available in all respective languages and contained all information about the project, participation and enabled direct access to the online questionnaires. Project partners also provided a link to the BeSeCu website on their particular homepage. Another strategy was direct contact (e.g. personal visits, mailing and telephone calls) with first responders, survivors or officials of affected regions (e.g. flood or earthquake). First responders were asked to inform their colleagues and possible survivors about the project. Many press releases in newspapers, newsletter or gazettes, radio interviews and discussions about BeSeCu on Television have been done in different countries. BeSeCu was also promoted on various conferences (e.g. 6th European Congress on Civil Protection and Disaster Management 2010 in Bonn/Germany, 12th International Conference on Fire Safety and Engineering in Nottingham/England, IV Scientific Conference – Man in extreme conditions: Earth, Water, Air).

Administration

The BeSeCu-S and BeSeCu-FR was available in a paper-and-pencil and an online version. Both versions had identical questions and the layout as well as response styles were kept similar. Questions and layout were identical across all languages also. Of the participants who answered the BeSeCu-FR field study questionnaire (n = 3,011), 52.2% (n = 1,571) filled out the paper-and-pencil questionnaire and 47.8% (n = 1,440) the online version. Of the participants who answered the BeSeCu-S questionnaire and experienced an incident in one of the partner countries (n = 1,112), 69.1% (n = 768) filled out the paper-and-pencil questionnaire,

25.6% (n = 285) the online version, and 5.3% (n = 59) filled out the questionnaire with support of one of the BeSeCu team members. For example, this was the case when older participants had trouble reading the questionnaire.

Final field study instruments

The BeSeCu-S comprised 145 items and was subdivided into two main parts. Part I comprised socio demographic items followed by questions regarding emergency relevant trust, knowledge, risk perception and experience (15 items). Part II addressed the specific incident. Questions regarding the incident were subdivided into four different stages: Beginning (14 items), Realization (26 items), Evacuation (31 items) and Aftermath (36 items). In the Beginning stage, setting relevant questions like the time and place of the event were surveyed. The Realization stage included questions concerning initial reactions and activities. The Evacuation stage concerned the process of evacuation and was therefore only mandatory for participants that either evacuated or had been rescued during the emergency situation and skipped by all other participants. In the last stage the events' consequences and impacts of the event were assessed.

The BeSeCu-FR comprised 159 items, representing 10 domains. The questionnaire started with the domain about demographic information (13 items) followed by questions regarding work characteristics (14 items) and theoretical knowledge and practical experience (18 items) regarding different emergency situations, fire brigade training and fire prevention/fire safety education. These domains were followed by questions on general risk perception (12 items) regarding six different emergency situations (i.e. domestic fire, fire in a public building, terrorist attack, flood, earthquake, and traffic accident). The next domain comprised questions about victims' behaviour in emergency situations (19 items) followed by questions about general communication with people on site, between first responders, and non-verbal communication (sign language) (27 items). Furthermore, general questions about a specific kind of emergency situation, i.e. fires in multiple-occupancy residential buildings (31 items) were asked (e.g. how often specific information is relayed to firefighters in advance of taking action, firefighters' perception of occupants' threat assessments etc.). The next domain contained questions about firefighters' stress and emotion regulation techniques in emergency situations (9 items) followed by questions about personal experience of threat in working life (2 items). In the last domain firefighter answered questions about the most stressful emergency situation they had professionally attended in the last 10 years (14 items).

References

Cann, A., Calhoun, L.G., Tedeschi, R.G., Taku, K., Vishnevsky, T., Triplett, K.N. et al. (2010). A short form of the Posttraumatic Growth Inventory. *Anxiety, Stress & Coping: An International Journal, 23 (2),* 127-137.

Cohen, S., Kamarck, T. & Mermelstein, R. (1983). A Global Measure of Perceived Stress. *Journal of Health and Social Behavior, 24 (4),* 385-396.

Collins, D. (2003). Pretesting survey instruments: An overview of cognitive methods. *Quality of Life Research, 12 (3),* 229-238. doi: 10.1023/A:1023254226592

Eremenco, S.L., Cella, D. & Arnold, B.J. (2005). A comprehensive method for the translation and cross-cultural validation of health status questionnaires. *Eval Health Prof, 28 (2),* 212-232. doi: 28/2/212 [pii] 10.1177/0163278705275342

Faulmann, F., Prüfer, P. & Rexroth, M. (2009). *Was ist eine gute Frage? Die systematische Evaluation der Fragenqualität* (1st ed.). Wiesbaden: VS Verlag für Sozialwissenschaften.

Fisher, H.W. (2010). *Future Research Needs. Response to disaster. Fact versus fiction and its perpetuation. The sociology of disaster* (pp. 201-202). Lanham, Maryland: University Press of America.

Freitag, S., Grimm, A. & Schmidt, S. (2011). Talking about traumatic events - A cross-cultural investigation. *Europe's Journal of Psychology, 7 (1),* 40-61.

Griffith, L.E., Cook, D.J., Guyatt, G.H. & Charles, C.A. (1999). Comparison of open and closed questionnaire formats in obtaining demographic information from Canadian general internists. *Journal of Clinical Epidemiology, 52 (10),* 997-1005. doi: 10.1016/S0895-4356(99)00106-7

Handa, V.L., Barber, M.D., Young, S.B., Aronson, M.P., Morse, A. & Cundiff, G.W. (2008). Paper versus web-based administration of the Pelvic Floor Distress Inventory 20 and Pelvic Floor Impact Questionnaire 7. [Article]. *International Urogynecology Journal, 19 (10),* 1331-1335. doi: 10.1007/s00192-008-0651-6

Kohnken, G., Milne, R., Memon, A. & Bull, R. (1999). The cognitive interview: A meta-analysis. *Psychology Crime & Law, 5 (1-2),* 3-27. doi: 10.1080/10683169908414991

Kroenke, K., Spitzer, R.L. & Williams, J.B.W. (2003). The Patient Health Questionniare-2: Validity of a Two-Item Depression Screener. *Medical Care, 41 (11),* 1284-1292.

Kuligowski, K.D. (2008). Modeling Human Behavior during Building Fires (p. 21): National Institute of Standards and Technology, *Technical Note 1619.*

Kuligowski, K.D. (2009). The Process of Human Behavior in Fires (p. 15): National Institute of Standards and Technology. *Technical Note 1632.*

Lin, Y.-H., Chen, C.-Y. & Chiu, P.-K. (2005). Cross-Cultural Research and Back-Translation. *The Sport Journal, 8* (4).

Martin, E., Hunter Childs, J., DeMaio, T., Hill, J., Reiser, C., Gerber, E. et al. (2007). *Guidelines for Designing Questionnaires for Administration in Different Modes.* U.S. Census Bureau: Washington, DC 20233.

Morgan, D.L. (1997). *Focus groups as qualitative research* (2nd ed.). Thousand Oaks, CA: Sage Publications.

Plummer-D'Amato, P. (2008). Focus group methodology Part 1: Considerations for design. *International Journal of Therapy and Rehabilitation, 15 (2),* 6.

Power, M. (2003). Development of a common instrument for quality of life. In: A. Nosiko & C. Gudex (Eds.), EUROHIS. *Developing Common Instruments for Health Surveys* (pp. 145-161). Amsterdam: Published on behalf of the Worlde Health Organization Regional Office for Europe by IOS Press.

Rubin, H.R., Pronovost, P. & Diette, G.B. (2001). From a process of care to a measure: the development and testing of a quality indicator. *Int J Qual Health Care, 13 (6),* 489-496. doi: 10.1093/intqhc/13.6.489

Sime, J., Creed, C., Kimura, M. & Powell, J. (1992). *Human Behaviour in Fires.* Department for Communities and Local Government. Not be printed.

Weiss, D.S. & Marmar, C.R. (1996). The Impact of Event Scale – Revised. In: J.P. Wilson & T.M. Keane (Eds.), *Assessing psychological trauma and PTSD* (pp. 399-411): New York: Guilford.

5 Field study on human behaviour in emergencies and disasters

5.1 Recruitment strategies across all centres

Daniela Knuth, Doris Kehl, Katrin Stegemann & Silke Schmidt

Each centre was responsible for the recruitment of their sample and used strategies that were most effective locally. The questionnaire was available in a paper-and-pencil version and an online version so various recruiting strategies could be applied. The online questionnaire was activated and thereby available for participants on June 8th 2010.

A field study manual was given to each project partner including instructions regarding recruitment. This included the requirement of a nationwide recruitment. Various strategies such as top down recruitment via fire brigades, radio interviews and possible contact partners were recommended. Additionally, all centres were asked to send a description of their nationwide recruitment strategies to the coordinating centre regularly as well as the sample numbers.

Among the 1,130 survivors who answered the BeSeCu-S questionnaire and met the inclusion criteria, 1,112 experienced the incident in one of the partner countries. The BeSeCu-FR questionnaire was answered by 3,011 firefighters. The country specific numbers for first responder and survivor participants with respect to administration mode are provided in Table 5.1 Number of participants, administration mode and country.

Table 5.1: Number of participants, administration mode and country

Country	First responder			Survivors			
	PP	Online	Total	PP	Online	Support	Total
Czech Republic	238	64	302	140	27	0	167
Germany	124	577	701	107	97	1	205
Italy	482	141	623	99	45	25	169
Poland	130	245	375	161	17	8	186
Spain	119	44	163	59	36	10	105
Sweden	9	172	181	47	36	0	83
Turkey	467	1	468	145	0	0	145
U.K.	2	196	198	10	27	15	52
Total	*1,571*	*1,440*	*3,011*	*768*	*285*	*59*	*1,112*

Notes: PP = Paper-pencil; support = questionnaire was read to the participant

The BeSeCu consortium was able to reach survivors of emergencies and disasters (see Fig. 5.1) and first responders (see Table 5.2) in all eight European countries and in numerous regions of each individual country.

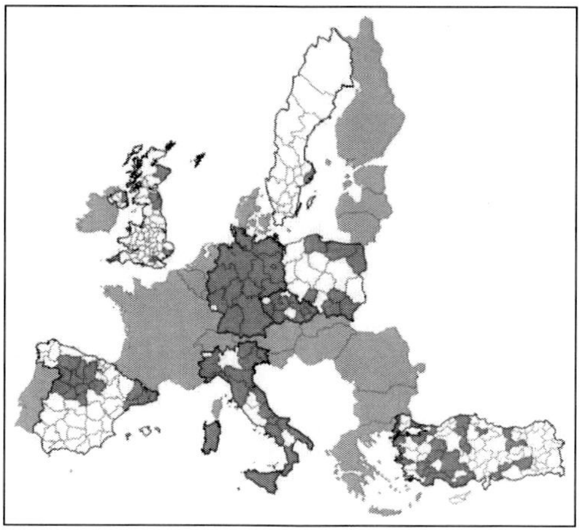

Fig. 5.1: European Regions of Civil Participants in the BeSeCu Field Study

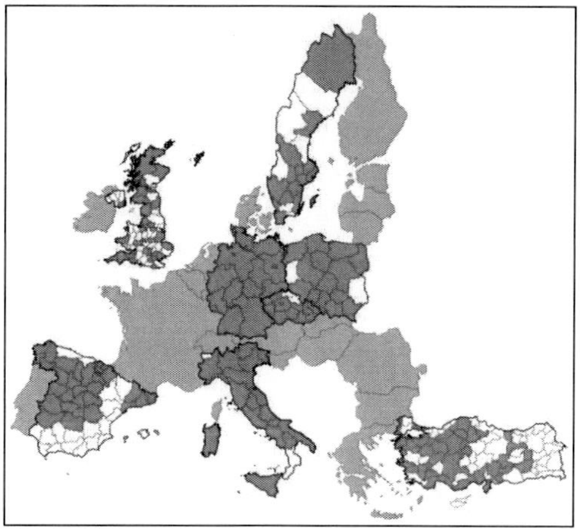

Fig. 5.2: European regions of First responders in the BeSeCu Field Study

5.1.1 Recruitment strategies of the Ernst-Moritz-Arndt-University Greifswald (EMAUG) and Hamburg Fire and Emergency Service Academy (HFESA)

Survivors

Online advertisement was used to reach as many people as possible nationwide. In Germany a large variety of different internet portals were used: www.local24.de, www.Kleinanzeigen.ebay.de, www.psychologie-heute.de, www.wer-weiß-was.de; www.gutefrage.net and www.Probanden-info.de. These different portals were used to advertise the BeSeCu project, to inform people about the project and the participation. Some platforms allow people to pose a question to experts like for example psychologists and first responders. Regarding the recruitment, we used these panels to get in contact with potential participants. Furthermore, it was asked for support of special firefighter homepages like www.feuerwehr.de, www.Berliner-feuerwehr.de and www.ub-feuerwehr.de. These homepages integrated a short announcement on their homepage addressing firefighter to inform and contact survivor about the BeSeCu project. Another form of online advertisement was the use of social networks like Facebook or StudiVZ/ MeinVZ. For the BeSeCu project the Facebook network was used to create a BeSeCu page that informs people about the project and how they can participate. Similar to the creation of own groups regarding the floods in Germany, fires and evacuation, we also advertised the BeSeCu project in existing groups regarding flood and fire. There are groups especially for people who survived a flood and experienced a fire in their own apartment. By posting the BeSeCu information in these groups, we were able to reach several people of the target population. Besides the special groups regarding flood and fire, we also used university groups to inform students and members of different universities about the project. This procedure was also used in firefighter groups, groups of different cities or states and groups of different civil protection organisations. By using this method we were able to inform more than 1,000 people at once about the project.

Another form to get in contact with inhabitants of affected flood regions was the direct contact of town officials. Citizens' offices and the mayor of the affected cities and towns of the flood in 2002 were contacted via telephone to ask for their support of the BeSeCu project. By using this recruitment strategy approximately 5,000 BeSeCu Flyer and more than 400 BeSeCu questionnaires for Survivors were sent out. In cooperation with the respective responsible person of each town further strategies of informing the people of the town were discussed and implemented. One very effective way to reach the inhabitants of small towns was the announcement in local newspapers and gazettes. A detailed research on house fires and floods enabled another way of personal contact with and recruitment of survivors. BeSeCu team members personally went to different regions and cities in Germany in order to present the project and interact with survivors. This strategy had the advantage of personal contact to survivors and therefore a greater commitment to fill out the questionnaire was achieved.

Another method, particularly to reach persons affected by house fires was the use of direct mailing. For the use of direct mailing, the knowledge of the street name and house number was required. Inhabitants of affected houses got a personal letter addressed to "All inhabitants of Example-street X" explaining the project and the reason of contacting them. Furthermore, newspapers were used to reach a wide range of people. The focus was mostly on local newspaper and local gazettes published by the citizen office in areas affected by flooding in the past years and in the recent months.

In order to inform the professional audience with respect to civil protection organisations and researchers in the field of disaster research, the BeSeCu project was also presented at different meetings and congresses (e.g. Interschutz 2010 in Leipzig/Germany, 6th European Congress on Civil Protection and Disaster Management 2010 in Bonn/Germany).

First responder

A major recruitment strategy for first responders was to get into personal contact with all the 102 major professional fire brigades in Germany.

The head of each professional fire brigade in Germany was contacted via a personal letter which included flyers and two questionnaires as specimen copies. After introducing the project via mail, fire brigades were contacted again by telephone in order to give them more information about the project and ask for their participation in the study by also informing their colleagues about the project. After their agreement during the call, a second personal letter including BeSeCu-flyers was sent out. They were asked to hang up the flyer on the bulletin-boards of their fire brigade. The flyer listed information about the project, about how to participate and included the link to the questionnaire. If first responders decided to participate via a paper-pencil questionnaire, they received a personalized letter, a flyer of the BeSeCu project, a questionnaire and a stamped return envelope, ensuring that there were no costs for the first responder. By using this recruitment strategy we were able to send out approximately 5,000 BeSeCu Flyer and more than 842 BeSeCu questionnaires for first responders. After sending out these materials, the relevant fire brigades were further supported via telephone and email.

Online advertisements were also used concerning the first responder recruitment. The BeSeCu project was advertised on several homepages which were especially designed for fire fighters and other first responders (e.g. www.feuerwehr.de, www.retter.tv, www.Berliner-feuerwehr.de and www.ub-feuerwehr.de). If possible, specific expert panels were opened for BeSeCu. As already described, in the part of the survivor-recruitment social networks like Facebook or StudiVZ/ MeinVZ were used to reach first responders.

Furthermore, all members of the Hamburg Fire Service were contacted via email (nearly 2,300). Students of the Hamburg High school of Applied Science, the faculties Rescue Engineering and the Hazard Control in the 4th and 5th semester were informed about the BeSeCu project. BeSeCu information and the link to the questionnaires were put on the homepage of the firefighter academy Hamburg.

By presenting the BeSeCu project at different meetings/ congresses, a wide range of professionals like fire brigades, civil protection organisations and researchers in the field of disaster research were reached and addressed.

5.1.2 Recruitment strategies of the University of Greenwich (UoG)

Survivors

The first strategy was to recruit survivors through the media. A press release about the study was circulated to over 400 media outlets, covering the four countries that comprise the UK. Both national and local press (particularly those covering parts of the UK that had been affected by significant emergencies) were targeted. A second press release was circulated to coincide with the inquests into the fatal 7th July 2005 ("7/7") London bombings. In addition, 11 radio interviews were conducted with national and regional broadcasters, again advertising the study. Furthermore, BeSeCu was mentioned in relevant professional journals (e. g. New Scientist).

To reach survivors of the 7/7 London bombings, help was requested from several organisations that provided support for victims of terrorism but UoG was informed that, due to changes in their funding/services, none were now in a position to assist. However, one general survivor support group, the charity Disaster Action, was able to help by forwarding an email on UoG's behalf to charity members who had been involved in 7/7.

With regards to fires in homes and public buildings, a charity involved in providing immediate help to survivors of emergencies was contacted. In addition, the National Flood Forum (NFF), a charity run by people who have experienced flooding/ worked with flood survivors, contacted UoG expressing interest in BeSeCu and this resulted in an advert for the study being displayed on their website. Similar help was requested from the Scottish Environment Protection Agency (SEPA), partners in the Scottish Flood Forum.

Furthermore, a search was conducted for media stories about large-scale emergencies (e.g. fires affecting multi-storey residential buildings) and then the relevant housing agencies, tenant associations, councils, etc. were contacted. A supportive response was received from one councilor who has worked with his flood-affected local community.

A search was also conducted for the Facebook pages of UK fire and rescue services and links to the survivor survey were posted on those pages. Facebook groups related specifically to survivors of UK fires were also searched for. Community-related Facebook groups were found, created by local authorities/members of the general public, for UK areas affected by major flooding and the link to the survivor survey was posted on them. For 7/7, UoG started their own Facebook group, with the aim of creating a public forum for anyone who was on the trains or in the stations directly affected by the bombs. In addition, UoG searched for 7/7-related Facebook pages created by members of the general public. Several memorial sites for 7/7 and/or other terror attacks existed and so adverts for BeSeCu were posted on those pages.

A UK BeSeCu Twitter account was set up and tweets were made about the study. UoG tagged to follow relevant organisations who had large numbers of followers (e.g. fire and rescue services, the British Red Cross) in the hope of getting the tweets noticed. Given the popularity of the video-sharing website YouTube, UoG searched the site for videos relating to major UK fires in domestic and public buildings, floods, as well as 7/7, and posted details of the study in the comments sections underneath these videos. Where appropriate and possible, UoG sent the person posting the footage a private message via YouTube asking them to take part in the survey if they themselves were a survivor.

Several online forums were searched for discussions or images relevant to BeSeCu. Where relevant discussion topics/ images were found, either private or public replies were posted requesting users take part in the study. General interest forums, such as discussion boards on major newspapers' websites, were also looked at and posts were made on threads relating to emergencies/terrorism. Furthermore, some Scottish and English universities were contacted to advertise the study through their electronic announcements systems (e.g. staff/student emails, electronic notice boards, intranets, etc.).

Safety officers from London Fire Brigade handed out BeSeCu leaflets directly to survivors, either while at the scene of the emergency or during later visits. Leaflets were also distributed by the UoG research team. The team began by viewing the publicly-available list of domestic fires that London Fire Brigade attended in

2009/2010. In the rare cases where specific addresses were available in the media (e.g. name of tower block, name of cul-de-sac), properties at those addresses were visited and details of the survey were delivered to residents. Similar efforts were undertaken to deliver leaflets to residents affected by serious floods in London. Furthermore, hotels that, according to media reports, had suffered significant fires were contacted directly via phone/email for help with study recruitment.

A similar recruitment strategy was adopted for contacting 7/7 survivors. Media reports were searched for survivor accounts and, where the survivor's real name was provided, UoG then undertook further, online searches to find publicly-available contact details. Correspondence with these survivors included an invitation to take part in the study and/or a request to pass on word of the research to other known survivors.

Finally, personal contacts in the fire and rescue profession, in academia, and in social circles (i.e. friends and family) were approached to see if they or anyone they knew had been involved in fires, floods, or the 7/7 bombings.

First responders

As mentioned in the section about survivors, a press release was circulated to over 400 media outlets. Similarly, the aforementioned 11 radio interviews with national and regional broadcasters, and the entries in the professional journals, included a call for firefighters to take part in the study. The main journal targeted for firefighters was Fire Risk Management.

Furthermore, the Chief Fire Officers Association (CFOA) was contacted and asked to promote the BeSeCu study to their members, the members being the managers of the various UK fire brigades (of which there are 46 in England, eight in Scotland, three in Wales and one in Northern Ireland). The CFOA agreed to do this and advertised the study through their official newsletter. They later added the study to their National Operations Policy Committee meeting agenda with the aim of getting the study promoted at a more regional level. While the initial response to the BeSeCu-FR was encouraging, it was noticed that participation following the CFOA endorsement only came from English fire brigades. Upon some research into the matter it was discovered that, due to the devolved nature of the UK (Scotland, Wales and Northern Ireland services operate under different legislative and administrative arrangements to those in England), the CFOA endorsement was not necessarily reaching the UK-wide audience expected. Thus a search was conducted for CFOA equivalents in the other UK countries. A little later, individual fire brigades (i.e. their managers or communications departments) were called/emailed directly and asked if they wished to be involved in BeSeCu. The result of these efforts was that several fire brigades advertised the study through their staff intranets, weekly circulars, e-bulletins, etc.

As mentioned in the section about survivor recruitment, a search was conducted for UK fire and rescue services with public Facebook pages. Posts to those pages included links to the firefighter survey, as well as to the survivor survey. However, the best response regarding the recruitment of firefighters was received from members of an online forum, UK Fire. The main users of this UK Fire forum are UK firefighters. Details of the study and a link to the online BeSeCu-FR were posted there and this generated good interest in the study as well as a good number of participants.

Leaflets, advertising the study, were distributed at relevant professional/academic meetings such as the 12th International Conference on Fire Safety and Engineering (Interflam 2010) held in Nottingham, England, and the Principles and Practice of Fire Modeling short course held in London, England, 2011.

Finally, personal contacts in the fire and rescue profession, in academia, and in social circles were approached to see if they knew of any first responders who might wish to take part in BeSeCu.

5.1.3 Recruitment strategies of the Institute of Public Security of Catalunya (ISPC)

Survivors

Concerning survivors of domestic fires contacts already established by the Spanish team in the recruitment process of the focus groups were used. Survivors' networks, victims' associations, and individual victims around the country were used and reached survivors were located in Barcelona, Gavà, Santa Coloma, Palencia, Huesca, Tarragona and Cornellà. Furthermore, media reports on domestic fires that had taken place during the last few years were explored, with a list of large-scale fires in the last 2 years elaborated. Direct mailing was used, sending letters to these buildings, addressed to the heads of neighbourhood associations. Additionally, BeSeCu project team's personal networks were used, through which we have reached survivors in Girona and Barcelona. Further strategies involved exploration of online social networks and forums such as Facebook.com and Loquo.com. In Catalonia, personal visits with a paper-and-pencil questionnaire were made to those who agreed to participate in the project. Outside of Catalonia, the questionnaires were distributed by post.

Although fires in public buildings were not a target situation for the ISPC within the BeSeCu project, contact with the Germans Trias Hospital (also known as "Can Ruti") in Badalona was established. This public hospital was subject to a fire in 2007 and the consequent evacuation of approximately 200 persons, including hospital staff and patients. The hospital's communications department proposed publication of the link to the online questionnaire on the hospital intranet to facilitate responses from hospital staff. This has required approval from the Board of Directors and discussion at a board meeting. Finally, an approval by the Board has been granted and the questionnaire was published at the intranet of the hospital.

Concerning survivors of Terrorist attacks contact was established with the two main "11 M" (March 11th) terrorist attacks victims' organisations: Asociación de Ayuda a las víctimas del 11M (ayuda11m.org) and Asociación 11-M afectados del Terrorismo (asociacion11m.org), both of which are based in Madrid. Contact with the first, Asociación de Ayuda a las víctimas del 11M, was initiated through electronic mail, and later, in order to explain the importance of their participation and to gain a compromise from the Association, a person from the ISPC BeSeCu team travelled to Madrid to establish personal contact with them. This proved a successful strategy as following the meeting the organisation agreed to participate in the project and have subsequently recruited a total of 25 of their members for the study. The second organisation, Asociación 11-M afectados del Terrorismo, was reached through the Associació Catalana de Víctimes d'Organitzacions Terroristes, who provided the Spanish team with direct contact with a representative member. To obtain their consent to participation, members of the team travelled once more to Madrid to provide an explanation of the project and of their potential involvement, as well as to explain in detail the research and methods. During this meeting, concerns were voiced by the representative as well as two psychologists working within the organisation. Their main concern surrounded the potential for emotional distress amongst respondents, who in many cases have spent years trying to recover psychologically. The organisation has been reluctant to collaborate in the research due to any potential psychological effects the questionnaire may have upon their members.

First responders

A general top-down approach throughout the country was difficult, because fire-fighting services in Spain are organised according to each of its 17 autonomous regions with two levels of administration: regional services (17) and local services (city councils of larger cities, approx. 100 services). Therefore, different levels of administration have been approached in different parts of the country. The ISPC has contacted by email 170 administrations, fire fighters services and individual fire stations covering all of Spain's autonomous regions. The team sent an invitation explaining the project and providing the link to the online assessment, as well as contact details for the ISPC staff working on the project. As a follow-up, those fire stations from which we did not receive any kind of response to the first email were later contacted again. In Catalonia, the ISPC's already established network has been utilised to a large extent. In order to formalize our visits to the fire stations, a letter was sent to the Director General of Prevention, Fire Extinction, and Rescues of Catalonia, with information on the project and the field study. To this date, personal visits with the paper-and-pencil questionnaire have been made to fire stations in the cities of Barcelona, Cambrils, Manresa, Puigcerdà, Reus, and Vic. The staff of one shift at each fire station have been informed about the study and "supervised' while filling out the questionnaire. Questionnaires have then been left at the stations for the rest of the shifts, and the chief fire officer of each fire station has been informed about the study in order to be able to distribute the questionnaire. The fire stations have also been provided with the link to the online questionnaire.

Furthermore, paper & pencil questionnaires were distributed among the promotion courses for firefighter corporals and sergeants at the ISPC. Additionally, information about the project, and the questionnaire for those interested, was distributed among the firefighters attending the seminar "La investigació d'incendis i explosions" arranged at the ISPC on November 10th 2010.

The link to the online assessment has been published on the Catalan fire fighters intranet (emergencies.intranet); on the webpage of the Spanish "Asociación Profesional de Técnios de Bomberos" (aptb.org), and on the emergency personnel online forum "E-mergencia" (e-mergencia.com).

A personal email with an invitation to participate in the study via online assessment has been sent to all firefighter trainers in Catalonia (approx. 200). The email was sent by the responsible professional for training in the firefighter School within the ISPC.

The most successful method so far has been the personal visits to the fire-stations with paper-and-pencil questionnaires conducted during station working hours and with the supervision of the ISPC BeSeCu research staff. However, this strategy is very time-consuming in terms of scheduling visits, travel and stay in the station while the questionnaires are being completed. The success rate for the questionnaires left at the fire stations has been low.

5.1.4 Recruitment strategies of the MTO – Säkerhet AB (MTO Safety AB)

Survivors

To be able to get in direct contact with fire survivors a recruitment strategy was to search for incidents that happened during the past few years, and to try to contact people on those addresses. Rescue services were asked to help with lists over incidents that occurred in their area. From the lists it was able to find incidents that were interesting to the study, evaluating the incidents with regard to fire and smoke spreading, injured people and other parameters. From the lists the addresses where the incidents occurred were found. It was also researched internet newspapers for addresses for where bigger incidents occurred. A general letter was sent by mail to people living at those addresses, inviting them to participate in the study, also containing information about the project. Within a few days these people were called to inform them about the project and ask them if they want to participate. The questionnaire was sent out to the people consenting to participation, by regular mail or by email. Furthermore, advertisement of the project and links to the questionnaires were also presented on the first page of our web page, www.mto.se.

First responders

Twenty rescue services were contacted via telephone and email. Some of them were unions covering several fire stations. We have been contacting fire fighters directly, leaders at a medium level of the organisation as well as heads of the fire stations. In some parts of the country the fire stations are organized in bigger unions, and in those cases we also contacted the heads of the unions. The heads of the fire stations were asked to give their employees the questionnaires in a paper pencil version or as online version, and to request their employees to fill out the questionnaires. Furthermore, rescue services were visited, and Swedish BeSeCu team members participated in meetings organized for leaders of rescue operations to inform about the project and to recruit participants. Furthermore, fire services were contacted all over the country. Information about the project and a link to the questionnaire was presented on the web page, www.mto.se.

5.1.5 Recruitment strategies of SGSP – Faculty of Fire Safety Engineering, Main School of Fire Service

For the centre SGSP the field study recruitment has been very much the same for survivors and fire fighters.

As one of the forms for recruiting survivors and first responders on-line advertisements were used. The information about the project and invitation for filling in the questionnaires was published at the web side of the Main School of Fire Service (www.sgsp.edu.pl) which proved to be effective since SGSP is the only one fire officers school in Poland, therefore visited by major number of fire fighters and academics. The information was also published through the web side of the National Headquarters of the State Fire Service, which again proved to be effective for our recruitment process. Because both web sides are used mainly by first responders this was the most effective way of reaching them and encourage them to fill in the on-line questionnaire.

Personal contacts were the most effective way of recruiting people for the study. Since the State Fire Service is a one centralized organisation for the whole country under one command of the Chief Commandant of the State Fire Service it was decided to take a use of this opportunity.

Top-down centralized network approach was used to carry out the study. It was cooperated with eight people working in the eight different Provincial Headquarters of the State Fire Service in Poland. This people were met at the beginning of the study and learned about the project and about the questionnaires themselves. Having that knowledge they started the recruitment process in their provinces

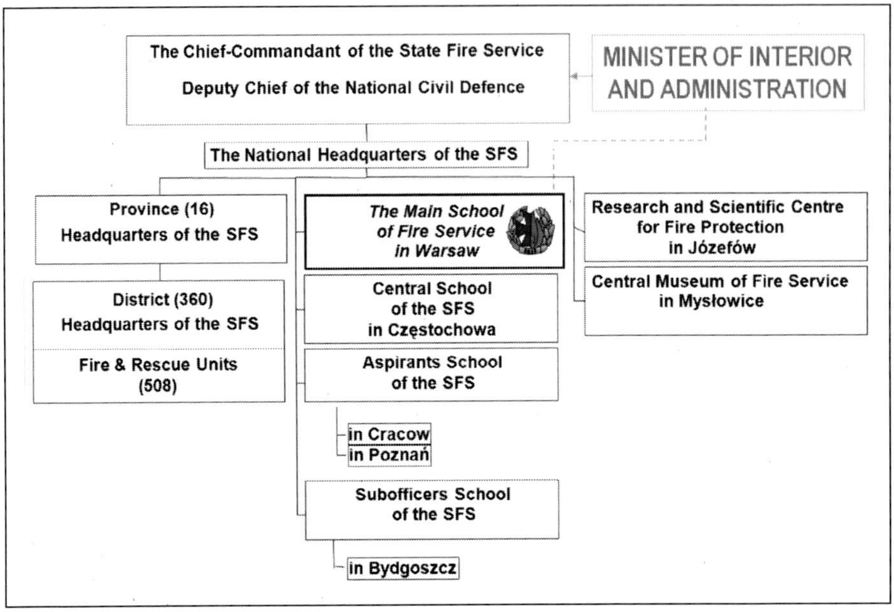

Fig. 5.3: Organisational chart of the State Fire Service in Poland

which enabled the collection of data from all over Poland. They reached the first responders through Municipal Headquarters from where the firefighters from numerous fire stations learned about the questionnaire. This was the most effective way of having first responders completed the on-line questionnaire. The eight people who cooperated with the Polish BeSeCu team also used the method of face-to-face meetings with firefighters at fire stations.

As it comes to survivors, they were recruited on the face-to-face basis mostly. In the Provincial Headquarters there is a central data base of all emergencies which happened in the given province. That's how knowledge about different cases like domestic fire, fire in a public building and floods was gained. Having the addresses of domestic fire and fire in public building cases each person appointed by the Polish team in the 8 provinces visited the fire scenes. People were asked if they took part in the evacuation process during these accidents or if they were involved in any way in that accidents and give out questionnaires to be completed by survivors. Direct contact with those survivors was essential to get a proper feedback. The similar approach was taken when it comes to flood survivors. Floods were very severe in Poland in 2010. Therefore there were many people involved in a flood situation. It was decided to focus on four provinces which were mostly affected by the flood and carried out the study there.

Another way used for promoting the BeSeCu project and the field study was during conferences and meetings. One of them was "IV Scientific Conference – Man in extreme conditions. Earth, Water, Air" on 22 October 2010. This conference was about evacuation of people from buildings, mass evacuation and behaviour of people during evacuation. Participants of the conference were interested in the BeSeCu project and were asked to disseminate information at their Universities and organisations.

5.1.6 Recruitment strategies of Prague Psychiatric Centre (PPC) – University of Prague

Survivors

Concerning survivors of domestic fires and fires in public buildings diverse strategies were undertaken.

A banner directing to a specially created website (http://www.pcp.lf3. cuni.cz/pcpout/besecu_uvod.htm) containing general information about the BeSeCu project and the questionnaire, inclusion criteria, contact information and form for registration into the project. This banner was posted on PPC external (http://www.pcp.lf3.cuni.cz/pcpout/) and internal website, so that general public as well as all PPC employees could get information about the project and could registered.

Posters and leaflets with basic information about the BeSeCu project and contact information were created and disseminated repeatedly on different types of places and in different regions of the Czech Republic (e.g. in PPC, different universities, conferences, medical clinics, municipal offices, letter boxes of survivors found on internet.

Oral presentation about the BeSeCu project was given in universities, conferences, seminars, workshops; both in formal and informal way, e.g. interdepartmental workgroup of employees of all rescue system professions designated for creation of standards of psychosocial help in the Czech Republic, appointed by the General Director of the Fire Rescue Service of the Czech Republic, meets on regular basis from the year 2006; workgroup of rescue workers and crisis managers from health service designated for creation of system of psychosocial intervention care in health service, appointed by the Czech Minister of Health, met in August 2009; educational seminar for staff of Charity Blansko, 26.11.2009; training workshop for policemen and clergy, 7.-12.12.2009, Slovakia; nationwide seminar for psychologists of Fire Rescue Service of CR, 2.2.2010; international V. Congress "Disaster Medicine", 4.-5.2.2010; workshop for members of Czech Red Cross, 15.-18.4.2010; team supervision "Psychosocial help in Critical Incident Stress Management" for Air Traffic Control of CR staff, 26.4.2010, 4.11.2010; 14. Prague Gerontological days 2010, 27.-28.5.2010; Educational Conference for nurses, 15.10.2010 in Brno, 30.10.2010 in Prague; Lecture for psychology students of Jihočeská univerzita, oral presentation, 15.10.2010 and 12.11.2010, České Budějovice.

In radio "Český rozhlas" an advertisement with basic information about the BeSeCu project was presented and broadcasted 4x/day before news for 14 days – 17.5.2010 – 31.5.2010. For this advertisement, an interview with a flood survivor was conducted, followed by a short interview with Markéta Holubová, who informed about the project, and after this, the advertisement was broadcasted for the first time. The interview (see above) was published on web of Český rozhlas (http://www.rozhlas.cz/strednicechy/aktualne/_zprava/734716), as well as many spontaneous articles containing the text from the interview on many other websites appeared: e.g. Enviweb, Týden, RSS Portál, Sběrnice.net, Monitor.cz, Aktuální zprávy.cz, iFarma, and Ekočtečka.cz.

Furthermore, Dr. Marie Sotolářová participated in a TV program on rescuers, broadcasted in May 2009 by Czech Television. She informed there the general public about the BeSeCu project (basic information about the BeSeCu project, its aims and objectives, target situations and people). She also participated in the movie "Grim reaper is afraid of us", which was also broadcasted by Czech Television, 16.3.2010. While the movie was created, she discussed the BeSeCu project with all people who were involved (film creators were interested in the study as potential inspiration for other movies).

A facebook group "Projekt BeSeCu" with general information about the project was created. It also contains link to PPC BeSeCu website, as well as link to the online questionnaire. In addition, post with general information about BeSeCu project was placed on "katastrofy.com" on Facebook.

Cooperation with director of Charity Blansko was established, in order to provide contacts and guarantee trustworthiness of PPC team members in the eyes of survivors who got help by the charity before. These persons were first informed by a leaflet and then they were visited personally.

Furthermore, domestic fires and fires in public buildings have been searched on special internet websites about emergency situations (e.g. http://www.pozary.cz/, http://www.katastrofy.com), internet and printed newspapers and journals, and in TV news. Afterwards, survivors of found fires were contacted via the leaflet and letter first, and then they were personally visited. Moreover, PPC hired psychologists of the Fire Rescue Service of the Czech Rep. and students to help with recruitment of fire survivors and data gathering. All hired individuals are professional psychologists or psychology students interested in emergency situations (or working in emergency situations), and of course, all get detailed information about the BeSeCu project and are trained in administration of the questionnaire before they start.

Concerning survivors of flood, participants were recruited by similar strategies as survivors of fires in domestic and public buildings. However, fewer strategies have to be adopted, because of easier access and easier localization of flood survivors. Contacts from focus groups (conducted earlier in the project) were used to get several flood survivors, but mainly PPC is cooperating with one Romany family, which, for small amount of money, helps with recruitment of Romany participants (who are also paid small amount of money for their participation). Further strategies were: banner on PPC external and internal website, advertisement in radio, personal contacts, paid help (for floods 2010), and Facebook – for more details see the previous section.

First responders

The major strategy in recruiting fire fighters was using professional contacts and help of PhD. Marie Sotolářová, who is a co-creator of establishing psychological service in Fire Rescue Service of the Czech Republic (FRS CR) and who was a head psychologist of Fire Rescue Service of the Czech Republic and a head of Department of Psychology and Sociology in Ministry of the Interior of the Czech Republic. The director of the Prague Psychiatric Center officially contacted the head-manager of Fire Rescue Service of the Czech Republic; firefighters from all regions of the Czech Republic were contacted, after permission of regional managers was obtained. In addition, cooperation with psychologists and members of post-traumatic care team of Fire Rescue Service of the Czech Republic was established to help with the recruitment process and organisation of meetings with firefighters from different Czech regions and towns.

5.1.7 Recruitment strategies of Association of Emergency Ambulance Physicians (AAHD)

Concerning recruitment of survivors of terrorist attacks, there were three terrorist attacks in closed settings between 2003 and 2007. The three establishments were selected because only terrorist attacks in close settings could be included into the study. Two of them refused to participate in the study. Only the shopping centre in Ankara was left for the survey. Concerning the recruitment of earthquake survivors, it was decided to collect data from survivors of the following three earthquakes: Marmara, Urla and Seferihisar earthquakes. To recruit survivors of domestic fires, firefighter departments and their managers were contacted via telephone. Hundred questionnaires were sent out to seven regions. With respect to fires in public buildings two hospitals in Izmir were selected. Official letters were sent to them and they agreed to participate.

Firefighters were recruited via the contacts with fire stations; 52 fire stations were contacted.

5.1.8 Recruitment strategies of University of Bologna (UoB)

Survivors

The recruitment of survivors was advertised by both newspapers and online journals like "Vivere Marche", "Vivere Europa", and "Il Resto del Carlino". Moreover, the BeSeCu Project was promoted by the Emergency Psychology research group web site of the University of Bologna (http://emergenze.psice.unibo.it/emergenze_eng). Several heads of psychological organisations and bloggers of emergency psychology were contacted by emails in order to promote BeSeCu Project in their web sites like "psicologiperipopoli", "psiconline.it", "psicologiaemergenza.blogspot.com", "psicoemergenza.it", "centrorampi.it", "opsoline.it" (by posting in groups of university students). A BeSeCu Italia web page was created on Facebook to illustrate the project and recruit participants. The Italian team also posted in groups of fire fighters where civilians, victims of emergency situations, usually post messages. Survivors who were willing to participate in the study contacted the team and the survivors got all necessary information to participate online or by the paper-and-pencil version of the questionnaire. Moreover, the BeSeCu Project was illustrated to students attending Psychology at the University of Bologna in order to promote and recruit participants. Private contacts were also used to recruit participants of specific situations both for earthquake and fires of domestic and public buildings.

Concerning recruitment of earthquake survivors, it was decided to focus on establishing contacts with survivors of the two main important earthquakes occurred in Italy in the last eleven years: Molise and Abruzzo Earthquakes in 2002 and 2009 respectively. Several Facebook groups regarding these situations were found and we promoted BeSeCu by these methods. Furthermore, we contacted personally several participants who were victims of these two situations (Abruzzo 2009 and Molise 2002) by phone and email. The majority of these people were reached by private contacts mainly. Because a high number of students were affected by the earthquake occurred in Abruzzo in April 2009, the project was presented during classes and questionnaires and flyers with a project description, contact details were handed out.

Concerning recruitment of survivors of domestic and public building fires, the Italian fire fighter official web site, social network, newspapers and online journals were used to find and obtain detail information regarding fires occurred in Italy (when, where, how many people involved etc.). Subsequently, people involved in those situations occurred in the areas of Bologna (Emilia Romagna), Ancona, Senigallia (Marche region) and Genova (Liguria) were visited personally. These cities were chosen for several reasons: presence of private contacts that introduced the Italian team to survivors facilitating the recruitment, easiness to reach the situations, low costs in terms of financial and human resources. With respect to domestic fires, six situations were visited personally and nearly 90 flyers were handed out personally or left in the letter box in Emilia Romagna; whereas five situations were visited in the area of Ancona (Marche region) and handed out nearly 20 flyers. In Genova (Liguria) survivors of three domestic fire situations were personally contacted and nearly 20 flyers were given to them. Especially for fire in public buildings, the organisation affected by the incident was contacted by email or phone in order to illustrate BeSeCu Project and recruit people. Resumed documents and flyers of the project were created and sent by email or gave personally to survivors both for domestic fires and fires in public building. Furthermore, each participant was given a symbolic gadget (i.e. pen, key-chain, notebook etc.) to increase motivation to participate. Concerning fire in public building, seven events were identified: four situations in Emilia Romagna, two in Liguria and one in Puglia regions; survivors were contacted personally and by telephone and email.

First responders

The Central Department of Italian firefighter Organisation was contacted by an official letter in which BeSeCu Project was explained in detail. In order to do that a document of the project description was made (partners of BeSeCu consortium, aims and tasks, description, contacts). The request was accepted and an official authorization from the Head of Italian firefighter Organisation was received. An email illustrating BeSeCu Project was sent to all 18 Regional Directions, 100 Provincial commands, 3 Autonomous Corps of Bolzano, Trento, Aosta of Italian firefighters and to 350 (voluntary and permanent) detached fire stations. Several provincial fire brigades contacted the Italian BeSeCu team showing interest in BeSeCu project and asking for additional information. Collaboration with all the fire stations that were interested in participating in the project was established; in order to do that it was accorded and negotiated a specific strategy to promote BeSeCu and recruit participants. To increase participants' motivation and to thank them a symbolic gadget was given to each fireman who participated in the study. Furthermore, firefighters were recruited via trade unions. The main firefighter trade unions were contacted by email and nearly 200 emails were sent to the Heads of the most important trade unions. Additionally, firefighters were recruited via Internet and Social Network. Messages were posted to illustrate BeSeCu Project and promote its recruitment in nearly 10 Italian firefighters groups found in Facebook. A BeSeCu Italia web page was also created on the Social Network Facebook. Furthermore, the BeSeCu Project was promoted by the Emergency Psychology research group web site of the University of Bologna (http://emergenze.psice.unibo.it/). Finally, several private contacts were used to promote and recruit participants in Bologna and Senigallia.

5.2 Results of the BeSeCu-S field study

Daniela Knuth on behalf of the BeSeCu group

Sample

A sample of 1,130 survivors answered the BeSeCu-S questionnaire and met the following inclusion criteria:

(a) experienced one of the following emergency situations: domestic fire, fire in a public building, flood, earthquake or terrorist attack;
(b) at least 18 years of age;
(c) knew that the emergency services attended the incident; and
(d) the incident was no longer than 11 years ago (i.e. occurred not earlier than 1999).

Criterion number three was not mandatory for earthquake, terrorist attack and flood survivors. Among the 1,130 survivors 1,112 experienced the incident in one of the partner countries: Czech Republic (n = 167), Germany (n = 205), Italy (n = 169), Poland (n = 186), Spain (n = 105), Sweden (n = 83), Turkey (n = 145), and UK (n = 52). A fire in a home was reported by 53.0%, a fire in a public building by 15.7%, a flood by 15.5%, an earthquake by 11.3% and 4.5% reported a terrorist attack. The mean time since the event was 3.21 years (SD = 3.39 years). The majority of participants was female (54.1%) and the mean age of all participants was 40.4 years (SD = 15.3) with age ranging from 18 years to 96 years.

Emergency assistance trust of BeSeCu survivors before the incident

Emergency assistance trust regarding different sources was assessed with the following question: *Before the incident occurred, to what extent did you believe you could rely on the following to assist you in an emergency?* Nine different sources of trust were examined and could be rated on 5-point-Likert scale from 1 = not at all to 5 = extremely. In total, participant had the most trust in the fire service as well as in themselves, family or friends and the medical service (Table 5.2). Less trust was felt towards the media, local authorities and strangers. Results of ANOVA analyses are the following: Self = $F(7,1021) = 10.18$, $p < .001$, $\eta = .26$; Family Friends = $F(7,1011) = 3.06$, $p < .01$, $\eta = .14$; Neighbours = $F(7,997) = 7.41$, $p < .001$, $\eta = .22$; Strangers = $F(7,983) = 1.46$, $p = .177$, $\eta = .10$; Medical service = $F(7,1005) = 7.53$, $p < .001$, $\eta = .22$; Police = $F(7,1004) = 7.35$, $p < .001$, $\eta = .22$; Fire service = $F(7,1012) = 6.69$, $p < .001$, $\eta = .21$; Local authorities = $F(7,999) = 2.66$, $p < .05$, $\eta = .14$; Media = $F(7,995) = 11.34$, $p < .001$, $\eta = .27$. Analyses did not include participants with multiple citizenships or a different citizenship than one

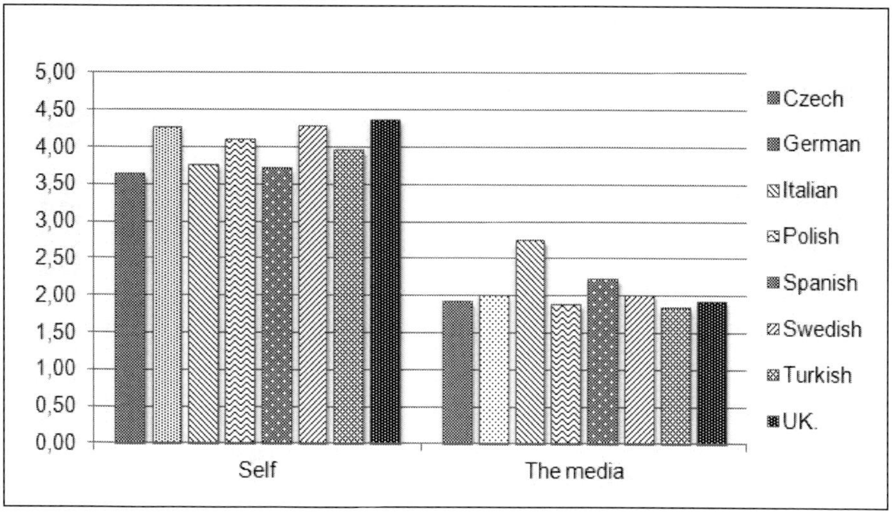

Fig. 5.4: Emergency assistance trust in oneself and the media depending on nationality

of the BeSeCu countries. The largest effects regarding the differences between different nationalities were found with respect to trust in oneself and trust in media (Fig. 5.4).

Table 5.2: Emergency assistance trust towards different sources according to participants' citizenship

	Czech (n = 165)		German (n = 203)		Italian (n = 168)		Polish (n = 172)		Spanish (n = 106)		Swedish (n = 75)		Turkish (n = 146)		UK (n = 39)		More (n = 18)		Other (n = 15)	
	M	SD	M	SD	M	SD	M	SD	M	SD	M	SD	M	SD	M	SD	M	SD	M	SD
Self	3.64	0.96	4.28	0.74	3.77	1.06	4.10	1.10	3.71	1.00	4.29	0.70	3.96	1.01	4.37	0.74	4.56	0.63	3.86	1.10
Family/Friends	3.97	0.82	4.18	0.88	4.01	0.94	3.88	1.04	3.69	0.95	3.90	1.19	4.00	0.92	3.85	0.86	4.33	0.72	3.57	0.94
Neighbours	2.75	0.95	3.17	1.04	2.77	1.07	3.07	1.03	2.56	1.00	3.26	1.03	3.18	0.90	3.07	0.92	3.38	0.81	2.64	1.22
Strangers	2.16	0.86	2.26	0.92	2.20	0.95	2.10	1.02	2.27	1.10	2.39	1.01	2.04	0.89	2.38	0.94	2.20	1.01	2.14	0.95
Medical service	3.73	0.86	4.09	0.93	3.73	0.92	3.78	1.01	3.79	0.85	4.34	0.82	3.60	0.87	3.92	0.81	3.88	0.72	3.57	1.09
Police	3.36	1.01	3.76	1.08	3.49	1.05	3.58	1.07	3.67	0.96	4.30	0.91	3.50	1.04	3.81	0.85	3.59	1.06	3.14	1.35
Fire service	4.02	0.85	4.27	0.85	3.84	1.07	4.26	0.86	4.10	0.81	4.54	0.73	3.98	0.97	4.26	0.71	4.00	0.79	4.00	1.18
Local authorities	2.56	1.12	2.83	1.07	2.98	1.19	2.60	1.21	2.93	1.12	2.87	1.13	2.86	1.08	2.77	1.24	2.60	0.91	2.43	1.09
Media	1.92	1.08	2.02	1.04	2.75	1.29	1.88	0.99	2.23	1.09	2.01	1.07	1.84	1.06	1.92	1.09	1.73	1.22	1.64	1.34

Emergency related knowledge

Emergency related knowledge was assessed with the following question: *Before the incident occurred, what knowledge did you have that would be of use in an emergency?* The following items were then rated on the 5-point-Likert scale ranging from 1 = not at all to 5 = extremely: *I had professional knowledge, gained from working for the emergency services; I had first aid knowledge, gained from a first aid course; I had fire safety knowledge, gained from being a warden/fire safety officer; I had taken part in fire drills at school; I had taken part in fire drills at work; I had read safety notices/evacuation plans in public places, such as in hotel rooms, train carriages, etc. and I had thought about what would happen if an emergency occurred in such a location and had prepared my own evacuation plan.* Mean values and standard deviation for each national subgroup are displayed in Table 5.3. Medium effects for the differences between nationalities were found for each item (Professional knowledge: $F[7,1034] = 14.38$, $\rho < .001$, $\eta = .30$; First aid knowledge: $F[7,1040] = 13.85$, $\rho < .001$, $\eta = .29$; Fire safety knowledge: $F[7,1023] = 16.44$, $\rho < .001$, $\eta = .32$; Fire drills [school]: $F[7,1020] = 9.76$, $\rho < .001$, $\eta = .25$; Fire drills [work]: $F[7,1028] = 17.10$, $\rho < .001$, $\eta = .32$; Read safety notices: $F[7,1031] = 9.46$, $\rho < .001$, $\eta = .25$; Prepared own evacuation plan: $F[7,1036] = 11.74$, $\rho < .001$, $\eta = .27$). The largest effects regarding the differences between nationalities were found for fire safety knowledge and fire drills at work (Fig. 5.5).

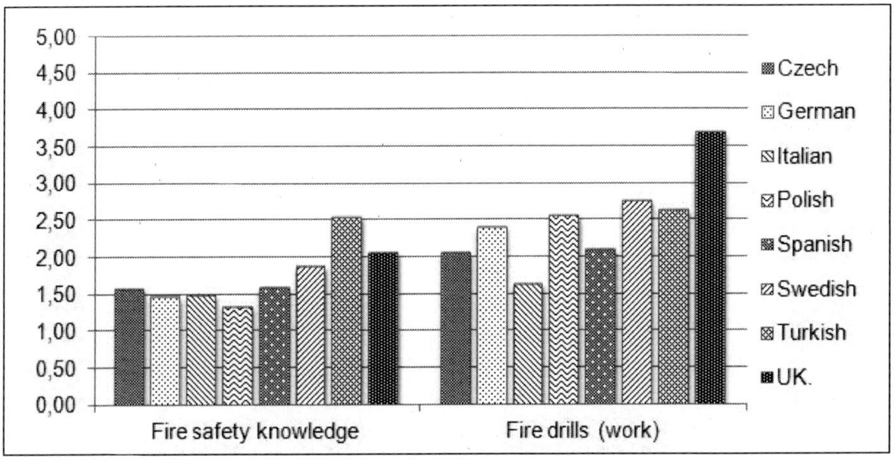

Fig. 5.5: Fire safety knowledge and experiences fire drills at work depending on nationality

Table 5.3: Emergency related knowledge before the event according to participants' citizenship

	Czech (n = 165)		German (n = 203)		Italian (n = 168)		Polish (n = 172)		Spanish (n = 106)		Swedish (n = 75)		Turkish (n = 146)		UK (n = 39)		More (n = 18)		Other (n = 15)	
	M	**SD**	**M**	**SD**	**M**	**SD**	**M**	**SD**	**M**	**SD**	**M**	**SD**	**M**	**SD**	**M**	**SD**	**M**	**SD**	**M**	**SD**
Professional	1.52	0.99	1.92	1.30	1.66	1.12	1.60	1.12	2.02	1.34	1.44	0.97	2.67	1.39	1.63	1.10	1.33	0.84	1.47	0.83
First aid	2.39	1.09	3.22	1.22	2.01	1.31	2.35	1.33	2.62	1.51	2.95	1.38	2.62	1.22	2.59	1.50	2.61	1.38	2.07	1.22
Fire safety	1.57	1.05	1.46	1.05	1.49	0.95	1.33	0.85	1.59	1.02	1.87	1.24	2.54	1.53	2.05	1.38	1.56	1.29	1.53	0.92
Fire drills (school)	2.42	1.10	2.72	1.31	2.49	1.34	2.15	1.29	1.76	1.14	2.88	1.42	2.54	1.31	3.16	1.28	2.50	1.15	2.47	1.25
Fire drills (work)	2.04	1.15	2.39	1.48	1.62	1.11	2.55	1.33	2.09	1.22	2.76	1.35	2.64	1.55	3.69	1.30	2.33	1.24	2.33	1.23
Read safety notices/ evacuation plans	2.25	1.05	2.95	1.30	2.43	1.26	2.23	1.33	2.71	1.29	3.09	1.22	2.67	1.28	3.15	1.18	2.56	1.34	2.93	1.22
Prepared own evacuation plan	1.78	1.00	2.45	1.33	1.78	1.21	2.45	1.31	1.91	1.11	2.57	1.30	2.57	1.34	2.72	1.38	2.17	1.34	2.27	1.33

Evacuation

In order to evaluate if participants had to evacuate during the event, the following question was asked: *Did you evacuate during this emergency situation?* One of the following response options had to be chosen: *Yes; No, but I was rescued by others* or *No.* In total most of the participants had to evacuate during the event (see Fig. 5.6). The distribution of these categories varies between incidents (χ^2 [8] = 58.318, $p < .001$, Cramér's V = .16) as well as between countries in which the incident happened (χ^2 [14] = 134.067, $p < .001$, Cramér's V = .25).

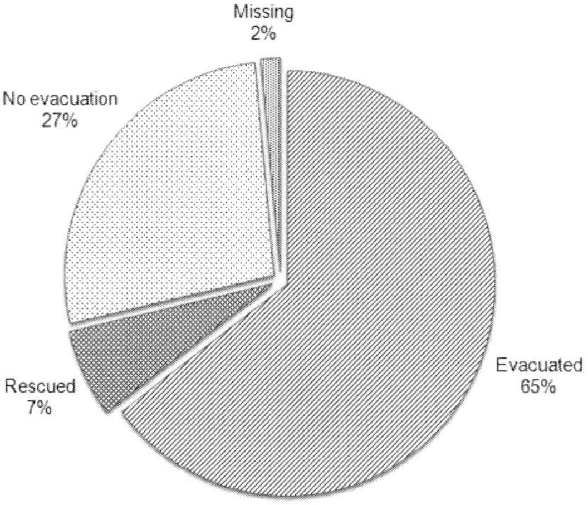

Fig. 5.6: Total evacuation characteristics (N = 1,112)

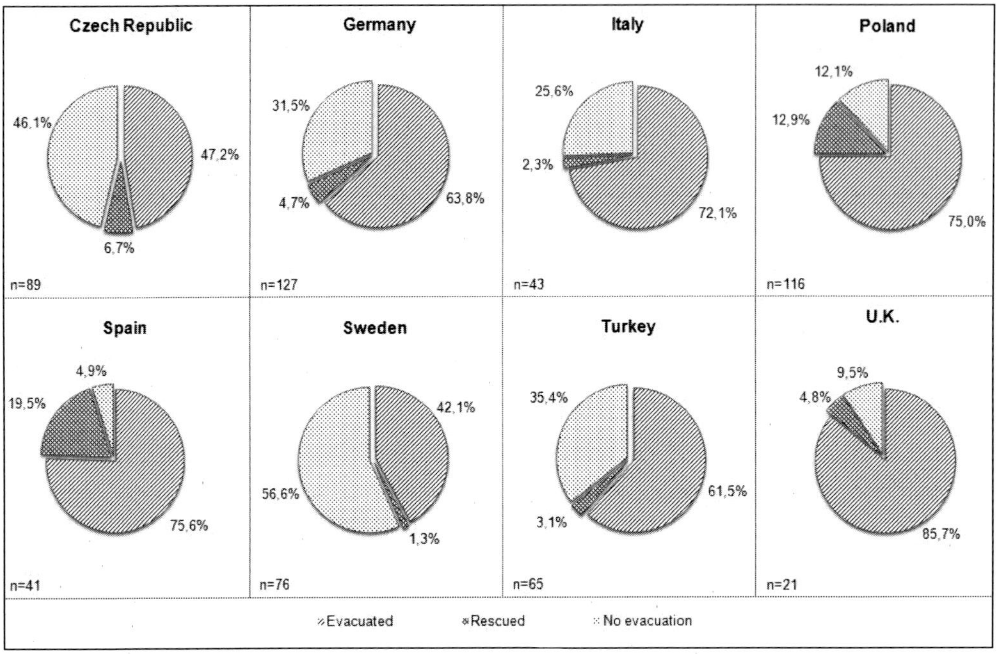

Fig. 5.7: Evacuations during home fires depending on the country of the incident

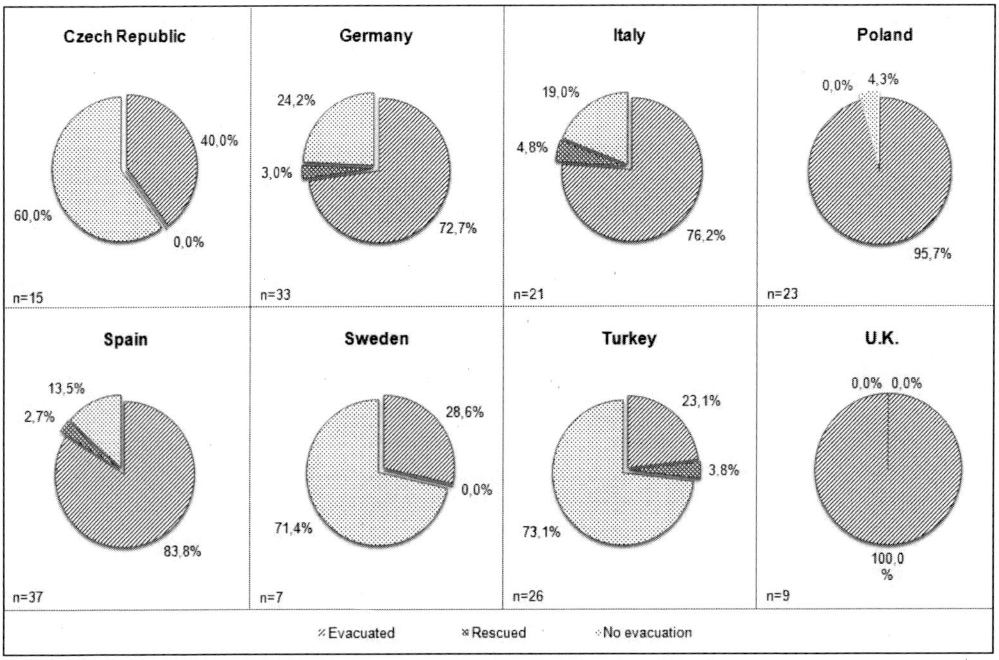

Fig. 5.8: Evacuations during public fires depending on the country of the incident

Especially for domestic fire events (χ^2 [14] = 87.271, $\rho < .001$, Cramér's V = .28) and public fire events (χ^2 [14] = 55.933, $\rho < .001$, Cramér's V = .40) the evacuation decisions differed greatly between the countries (see Fig. 5.7 and Fig. 5.8). In Germany, Italy Poland, Spain and the UK most people did evacuate during fire incidents. Almost half of the participants who experienced a fire event in the Czech Republic did not evacuate during the incident. In Sweden most participants did not evacuate either whereas in Turkey, evacuation was very frequent in home fires but not in public fires.

Evacuation decisions during terrorist attacks (see Fig. 5.9) also differed between the incident countries Spain, Turkey and the UK (χ^2 [4] = 11.491, $\rho < .05$, Cramér's V = .34). In Turkey two out of three participants did not evacuate whereas the incidents in the UK and Spain were very comparable in this respect (χ^2 [2] = .821, $\rho = .66$, Cramér's V = .14).

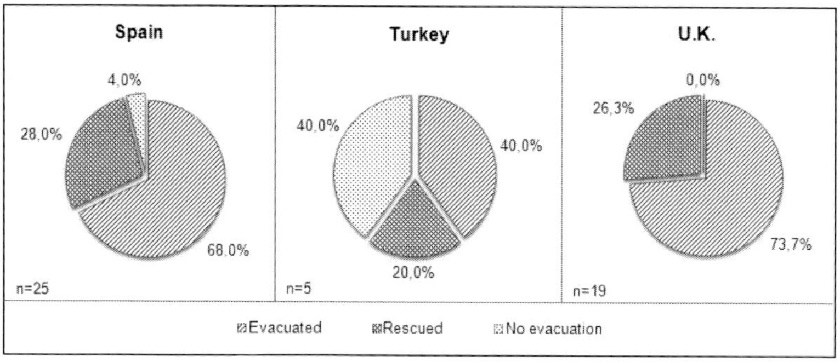

Fig. 5.9: Evacuations during terroristic attacks depending on the country of the incident

Participants with experiences of flood incidents in the Czech Republic, Germany, Italy and Poland (see Fig. 5.10) also varied with respect to the evacuation decisions (χ^2 [6] = 32.989, $\rho < .001$, Cramér's V = .31).

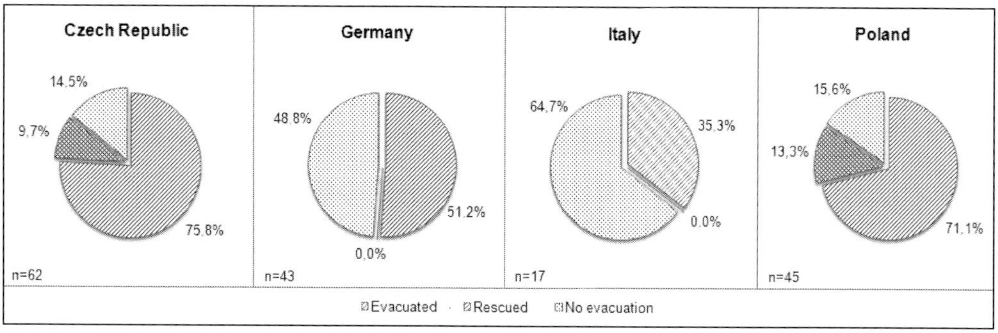

Fig. 5.10: Evacuations during floods depending on the country of the incident

The evacuation decisions of earthquake survivors in Turkey and Italy (see Fig. 5.11) were similar (χ^2 [2] = .901, ρ = .637, Cramér's V = .09).

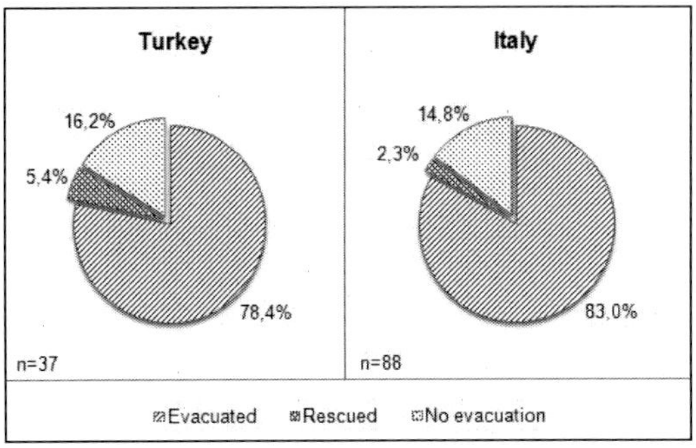

Fig. 5.11: Evacuations during earthquakes depending on the country of the incident

If an evacuation was needed, participants were also asked on how they were able to exit the building or the facility they were in. Small effects were found regarding differences between the incidents [Habit: χ^2 (4) = 53.255, ρ < .001, Cramér's V = .26; Retracing steps: χ^2 (4) = 9.624, ρ < .05, Cramér's V = .11; Recalling the layout of location: χ^2 (4) = 30.973, ρ < .001, Cramér's V = .20; Chance: χ^2 (4) = 2.330, ρ = .675, Cramér's V = .06; Followed other people: χ^2 (4) = 50.908, ρ < .001, Cramér's V = .26; Directed/forced: χ^2 (4) = 14.209, ρ < .01, Cramér's V = .14; Lighting/signage: χ^2 (4) = 42.068, ρ < .001, Cramér's V = .23; Quickest/closest way out: χ^2 (4) = 15.742, ρ < .01, Cramér's V = .14] and between different nationalities [Habit: χ^2 (7) = 29.918, ρ < .001, Cramér's V = .20; Retracing steps = χ^2 (7) = 26.351, ρ < .001, Cramér's V = .19; Recalling the layout of location: χ^2 (7) = 25.646, ρ < .01, Cramér's V = .19; Chance: χ^2 (7) = 19.970, ρ < .01, Cramér's V = .17; Followed other people: χ^2 (7) = 21.363, ρ < .01, Cramér's V = .17; Directed/forced: χ^2 (7) = 17.680, ρ < .05, Cramér's V = .16; Lighting/signage: χ^2 (7) = 30.073, ρ < .001, Cramér's V = .20; Quickest/closest way out: χ^2 (7) = 16.585, ρ < .05, Cramér's V = .15]. The usage of different strategies for public and domestic fires is illustrated in Fig. 5.12. The most commonly used strategy, especially in case of domestic fires, was habit; with people exiting a building the way they usually do. Using lighting and signage was a common strategy in case of public fires, especially for UK participants. It must be noted thought that some national subsamples especially for public fires were very small [public fires: Czech (n = 6), Germany (n = 22), Italian (n = 17), Polish (n = 18), Spanish (n = 32), Swedish (n = 2), Turkish (n = 5) and UK (n = 9); domestic fires: Czech (n = 48), Germany (n = 83), Italian (n = 31), Polish (n = 89), Spanish (n = 36), Swedish (n = 27), Turkish (n = 35) and UK (n = 15)].

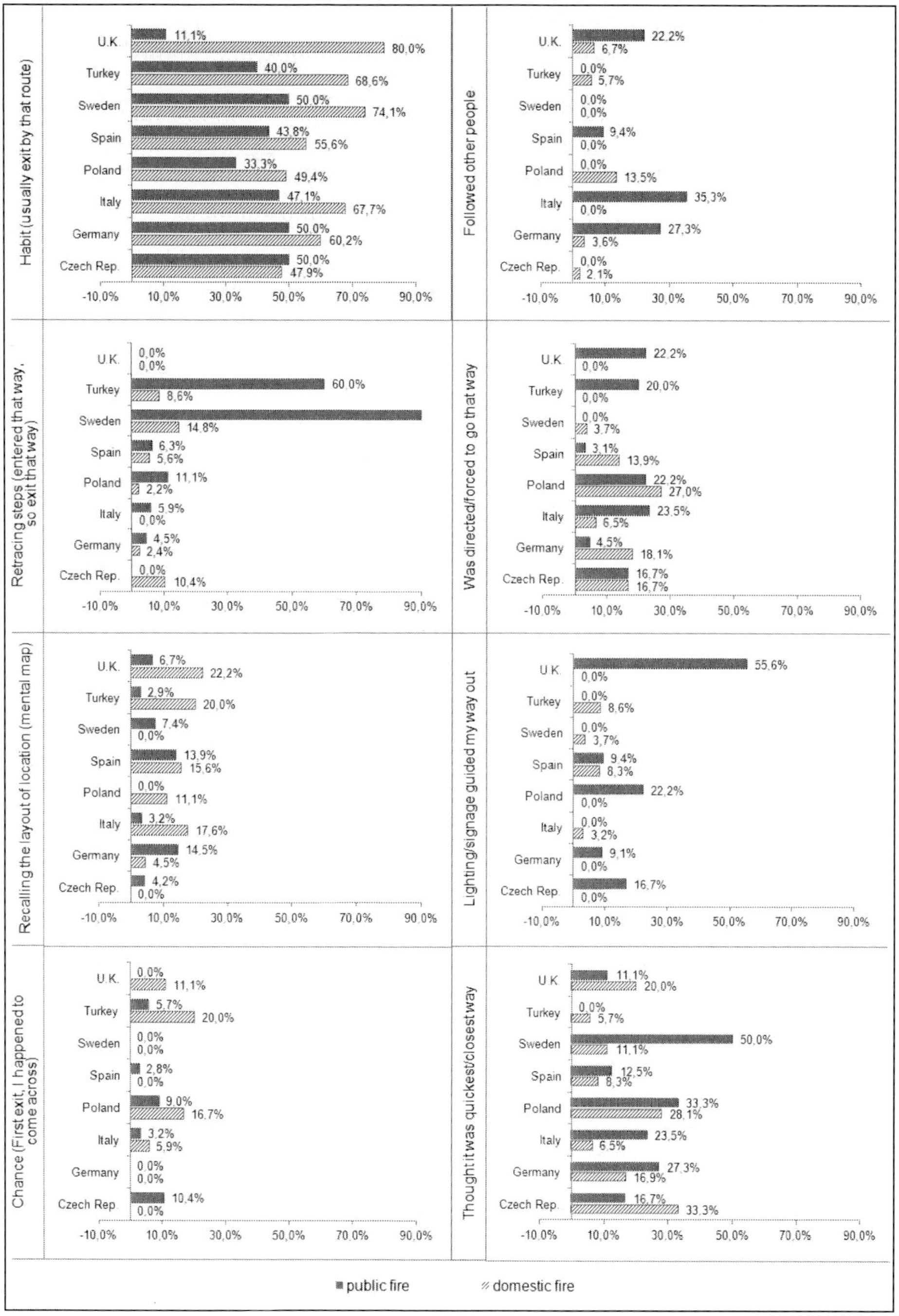

Fig. 5.12: Wayfinding behaviour for public fires (left) and domestic fires (right) depending on the nationality of the participants

Information seeking and information need during the event

In order to find out if survivors sought more information in the course of the event, the following questions were asked: *What was the first thing you did/ what else did you do when you understood something was happening?* All participants who chose the option *"I actively sought further information"* at least once are displayed in Fig. 5.13. Differences in information seeking behaviour were found with respect to the country of the incident (χ^2 [7] = 26.264, $\rho < .001$, Cramér's V = .16) and the type of event (χ^2 [4] = 46.508, $\rho < .001$, Cramér's V = .21).

In total 20% of the domestic fire survivors did actively seek further information and some point of the event (28% in terrorist attack, 35% in a flood, 44% in a public building fire and 21% in an earthquake). Information seeking behaviour was most common if a fire in a public building occurred or during the terrorist attacks in Turkey and the UK.

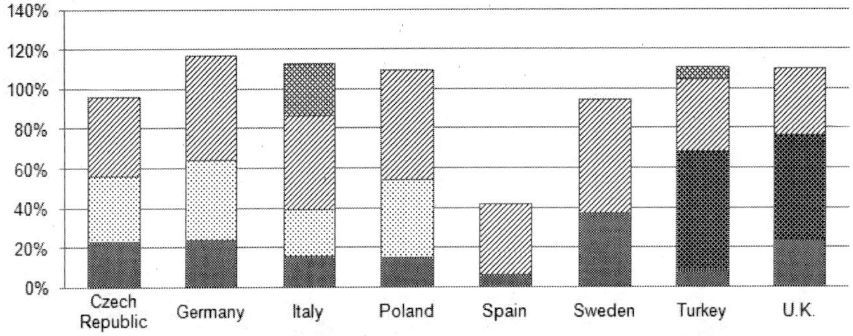

	Czech Republic	Germany	Italy	Poland	Spain	Sweden	Turkey	U.K.
Earthquake			26,2%				6,3%	
Public building fire	40,0%	53,1%	47,4%	55,0%	36,1%	57,1%	36,4%	33,3%
Flood	33,3%	40,5%	23,5%	39,0%				
Terrorist attack					0,0%		60,0%	52,6%
Fire in a home	22,7%	23,2%	15,4%	15,0%	5,7%	37,0%	7,9%	23,8%

Fig. 5.13: Information seeking in different incidents and their corresponding countries

The frequencies for seeking behaviour as a first response to an event ranged from 5% in an earthquake to 20% in a public building fire (see Fig. 5.14). In order to find out what kinds of information are important for participants, they were asked: *What type of information were you seeking?* The answer options were the following: *Information about the nature of the incident.; Information about the type of threat the incident posed to me.; Information about what I should do.; Information about what means of communication were available.; Information about what means of evacuation were available.; Information regarding the official response to the emergency (e.g. Did staff at the location/emergency services actually know about the problem? What were they doing to resolve it?)* and *Information about how soon professional help would arrive.* Fig. 5.14 displays information which was actively sought by the participants as a first action during the event. Information regarding the nature of the event was needed, especially in a terrorist attack or a domestic fire. In natural incidents like floods or earthquakes, information regarding the type of threat and further instructions were sought.

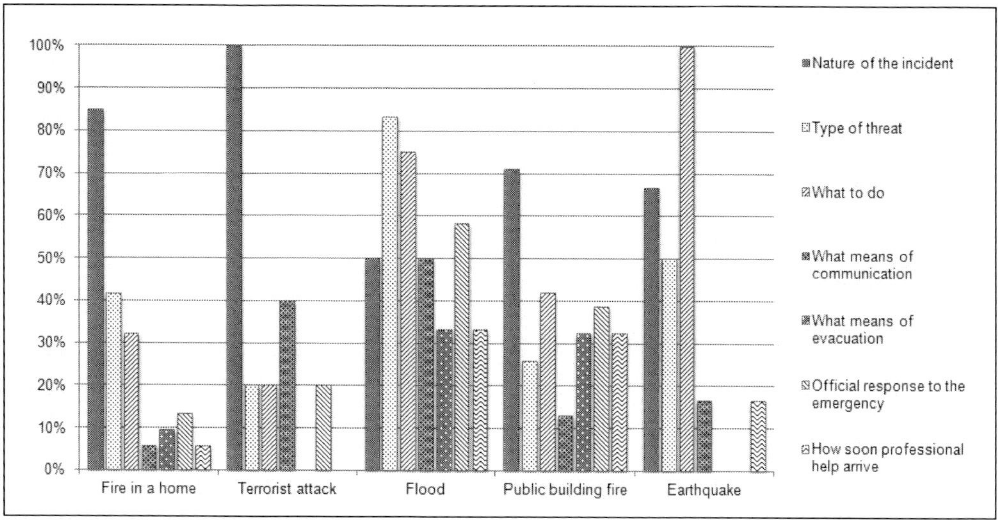

Fig. 5.14: Information seeking as a first response to the event

In addition to information seeking as a first action, participants were further asked about any information they might have needed during the event (regardless of seeking activities for this information). About 41% of all participants would have needed more information during the event, with most terrorist attack survivors (64%) needing more information. Fig. 5.15 illustrates the type of information which was requested. The nature of the incident, the type of threat and information about what to do next was the most frequently requested information. In terrorist attacks information on evacuation possibilities were deemed important.

No significant differences between incident types were found with respect to information need regarding the nature of the event (χ^2 [4] = 7.854, ρ = .097, Cramér's V = .13), the type of threat (χ^2 [4] = 2.987, ρ = .560, Cramér's V = .08), on what to do next (χ^2 [4] = 8.436, ρ = .077, Cramér's V = .14) and the official response to the emergency (χ^2 [4] = 9.217, ρ = .056, Cramér's V = .14). Significant differences, but also only small effects, were found for information regarding the means of communication (χ^2 [4] = 12.220, ρ < .05, Cramér's V = .17) and information on how soon professional help would arrive (χ^2 [4] = 10.574, ρ < .05, Cramér's V = .15). The differences in information need regarding evacuation possibilities χ^2 [4] = 29.259, ρ < .001, Cramér's V = .26) can be interpreted as a medium effect.

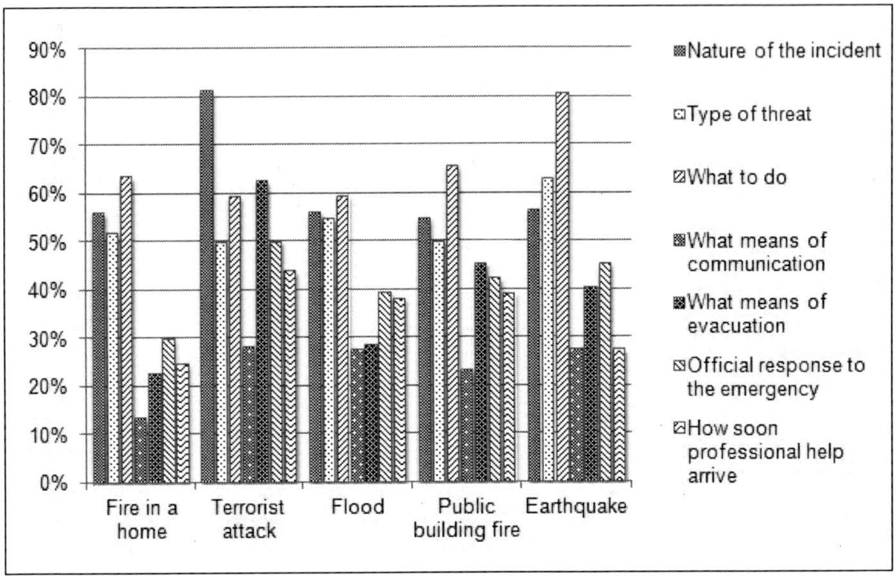

Fig. 5.15: Information need during the course of the event

Communication during the events

The involvement of the emergency service during fire incidents was one criterion for all BeSeCu participants. In order to find out if the participant actually communicated with the emergency service the following question was asked: *Did you communicate with the emergency services at all during the incident?* In total 59.4% of the BeSeCu participants did communicate during the event. Differences are present between the different countries of the event (χ^2 [7] = 110.718, $\rho < .001$, Cramér's V = .32) and the incident type (χ^2 [4] = 183.670, $\rho < .001$, Cramér's V = .41).

Fig. 5.17 illustrates that communication with the emergency service was very frequent in fire events but not in the earthquake events. The comparison of different countries revealed a less frequent communication in events which happened in Italy (see Fig. 5.16). In this context Fig. 5.18 reveals that a less frequent communication in Italy was present not only in earthquake but also in cases of public fires and floods.

Communication during domestic fires (χ^2 [7] = 7.887, $\rho = .343$, Cramér's V = .12), terrorist attacks (χ^2 [2] = 1.380, $\rho = .501$, Cramér's V = .17) and earthquakes (χ^2 [1] = 1.219, $\rho = .269$, Cramér's V = .10) only show small effect sizes regarding the differences between the corresponding countries of the event. Medium effects were found for communication in floods (χ^2 [3] = 19.781, $\rho < .001$, Cramér's V = .35) and public fires (χ^2 [7] = 12.133, $\rho = .096$, Cramér's V = .27).

Communication quality was also assessed with the question: *Did both parties understand what the other was trying to communicate?* Participants evaluated the

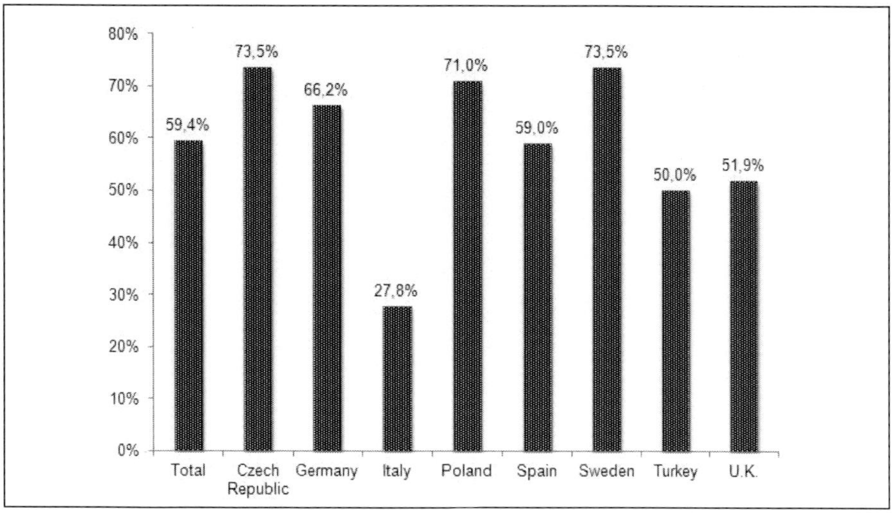

Fig. 5.16: Communication with emergency service depending on the incident country

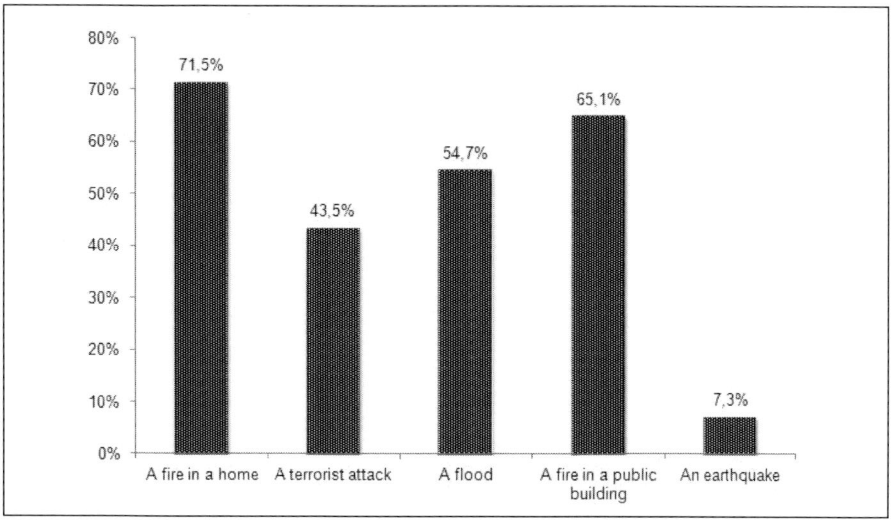

Fig. 5.17: Communication with emergency service depending on the type of event

quality on 5 point Likert scale which ranged from 1 = not at all, 2 = a little bit, 3 = moderately, 4 = quite a bit to 5 = extremely. Global differences are displayed in Table 5.4 Bonferroni corrected posthoc tests for communication quality in domestic fires revealed significant differences between Sweden and the Czech Republic, Germany, Spain, Turkey and between Poland and Turkey. With respect to flood a significant difference was found between the Czech Republic and Poland and in case of public fires the values of Germany did significantly differ from the Czech

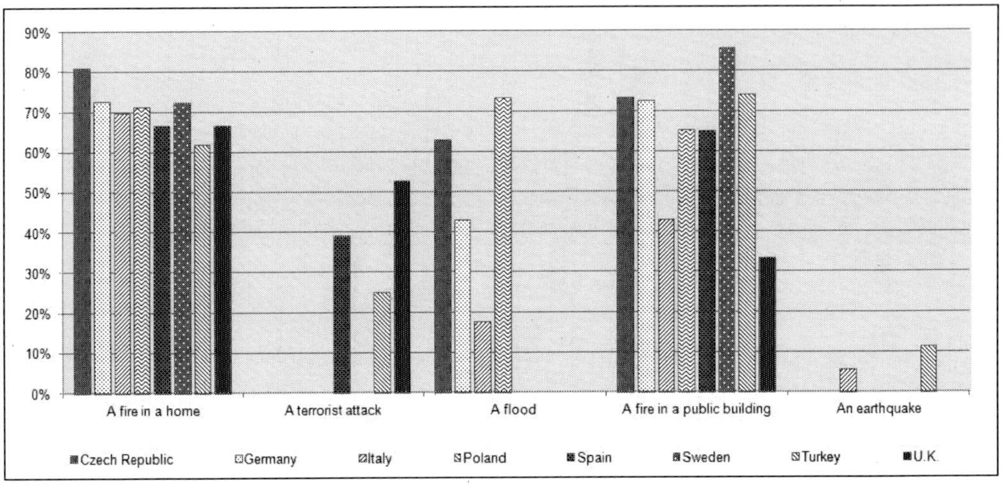

Fig. 5.18: Communication with the emergency service depending on type and country of the event

Republic and from Spain. In total 83.4% of the participants who communicated with the emergency service (n = 614) evaluated that both parties understood each other quite a bit or extremely.

Table 5.4: Communication quality depending on the country and type of incident

	Czech Republic		Germany		Italy		Poland		Spain		Sweden		Turkey		UK		F (df1/ df2)	η
	M	SD	M	SD	M	SD	M	SD	M	SD	M	SD	M	SD	M	SD		
Total	3.98	0.76	4.19	1.07	4.07	0.89	4.30	0.77	3.91	0.94	4.71	0.62	3.80	0.99	4.08	1.21	6.464 (7/608)***	.26
Home fire	4.03	0.72	4.00	1.18	4.10	0.94	4.23	0.84	4.00	0.72	4.70	0.64	3.62	0.89	4.25	1.14	5.344 (7/383)***	.30
Terrorist attack[a]									3.63	1.30			3.00	.	3.80	1.40	0.074 (1/16)	.07
Flood[b]	3.97	0.80	4.39	0.85	4.33	0.58	4.56	0.56									5.820 (2/84)**	.35
Public fire[c]	3.73	0.90	4.74	0.45	3.89	0.93	4.13	0.64	3.92	1.02	4.83	0.41	4.21	1.13	4.50	0.71	3.288 (6/100)**	.41
Earth-quake[d]					4.00	0.82							3.67	0.58				

Note.: * $p < .05$, ** $p < .01$, *** $p < .001$; [a] = Turkey was excluded from ANOVA analysis because n = 1; [b] = Italy was excluded from ANOVA analysis because n = 3; [c] = UK was excluded from ANOVA analysis because n = 2; [d] = No further ANOVA analysis since n = 4 for Italy and n = 3 for Turkey

5.3 Results of the BeSeCu-FR field study

Doris Kehl on behalf of the BeSeCu group

Sample

The BeSeCu-FR field study questionnaire answered 3,011 firefighters (Czech Republic [n = 302], Germany [n = 701], Italy [n = 623], Poland [n = 375], Spain [n = 163], Sweden [n = 181], Turkey [n = 468], UK [n = 198]). Participants could be included if they gave their informed consent and met the following inclusion criteria: a) at least 18 years of age and b) they were a firefighter and their last operation was no longer than ten years ago.

Of the 3011 firefighters were 97.0% male. The average age of the participants was 37.2 years (SD = 9.6, range: 18–66 years). The lowest formal qualification had 5.0% of the participants, 22.7% the intermediary secondary, and 72.4% had a completed secondary qualification or university degree. In a relationship were 78.9% of the participants. Only 4.6% (n = 137) of participants had a migrant background. About three-fourths of the participants (81.6%) were employed as fire fighter and 18.4% were honorary members (unpaid). Among the participants 62.3% worked as operational and 37.7% as leading operational personnel. On average participants have been working 13.5 years as a fire fighter (SD = 8.8, range: 0–52). Of the participants 34.3% had attended more than 100 operations in the past with respect to domestic fires, 19.1% attended 51 to 100 operations, 31.7% attended 11 to 50 operations and 14.9% attended less or equal than 10 operations.

Significant differences between national samples with respect to all the participants' demographic and work characteristics were observed (see Table 5.5 and 5.6): gender, χ^2 (7) = 22.45, $\rho < .01$, Cramér's V = .09; age, F (7, 2,989) = 80.41, $\rho < .001$, $\eta = .40$; education, χ^2 (14) = 651.64, $\rho < .001$, Cramér's V = .33; income, χ^2 (14) = 756.26, $\rho < .001$, Cramér's V = .36; relationship status, χ^2 (7) = 80.47, $\rho < .001$, Cramér's V = .16; migrant background (yes/no), χ^2 (7) = 47.69, $\rho < .001$, Cramér's V = .13; working arrangement, χ^2 (7) = 1,277.61, $\rho < .001$, Cramér's V = .65; rank/role, χ^2 (7) = 204.98, $\rho < .001$, Cramér's V = .26; years of service, F (7, 2,994) = 30.24, $\rho < .001$, $\eta = .26$; and number of operations in the past with respect to domestic fires, χ^2 (21) = 600.07, $\rho < .001$, Cramér's V = .26.

Communication with people on site, between first responders, and non-verbal communication

Communication with civilians when at the scene of an emergency was assessed with the following question: *"How frequently do you communicate in the following ways with victims during an operation?"* with respect to five different channels

Table 5.5: Demographic characteristics divided for each national sample

Demographic characteristics	Czech Republic n = 302 N%	Germany n = 701 N%	Italy n = 623 N%	Poland n = 375 N%	Spain n = 163 N%	Sweden n = 181 N%	Turkey n = 468 N%	U.K. n = 198 N%	Missing %
Male Gender	98.68	97.00	94.84	98.93	97.55	95.00	98.08	96.92	0.2
Age M (SD)	36.64 (7.77)	32.47 (10.39)	40.87 (8.25)	32.78 (7.08)	40.67 (8.77)	42.04 (10.49)	38.23 (8.41)	42.44 (7.93)	0.5
Education									0.1
Lowest formal	0.66	12.71	0.16	0.00	5.52	4.42	8.33	1.01	
Intermediary secondary	0.99	40.86	32.85	0.27	27.61	3.87	13.25	36.87	
Completed secondary or university degree	98.34	46.43	66.99	99.73	66.87	91.71	78.42	62.12	
Income									1.1
< 70% of annual net	2.01	21.20	6.01	7.49	1.26	0.56	8.59	0.51	
70% ≤ x ≥ 150% of annual net	43.14	45.27	82.95	52.41	18.24	29.44	26.65	36.36	
> 150% annual net	54.85	33.52	11.04	40.11	80.50	70.00	64.76	63.13	
In a relationship	77.74	71.00	80.65	72.27	76.69	88.89	87.31	88.89	0.3
Migrant background	5.63	6.56	3.22	2.93	1.24	10.5	1.28	9.09	0.3

Table 5.6: Work characteristics divided for each national sample

Work characteristics	Czech Republic n = 302 N%	Germany n = 701 N%	Italy n = 623 N%	Poland n = 375 N%	Spain n = 163 N%	Sweden n = 181 N%	Turkey n = 468 N%	U.K. n = 198 N%	Missing (%)
Working arrangement									0.4
Employed	99.34	36.15	89.87	93.33	90.80	99.44	99.78	100.00	
Honorary	0.66	63.85	10.13	6.67	9.20	0.56	0.22	0.00	
Rank/role									0.4
Operational personnel	68.21	52.43	72.35	72.85	81.60	43.89	64.29	32.49	
Leading operational personnel	31.79	47.57	27.65	27.15	18.40	56.11	35.71	67.51	
Years of service M (SD)	12.88 (7.17)	13.05 (9.26)	14.85 (8.95)	10.25 (6.87)	15.07 (8.85)	17.38 (11.25)	11.43 (7.30)	18.48 (8.43)	0.3
Number of operations in the past with respect to domestic fires									0.9
1-10	22.19	25.04	14.70	8.02	16.88	11.11	5.65	4.19	
11-50	43.71	42.20	33.76	33.42	22.50	35.56	12.39	14.66	
51-100	20.20	16.88	23.10	24.33	25.63	18.33	13.04	12.04	
>100	13.91	15.88	28.43	34.22	35.00	35.00	68.91	69.11	

Table 5.7: Different use of communication channels between national samples

	Czech Republic	Germany	Italy	Poland	Spain	Sweden	Turkey	U.K.
	M (SD)	M (SD)	M (SD)	M (SD)	M (SD)	M (SD)	M (SD)	M (SD)
Face-to-face verbal communication i.e. in person [a]	4.08 (0.82)	3.93 (0.90)	4.14 (0.78)	3.86 (0.92)	4.47 (0.56)	4.15 (0.68)	4.15 (0.99)	4.41 (0.67)
Face-to-face non-verbal communication – body language/ hand signals [b]	3.19 (0.96)	3.07 (0.94)	2.77 (0.96)	3.21 (0.92)	2.93 (0.83)	2.97 (0.91)	3.12 (1.12)	3.19 (1.02)
Face-to-face non-verbal communication – pictorial signs [c]	1.88 (0.87)	2.06 (0.87)	1.77 (0.83)	2.21 (0.95)	2.12 (0.84)	1.57 (0.67)	1.98 (1.13)	1.87 (0.83)
Remote verbal communication [d]	2.13 (0.81)	2.09 (0.78)	2.21 (0.90)	2.30 (0.94)	2.17 (0.79)	1.77 (0.90)	2.91 (1.16)	1.92 (0.76)
Telecommunications [e]	2.08 (0.96)	1.75 (0.86)	2.79 (1.08)	2.24 (1.01)	2.79 (0.95)	2.20 (1.03)	2.88 (1.28)	2.14 (1.00)

Notes: [a] $F(7,2984) = 17.41$, $p < .001$, $\eta = .20$; [b] $F(7,2956) = 11.39$, $p < .001$, $\eta = .16$; [c] $F(7,2941) = 15.16$, $p < .001$, $\eta = .19$; [d] $F(7,2955) = 48.72$, $p < .001$, $\eta = .32$; [e] $F(7,2951) = 76.17$, $p < .001$, $\eta = .39$.

(Likert items: 1 = never to 5 = always). In total, firefighters often communicate verbal face-to-face i.e. in person ($M = 4.08$; SD = 0.86) and sometimes via body language and hand signals ($M = 3.04$; SD = 0.98). Pictorial signs ($M = 1.95$; $SD = 0.91$), remote verbal communication systems e.g. loudhailer, public address system, intercom ($M = 2.24$; SD = 0.95) and telecommunication e.g. phone call ($M = 2.34$; $SD = 1.12$) were seldom used. There were significant differences between national samples with respect to the frequency of use of the different communication channels during an operation (see Table 5.7).

Additionally, firefighters were asked: *"In your opinion, what would be the most efficient way to communicate with victims in evacuation situations where verbal communication is impossible?"* With respect to the following three options: body language (e.g. hand signals, gestures), pictorial signs/pictograms, and digital signs/ LCD display. In total, more than seventy percent of firefighters (70.6%) assessed body language as the most efficient way to communicate where verbal communication is impossible, whereas only 15.4% assessed pictorial signs/ pictograms and 14.0% digital signs/LCD display as the most efficient way to communicate. Again, significant differences between national samples were observed, $\chi^2(14) = 482.50$, $p < .001$, Cramér's V = .29 (see Fig. 5.19). Of interest, more than ninety percent of Turkish firefighters assessed body language as the most efficient way to communicate compared to only 42% of German firefighters.

Furthermore, firefighters were asked: *"If verbal communication was impossible during an evacuation situation, which of the following instructions would be used most frequently as signs or gestures? Please choose the 10 signs/gestures that are most common and helpful in your opinion."* In total, firefighters assessed the following ten signs (out of 19) as most common and helpful: go down/ down the stairs (47.0%), are you able to walk (58.4%), come here (62.8%), attention

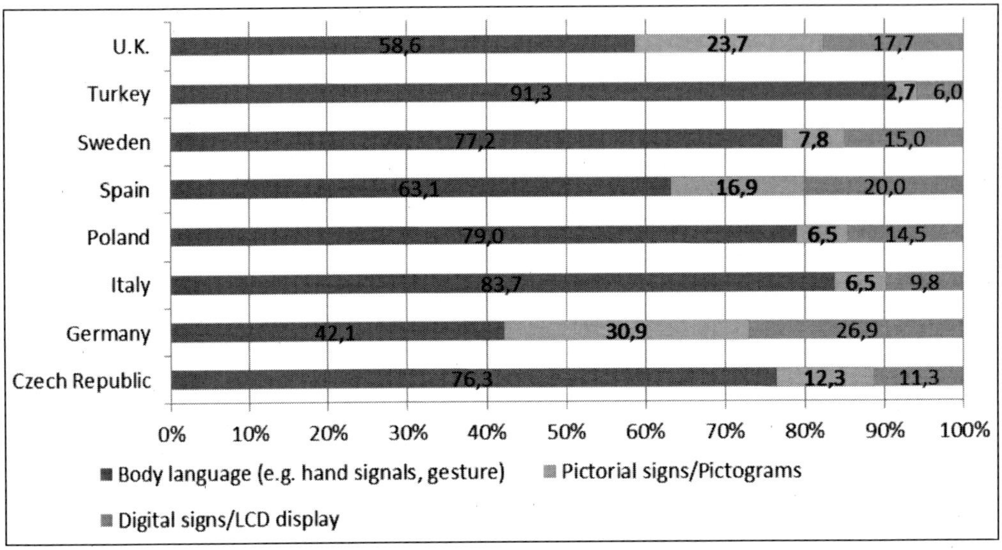

Fig. 5.19: Communication with victims in evacuation situations where verbal communication is impossible

(66.3%), go this/ that way (67.0%), are you injured (72.0%), stop/stand by (76.7%), evacuate/leave the building (78.5%), calm down (79.1%), follow me (82.0%). Differences between national samples were revealed with respect to the estimated use of different signs/ gestures when verbal communication is impossible (see Table 5.8).

Communication difficulties during an operation were assessed by asking: *How often would you say there are communication difficulties during an operation with the following groups?* (five Likert items: 1 = never to 5 = always). In total, firefighters assessed the frequency of communication difficulties with children (M = 2.61, SD = 0.91), people with disabilities (M = 2.77, SD = 0.90), general public (M = 2.85, SD = 0.77), elderly (M = 3.04, SD = 0.84) and people with migrant background (M = 3.24, SD = 0.99) in ascending order. There were significant differences between national samples with respect to the frequency of communication difficulties (see Table 5.9). If there are communication difficulties with victims, on average it does moderately affect firefighters work during operations (M = 3.04, SD = 0.97) with significant differences between national samples, $F(7,2982) = 19.11$, $\rho < .001$, $\eta = .21$: Czech Republic (M = 2.61, SD = 0.80), Germany (M = 3.25, SD = 0.86), Italy (M = 3.17, SD = 1.03), Poland (M = 2.85, SD = 0.90), Spain (M = 3.20, SD = 0.87), Sweden (M = 2.91, SD = 0.81), Turkey (M = 3.98, SD = 1.17), U.K. (M = 3.00, SD = 0.88).

Additional, firefighters rated the efficiency of the communication of firefighters with other emergency service personnel (Likert items: 1 = never efficient to 5 = always efficient). In total, fire fighters assessed the communication with civil

Table 5.8: Estimated use of different signs/ gestures (in percent) when verbal communication is impossibl

	Czech Republic	Germany	Italy	Poland	Spain	Sweden	Turkey	U.K.	Total
Stop/stand by [a]	83.1	80.3	80.4	81.6	82.6	51.9	66.2	75.3	76.7
Evacuate/leave the building [b]	71.5	92.0	63.8	80.7	74.5	95.0	70.7	89.4	78.5
Help me/him/her [c]	39.1	24.9	26.1	40.8	29.2	44.2	22.5	29.8	29.9
Come here [d]	70.9	66.9	66.0	50.0	68.3	50.8	55.0	75.3	62.8
Go up/up the stairs [e]	27.8	28.1	27.7	34.1	24.2	16.0	21.0	22.2	26.3
Lay on the floor [f]	28.5	28.3	28.6	37.4	49.7	8.8	37.3	14.6	30.0
Attention [g]	75.5	61.7	71.5	69.9	54.0	64.1	65.4	59.6	66.3
Run [h]	38.1	19.0	23.5	33.1	15.5	12.7	39.3	8.6	25.5
Go this/that way [i]	68.9	72.4	82.5	56.7	75.2	63.5	35.2	86.4	67.0
Move back [j]	26.2	37.7	31.4	46.0	32.3	35.9	21.7	54.0	34.5
Go down/down the stairs [k]	50.7	54.9	49.0	45.7	46.6	34.3	34.8	50.5	47.0
Crawl [l]	7.6	27.0	8.9	24.5	14.9	33.7	24.3	18.7	19.8
Follow me [m]	91.4	85.4	76.9	85.3	91.3	69.6	72.4	91.9	82.0
Calm down [n]	72.2	79.6	82.0	76.7	88.2	57.5	85.0	81.8	79.1
Are you able to walk [o]	60.3	52.9	62.1	64.2	62.1	53.0	55.0	62.1	58.4
Are you injured [p]	80.5	69.6	75.2	71.3	78.9	67.4	62.0	80.3	72.0
Leave your belongings [q]	32.5	53.3	34.5	32.0	23.6	50.3	14.4	54.5	37.0
Hurry [r]	29.5	49.0	34.3	41.3	32.3	39.2	63.0	40.4	43.1
Others [s]	6.3	6.6	3.4	1.9	8.7	5.0	5.6	4.0	5.0

Notes: [a] χ^2 (7s) = 115.58, ρ < .001, Cramér's V = .20 · [b] χ^2 (7) = 226.05, ρ <. 001, Cramér's V = .28
[c] χ^2 (7) = 75.65, ρ < .001, Cramér's V = .16 · [d] χ^2 (7) = 80.41, ρ < .001, Cramér's V = .16 ·
[e] χ^2 (7) = 32.62, ρ < .001, Cramér's V = .10 · [f] χ^2 (7) = 113.82, ρ < .001, Cramér's V = .20
[g] χ^2 (7) = 43.07, ρ < .001, Cramér's V = .12 · [h] χ^2 (7) = 153.67, ρ < .001, Cramér's V = .23
[i] χ^2 (7) = 344.58, ρ < .001, Cramér's V = .34 · [j] χ^2 (7) = 103.91, ρ < .001, Cramér's V = .19
[k] χ^2 (7) = 60.60, ρ <. 001, Cramér's V = .14 · [l] χ^2 (7) = 133.09, ρ < .001, Cramér's V = .21
[m] χ^2 (7) = 107.70, ρ < .001, Cramér's V = .19 · [n] χ^2 (7) = 83.25, ρ < .001, Cramér's V = .17
[o] χ^2 (7) = 24.44, ρ <. 001, Cramér's V = .09 · [p] χ^2 (7) = 51.52, ρ < .001, Cramér's V = .13 ·
[q] χ^2 (7) = 241.09, ρ < .001, Cramér's V = .28 · [r] χ^2 (7) = 134.00, ρ < .001, Cramér's V = .21
[s] χ^2 (7) = 20.98, ρ < .01, Cramér's V = .08.

protection as sometimes efficient (*M* = 3.18, *SD* = 1.08) and the communication often efficient with police (*M* = 3.69, *SD* = 0.85), emergency medical service (*M* = 3.98, *SD* = 0.79) and firefighters (*M* = 4.31, *SD* = 0.67). There were significant differences between national samples with respect to the efficiency of the communication (see Table 5.10). Another question was: *How frequently do you lack information that is important to perform an efficient operation?* (Likert item: 1 = never to 5 = always). In total, firefighter sometimes lack information that is important to perform an efficient operation (*M* = 3.00, *SD* = 0.84) with significant differences between national samples, $F(7,2984) = 11.78$, ρ < .001, η = .16: Czech Republic (*M* = 2.95, *SD* = 0.75), Germany (*M* = 3.14, *SD* = 0.77), Italy (*M* = 3.09,

Table 5.9: Communication difficulties with different population groups (n = 3,011)

	Czech Republic		Germany		Italy		Poland		Spain		Sweden		Turkey		U.K.	
	M	SD	M	SD	M	SD	M	SD	M	SD	M	SD	M	SD	M	SD
Children [a]	2.56	0.76	2.66	0.79	2.39	0.91	2.75	0.86	2.50	0.80	2.31	0.65	2.87	1.25	2.78	0.66
Elderly [b]	3.26	0.75	3.18	0.74	2.95	0.80	3.13	0.82	2.88	0.68	2.58	0.70	3.02	1.14	2.97	0.69
People with disabilties [c]	2.73	0.83	2.97	0.78	2.60	0.84	2.83	0.94	2.59	0.81	2.37	0.70	2.93	1.23	2.65	0.59
Adults with migrant background [d]	3.13	0.96	3.59	0.78	3.45	0.88	2.86	1.10	3.30	0.88	3.02	0.82	2.78	1.25	3.30	0.80
General public [e]	2.67	0.61	2.81	0.66	2.89	0.72	2.89	0.75	2.77	0.67	2.46	0.57	3.11	1.14	2.83	0.55

Note: [a] $F(7,2971) = 16.86, \rho < .001, \eta = .20$ · [b] $F(7,2957) = 16.43, \rho < .001, \eta = .19$
[c] $F(7,2943) = 17.29, \rho < .001, \eta = 20$ · [d] $F(7,2922) = 42.60, \rho < .001, \eta = 30$
[e] $F(7,2963) = 17.54, \rho < .001, \eta = .20$.

Table 5.10: Efficiency of the communication of firefighters with other emergency personnel

	Czech Republic	Germany	Italy	Poland	Spain	Sweden	Turkey	U.K.
	M (SD)	M (SD)	M (SD)	M (SD)	M (SD)	M (SD)	M (SD)	M (SD)
Firefighter colleagues [a]	4.46 (0.56)	4.24 (0.55)	4.26 (0.73)	4.60 (0.56)	4.37 (0.53)	4.08 (0.43)	4.28 (0.90)	4.13 (0.64)
Police [b]	3.71 (0.73)	3.59 (0.77)	3.75 (0.85)	3.92 (0.78)	3.74 (0.67)	3.44 (0.74)	3.76 (1.10)	3.37 (0.76)
Emergency medical service [c]	3.94 (0.78)	4.11 (0.61)	3.89 (0.85)	4.18 (0.66)	3.82 (0.76)	3.62 (0.67)	4.12 (0.94)	3.56 (0.76)
Civil protection [d]	2.85 (0.94)	3.56 (0.83)	2.80 (1.11)	3.40 (0.98)	3.01 (1.00)	2.82 (0.77)	3.44 (1.38)	2.96 (0.86)

Notes: [a] $F(7,2972) = 20.12, \rho < .001, \eta = .21$ · [b] $F(7,2969) = 13.05, \rho < .001, \eta = .17$
[c] $F(7,2972) = 25.91, \rho < .001, \eta = .24$ · [d] $F(7,2948) = 41.51, \rho < .001, \eta = .30$.

SD = 0.83), Poland (*M* = 2.76, *SD* = 0.83), Spain (*M* = 3.19, *SD* = 0.68), Sweden (*M* = 2.92, *SD* = 0.74), Turkey (*M* = 2.86, *SD* = 1.05), and U.K. (*M* = 3.05, *SD* = 0.73).

With respect to fires in multiple occupancy residential buildings firefighters were asked: *In general, how often is the following information relayed to you in advance of taking action at such an incident?* (Likert items: 1 = never to 5 = always). In total, firefighters reported that the number of other fire engines attending the scene (*M* = 3.98, *SD* = 1.16) and the number of units (i.e. individual homes) directly affected by the fire (*M* = 3.52, *SD* = 1.09) are often relayed to them in advance of taking action. However, the number of people who need to evacuate (*M* = 3.03, *SD* = 1.17), information regarding type of action already taken to rescue victims (*M* = 2.97, *SD* = 1.14) and information regarding type of action required to be taken to rescue victims (*M* = 2.91, *SD* = 1.28) is only sometimes relayed to them. Firefight-

Table 5.11: Information relayed to firefighters in advance of taking action at fires in multiple-occupancy residential building

	Czech Republic	Germany	Italy	Poland	Spain	Sweden	Turkey	U.K.
	M (SD	**M (SD)**	**M (SD)**	**M (SD)**	**M (SD)**	**M (SD)**	**M (SD)**	**M (SD)**
Number of other fire engines attending the scene [a]	4.07 (0.92)	3.50 (1.41)	3.96 (1.14)	4.10 (0.94)	4.43 (0.76)	4.32 (0.85)	4.08 (1.18)	4.51 (0.72)
Number of units (i.e. individual homes) directly affected by the fire [b]	3.25 (1.01)	3.25 (1.16)	3.68 (1.02)	3.98 (0.89)	3.90 (0.73)	3.16 (0.99)	3.80 (1.17)	3.12 (1.00)
Number of people who need to evacuate [c]	2.71 (1.05)	2.86 (1.23)	3.00 (1.09)	3.54 (0.99)	2.76 (0.98)	2.63 (0.96)	3.75 (1.19)	2.49 (1.03)
Profile of the victims (e.g. ages, cultural background) [d]	1.95 (0.92)	1.81 (0.92)	2.20 (1.01)	2.58 (1.08)	2.27 (0.93)	1.80 (0.76)	2.83 (1.29)	1.72 (0.76)
Suspected cause of the fire [e]	2.15 (0.92)	2.07 (0.94)	2.49 (1.06)	2.73 (1.02)	2.39 (0.94)	2.06 (0.84)	3.55 (1.22)	2.04 (0.88)
What type of action already taken to rescue victims [f]	2.43 (1.02)	3.14 (1.19)	2.81 (1.02)	3.39 (0.98)	2.76 (0.98)	2.62 (0.78)	3.43 (1.26)	2.57 (1.19)
What type of action required to be taken to rescue victims [g]	2.46 (1.17)	3.04 (1.35)	2.70 (1.14)	3.17 (1.14)	2.69 (1.09)	2.39 (1.06)	3.70 (1.20)	2.48 (1.31)

Notes: [a] $F(7, 2664) = 30.32, p < .001, \eta = .27$ · [b] $F(7, 2658) = 32.56, p < .001, \eta = .28$
[c] $F(7, 2656) = 47.84, p < .001, \eta = .33$ · [d] $F(7, 2648) = 53.15, p < .001, \eta = .35$
[e] $F(7, 2649) = 89.07, p < .001, \eta = .44$ · [f] $F(7, 2652) = 36.24, p < .001, \eta = .30$
[g] $F(7, 2660) = 41.47, p < .001, \eta = .31$.

er reported that information about the suspected cause of the fire (*M* = 2.46, *SD* = 1.12) and about the profile of the victims e.g. ages, cultural background (*M* = 2.15, *SD* = 1.06) is seldom relayed to them in advance of taking action. Significant differences between national samples were observed (Table 5.11). The largest difference between national samples was observed with respect to information about the suspected cause of fire. Turkish firefighter reported that they often receive this information, whereas British, Czech, German and Swedish firefighters reported that they seldom receive information about the suspected cause of fire.

Furthermore, firefighters were asked: *What information given to you on site could lead to a more effective operation?* Participants were asked to allocate each type of information a number, starting with 1 (most important) to 7 (least important). The number of missing persons was assessed as the most important information (*M* = 2.55, *SD* = 1.98) followed by the number of people in the building (*M* = 2.70, SD = 1.99), existence of hazardous materials (*M* = 2.81, *SD* = 2.06), number of people who need to evacuate (*M* = 3.03, *SD* = 2.01), if there are people with special needs in the building e.g. disabled, deaf people (*M* = 3.14, *SD* = 2.03) and building geometry (*M* = 3.64, *SD* = 2.14). Information with respect to the nationalities of people involved (e.g. to prepare for language differences) was assessed by firefighters as the least important information (*M* = 5.23, *SD* = 2.12). Again, significant differences between national samples were observed (Table 5.12). Large differences between national samples were observed with respect to

Table 5.12: Firefighters' assessment of a more effective operation due specific information

	Czech Republic	Germany	Italy	Poland	Spain	Sweden	Turkey	U.K.
	M (SD)	M (SD)	M (SD)	M (SD)	M (SD)	M (SD)	M (SD)	M (SD)
Building geometry [a]	2.85 (1.93)	4.21 (2.00)	3.14 (2.01)	4.99 (1.84)	3.44 (2.00)	3.63 (1.97)	2.49 (2.14)	4.36 (1.87)
Existence of hazardous materials [b]	1.94 (1.71)	3.64 (1.90)	2.27 (2.16)	3.28 (1.95)	2.48 (1.93)	2.73 (1.83)	2.50 (2.31)	2.94 (1.45)
If there are people with special needs in the building [c]	2.25 (1.80)	3.53 (1.80)	2.69 (2.15)	3.47 (1.84)	3.41 (1.95)	3.41 (1.90)	2.64 (2.32)	4.49 (1.33)
Nationalities of people involved [d]	4.54 (2.06)	5.83 (1.80)	4.65 (2.19)	5.75 (1.80)	5.59 (1.87)	5.46 (1.97)	4.06 (2.50)	6.66 (0.72)
Number of missing persons [e]	2.02 (1.78)	1.99 (1.59)	3.01 (2.28)	3.72 (1.76)	3.16 (2.01)	2.12 (1.81)	2.59 (2.15)	1.58 (0.95)
Number of people in the building [f]	1.99 (1.72)	2.59 (1.72)	2.66 (2.12)	2.57 (1.97)	3.23 (2.08)	3.28 (2.06)	2.64 (2.21)	3.68 (1.65)
Number of people who need to evacuate [g]	2.00 (1.65)	3.55 (1.77)	2.94 (2.19)	2.89 (1.77)	2.88 (2.01)	3.02 (2.00)	2.69 (2.30)	4.10 (1.43)

Notes: [a] $F(7,2922) = 68.86$, $p < .001$, $\eta = .38$ · [b] $F(7,2926) = 37.74$, $p < .001$, $\eta = .29$
[c] $F(7,2924) = 37.41$, $p < .001$, $\eta = .29$ · [d] $F(7,2881) = 59.45$, $p < .001$, $\eta = .36$
[e] $F(7,2906) = 49.67$, $p < .001$, $\eta = .33$ · [f] $F(7,2915) = 17.49$, $p < .001$, $\eta = .20$
[g] $F(7,2913) = 30.32$, $p < .001$, $\eta = .26$.

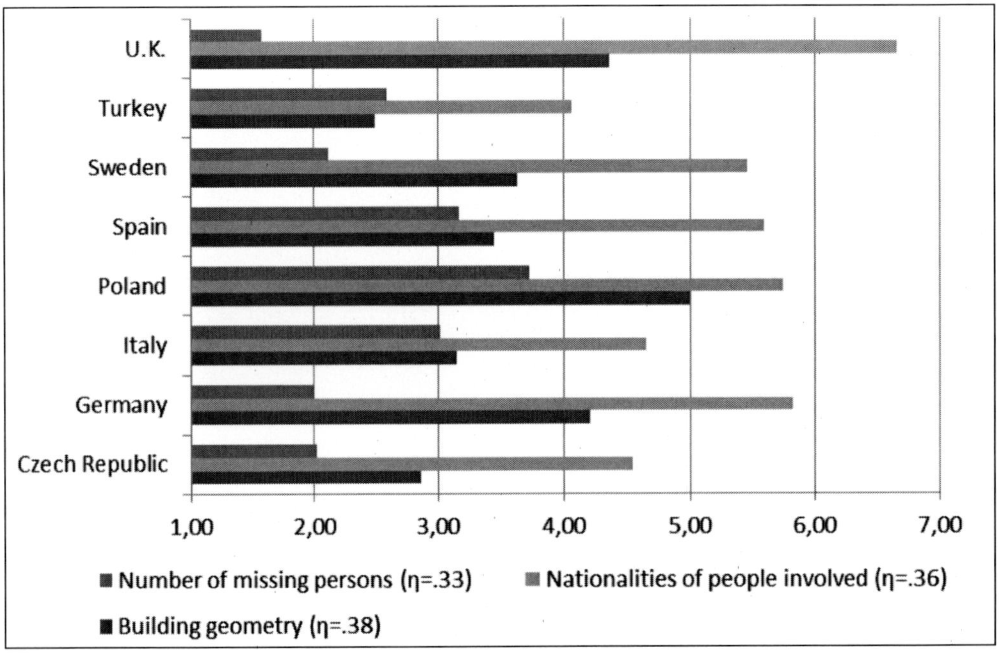

Fig. 5.20: Type of information given to firefighters on site leading to a more effective operation

building geometry, nationalities of people involved and number of missing persons as displayed in Fig. 5.20.

Behaviour of civilians in emergency situation

Firefighter assessed how frequently they have seen victims display diverse reactions (Likert items: 1 = never to 5 = always). Differences between national samples were observed as displayed in Table 5.13. In total, firefighters assessed that victims most frequently display panic-like behaviour, misinterpreting the situation

Table 5.13: Firefighters' assessment of how frequently they have seen different victim reactions in emergency situation

	Total	Czech Republic	Germany	Italy	Poland	Spain	Sweden	Turkey	U.K.
	M (SD)	M (SD)	M (SD)	M (SD)	M (SD)	M (SD)	M (SD)	M (SD)	M (SD)
Panic-like behaviour [a]	3.44 (0.93)	3.33 (0.70)	3.38 (0.83)	3.52 (0.88)	3.36 (0.89)	3.30 (0.76)	2.74 (0.92)	3.89 (1.17)	3.54 (0.75)
Starting the evacuation too late [b]	2.78 (1.02)	2.80 (0.94)	2.77 (1.06)	2.65 (0.99)	2.62 (0.90)	2.76 (0.87)	3.02 (0.93)	2.67 (1.15)	3.47 (0.81)
Not evacuating at all even though it is required [c]	2.42 (1.05)	2.55 (0.99)	2.26 (1.03)	2.25 (0.98)	2.46 (0.97)	2.40 (0.88)	2.70 (0.97)	2.25 (1.20)	3.35 (0.78)
Moving too slow during evacuation [d]	2.52 (1.01)	2.52 (0.86)	2.57 (1.04)	2.35 (0.98)	2.55 (0.90)	2.50 (0.81)	2.93 (0.98)	2.26 (1.17)	3.08 (0.84)
Moving towards the danger [e]	2.44 (1.02)	2.19 (0.84)	2.67 (0.96)	2.31 (1.04)	2.23 (0.93)	2.54 (0.95)	2.08 (0.77)	2.74 (1.27)	2.46 (0.81)
Misinterpreting the situation [f]	3.12 (0.99)	3.09 (0.84)	3.54 (0.79)	3.07 (0.95)	3.00 (0.95)	3.11 (0.85)	3.06 (0.82)	2.56 (1.27)	3.39 (0.79)
Incorrect priorities (e.g. fire fighting instead of evacuation) [g]	2.62 (1.01)	2.49 (0.87)	2.75 (1.00)	2.56 (0.97)	2.42 (0.93)	3.07 (0.85)	2.60 (0.74)	2.45 (1.30)	2.95 (0.77)
Supportive behaviour [h]	3.18 (0.95)	3.00 (0.79)	2.90 (0.88)	3.38 (0.97)	3.14 (0.88)	3.55 (0.74)	2.93 (0.81)	3.42 (1.23)	3.26 (0.68)
Refusing to follow instructions [i]	2.70 (0.99)	2.98 (0.87)	2.97 (0.92)	2.50 (0.98)	2.70 (0.95)	2.70 (0.80)	2.41 (0.74)	2.34 (1.26)	2.97 (0.74)
Misunderstanding the emergency services interventions [j]	2.74 (0.95)	2.71 (0.74)	2.91 (0.89)	2.78 (0.92)	2.66 (0.92)	2.94 (0.88)	2.48 (0.80)	2.37 (1.22)	3.02 (0.82)
Verbal attacks [k]	2.81 (1.00)	2.69 (0.77)	2.91 (0.95)	2.72 (0.94)	2.68 (0.88)	2.52 (0.83)	2.15 (0.79)	3.31 (1.31)	2.93 (0.80)
Physical attacks [l]	1.94 (0.91)	1.74 (0.71)	1.84 (0.82)	1.70 (0.77)	2.04 (0.77)	1.52 (0.65)	1.52 (0.57)	2.75 (1.19)	2.16 (0.74)

Notes: [a] $F(7,2969) = 35.15$, $p < .001$, $\eta = .28$ · [b] $F(7,2954) = 18.51$, $p < .001$, $\eta = .20$
[c] $F(7,2950) = 33.48$, $p < .001$, $\eta = .27$ · [d] $F(7,2959) = 20.79$, $p < .001$, $\eta = .22$
[e] $F(7,2960) = 21.46$, $p < .001$, $\eta = .22$ · [f] $F(7,2964) = 46.54$, $p < .001$, $\eta = .31$
[g] $F(7,2962) = 14.89$, $p < .001$, $\eta = .18$ · [h] $F(7,2954) = 24.58$, $p < .001$, $\eta = .23$
[i] $F(7,2950) = 28.89$, $p < .001$, $\eta = .25$ · [j] $F(7,2942) = 19.14$, $p < .001$, $\eta = .21$
[k] $F(7,2952) = 34.59$, $p < .001$, $\eta = .28$ · [l] $F(7,2953) = 84.75$, $p < .001$, $\eta = .41$.

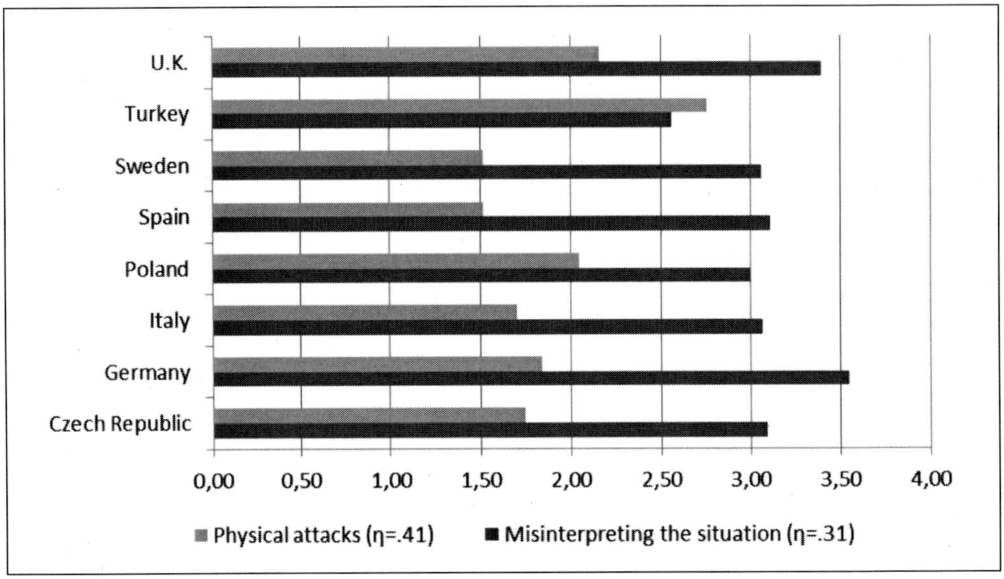

Fig. 5.21: Behaviour of civilians in emergency situation

(e.g. underestimation of the danger) and supportive behaviour. Large differences between national samples were observed with respect to physical attacks and misinterpreting the situation as displayed in Fig. 5.21.

Furthermore, firefighters assessed how frequently they have encountered incorrect behaviour (Likert items: 1 = never to 5 = always). In total, firefighters

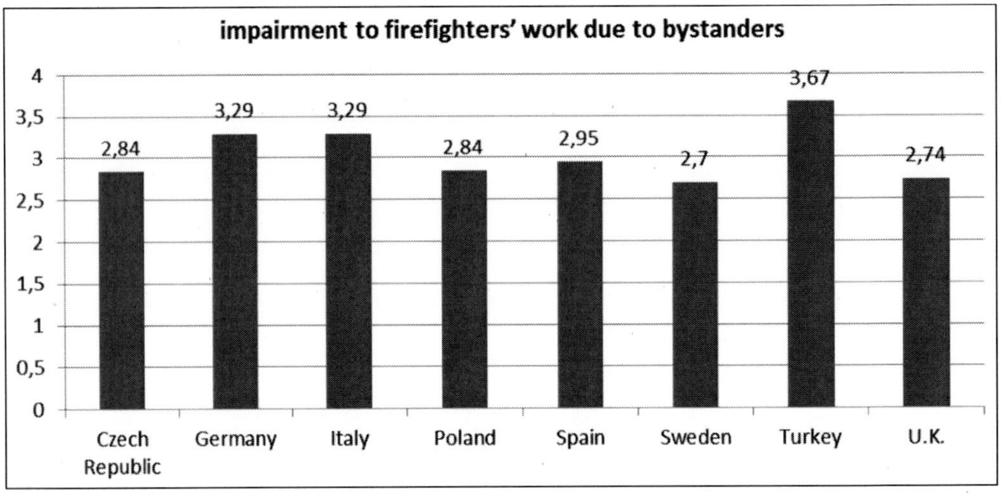

Fig. 5.22: Impairment to firefighters' work due to bystanders

Table 5.14: Firefighters' assessment of how frequently they have encountered incorrect behaviour among different population groups

	Czech Republic	Germany	Italy	Poland	Spain	Sweden	Turkey	U.K.
	M (SD)	M (SD)	M (SD)	M (SD)	M (SD)	M (SD)	M (SD)	M (SD)
Children [a]	2.41 (0.91)	2.61 (1.02)	1.68 (0.93)	2.48 (0.97)	1.98 (0.89)	2.18 (0.87)	2.71 (1.25)	2.85 (0.97)
Elderly [b]	3.17 (0.83)	3.11 (0.91)	2.42 (0.97)	2.78 (0.91)	2.90 (0.76)	2.68 (0.87)	2.88 (1.18)	2.17 (0.92)
People with disabilities [c]	1.96 (0.88)	2.33 (0.98)	1.71 (0.83)	2.19 (0.92)	1.69 (0.78)	1.90 (0.84)	2.45 (1.19)	1.69 (0.81)
Adults with migrant background [d]	2.55 (1.09)	3.29 (0.99)	2.90 (1.06)	1.90 (0.99)	2.78 (1.02)	2.76 (1.00)	2.46 (1.16)	2.42 (1.00)
General public [e]	2.82 (0.65)	3.04 (0.70)	2.76 (0.81)	2.84 (0.75)	2.81 (0.68)	2.54 (0.69)	3.35 (1.12)	2.90 (0.79)

Notes: [a] $F(7,2947) = 65.65$, $\rho < .001$, $\eta = .37$ · [b] $F(7,2929) = 44.83$, $\rho < .001$, $\eta = .31$
[c] $F(7,2908) = 40.77$, $\rho < .001$, $\eta = .30$ · [d] $F(7,2888) = 72.31$, $\rho < .001$, $\eta = .39$
[e] $F(7,2956) = 31.11$, $\rho < .001$, $\eta = .26$.

encountered incorrect behaviour seldom among disabled (*M* = 2.06, *SD* = 0.98) and children (*M* = 2.35, *SD* = 1.08) and sometimes among adult migrants (*M* = 2.73, *SD* = 1.13), elderly (*M* = 2.80, *SD* = 0.99), and the general public (*M* = 2.93, *SD* = 0.83). Significant differences between national samples were observed with respect to the different population groups (see Table 5.14).

If victims display incorrect behaviour, on average, it does moderately affect firefighters work during operations (*M* = 2.86, *SD* = 1.03) with significant differences between national samples, $F(7,2986) = 9.17$, $\rho < .001$, $\eta = 15$: Czech Republic (*M* = 2.67, *SD* = 0.89), Germany (*M* = 3.05, *SD* = 0.98), Italy (*M* = 2.85, *SD* = 1.12), Poland (*M* = 2.72, *SD* = 0.93), Spain (*M* = 2.86, *SD* = 0.93), Sweden (*M* = 2.56, *SD* = 0.86), Turkey (*M* = 2.98, *SD* = 1.23), U.K. (*M* = 2.79, *SD* = 0.91). The frequency of impairment to firefighters' work due to bystanders was assessed by asking: In general, how frequently do bystanders interfere with your work? (Likert item: 1 = never to 5 = always). In total, firefighter assessed that bystander sometimes interfere with their work (*M* = 3.16, *SD* = 0.92). A large effect of country on impairment to firefighters' work due to bystanders was observed, $F(7,2990) = 54.31$, $\rho < .001$, $\eta = .34$ (see Fig. 5.22).

Victims' compliance to firefighters' command

Victims' compliance to firefighters' command with respect to fires in multiple- occupancy residential buildings was assessed by asking: *When attempting to rescue occupants from multiple residential buildings, what makes them most likely to follow your command?* (Likert items: 1 = not at all to 5 = extremely). "Giving impression of being cool and calm" (*M* = 4.12; *SD* = 0.79), "making them feel they are

Table 5.15: Behaviour strategies of firefighters and victims' compliance to fire fighters command

	Czech Republic	Germany	Italy	Poland	Spain	Sweden	Turkey	U.K.
	M (SD)	M (SD)	M (SD)	M (SD)	M (SD)	M (SD)	M (SD)	M (SD)
The uniform [a]	3.54 (0.82)	3.47 (1.09)	4.04 (0.89)	4.07 (0.86)	3.97 (0.71)	3.93 (0.90)	4.03 (1.05)	4.05 (0.87)
Giving impression of being cool and calm [b]	3.84 (0.75)	4.03 (0.71)	4.11 (0.90)	4.23 (0.73)	4.05 (0.54)	4.41 (0.67)	4.26 (0.87)	4.19 (0.77)
Showing empathy [c]	2.62 (1.03)	3.36 (0.96)	3.29 (1.20)	2.91 (1.15)	3.75 (0.94)	4.11 (0.72)	3.70 (1.10)	3.28 (0.92)
Shouting, being forceful [d]	2.91 (0.92)	1.77 (0.88)	1.97 (1.03)	2.09 (0.96)	2.24 (0.91)	2.04 (0.93)	2.89 (1.24)	2.96 (0.99)
Informing them fully of the situation [e]	3.53 (0.81)	2.93 (1.04)	3.46 (1.05)	3.44 (0.89)	3.60 (0.90)	3.56 (0.98)	3.81 (1.02)	3.31 (0.97)
Making them feel they are taking an active role in their own rescue [f]	3.22 (0.91)	3.50 (0.98)	3.78 (1.11)	3.52 (0.93)	3.39 (0.92)	3.13 (0.99)	4.27 (0.87)	2.88 (1.06)

Notes: [a] $F(7,2646) = 27.94$, $p < .001$, $\eta = .26$ · [b] $F(7,2661) = 12.94$, $p < .001$, $\eta = .18$
[c] $F(7,2631) = 48.45$, $p < .001$, $\eta = .34$ · [d] $F(7,2636) = 82.99$, $p < .001$, $\eta = .42$
[e] $F(7,2650) = 32.61$, $p < .001$, $\eta = .28$ · [f] $F(7,2658) = 53.85$, $p < .001$, $\eta = .35$.

taking an active role in their own rescue" (*M* = 3.56; *SD* = 1.05) and the uniform per se (*M* = 3.84; *SD* = 0.98) were assessed as the most effective strategies to get victims' compliance with respect to following firefighters command. Firefighter assessed that "informing them fully of the situation" (*M* = 3.38; *SD* = 1.02) and "showing empathy" (*M* = 3.32; *SD* = 1.11) affects victims' compliance moderately.

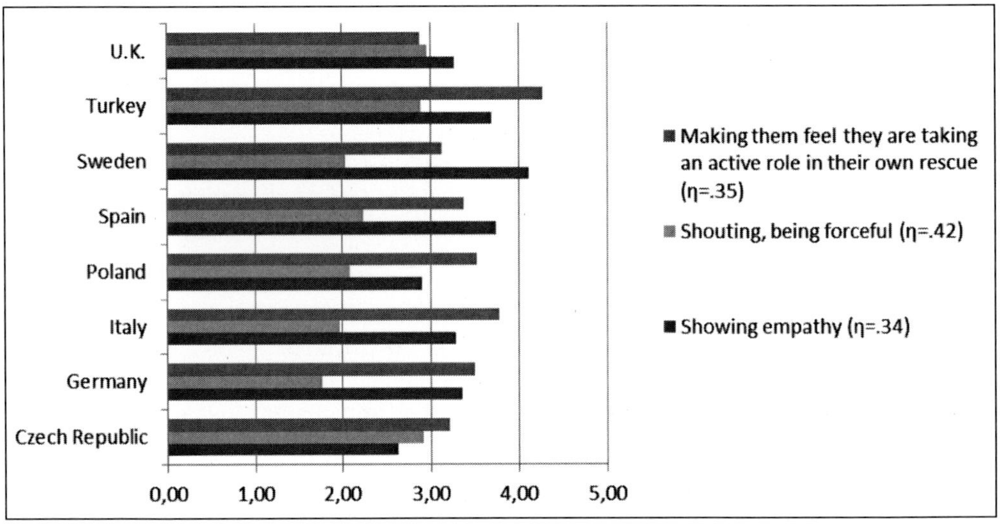

Fig. 5.23: Victims' compliance to firefighters' command

"Shouting, being forceful" ($M = 2.25$; $SD = 1.09$) was assessed as the least effective way to make victims following firefighters command. Significant differences between national samples were observed (see Table 5.15). A large effect of country was observed for the following three strategies: "Shouting, being forceful", "showing empathy" and "making them feel they are taking an active role in their own rescue" (see Fig. 5.23).

Fire brigade training and fire prevention/fire safety education with specific groups

Firefighters were asked: *Have you received fire brigade training on how people (e.g. occupants, bystander) behave in emergency situations?* With the following three options: (1) yes, sufficient training, (2) yes, but would like additional training, and (3) no, no training. In total, 31.4% had received sufficient training and 53.2% had received training, but would like additional training. Thus 15.3% of the firefighters received no training at all. Differences between national samples were observed with respect to fire brigade training on how people behave in emergency situations, χ^2 (14) = 224.16, $p < .001$, Cramér's V = .19 (see Fig. 5.24).

Additionally, firefighters were asked: *Have you received fire brigade training on how you are supposed to communicate with, and behave towards, the following groups?* With the following three options: (1) yes, sufficient training, (2) yes, but would like additional training, and (3) no, no training. In total, three-quarters of the firefighters or more received no or not sufficient training with respect to the differ-

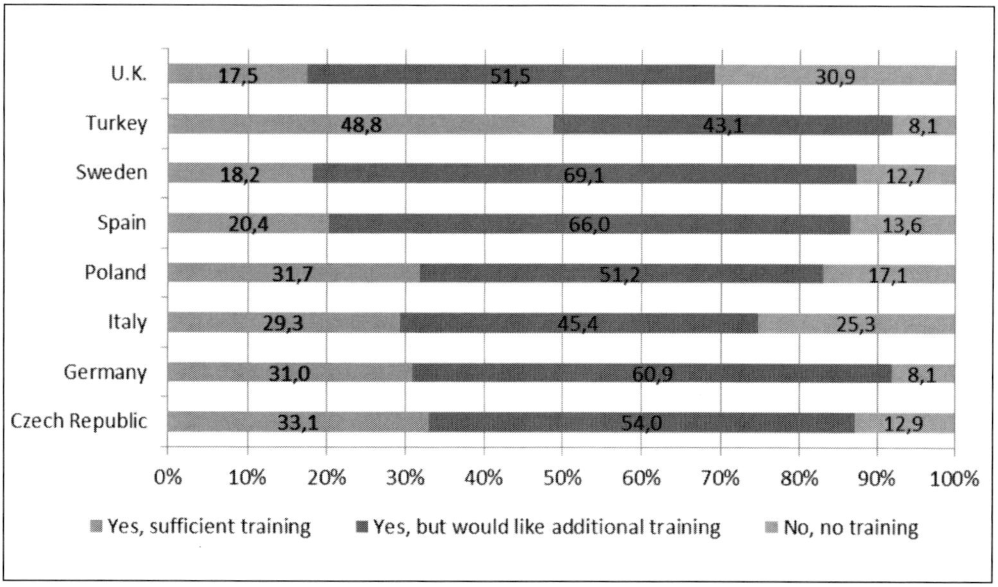

Fig. 5.24: Fire brigade training on how people behave in emergency situation

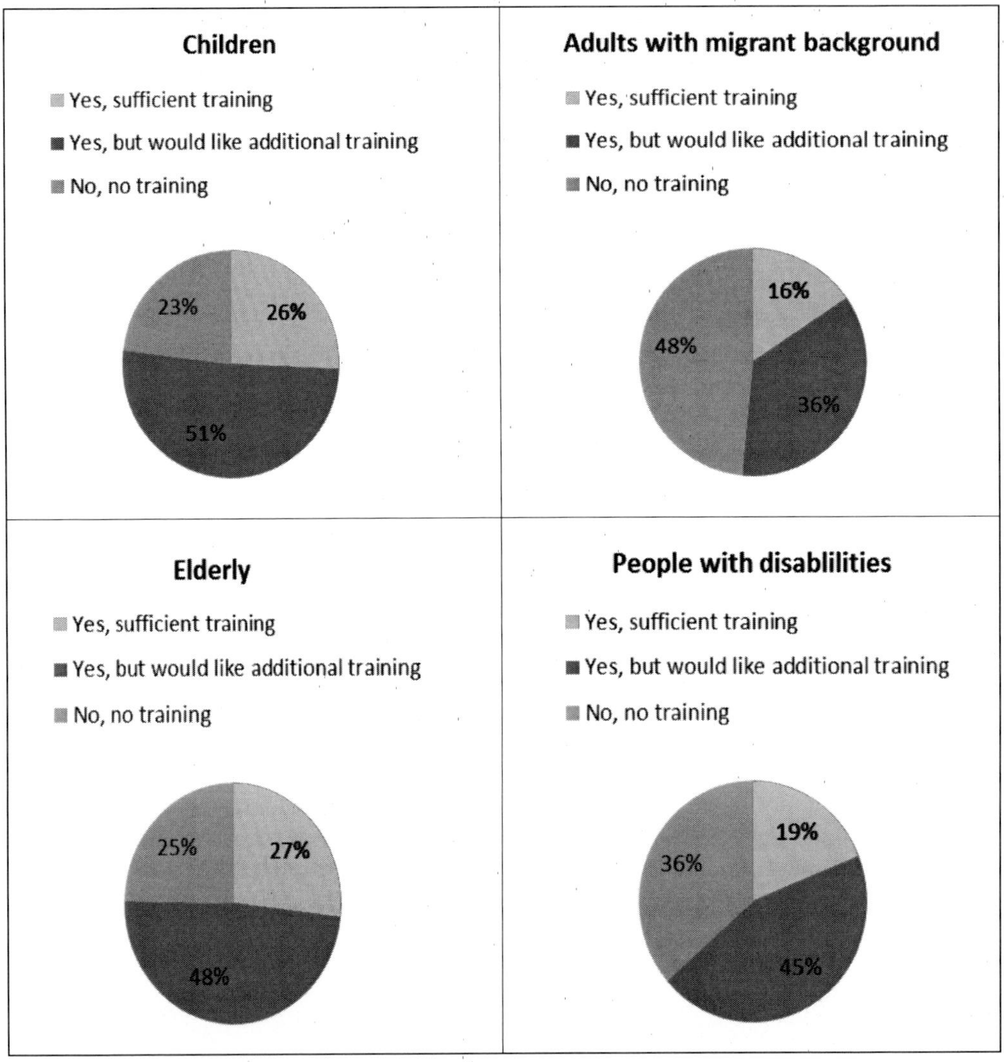

Fig. 5.25: Fire brigade training with respect to different population groups

ent population groups (see Fig. 5.25). Differences between national samples were observed with respect to the different population groups (see Table 5.16).

Furthermore, firefighters were asked: *With which population groups does your fire brigade actively work on providing fire prevention/fire safety education?* with respect to the following population groups: children, elderly, people with disabilities, adults with migrant background and the general public. In total, seventy percent of the firefighters reported that fire prevention/fire safety education to children and the general public is provided. However, only 14% of the firefighters reported

Table 5.16: Estimated fire brigade training (in percent) on how firefighter is supposed to communicate with, and behave towards different population groups

	Czech Republic	Germany	Italy	Poland	Spain	Sweden	Turkey	U.K.
Adults with migrant background [a]								
Yes, sufficient training	16.9	15.7	14.5	15.9	7.4	6.1	23.9	13.2
Yes, but would like additional training	37.1	41.1	26.9	34.8	35.0	44.8	35.1	42.1
No, no training	46.0	43.2	58.5	49.3	57.7	49.2	41.1	44.7
People with disabilities [b]								
Yes, sufficient training	25.5	16.3	15.3	21.6	9.8	9.9	27.8	20.7
Yes, but would like additional training	53.3	43.7	39.6	58.4	42.3	39.2	40.7	40.4
No, no training	21.2	40.0	45.1	20.0	47.9	50.8	31.5	38.9
Elderly people [c]								
Yes, sufficient training	36.2	28.1	22.9	26.1	19.0	13.3	34.6	24.7
Yes, but would like additional training	54.5	48.0	40.5	59.8	64.4	51.9	44.8	35.9
No, no training	9.3	23.9	36.6	14.0	16.6	34.8	20.6	39.4
Children [d]								
Yes, sufficient training	32.5	26.0	20.1	27.3	16.6	11.0	36.1	27.3
Yes, but would like additional training	58.3	55.7	43.3	60.4	64.4	54.7	44.5	33.3
No, no training	9.3	18.3	36.6	12.3	19.0	34.3	19.5	39.4

Notes: [a] χ^2 (14) = 88.75, $p < .001$, Cramér's V = .12 · [b] χ^2 (14) = 157.61, $p < .001$, Cramér's V = .16
[c] χ^2 (14) = 191.47, $p < .001$, Cramér's V = .18 · [d] χ^2 (14) = 230.77, $p < .001$, Cramér's V = .20.

Table 5.17: Fire prevention/ fire safety education with different population groups (in percent)

	Czech Republic	Germany	Italy	Poland	Spain	Sweden	Turkey	U.K.	Total
Children [a]	92.1	91.6	43.1	70.7	65.2	89.5	61.9	95.5	73.1
Elderly people [b]	9.9	29.2	13.1	18.4	24.2	49.2	18.1	89.4	25.8
People with disabilities [c]	10.6	24.1	8.5	20.3	6.2	23.8	14.8	72.7	19.9
Adults with migrant background [d]	2.0	16.0	6.3	2.1	6.2	43.6	8.9	70.2	14.5
General public [e]	45.7	73.0	70.5	58.7	50.9	87.8	78.4	91.9	69.7
None [f]	4.6	2.6	17.6	7.2	9.9	1.7	4.4	0.0	6.9

Notes: [a] χ^2 (7) = 572.65, $p < .001$, Cramér's V = .44 · [b] χ^2 (7) = 591.84, $p < .001$, Cramér's V = .44
[c] χ^2 (7) = 449.85, $p < .001$, Cramér's V = .39 · [d] χ^2 (7) = 760.12, $p < .001$, Cramér's V = .50
[e] χ^2 (7) = 225.97, $p < .001$, Cramér's V = .28 · [f] χ^2 (7) = 162.24, $p < .001$, Cramér's V = .23.

that fire prevention/fire safety education is provided to adults with migrant background (see Table 5.17). Differences between national samples were observed with respect to the different population groups (see Table 5.17). Of interest, 17% of the Italian firefighters reported that fire prevention/fire safety education is provided to none of the different population groups looked at, whereas zero percent of the British firefighters reported that. Also, almost three-quarters of the British firefighters reported that fire prevention/fire safety education is provided to adults with migrant background, whereas only 2% of Czech and Polish firefighters reported this.

5.4 Situational characteristics of survivor data

Daniela Knuth & Doris Kehl

In order to evaluate the severity of the events and have an objective measure, situational characteristics of the events which survivor experienced were collected. For all available events the number of injured persons as well as the number of fatalities is displayed in Table 5.18 to Table 5.22. Event characteristics were collected with help of first responders and information available online. Incident data were found for 56 participants (N) who experienced a fire in a home in Germany (see Table 5.18). These 56 participants experienced 43 different fire events (N_{Inc}), which means that some participants experienced the same event. Furthermore 57% of these 56 participants experienced an event without any casualties and 94% of the events happened without fatalities (N_0 %). Moreover the mean number of injured/killed persons as well as the range is displayed in Table 5.18. In comparison incident information from Spanish home fires was available for 24 participants who experienced only four different events which all included casualties and only 4.2% of the participants experienced an event without fatalities. Although this information was only available for some events, it might be a hint on how severe these events were. Furthermore the number of different events becomes apparent. In total 37 participants experienced a public fire in Spain and 35 of these participants experienced the same event which resulted in one casualty and no fatalities. In total the BeSeCu project collected information from at least 10 different floods, 151 domestic fires, 35 public fires, 4 terrorist attacks and 16 different earthquakes.

Table 5.18: Numbers of injuries and fatalities for fire in a home incidents (n = 589)

	Incident information about injured persons								Incident information about fatalities							
	N	M%	N_0%	*M*	*SD*	Min	Max	N_{Inc}	N	M%	N_0%	*M*	*SD*	Min	Max	N_{Inc}
Czech Republic (n = 89)	34	61.8	91.2	0.2	0.7	0	4	16	34	61.8	100	0.0	0.0	0	0	16
Germany (n = 128)	56	56.3	57.1	2.2	4.6	0	21	43	53	58.6	94.3	0.1	0.5	0	2	41
Italy (n = 43)	43	0.0	65.1	1.6	2.5	0	9	30	43	0.0	100	0.0	0.0	0	0	30
Poland (n = 118)	89	24.6	41.6	1.5	2.1	0	8	40	89	24.6	95.5	0.0	0.2	0	1	40
Spain (n = 41)	24	41.5	0.0	19.6	8.0	1	30	4	24	41.5	4.2	3.4	3.0	0	9	4
Sweden (n = 76)	10	86.8	50.0	0.9	1.2	0	3	5	10	86.8	100	0.0	0.0	0	0	5
Turkey (n = 73)	0	100	–	–	–	–	–	–	0	100	–	–	–	–	–	–
UK (n = 21)	18	14.3	83.3	0.3	0.8	0	3	13	19	9.52	100	0.0	0.0	0	0	14
Total (n = 589)	274	53.3	54.0	3.0	6.2	0	30	151	272	53.8	89.0	0.3	1.3	0	9	150

Notes: N = number of participants with incident information; M% = Missing; N_0% = percentage of participants that experienced an incident with zero injured/deceased persons; N_{inc} = number of different incidents.

Table 5.19: Numbers of injuries and fatalities for public fire incidents (n = 175)

	Incident information about injured persons								Incident information about fatalities							
	N	M%	N_0%	*M*	*SD*	Min	Max	N_{Inc}	N	M%	N_0%	*M*	*SD*	Min	Max	N_{Inc}
Czech Republic (n = 15)	12	20.0	66.7	0.8	1.7	0	6	6	12	20.0	75.0	0.3	0.5	0	1	6
Germany (n = 33)	20	39.4	25.0	1.5	1.1	0	4	10	20	39.4	95.0	0.1	0.2	0	1	10
Italy (n = 21)*	20*	4.8	94.7	0.2	0.9	0	4	9	20	4.8	95.0	0.2	0.7	0	3	9
Poland (n = 23)	9	60.9	66.7	0.7	1.0	0	2	3	9	60.9	66.7	0.7	1.0	0	2	3
Spain (n = 37)	35	5.4	0.0	1.0	0.0	1	1	1	35	5.4	100	0.0	0.0	0	0	1
Sweden (n = 7)	0	100	–	–	–	–	–	–	0	100	–	–	–	–	–	–
Turkey (n = 30)	22	26.7	100	0.0	0.0	0	0	2	22	26.7	100	0.0	0.0	0	0	2
UK (n = 9)	4	55.6	75.0	0.3	0.5	0	1	4	4	55.6	100	0.0	0.0	0	0	4
Total (n = 175)	122	30.3	51.2	0.7	1.0	0	4	35	122	30.3	93.4	0.1	0.4	0	3	35

Notes: n = number of participants with incident information; M% = Missing; N_0% = percentage of participants that experienced an incident with zero injured/deceased persons; N_{inc} = number of different incidents. *one outlier was excluded (300 injured persons).

Table 5.20: Numbers of injuries and fatalities for terrorist attacks (n = 50)

	Incident information about injured persons								Incident information about fatalities							
	N	M%	N_0%	*M*	*SD*	Min	Max	N_{Inc}	N	M%	N_0%	*M*	*SD*	Min	Max	N_{Inc}
Spain (n = 26)	25	3.8	0.0	1857.0	0.0	1857	1857	1	25	3.8	0.0	191.0	0.0	191	191	1
Turkey (n = 5)	3	40.0	0.0	20.0	0.0	20	20	1	3	40.0	100	0.0	0.0	0	0	1
UK (n = 19)	13	31.6	0.0	646.2	193.9	1	700	2	14	26.3	14.3	48.0	20.3	0	56	3
Total (n = 50)	41	18.0	0.0	1338.7	682.2	1	1857	4	42	16.0	11.9	129.7	77.0	0	191	5

Notes: n = number of participants with incident information; M% = Missing; N_0% = percentage of participants that experienced an incident with zero injured/deceased persons; N_{inc} = number of different incidents.

Table 5.21: Numbers of injuries and fatalities for floods (n = 172)

	Incident information about injured persons								Incident information about fatalities							
	N	M%	N_0%	*M*	*SD*	Min	Max	N_{Inc}	N	M%	N_0%	*M*	*SD*	Min	Max	N_{Inc}
Czech Republic (n = 63)	0	100	–	–	–	–	–	–	26	58.7	0.0	12.9	5.8	5	17	7
Germany (n = 43)	2	95.4	50	10.0	14.1	0	20	2	33	23.3	9.1	9.7	9.2	0	21	7
Italy (n = 17)	4	76.5	0.0	73.8	42.5	10	95	4	15	11.8	53.3	8.1	12.4	0	31	9
Poland (n = 45)	45	0.0	0.0	60.0	0.0	60	60	3	45	0.0	0.0	25.0	0.0	25	25	1
Spain (n = 1)	0	100	–	–	–	–	–	–	0	100	–	–	–	–	–	–
UK (n = 3)	1	66.7	0.0	1.0	0.0	1.0	1	1	3	0.0	100	0.0	0.0	0	0	3
Total (n = 172)	52	69.8	1.9	58.0	16.9	0	95	10	122	29.1	11.5	15.6	10.2	0	31	27

Notes: n = number of participants with incident information; M% = Missing; N_0% = percentage of participants that experienced an incident with zero injured/deceased persons; N_{inc} = number of different incidents.

Table 5.22: Numbers of injuries and fatalities for earthquakes (n = 126)

	Incident information about injured persons								Incident information about fatalities							
	N	M%	N_0%	*M*	*SD*	Min	Max	N_{Inc}	N	M%	N_0%	*M*	*SD*	Min	Max	N_{Inc}
Germany (n = 1)	0	100	–	–	–	–	–	–	0	100	–	–	–	–	–	–
Italy (n = 88)	59	33.0	20.3	1045.9	752.5	0	1600	12	62	29.6	25.8	192.4	147.0	0	308	13
Turkey (n = 37)	30	18.9	0.0	39724.0	12925.6	11	43953	4	31	16.2	3.2	15565.4	6008.7	0	17840	5
Total (n = 126)	89	29.4	13.5	14083.5	19837.3	0	43953	16	93	26.2	18.3	5316.7	8054.6	0	17840	18

Notes: n = number of participants with incident information; M% = Missing; N_0% = percentage of participants that experienced an incident with zero injured/deceased persons; N_{inc} = number of different incidents.

The following sections display correlations of objective measures with emotions and cognitions of the survivors of different incident types as well as the relationship to later risk perception concerning the events. Although these results might be a first hind concerning these associations, it must be noted that these objective information were not available for all national samples and all incidents. Fig. 5.26 to Fig. 5.30 display the relations between the number of injured and killed participants in the event with perceived threat, emotional distress and the ability to deal with the situation. These correlations arte displayed according to their respective stages: realization, during evacuation and upon exiting. For domestic fire (see Fig. 5.26) as well as earthquake survivors (see Fig. 5.29) none of the correlations passed the limit of $r = .30$ for medium effects. Solely the correlation of perceived threat in the stage of realization showed a correlation with the number of injured persons which was close to that limit. For public fire survivors (see Fig. 5.27) the correlations for emotional distress in all three stages and perceived threat during the evacuation showed correlation greater than .30 with the number of killed persons during the event. For emotional distress during evacuation and upon exiting the correlations were close to the limit of $r = .50$ for large effects. Medium positive correlations between the number of injured persons with emotional distress during the evacuation and upon exiting were observed for terrorist attacks survivors (see Fig. 5.28). On the other hand, negative correlations with medium effects were found for the ability to deal with the situation and the number of injured persons. These negative correlations were also found for flood survivors (see Fig. 5.30). Positive correlations were found the amount of perceived stress and emotional distress with the number of deaths during the flood as well as with the number of injured persons during the event.

With respect to risk perception for different incidents, the following results were found: For domestic fire (see Fig. 5.31) and flood (see Fig. 5.33) survivors, no positive or negative correlations of risk perception and objective data of the experienced event were found that exceeded the limit of $r = .30$. Public fire (see Fig. 5.32) and terrorist attack (see Fig. 5.35) survivors showed a negative correlation greater than $r = .30$ of the number of injured persons during the event with risk perception for future earthquakes. In the sample of earthquake survivors on the other hand, solely positive correlation of objective measures with risk perception values were observed (see Fig. 5.34). The correlations with risk perception for terrorist attacks and for floods reached the limit for medium effects.

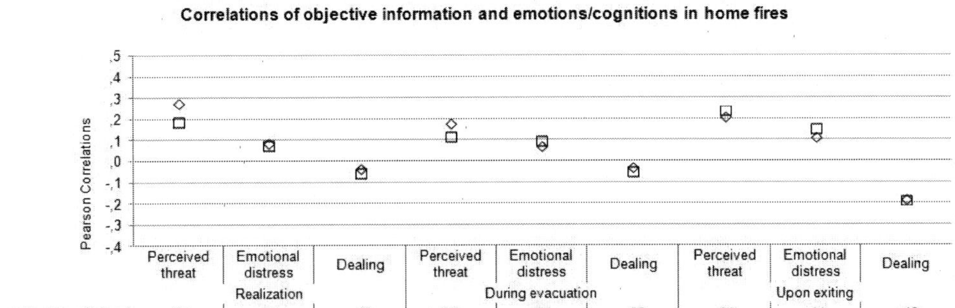

	Perceived threat	Emotional distress	Dealing	Perceived threat	Emotional distress	Dealing	Perceived threat	Emotional distress	Dealing
		Realization			During evacuation			Upon exiting	
◇ Number of injured	,27	,09	-,03	,18	,07	-,03	,21	,11	-,18
□ Number of deaths	,19	,08	-,05	,12	,10	-,05	,24	,15	-,19

Fig. 5.26: Correlations for domestic fire survivors (Correlations |r| ≥ .13, |r| ≥ .17 and |r| ≥ .24 were statistically significant with $p < .05$, $p < .01$ and $p < .001$ respectively)

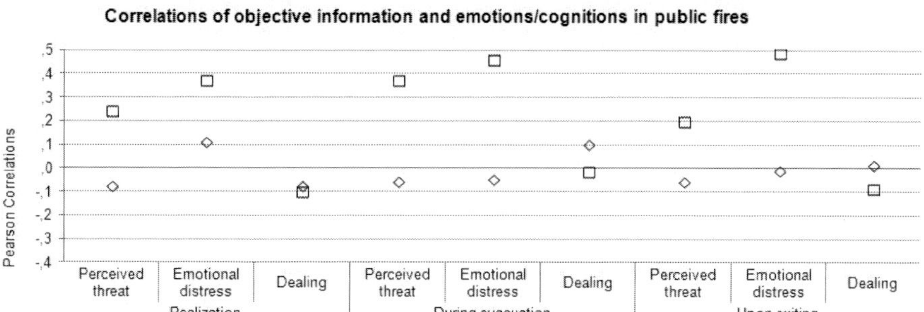

	Realization: Perceived threat	Realization: Emotional distress	Realization: Dealing	During evacuation: Perceived threat	During evacuation: Emotional distress	During evacuation: Dealing	Upon exiting: Perceived threat	Upon exiting: Emotional distress	Upon exiting: Dealing
◇Number of injured	-,07	,11	-,07	-,05	-,04	,10	-,06	-,01	,02
□Number of deaths	,24	,38	-,10	,37	,46	-,01	,20	,49	-,09

Fig. 5.27: Correlations for public fire survivors (Correlations |r| ≥ .21, |r| ≥ .24 and |r| ≥ .35 were statistically significant with p < .05, p < .01 and p < .001 respectively)

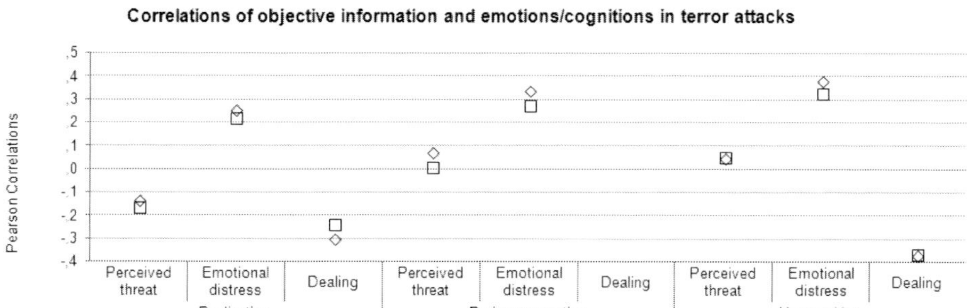

	Realization: Perceived threat	Realization: Emotional distress	Realization: Dealing	During evacuation: Perceived threat	During evacuation: Emotional distress	During evacuation: Dealing	Upon exiting: Perceived threat	Upon exiting: Emotional distress	Upon exiting: Dealing
◇Number of injured	-,14	,25	-,30	,07	,34	-,42	,04	,38	-,37
□Number of deaths	-,16	,22	-,24	,01	,27	-,42	,05	,33	-,37

Fig. 5.28: Correlations for terror survivors (Correlations |r| ≥ .37 and ≥ .42 were statistically significant with p < .05 and p < .01 respectively)

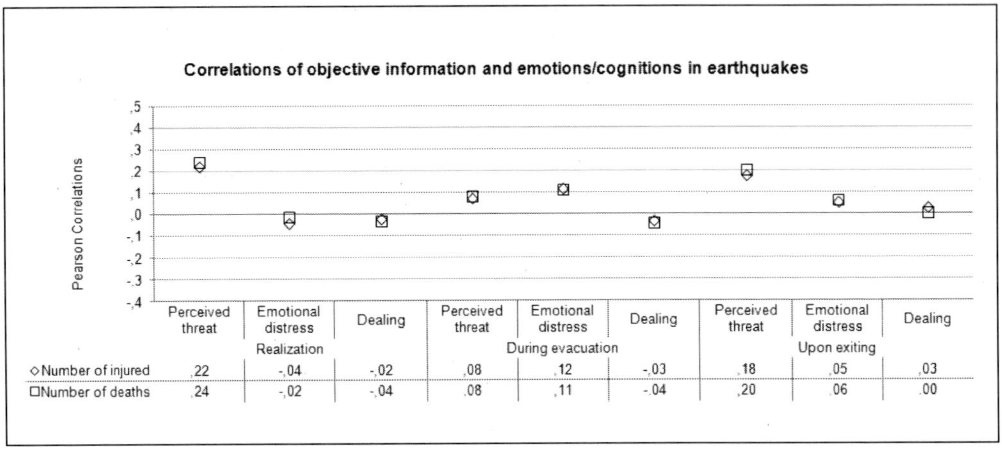

Fig. 5.29: Correlations for earthquake survivors (Correlations |r| ≥ .23, |r| ≥ .28 and |r| ≥ .36 were statistically significant with $p < .05$, $p < .01$ and $p < .001$ respectively)

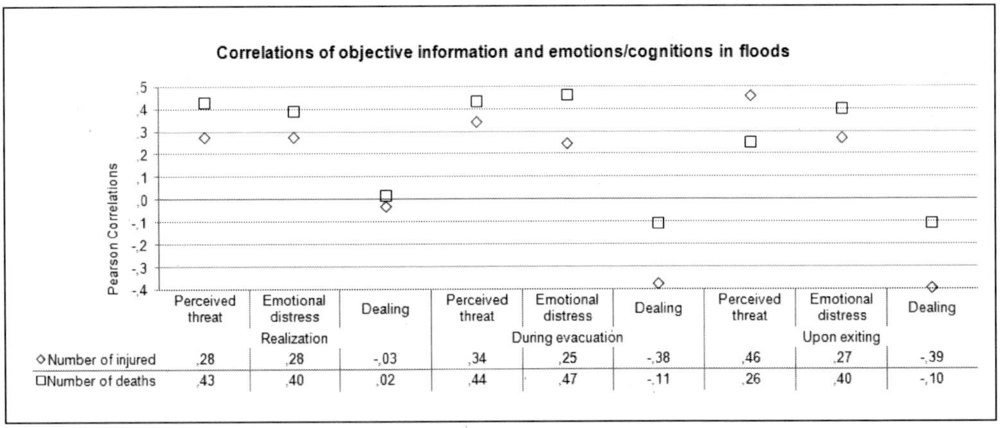

Fig. 5.30: Correlations for flood survivors (Injured correlations: |r| ≥ .28 and |r| ≥ .46 were statistically significant with $p < .05$ and $p < .01$ respectively; Deaths correlations: |r| ≥ .19 and |r| ≥ .40 were statistically significant with $p < .05$ and $p < .001$ respectively)

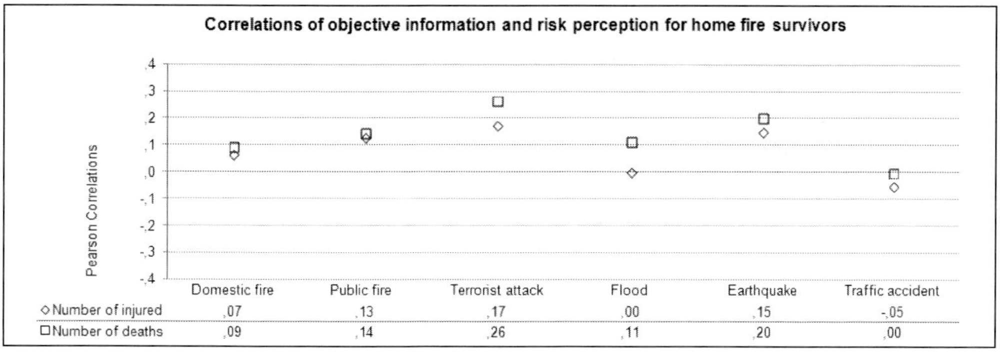

	Domestic fire	Public fire	Terrorist attack	Flood	Earthquake	Traffic accident
◇Number of injured	,07	,13	,17	,00	,15	-,05
□Number of deaths	,09	,14	,26	,11	,20	,00

Fig.5.31: Correlations for domestic fire survivors (Correlations |r| ≥ .13, |r| ≥ .17 and |r| ≥ .24 were statistically significant with $p < .05$, $p < .01$ and $p < .001$ respectively).

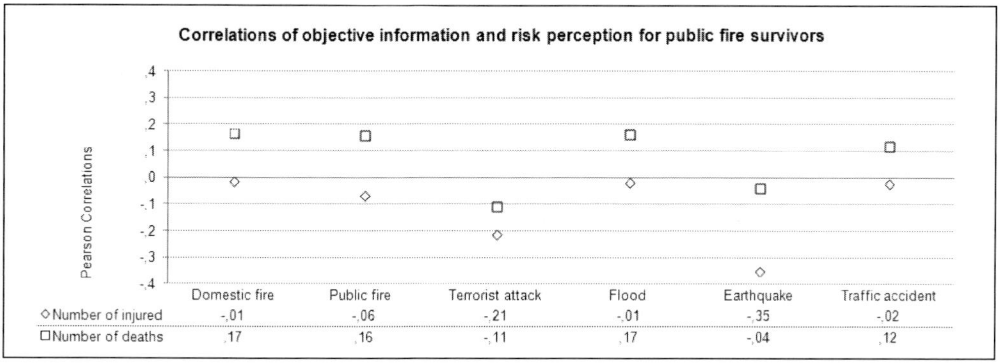

	Domestic fire	Public fire	Terrorist attack	Flood	Earthquake	Traffic accident
◇Number of injured	-,01	-,06	-,21	-,01	-,35	-,02
□Number of deaths	,17	,16	-,11	,17	-,04	,12

Fig. 5.32: Correlations for public fire survivors (Correlations |r| ≥ .21, |r| ≥ .24 and |r| ≥ .35 were statistically significant with $p < .05$, $p < .01$ and $p < .001$ respectively)

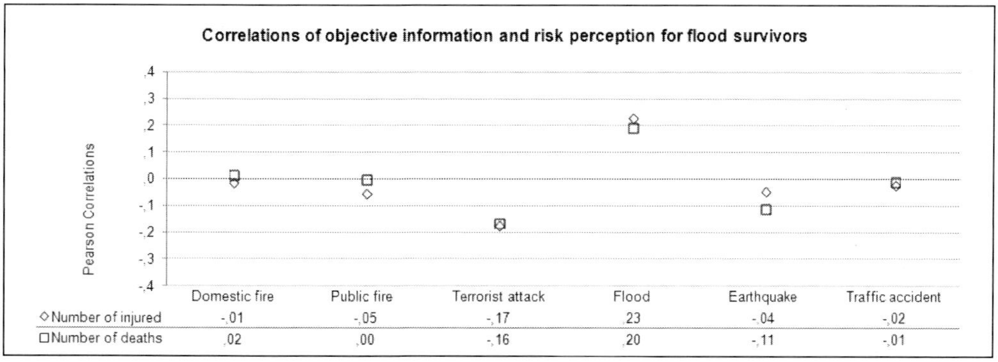

	Domestic fire	Public fire	Terrorist attack	Flood	Earthquake	Traffic accident
◇Number of injured	-,01	-,05	-,17	,23	-,04	-,02
□Number of deaths	,02	,00	-,16	,20	-,11	-,01

Fig. 5.33: Correlations for flood survivors (Injured correlations: |r| ≥ .28 and |r| ≥ .46 were statistically significant with $p < .05$ and $p < .01$ respectively; Deaths correlations: |r| ≥ .19 and |r| ≥ .40 were statistically significant with $p < .05$ and $p < .001$ respectively)

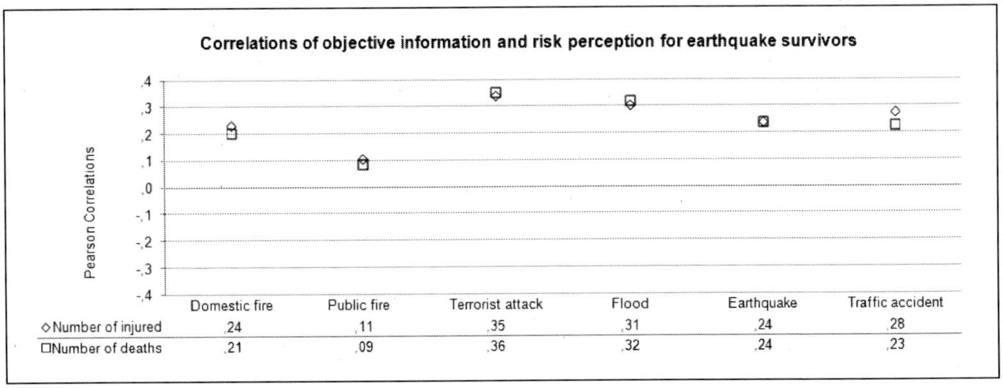

Fig. 5.34: Correlations for earthquake survivors (Correlations |r| ≥ .23, |r| ≥ .28 and |r| ≥ .36 were statistically significant with $p < .05$, $p < .01$ and $p < .001$ respectively)

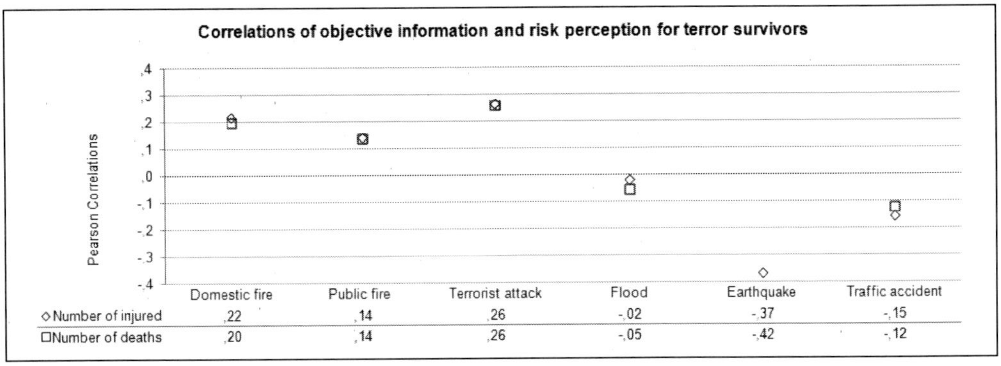

Fig. 5.35: Correlations for terror survivors (Correlations |r| ≥ .37 and |r| ≥ .42 were statistically significant with $p < .05$ and $p < .01$ respectively)

In conclusion, it can be assumed that objective measures like the number of people that were killed and injured cannot explain the full extents of psychological reactions during and after the events. It seems that there are differences between the type of event, with higher correlations of peri-event responses with object measures for public fires, terrorist attacks and floods. In the context of risk perception much research focuses on comparisons of objective and subjective risk. The results in this chapter had a different approach. It has been shown that the (possibly) severity of an experienced event did have no (or only marginal) relations to the risk perception values for future incidents. This supports the hypothesis that subjective psychological responses are more important. With respect to some limitations and the incomplete objective data available for the events, it must also be noted, that the correlations might be biased by differences between the national samples.

6 Development of evacuation gestures

Pawel Kepka, Jerzy Wolanin & Grzegorz Beltowski

Managing evacuation is one of the most difficult tasks to execute by all rescue and aid entities taking part in its planning, coordinating, direct leading and realization. In order to provide efficient evacuation of people a correct preparation is needed which surely consists of providing and securing the following: transport, technical support, order-security, sanitary and medical social-living conditions and means of communication. However, given the diversity of societies, inter alia, in terms of multilateralism or multiculturalism the introduction of the non-verbal evacuation seems to be justified in order to eliminate some of the problems in communication. Creating and common usage of a well-known evacuation language would occur to be very useful and it would lead to improving evacuation conditions in many problematic and complicated situations. Such a "language" would consist of several simple gestures expressing the need of doing certain actions such as: follow me, stop, go this way, run and so on. Apparently these simple and mostly easily understandable gestures could lead to the rapid and efficient evacuation.

6.1 Evacuation possibilities using nonverbal communication

In order to provide efficient evacuation of people a correct preparation is needed which surely consists of providing and securing the following: transport, technical support, order–security, sanitary and medical social – living conditions and means of communication.

Evacuation consists of moving people out of buildings or places, in which life or health might be endangered, into safe places. It is a method of protection against dangerous events in both preventing and rescue meaning. Taking into consideration conditions, which result from the character of dangers, we can mark out two types of evacuations: planned and emergency (ad-hoc). The planned evacuation consists of early moving people out of structures, potentially threatened areas, where the risk of occurring danger is high. It is planned in normal time (of peace), and is executed in situations when symptoms of danger occur. Taking into consideration the fact that public utility and collective residence buildings are often equipped in different kinds of fire protection systems, we can assume that in such structures the planned evacuation occurs in most cases. The emergency (ad-hoc) evacuation consists of immediate moving people out of structures and areas in which unfavourable for life and health situations occur. The emergency (ad-hoc) evacuation occurs more seldom and it is connected with unpredicted events, for which such a scenario and plan was not prepared. The events, like earthquakes, floods and typhoons, etc. evoke danger suddenly and threaten large amount of people causing a need for the emergency (ad-hoc) evacuation.

In order to provide efficient evacuation of people a thorough preparation is needed, which consists of providing and securing different aspects.

1. The means of transportation consisting of precise planning the adequate amount of transportation means for moving evacuated people out of evacuation structures/areas into safe structures/areas. When planning transportation we should consider railway transport, car transport, private means of transportation and (in case of inability to provide means of transportation) walking evacuation.
2. Technical support, consisting of technical help points, and means of communication and equipment for entities and institutions responsible for evacuation.
3. Order – security consisting of maintaining order, securing belongings left in evacuated buildings/areas, control of movement on evacuation lanes.
4. Sanitary and medical service consisting of first aid and sanitary-epidemiology care.
5. Social-living conditions, essential consumer goods (food, water, clothing, electricity, etc.). This includes accommodation as well and sixth means of communication consisting of reporting, commanding and co-operation communication.

There are a lot of problems connected with carrying out the evacuation. Some of them are caused by not abiding the fire protection regulations or by not preparing for the evacuation, others by behaviour of evacuated people or specific groups of people (handicapped, criminals, children etc.). During the process of evacuation we can find out some patterns of behaviour for the above groups of people. The groups are as follows: healthy people, elderly people, physically disabled, deaf and blind, mentally disabled, injured, criminals, foreigners, illegal immigrants, children, etc.

In modern times, when societies are multicultural, there is a need for "commonality" of certain activities which may have an impact on improving public safety. One of these needs is the development of such evacuation signs, shown by a firefighter or a person responsible for the evacuation, which could be understood without verbal communication. Such a non-verbal language is already used successfully, inter alia, by the police (at the crossroads) or by the divers. Creating and common usage of well-known evacuation language would occur to be very useful and it would lead to improving evacuation conditions in many problematic and complicated situations. Such a language would have to consist of several simple gestures expressing the need of doing certain actions such as: follow me, stop, go this way, run, etc. The next step was to determine whether these words can be supported with gestures or replaced by gestures. To introduce and spread the non-verbal language for evacuation it is necessary to develop substantial objectives, descriptions, and then execute short instructional videos for each gesture.

Fig. 6.1: Stop!

Fig. 6.2: Go up!

Taking this into account, a survey to the potential willingness and capacity to use evacuation language were carried out. It was conducted on a group of 69 people in two groups: 59 firefighters from various levels of government on the one hand and 10 people who do not deal with rescue operations.

Firstly, frequently used phrases in the verbal evacuation were identified. On the basis of the study the most useful gestures are (in descending order): STOP, look at me, go down, go up, calm down, move back, come to me, crawl, follow me, run, jump, go this way, help me, hurry up, lay on the floor and are you okay. For these gestures 16 short films were complied. These films have to give the real conditions of the evacuation, such as firefighter wears dark gloves, room lighting is dim (although it should be even darker), some gestures coincide with the silhouette of a fireman, and therefore may be difficult to read, the number of gestures that can be learned should be taken into account (approx. 12-16). Therefore, the limitations to the use and technical assumptions (making real) of the gestures for evacuation instructions in the absence of verbal communication were defined. The examples of situations where gestures cannot be applied for evacuation are e.g. in dense smoke, evacuation at night/dusk, buildings for people with limited mobility, evacuation of children, evacuation of unconscious people, signing across large distances, etc. technical assumptions for the development of gestures were that the firefighter is dressed in a protective uniform ("nomex" type) which makes it difficult to perform certain gestures. The firefighter has gloves on his hands which prevents finger gestures and wears a helmet which prevents facial expressions.

Fig. 6.3: Crawl!

Fig. 6.4: Hurry up!

Moreover it has to be considered that the firefighter carries about 30 kg of equipment which prevents him from forceful movements.

SGSP prepared a questionnaire which served as a research tool. The research was carried out among first responders and civilians. The partners from Germany, Italy, Turkey and UK carried out the questionnaire showing the short movies with hand signals on a sample of 610 people.

The generation of items for the BeSeCu-FR instrument consisted of three steps: literature research, expert consultation and focus groups with emergency personnel. Thus items were generated via a deductive and inductive approach. The item pool of the BeSeCu-FR was afterwards pretested.

A comprehensive literature review has been done in order to acquire an overview of the literature that have dealt with our project topic and focused on national and international scientific evidence on security research and human behaviour.

The project consortium consisted of research partners and emergency personnel (e.g. fire fighter, emergency medical services) and their research bodies. The emergency personnel gave us the information about the knowledge they need.

The hand signals were used in the silent evacuation experiment carried out at the Main School of Fire Service on 30 of April during the Warsaw Project Meeting. The main scope of the experiment was the research on effectiveness and the effect observation of the non-verbal gestures, which could be used for guiding people out of the building during unannounced evacuation. There were around 150 students and teachers evacuated during their classes. They were familiar with the building bud did not know anything about the hand signals. At international scientific and technical conference on "Emergency Evacuation of People from Buildings" was organized by SGSP on 31.04.–01.05.2011. It gathered wide audience (app. 200) from all over Europe but also from other countries. The Security Research Conference is an annual event hosted by the country holding the Presidency of European Council being also the largest European meeting focused on security research and at complex evacuation of people from the sports facility and a hotel (University of the Safety of Life in Lviv).The conference is a communication platform bringing together policy makers, researchers, industry representatives and end users from across Europe to foster the debate on future research priorities and the technological, legal and organisational solutions answering current public security threats.

SGSP have done a worldwide research on existing hand signals/non-verbal signs for communication which operate at present but with little effect.

SGSP proposed to work out and establish set of signs/hand signals which can enhance and improve communication between survivors and first responders regardless of country or ethical background. The set of hand signals were elaborated on the basis of survey with polish firefighters. All the centres were invited to analyze and assess the set of signals with further remarks, proposals and corrections.

On that basis 16 hand signals were established and chosen as a way of non-verbal communication and the video films were produced in order to make a wider European survey.

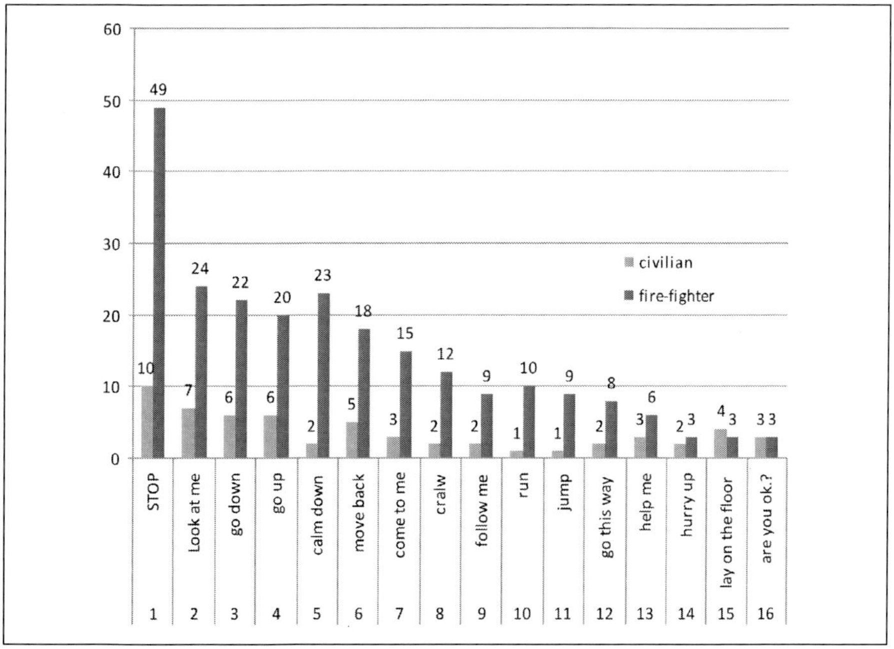

Fig. 6.5: Gestures used for evacuation instructions in the absence of verbal communication

6.2 Results of the non-verbal communication study

After that experiment there were several remarks, which limit several hand signals. "Go up', "Go down' and "Go this way' can be communicated by one universal signal "Go this way' showing the direction of movement. "Hurry up" and "Run" are also too close to be two separate signals. They can be merged. The hand signal "do not do it" was added.

The hand signals which were universally understandable are as follows: Stop, Follow me, Run, Hurry up, Go this way, Calm down, Come to me, Move back, Crawl, Jump down, Lay on the floor, Help me and Do not do it.

Given the diversity of societies, inter alia, in terms of multilateralism or multiculturalism the introduction of the non-verbal evacuation (gestures) seems to be justified in order to eliminate some of the problems in communication.

Conditions in which the evacuation is being conducted seem to be a problem as well: Stress, chaos and nerves. These factors have a destructive influence on communication and smooth evacuation process. The presented language of gestures should be introduced to the society and implemented to be executed. Apparently, these are quite simple and easy to understand gestures and their global introduction could be very useful. In the era of European Union implementing and wide using the non-verbal language seems to be realistic. The idea to be successful only needs engaging proper organs to implement it.

7 Field trial on evacuation responses

Ed Galea, Lazaros Filippidis, Steven J. Deere & Gary Sharp

7.1 Background

The aim of the BeSeCu (Behaviour, Security and Culture) project is to investigate cross-cultural and ethnic differences of human behaviour in crisis situations in order to better tailor security related communication, instructions and procedures with a view to improving evacuation and protection. The project will provide evidence that will be useful to first responders, building designers and those involved in the development of emergency operating procedures for buildings. Project BeSeCu was funded by the EU Seventh Framework Program of security research, BeSeCu (project no. 218324) with a budget of Euro 2.1 million and ran from 2008 to 2011.

The BeSeCu project consists of two main research streams, a field study involving interviews with people who have experienced crisis situations and a series of experimental evacuation trials. In the field study a cross-cultural survey of individual experiences was conducted to identify determinants of inter-individual differences in people who have experienced evacuation situations, fire disaster survivors and survivors of similar crisis situations, but also workers and first responders as well as those affected in the community. The egress trials were intended to investigate if culture plays a significant role in evacuation. A series of three evacuation trials were conducted under similar conditions (structure, population and evacuation circumstances) in three different countries with different cultural backgrounds. Egress data such as occupant response times were determined through video analysis and compared across the three trials to identify similarities and differences. In addition, an evacuation model validation data set was compiled from appropriate data collected from the trials. The model validation work is not described here but is described in detail in Galea, Filipidis, Deere, Sharp & Sauter, 2012.

Project BeSeCu was carried out by a consortium of eight European partners, namely: Institute of Psychology, Ernst Moritz Arndt University of Greifswald (GERMANY); Fire Safety Engineering Group (FSEG) at the University of Greenwich (UK); the University Medical Centre of Hamburg, Institute of Medical Psychology (GERMANY); Institute of Public Security of Catalunya (SPAIN); Hamburg Fire and Emergency Service Academy (GERMANY); Man-Technology-Organisation Psychology (SWEDEN); Faculty of Fire Safety Engineering, The Main School of Fire Service (POLAND); Prague Psychiatric Centre, University of Prague (CZECH REPUBLIC); and Association of Emergency Ambulance Physicians (TURKEY), and The Crisis and Disaster Psychology Research Group of the University of Bologna (ITALY).

7.2 Culture and human behavioural responses to emergencies and disasters

The aim of the experimental component of project BeSeCu is to study how people react in an emergency, and to determine whether there are any cultural factors – both social culture and fire safety culture – which impact emergency behaviour. By social culture we mean a society's shared system of values, beliefs and attitudes that influences that society's perception of the world and its behavioural response to both every day encounters and unusual incidents. When discussing social cultures it must be emphasized that we are not talking about individuals but of large populations and so are attempting to compare one normal distribution of behavioural response for one population with that of another. Aspects of social culture which may differ from one society to another include degree of physical contact, nature and extent of eye contact, degree of physical social separation, sense of community, feelings of fatalism, levels of machismo, risk perception, response to authority, acceptable levels of public and private signs of emotion, etc. By fire safety culture we mean the regulatory fire safety framework, supported by legislation, prescriptive guidance, education efforts, performance guides and most important enforcement that exists within a society. This top-down safety culture (where safety levels are imposed) is, to some degree, supported by a bottom-up expectation of the public regarding safety levels in general. This extends far beyond fire safety with the public having high expectations regarding the functionality and safety levels reached in all aspects of life.

It is often suggested that differences in culture may influence the response of the public to emergency procedures. Specifically, it is hypothesized that the differences in both the social and fire cultures may result in differences in response behaviours and response times. The evacuation process can be considered to comprise two broad phases, called the Response Phase and Evacuation Movement Phase (Galea, 2009). The experimental component of project BeSeCu addresses issues associated with Response Phase behaviours (Galea, 2009), in particular response time, and the impact of culture.

In practical fire engineering applications it is common practice to assume that evacuation related data, such as response time, can be reliably applied more widely than the context from which the data was collected. In particular, this type of data is often applied to situations within cultural environments – both social and fire – different to that from which the data was collected. The majority of readily available published evacuation data (both response time and total evacuation time) that is used in fire engineering applications throughout the world originates from a small number of countries with broadly similar cultural backgrounds; i.e., UK, USA, Canada, Australia and New Zealand (Sime, 1992; Sime, 1990; Proulx, 1994; Proulx and Sime, 1991; Shields & Boyce, 2000; Proulx, 1995; Brennan, 1997). There has been very little effort in exploring the impact of culture on fire evacuation behaviour, especially outside of the small number of countries mentioned. Here we take culture to mean the social culture of the society that the occupants belong to. This begs the question, can response time data collected from predominately Western European/North American type social cultures (UK, Australia, Canada, USA, New Zealand) be applied in significantly different social cultures such as in Japan, China, Korea, Turkey, Czech Republic, Brazil, etc.? Is there a cultural component to the time required to complete the Response Phase?

7.3 The basis for the experimental trials

7.3.1 Trial rationale

To investigate potential cultural differences in human behaviour in crisis situations, three unannounced evacuation experiments were undertaken in three European countries, Czech Republic, Poland and Turkey. The purpose of these experiments is to explore the differences and similarities in observed emergent behaviours (during the response phase) of the test populations under emergency evacuation situations. Thus the unannounced nature of these trials is essential as this will instill in the test population a feeling that this could be a real situation requiring evacuation.

In order to expand the set of useful data, the data derived from the BeSeCu trials is compared with data collected from an evacuation trial conducted in the UK by the Fire Safety Engineering Group (FSEG) of the University of Greenwich (Gwynne, Galea, Parke & Hickson, 2003; Gwynne, 2007). The FSEG trial was conducted in a university library building and so to maintain a basis for comparison, the BeSeCu trials are all conducted in university library buildings. There are a number of advantages in using library buildings as the selected target structure for this cross-cultural study. These include:

- The nature of the target population found in university libraries is similar across different countries.
- The nature of university library buildings is similar across different countries.
- University library buildings are relatively straight forward to evacuate and do not involve any essential service or business disruption.
- As the library building is administered by a single authority, it is relatively easy to obtain permission to evacuate such buildings.
- There are fewer ethical issues as the target population is not generally considered at risk, vulnerable or involving minors.
- The project already has access to a UK data set for this type of building which can be used as a basis for comparison.

7.3.2 Research question

The aim of these trials is to determine if there are significant differences or similarities between cultures in response to emergency evacuation situations. In order to investigate this issue data was collected in several forms, including manual

measurements with stop watches, video recording and post evacuation questionnaires. This range of data collection techniques enable:
- Objective measurements made through systematic analysis of video footage and manual measurements.
- Subjective experiences captured through post evacuation questionnaire analysis.
- Behavioural observations made through analysis of video footage.

The data derived from these various sources was then compared to identify similarities and differences in:
- The range of occupant response times.
- Nature (shape) of response time distributions.
- Type and frequency of response phase behaviours.
- Response to authority figures during response phase.

In addition, data suitable for the validation of evacuation models was collected from the trials. This involved:
- Full building evacuation data.
- Component data such as: exit flow rates, crowd densities as a function of time, exit times, etc.

The collected validation data sets and evacuation modelling using the building EXODUS evacuation software (Galea, Sharp & Lawrence, 2008; Gwynne, Galea & Lawrence, 2008; Galea, Sharp, Lawrence & Holden, 2008) is not described here but is presented elsewhere (Galea, 2012; Galea, Sauter, Deere & Filippidis, 2011; Galea, Sharp, Sauter, Deere & Filippidis, 2012).

7.4 Response phase behavioural framework

7.4.1 Response time

It is now widely accepted that a key factor which can determine the success of an evacuation is the speed with which occupants respond to the call to evacuate and begin purposeful movement to a place of safety (Sime, 1992; Sime, 1990; Proulx, 1994; Proulx and Sime, 1991; Shields & Boyce, 2000; Proulx, 1995; Brennan, 1997). Indeed, in some cases, the time required to complete the Response Phase may be greater than the time required to complete the Evacuation Movement Phase and travel to the place of safety.

The Response Phase can entail a number of different factors such as; gathering belongings, switching off computers, completing emails, securing valuables and investigation of the incident before the movement phase commences. Since these behaviours are not part of the direct egress phase, they constitute what is generally known as Response Phase. The duration of the Response Phase is here called the response time (sometimes also referred to as the pre-movement time or pre-evacuation time).

Over the years, much response time data has been collected (Shields & Boyce, 2000; Proulx, 1995; Brennan, 1997) and published. However, as this data is generally published as mean response times, it is of limited practical use to modern evacuation models which requires a response time distribution. More recently, response time data is being published which provides the actual distribution of response times (Gwynne, Galea, Parke & Hickson, 2003; Charters, Holbourn & Townsend, 2001; Proulx & Fahy, 1997; Purser, 1998; Tavares, Gwynne & Galea, 2006; Galea, Sharp, Lawrence & Dixon, 2007; Galea, Deere, Sharp, Filippidis, Lawrence & Gwynne, 2007). From these studies, the generally accepted form of the response time distribution is a log-normal curve whose mode and length of tail varies depending on the nature of the evacuation scenario (Purser, 1998).

The response time is a key factor measured in the egress trials and compared across the various cultural groups. As evacuation data, in particular response time data, used in engineering calculations is generated from countries such as; UK, USA, Australia and New Zealand, the countries in which the BeSeCu evacuation trials were conducted are: Turkey, Poland and the Czech Republic. These countries are drawn from the BeSeCu partners and represent countries which are culturally different from the core countries from which the majority of evacuation data is drawn.

The response time generally depends on the following factors: the type of structure, the occupying population, the experience of occupants with regards to training, false alarms and previous real incidents, the type of cues related to the incident occupants may receive, the structure of management within the building with regards handling these types of situation and so forth. Response times can vary from just a few seconds with good training, previous experience of real incidents, the presence of assertive staff and a voice alarm system to an extended period of many minutes should people be asleep, isolated, used to frequent false alarms, or overly familiar with the building they are in.

The operational definition of response time for the purposes of the BeSeCu experimental trials is taken as:

> *"The time taken, after the sounding of the alarm, by an individual to purposefully initiate evacuation".*

There are numerous activities that may be undertaken during the Response Phase such as disengaging from any task at which they had previously been occupied, collect coats, engaging in discussion, breaking off social activities, etc. Activities such as those described above contribute to the extent of the overall response phase and hence the response time. Therefore, the time interval from the sounding of the alarm to the point at which the individual initiates their evacuation is the period that defines the response time for the individual.

7.4.2 The response phase behavioural framework

The comparative studies of evacuation behaviour described in this report are based not simply on response times, but on a framework developed as part of project BeSeCu, to describe Response Phase behaviours. Within the proposed evacuation behaviour framework (Galea, 2009), the evacuation process is considered to comprise of two broad phases; the Response Phase and Evacuation Movement Phase (see Fig. 7.1). The framework attempts to convey the nature of the human factors processes that characterize Response Phase behaviours. This description not only provides a consistent method for describing Response Phase behaviour, but also provides a useful framework for classifying and quantifying the Response Phase other than simply using the overall response time. Using this framework we may eventually be able to develop predictive models to estimate response times. A key part of the Response Phase analysis is the determination of the Notification, Cognition and Activity stage start and end points (Galea, 2009) (see Fig. 7.1).

Notification stage

The first stage of the Response Phase is the Notification stage (see Fig. 7.1). In the Notification stage, notification cues such as an alarm convey to the occupants that an unusual and potentially hazardous event has occurred, requiring the occupants to evacuate. The notification cues may be a traditional alarm such as a siren or an alarm bell, a voice alarm, intervention by staff or environmental cues such as the smell of smoke etc. The start of the Notification stage is marked by the occupants being exposed to the first cues. During the Notification stage the occupant may (knowingly or unknowingly) ignore the cues and continue with their normal activities as they have not accepted or recognized that the cues are relevant to their situation. For each exposed occupant, the end of the Notification stage is marked by the occupants responding to the notification cues by mentally and/or physically disengaging from the tasks they were previously involved in and the recognition that the cue(s) they have been subjected to indicate that something unusual may be occurring in their environment. At the end of the Notification stage, while the occupants are alerted that something unusual is occurring in their environment, they have not started to physically react to the situation. The end of the Notification stage marks the beginning of the Cognition stage.

Cognition stage

During the Cognition stage the alerted occupants interpret the information provided by the initial notification cues, and potentially other sources of information (e.g. further incident related cues, staff intervention, etc.), and decide how they should respond (see Fig. 7.1). There are essentially three broad types of response the occupant may decide to undertake:

- In the first type of response, the initial notification cues have been insufficient to convey to the occupant the immediate need for evacuation and so the occupant re-engages in their previous activity until further cues or information is received.

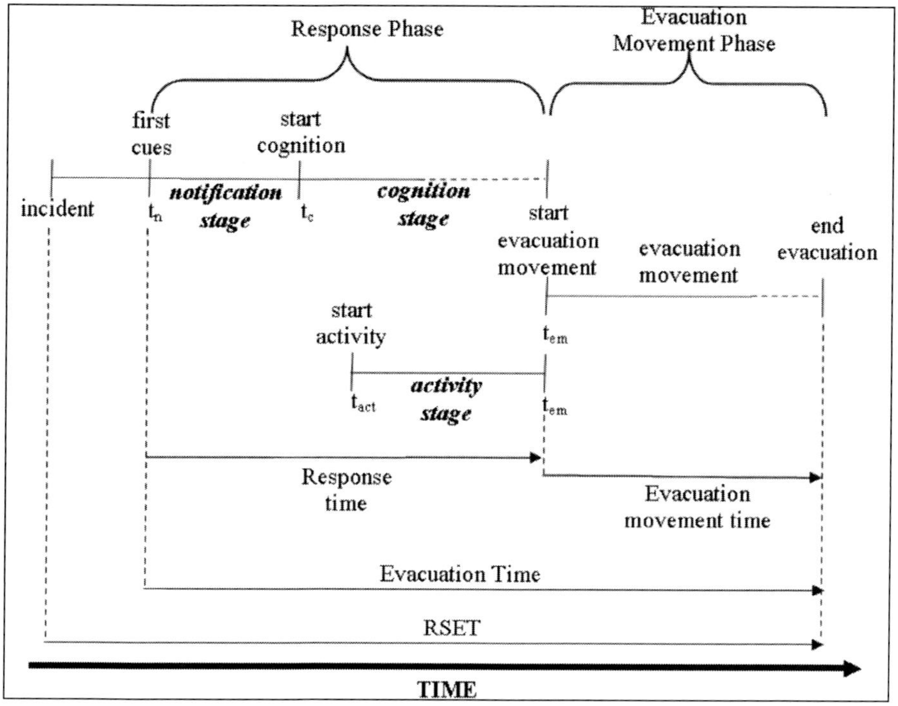

Fig. 7.1: Framework for describing evacuation behaviour

In this case, the Cognition stage continues until one of the other two possible responses occur.

- In the second type of response, the occupant has recognized the initial notification cues and as a result, immediately commences evacuation movement without undertaking any other activity. Alternatively, the occupant may have ignored the initial notification cues and re-engaged in their pre-notification activity but then acknowledges additional cues and as a result immediately commences evacuation movement without undertaking any other activity. In these cases the end of the Cognition stage also marks the end of the Response Phase and the beginning of the Evacuation Movement Phase.
- In the third type of response, the occupant acknowledges that the notification cues indicate that something potentially hazardous is occurring in their environment and as a result undertakes a series of Action and/or Information tasks, marking the start of the Activity stage. In this case, cognitions may be occurring at the same time as activities, activities could be sparking new cognitions and cognitions could initiate one or more new activities. As a result, the Activity stage can run in parallel to the Cognition stage. However, the physical duration of the Cognition stage is less well defined as it may have several possible end points and so is taken to run to the end of the Activity stage.

Activity stage

At the start of the Activity stage the occupant performs a series of Information and/or Action tasks (Galea, 2009; Galea, Hulse, Day, Siddiqui, Sharp, Shields, Boyce, Summerfield, Canter, Marselle & Greenall, 2010; Galea, Shields, Canter, Boyce, Day, Hulse, Siddiqui, Summerfield, Marselle & Greenall, 2006) which were conceived during the Cognition stage (see Fig. 7.1). These are defined as follows:

- An Action task involves the occupant physically undertaking an activity such as: shutting down a work station; packing work items; packing/collecting personal belongings in the immediate vicinity; physically moving to another location to perform an action (e.g. fight fire, collect an item).
- An Information task involves the occupant seeking, providing or exchanging information concerning the incident or required course of action and may include; calling someone on the phone to seek/provide information; seeking/providing information in person; engaging with electronic media (e.g. television, radio, text services, etc.); investigating the incident. Information tasks may thus involve the physical movement of the occupant; however, what distinguishes this activity from an Action task is the end purpose of the movement i.e. to obtain information or to undertake a physical task.

It is hypothesized that the Cognition stage may run in parallel to the Activity stage, and so the occupant may return to the Cognition stage to interpret new information gained, assess their current situation and contemplate their next course of action, which may in turn require further Action/Information tasks to be executed. Thus, during the Activity stage, there may be brief periods where the occupant appears to be undertaking no specific task. The start of the Activity stage is marked by the commencement of the planned tasks while the end of the Activity stage is marked by the completion of all tasks conceived during the Cognition stage. The end of the Activity stage usually denotes the end of the Response Phase and the beginning of the Evacuation Movement Phase. It is only at the start of the Evacuation Movement Phase that the occupant begins their purposeful movement to an exit or stair or place of safety.

Response phase parameters

Based on the Response Phase Behavioural Framework, key parameters that define the Response Phase for each member of the population are:

- Response Time (sec).
- Notification Time (sec).
- Number of Action Tasks undertaken.
- Number of Information Tasks undertaken.
- Action Task duration (sec).
- Information Task duration (sec).

From these individual parameters a parameter set representative of the population as a whole can be determined by taking the average for each individual parameter. In this way the Response Phase for a particular evacuation can be defined by specifying the average duration of the Notification stage (NT), the average number of Action Tasks (AT) undertaken, the average number of Information Tasks (IT) undertaken, the average duration of an Action Task (ATT), the average duration of an Information and Task (ITT) and the average Response Time (RT).

Each of these average Response Phase parameters (i.e. NT, AT, IT, ATT, ITT), average response time and response time distributions are dependent on:

- The type of the structure and hence the nature of the activities the population will be involved in pre-alarm, e.g. library building, supermarket, high rise residential building, high rise office building, airport, rail station, etc.
- The nature of the notification process, e.g. voice alarm, staff intervention, tone alarm, etc.
- The demographics of the population, e.g. age and gender, and,
- The nature of the population, e.g. degree of familiarity with the structure, degree of training, etc.

Thus the Response Phase parameter set (i.e. NT, AT, IT, ITT and ATT) associated with a university library with a voice alarm is likely to be significantly different to that for an airport building with voice alarm. This will lead to different average response times and different response time distributions for these different structures. However, for identical building types, with identical notification systems, identical population demographics with identical levels of familiarity and training it is expected that the Response Phase parameter set, average response times and response time distributions would be similar. Thus for the three BeSeCu libraries, it is expected that the Response Phase parameter set will be similar.

However, if the Response Phase parameter set and hence the average response time and response time distribution are also dependent on culture, it is possible that the average response time, response time distributions and Response Phase parameter set will be significantly different for each of the three BeSeCu libraries.

7.5 The trials

A series of three unannounced evacuation trials were undertaken at three different locations as part of project BeSeCu:

- Czech Republic: VSB-Technical University of Ostrava, 21 October 2009
- Turkey: Izmir Institute of Technology, 2 March 2010
- Poland: University of Warsaw Library, 26 May 2010

A similar evacuation protocol was implemented at each site. This involved the activation of a voice alarm to initiate the evacuation. The precise wording of the message used in the voice alarm was agreed with each of the three participating sites. As a result, while the message at each site was different, an attempt was made to make them as similar as possible. Each evacuation was unannounced and so staff and students at the three sites did not know beforehand that a trial evacuation was taking place. In addition, all three buildings are similar, being multi-floor buildings with multiple exit points (see Fig. 7.2).

(a) Czech Republic (b) Turkey (c) Poland

Fig. 7.2: The three libraries used in the BeSeCu study

7.5.1 Outline of trial protocol

The primary data that was collected is in the form of video footage from strategically located video cameras and from participant responses to a post-trial questionnaire. A significant amount of effort was invested in selecting the locations for the video cameras. This was done weeks prior to the trials taking place and was determined through site visits by the FSEG team. The camera locations were determined so as to achieve a good coverage of the occupied library spaces and to ensure that students involved in a variety of activities would be captured. These visits also identified the number of cameras that were required and the type of mounting system that would be required. A thorough understanding of the library layout was also necessary in order to ensure that the questionnaire was relevant to the specific trial site. The questionnaire had to be prepared well in advance of each trial as it needed to be translated into the host language.

Scheduling the trials was quite difficult as the trial dates must coincide with a likely high occupancy, should not coincide with exam periods, should not be in a seasonally difficult time (e.g. snow), should not be too close to each other and should allow sufficient time to perform some of the required detailed data analysis. In addition, it was desirable to have the Ostrava library as the first trial as it is the least difficult of the three and have the Warsaw library last as it is the most challenging.

Several weeks prior to undertaking the trials, the trial equipment and questionnaires were shipped to the trial site. A couple of days prior to the trial, the FSEG team travelled to the trial site and setup a base of operations. The trial team consisted of 5 FSEG team members experienced in managing evacuation trials, 0 to 2 other BeSeCu team members and 6 to 20 volunteers from the local site. The night prior to the trial, the FSEG team would setup the video equipment so that staff and students are not alerted to the activity. The video cameras were activated in the morning prior to the opening of the library. The time at which the trial would take place was determined beforehand. This was to ensure that the library staff was unaware of the precise time that the trial would take place. The trial was started when it was determined that the maximum number of people were within the library. At this point the alarm would be activated and the library evacuated following the standard procedures in place at each site. As each person left the library they would be given a questionnaire and a pencil and asked to complete and return the questionnaire. Following each evacuation trial, the video equipment would be taken down and the video footage briefly examined. The day following each trial a de-brief would take place where the FSEG team would give a brief presentation to the library staff and identify good and bad in the evacuation procedure and evacuation performance. The equipment and completed questionnaires were packed and shipped back to the UK by road freight. When the equipment arrived back in the UK the video footage would be removed from the cameras and transferred to an archival system and backed up. The video footage is then edited down to the required portion of footage and converted to WMV format to reduce storage requirements and for ease of use. When this is completed the data analysis would begin. The questionnaire data would also be extracted from the questionnaires and entered into a database for analysis.

7.5.2 Trial sites

Each of the three trial sites will be described in turn, including a description of: The library and its staff, the alarm system and the video camera setup.

Czech Republic: VSB-Technical University of Ostrava

The building

The library has a floor area of some 15,000 m^2 and has 5 floors, although only 2 floors are used by students. The students have access to two stairs and three routes out of the library. The library building has mixed occupancy and accommodates staff offices, computer rooms, classrooms, study areas, reading rooms and auditoria. The library has 25 members of staff and an average monthly usage of 5,000 visitors. The staff of the library receives procedural training every two years and fire drills are only run at the request of the local fire brigade. There had not been a fire drill in the library for several years.

The alarm

The alarm system within the library is zoned and consists of a combination of tones, recorded voice and live voice messages. The nature of the alarm message is to first inform the entire campus population that there is an incident on the campus, and then to inform the appropriate sub-population of the need to commence the evacuation process. The nature of the alarm messaging that was agreed to be used on the day of the trial was as follows:

- Alarm Tone, Alarm Tone (short burst),
- Recorded Voice Message 1:
  "Warning! Warning! I announce an emergency situation. I ask all workers and

students and other people present to stay calm, prepare to evacuate and wait for instructions."

There would then be a short gap as the security staff check the nature of the alarm and decide which building to evacuate. For the purposes of this trial we had agreed that there would be no more than a 10 sec gap between the end of Recorded Message 1 and Live Message 2.

- Live Voice Message 2:
  "Please evacuate the library building as quickly as possible. Please evacuate the library building as quickly as possible".

Unfortunately, on the day of the trial, the alarm sequence did not occur as planned.

The team

A team of five from FSEG travelled to Ostrava in the Czech Republic to setup the required equipment and manage and conduct the evacuation trial. The team to run these trials consisted of 16 people. These consisted of:

- 5 staff from FSEG (four in the camera team and overall trial controller),
- Mr. Petr Kucera from VSB who acted as the liaison with VSB.
- Mr. Jaroslav Soukup and Mr. Kamil Coufal, VSB MSc students who assisted with: Equipment setup, entering questionnaire responses into database.
- 9 VSB MSc students in three teams of three people to manage the exits, give out questionnaires.

The video equipment

In total six cases of equipment weighing 126 kg were shipped to Ostrava for use in the trials (see Fig.7.3). A total of 22 video cameras and associated clamps and mounts, walkie-talkies, power supplies, stop watches, questionnaire distribution bags, pencils, portable hard disks, questionnaire collection bins, etc.

Once the FSEG team arrived in Ostrava, one of the first tasks was to prepare all of the equipment for installation. On the day before the trial and after the library has officially closed, the camera team setup the 22 video cameras throughout the library at the pre-defined locations (see Fig. 7.4) , 9 on the ground floor and 13 on the first floor. This process took just over 2 hours to complete and was finished just after mid night on the night before the trial. Depicted in Fig. 7.5 is an example of the FSEG team setting up the video cameras. The following morning, on the day of the trial, the team entered the library at 06:00, well before official opening to set

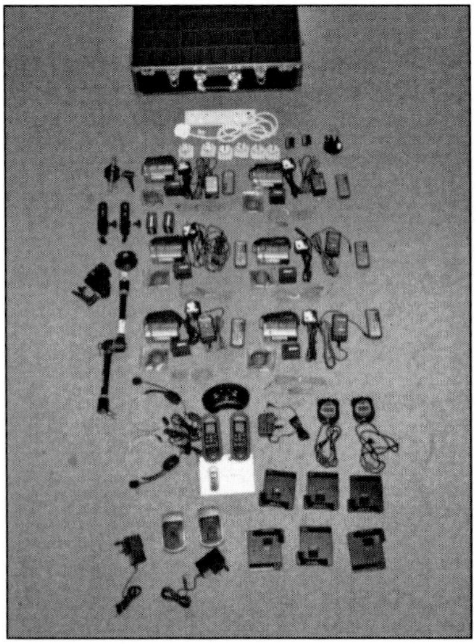

Fig.7.3: FSEG equipment required for Czech Republic trial

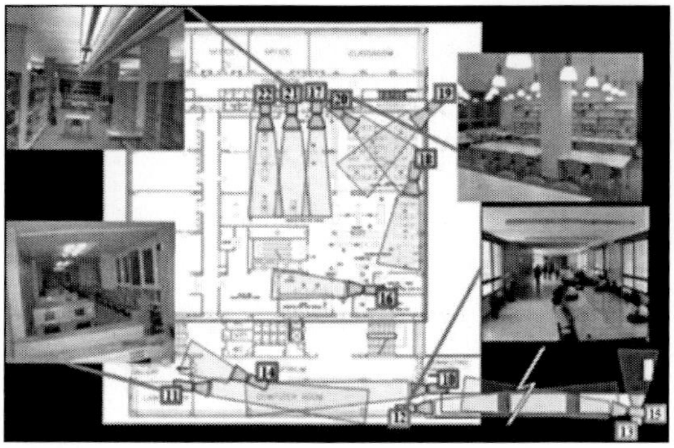

Fig. 7.4: First floor layout with camera locations and views from selected cameras

Fig. 7.5: FSEG team setting up video cameras in Ostrava library

up the cameras that could not be setup the night before. Just before the library opened all of the cameras were activated so that they would record continuously from the start of the day up to the end of the evacuation.

Turkey: Izmir Institute of Technology

The building

The library has two floors each with an area of 3,050 m^2 and students have access to two stairs, two elevators. There are two routes out of the library, the main entrance, with two doors, and an emergency exit which is normally locked and not in normal use. To exit the building via the main exit, occupants must first pass through a turnstile. In normal usage, students must pass their ID cards over a card reader while during emergency situations the turnstile is set to free-swing. The library building has mixed occupancy and accommodates staff offices, computer rooms, study areas, reading rooms and a canteen. The library has 19 members of staff and an average daily usage of 800–900 visitors. At any one time there may be between 50 and 300 visitors within the library. Apart from the evacuation trial conducted for this project, there had never been a fire drill in the building. There are no formal procedures that staff would be required to follow in the event of an evacuation and staff is not trained to handle an evacuation.

The alarm

The alarm system within the library consists of a combination of tones and a recorded voice message which are run concurrently. To the best knowledge of the library staff, the fire alarm system had never been tested and a recorded message had not been set by the staff. An alarm message was recorded which requested the immediate evacuation of the library. The alarm tone and the voice message were run simultaneously. The 7.5 s duration message was repeated con-

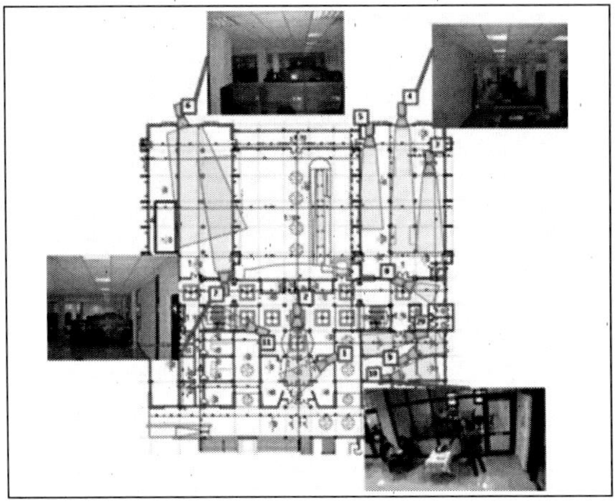

Fig. 7.6: Ground floor layout with camera locations and views from selected cameras

Fig. 7.7: FSEG team setting up video cameras in Izmir library

tinuously throughout the evacuation. The recorded voice message used in the trial was:

- "Attention please, Attention please, due to a suspected fire in the library, please leave the building immediately. Please proceed to your nearest exit."

The team

A team of five from FSEG travelled to Izmir in Turkey to setup the required equipment, manage and conduct the evacuation experiment. The team to run these trials consisted of 14 people. These consisted of:

- 5 staff from FSEG, four in the camera team and overall trial controller
- Mr. Gultekin Gurdal library Director
- Dr. Zeynep Baskaya Sofuoglu (Association of Emergency Ambulance Physicians and BeSeCu partner) liaison with library
- 7 doctors/nurses from Izmir 112 Ambulance Service who constituted the door teams to manage the exits and give out and collect questionnaires: 1 team of four people (main exit) and 1 team of three people (emergency exit).

The video equipment

In total six cases of equipment weighing 109 kg were transported to Izmir for use in the trials. A total of 28 video cameras and associated clamps and mounts, walkie-talkies, power supplies, stop watches, questionnaire distribution bags, pencils, portable hard disks, questionnaire collection bins, etc.

When the FSEG team arrived in Izmir, the first task was to prepare all of the equipment for installation. On the day before the trial and after the library has officially closed, the camera team setup the 28 video cameras throughout the library at the pre-defined locations (see Fig. 7.6 and Fig. 7.7), 11 on the ground floor and

17 on the first floor. This process took just over 2.5 hours to complete, starting at 23:00 on the day before the trial and was completed at 01:30 on the day of the trial. The following morning, on the day of the trial, the team entered the library at 07:00, well before official opening to set up the cameras that could not be setup the night before. Just before the library opened all of the cameras were activated so that they would record continuously from the start of the day up to the end of the evacuation.

Poland: University of Warsaw Library

The building

The library has seven floors including a roof garden which is opened to users of the library in the spring and summer seasons. The approximate area of the building is 60,970 m^2 with a usable area of 49,205 m^2. The building has nine stairs and 13 open spiral stairs, with 19 lifts. There are five normal and 13 emergency exits in the building, seven of which are normally accessible by students. The building is mixed use in that the building is divided into three parts: the library, a commercial section with retail outlets and the Law and Administration Faculty of Warsaw University. The Law and Administration Faculty is a separate building and constitutes a separate fire zone. The commercial part of the building has restaurants, kiosks, a bookshop, buffet areas, etc. These are also separate from the main library and in the event of a drill would not need to be evacuated. For the purposes of this trial, only the main library was evacuated.

The building has 820 employees. The monthly usage of the library building is approximately 27,200 to 211,100, with an average of around 94,600. The maximum occupancy of the building is 2,200. The building has fire drills every two years; the last one was in 2007. The drills involve evacuation of the building and it is also possible to evacuate only parts of the building. Once the alarm is broadcast through the loudspeakers there is an announcement which can involve either the threat i.e. fire or explosive material or it can be announced that there is an emergency without giving any further details. Staff, executives and users have formal procedures to follow in the event of an emergency and the staff receives training in these procedures once a year.

The alarm

The alarm is both an audible signal as well as a voice system. It can be announced in the whole of the building or restricted to parts of the building divided into special audible zones. When the Alarm is sounded, a fire curtain immediately begins to lower in the central part of the building, and is fully lowered within 5-10 seconds. For the purposes of the trial, the fire curtain will not be deployed. The alarm tone and the voice message were run simultaneously. The 17s duration message was repeated continuously throughout the evacuation. The recorded voice message used on the day was:

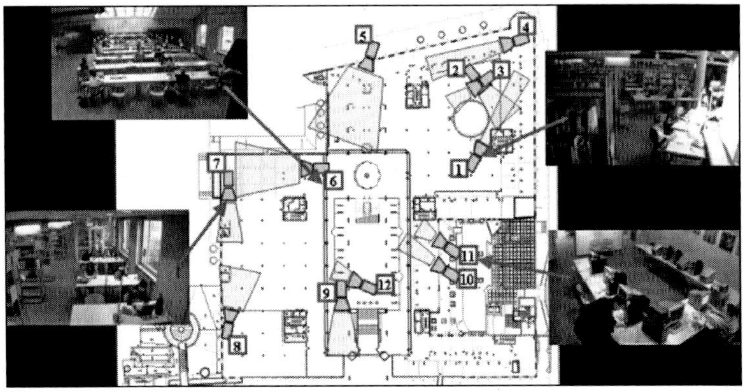

Fig. 7.8: Ground floor (Level 1) layout with camera locations and views from selected cameras

Fig. 7.9: FSEG team setting up video cameras in the Warsaw library

- English: "Ding Dong" (sound of alarm), "Attention please, attention please, due to a fire, please leave the building. Please, stay calm and proceed to your nearest exit", "Ding Dong".

The team

A team of five from FSEG travelled to Warsaw in Poland to setup the required equipment, to manage and conduct the evacuation experiment. The team required to run these trials consisted of 26 people. These consisted of:

- 5 staff from FSEG four in the camera team and overall trial controller),
- Mr. Grzegorz Beltowski from SGSP who acted as the liaison with the library.
- Mr. Adam Kolad and Mr. Grzegorz Ratajczyk, MSc students who assisted with: equipment setup, entering questionnaire responses into database, data analysis
- 18 SGSP students in 9 teams of two people to manage the exits, give out questionnaires.

The video equipment

In total six cases of equipment weighing 120 kg were transported to Warsaw for use in the trials. A total of 30 video cameras and associated clamps and mounts, walkie-talkies, power supplies, stop watches, questionnaire distribution bags, pencils, portable hard disks, questionnaire collection bins, etc.

When the FSEG team arrived in Warsaw, the first task was to prepare all of the equipment for installation. On the day before the trial and after the library has officially closed, the camera team setup the 30 video cameras throughout the library at the pre-defined locations (see Fig. 7.8), 12 on Level 1 (ground floor), 11 on Level 2 and seven on Level 3. This process took just over 2.5 hours to complete, starting at 21:30 on the day before the trial and was completed at midnight on the night before the trial. Depicted in Fig. 7.9 is an example of the FSEG team setting up the video cameras. The following morning, on the day of the trial, the team entered the library at 06:00, well before official opening to setup the cameras that could not be setup the night before. Just before the library opened all of the cameras were activated so that they would record continuously from the start of the day up to the end of the evacuation.

UK: University of Greenwich Library (Dreadnought Library)

The building

The library has three floors each with a usable area of 3,000 m^2 with dimensions of each floor approximately 50 m x 60 m. The structure has six staircases and eight exits, of which only one is in normal use, the other seven being emergency exits. The library building has mixed occupancy and accommodates staff offices, computer rooms, study areas, reading rooms, discussion rooms etc. The library has 27 members of staff and an average monthly usage of 5,200 visitors. The library has three unannounced evacuation drills per year in which the entire library is evacuated. Staff members are trained to ensure that their section of the library is cleared prior to evacuating. Academic staff members with classes in the library are also trained to ensure that their class evacuated prior to leaving the building. The evacuation trial took place on the 22 January 2007.

The alarm

The alarm system consists of a simple alarm bell. In this evacuation the following procedure was employed: the alarm sounded; a large number of staff performed a sweep encouraging the population to evacuate; evacuees then moved to a designated assembly point.

The video equipment

Unlike the other three evacuation trials, in-house CCTV cameras were used to collect the required data. A total of 22 rooms in the library were under surveillance through CCTV cameras, of which a total of 15 proved useful for analysis. Thus, data from 15 internal CCTV cameras were used in this analysis.

Ethics approval

All research conducted by University of Greenwich staff and students involving human participants requires ethical consideration by the university's research ethics committee (UREC). UREC consists of a panel of 21 individuals drawn from a broad variety of disciplines and organisations, who meet on only five occasions during an academic year. Applications for ethical approval must be submitted to the panel at least two weeks prior to a meeting. The application form must include details about the project including its aims, research questions and methodology, information about the personnel and participants involved, and ethical issues to be addressed, including data handling. Furthermore, applicants must include all materials to be administered to participants and letters of agreement from interested parties (e.g. building owners).

UREC reviews the application and decides on one of four actions: to accept the application outright; accept the application following minor amendments; reject the application with suggestions for major amendments and resubmission; or reject the application outright. Applicants will be informed of UREC's decision a few weeks after the meeting. If the decision is to accept the application, the applicant may then begin their research.

The FSEG team submitted their application for ethics approval associated with the BeSeCu trials and were granted ethics approval to conduct the evacuation trials.

Video data analysis

Video footage collected from evacuation trials can be analyzed to determine response times and Response Phase behaviours. This analysis is undertaken frame by frame using software tools such as Adobe Premiere. In this type of analysis, for the most part, it is not possible to determine the end of the Notification and start of the Cognition stages. This is because from the video footage alone it is difficult to determine when incident related cognitions occur. However, using the video footage it is possible to determine when someone's behaviour changes from that which they were involved in prior to the Notification stage to those behaviours defined in the Activity stage such as seeking information, packing away belongings and shutting down equipment, etc. Thus, in the video analysis, the Cognition and Activity stages are combined and referred to simply as the Activity stage. As a result the video analysis provides the following Response PhaseThe start of the Response Phase (i.e. the start of the Notification Stage) which is indicated by the first notification cues e.g. the sound of the alarm or staff intervention.

- The end/start of the Notification/Activity Stage where people begin to perform action and information tasks prior to starting the Evacuation Movement Phase.
- The number, type and duration of Action and Information tasks performed.
- Whether or not staff intervention was involved in getting person started, or intervention by any other person.
- Time at which member of staff/other person intervened.
- The end point of the Activity Stage and the commencement of the Evacuation Movement Phase.
- Response Time

From this information it will be possible to determine the following key Response Phase parameters for each individual:

- Response Time (sec).
- Notification Time (sec).
- Number of Action Tasks undertaken.
- Number of Information Tasks undertaken.

- Action Task duration (sec).
- Information Task duration (sec).

From this data, representative averages can be determined to characterize the population. In addition the following contextual information will be collected:

- Gender of person.
- Approximate age (e.g. provide three or four broad age bands to identify: child, young person (student), older person (staff), elderly person).
- Role of person (staff or student).
- Group status.
- Number of people in room at time of alarm or if not in a room, number of people in immediate vicinity.
- Room type (large open plan study area, small study area, computer area, shelving area, circulation space).

Where possible, data for evacuation model validation will also be collected. This includes:

- Total number of people in the various locations.
- Exit route taken by individuals
- Exit used by individuals.
- Exit flow rates achieved.
- Exit flow counts.
- Density as a function of time at key locations.

Prior to commencing analysis of trial video footage, a set of definitions relating to the key Response Phase stages was developed. These clearly specify how to identify the start/end points of the Notification and Activity stages and identify a range of Action and Information tasks that may be undertaken during the Activity stage. The Action/Information tasks include 15 Action tasks (e.g., collect belongings, shut down computer, pickup bag, etc.) and seven Information tasks (e.g., engage in information exchange, provide information/instructions to others, move to another location to acquire information, etc.). The analysis team was then trained in identifying and categorizing the various Response Phase stages and Activity stage tasks. Finally, prior to commencing data extraction, the analysis team must successfully complete an interrater testing process to ensure that they can consistently identify the required data. Full details concerning the video data analysis can be found in Galea, 2009.

The questionnaire

The questionnaire was written in the native language of the host country and consisted of 29 questions arranged in eight logical sections. These addressed:

- **Demographics (Questions 1 to 4):** This section concerned the age, gender and year of study of the participants. The participants were also asked to identify any disabilities they may have. This section was the same for all three sites.

- **Experience (Question 4 to 8):** This section assessed the participants' experience of previous evacuation trails and level of evacuation training. This section was the same for all three sites.
- **Risk Perception (Questions 9, 13, 19, 24 and 28):** This question was asked five times and attempts to measure the perception of risk: in normal usage of the building (Q9), when the participant heard the alarm (Q13), when the participant decided to evacuate (Q19), when the participant was in the process of evacuating (Q24) and finally when they exited the building (Q28). This series of questions attempts to map the change in risk perception throughout the evacuation process. This section is the same for all three sites
- **Initial Response to Alarm (Questions 10 to 19):** While most of this section is the same for all three sites, there are several exceptions. Furthermore, several changes were made to this section in light of the Czech Republic experience. Firstly, the options in Q14 are specific to each site. Following the evacuation trial in the Czech Republic, it was noted that in some circumstances not everyone could hear the alarm. Q14, Q15 and Q16 were modified to ensure that if occupants do not hear the alarm but learn of the need to evacuate from someone else they can still answer the questions.
- **Estimation of Response Time (Question 20):** The participant was asked to estimate how long they took before they started to move towards the exit. This question was the same for all three sites.
- **Group Information (Questions 21 and 22):** The participant was asked to identify if they were alone, in groups of friends or groups of strangers when they heard the alarm and when they exited the building. This section is the same for all three sites.
- **Evacuation Movement Phase (Questions 23 to 28):** These questions addressed the experience of the participant during their movement towards the exit. Questions such as which exit did they use, what factors influenced their route choice, did they require guidance information, how congested the stairs were etc. Only the question related to which exit did they use was altered for each site so that it was relevant for the particular building.
- **Ethnic Information (Question 29):** This question addressed the ethnicity of the participant. This question was modified for each of the three sites.

The full questionnaire, written in English and each of the trial languages can be found in Galea, 2009.

7.6 Evacuation trial results

The results from each trial relating to the observed Response Phase behaviours are presented and discussed. Each trial is analyzed using a similar approach, with key Response Phase parameters determined for each trial. In addition, an empirical model used to predict average response times is developed and assessed using data generated from each trial.

Czech Republic: VSB-Technical University of Ostrava

Alarm sequence

Unfortunately, on the day of the trial, a fault in the alarm system meant that the alarm system failed to operate throughout the library. The alarm could only be heard by the population in the large open study area. For the remainder of the population in the library, the evacuation was initiated by staff intervention – where members of staff went around the library informing the population that they needed to evacuate the library immediately due to a suspect fire. Furthermore, the alarm messaging did not occur as originally planned, with the live voice messages being considerably longer than anticipated. The alarm actually consisted of several messages; a translation of the messages that occurred on the day is as follows:

- Alarm Sequence 1, t = 0 sec: Alarm Tone, Alarm Tone – 54 sec duration.
- Alarm Sequence 2, t = 54 sec: Recorded Voice Message 1:
- "Attention! Attention! I declare the emergency situation. Attention! Attention! I declare the emergency situation. I am asking for all employees, students and everybody else to stay calm and wait for next information. Prepare for evacuation. Attention! Attention! Prepare for evacuation and wait for next information. Prepare for evacuation and wait for next information." – 24 sec duration.
- Pause – 35 sec duration.
- Alarm Sequence 3, t = 113 sec; Live Voice Message 2:
- "Library, Attention, the evacuation is only for the new library building. The other buildings are not endangered. For evacuation of the New library use the main entrance from library, on the second floor use the corridor to the Aula building and continue to Aula or continue to the building A – B. Do not use lifts and on the stairs people coming down floor above have priority. Be careful about your personal safety and the new library building leave as fast as possible."
- "Attention, all of this information is only for the new library building. I repeat, carry out all spaces of the new library building. For evacuation of the new library use the main entrance from library, on the second floor use the corridor to the Aula building or continue to the building B. Attention, the evacuation is only for the new library building. The other buildings are not in danger. I am asking for all students, employees and everybody else to stay calm and wait for next information. I repeat, fire alarm is declared only for the new library building, other buildings are not endangered. Wait for the next information." – 89 sec duration.
- Pause – 184 sec duration.
- Alarm Sequence 4, t = 386 sec: Live Voice Message 3:
- Content not clear. – 80 sec duration.
- Entire alarm sequence is 466 sec (7 min 46 sec) long.

The entire alarm sequence took almost 8 minutes and conveyed far too much information to be effective. This may have contributed to the delay in people commencing their evacuation.

Population characteristics

A total of 68 questionnaires were returned. From the returned questionnaires, at the time of the alarm there were 68 students within the library, 54 within the main part of the library and 14 within the study area. According to the video analysis, there were 70 students within the library for which response time data could be determined, 47 within the main part of the library and 23 within the study area.

From the questionnaire, 78% (53) of the student population was male, 22% (15) were female and 93% (63) were in the age range 18-24; 6% (4) were in the age range 25-34 and 1% (1) was in the age range 35-44. Furthermore, 45% (30) were in the first year of study at the University; 12% (8) were in the second year; 18% (12) were in the third year; 25% (17) were in the fourth or more year of study at the University (note, one student did not specify their year of study).

Concerning evacuation experience, 75% (51) stated that they had not experienced an evacuation exercise in the past 12 months. When asked if they had experienced a fire alarm in the library building 94% (29/31) stating that they had never experienced an alarm in the library. However, 71% (30/42) had stated that they had received specific instructions or training concerning evacuation procedures for the library. The majority of participants (50% (16/32)) identified that the training that they received was at the start of their course. Only 17% (11/68) of the participants had knowledge of only one exit, with 28% (19/68) knowing of more than four exits and so the majority of the participants had good familiarity with the building.

The participants were asked to rate their perceived risk of serious injury due to fire at several times during the evacuation process; when normally using the library, when they heard the alarm, when they decided to evacuate, during the evacuation process and when they exited the building. The perceived risk varied as shown in Table 7.1. Note the "heard alarm" category consists of only 40 people. There were only 23 people in the section of the library that heard the alarm. It is assumed that some of the participants who experienced the staff intervention understood the staff intervention to be the alarm and replied to this question however, the majority of the participants who were exposed to the staff intervention did not reply to this question. Normally, 47% of the population consider themselves to be at no risk due to fire when in the library. Surprisingly, this increased by 34% during the evacuation process and reached a maximum of 65% on exiting the library.

Table 7.1: Risk perception during the Czech library evacuation

	No Risk	Low Risk	Moderate Risk	High Risk	Number of people
Normally	47%	38%	12%	3%	68
Heard Alarm	57%	43%	–	–	40
Decided to Evacuate	57%	36%	8%	0%	67
During Evacuation	63%	31%	6%	0%	67
On Exit	65%	30%	5%	0%	63

Normally, the population consider the library to be a safe environment as 85% of the population consider that there is no or low risk of serious injury due to fire. Only 15% of the population consider themselves normally to be at Moderate (12%) or High (3%) risk of serious injury due to fire. During the evacuation process, the perception of risk of serious injury due to fire decreased.

Based on the video analysis at the time of the alarm, 71% of the entire population was working at a computer, 21% were engaged in other work related activities and 7% were engaged in other social activities. Thus 92% of the population was engaged in a work related activity at the time of the alarm with 71% engaged in computer activities.

Response times

Given the failure of the alarm system, there were two student populations for which the response time was determined. Population 1 (Pop1) consisted of the students who did not hear the alarm but responded to staff intervention – a total of 47 people. The second group, Population 2 (Pop2), consisted of the population who reacted to the sound of the alarm – a total of 23 people. For Pop1 the response time was determined from the point of staff intervention (first cue and start of the Notification Stage), to the point where the person began purposive movement towards an exit (end of Activity Stage and start of Evacuation Movement Phase). The response time distribution for Pop1 is presented in Fig. 7.10. As can be seen from Fig. 7.10, the response time distribution follows the typical log-normal profile, with over 48.9% of the population responding within 40 sec. The maximum response time for this population is in the range 80 to 100 sec (2.1% of the population).

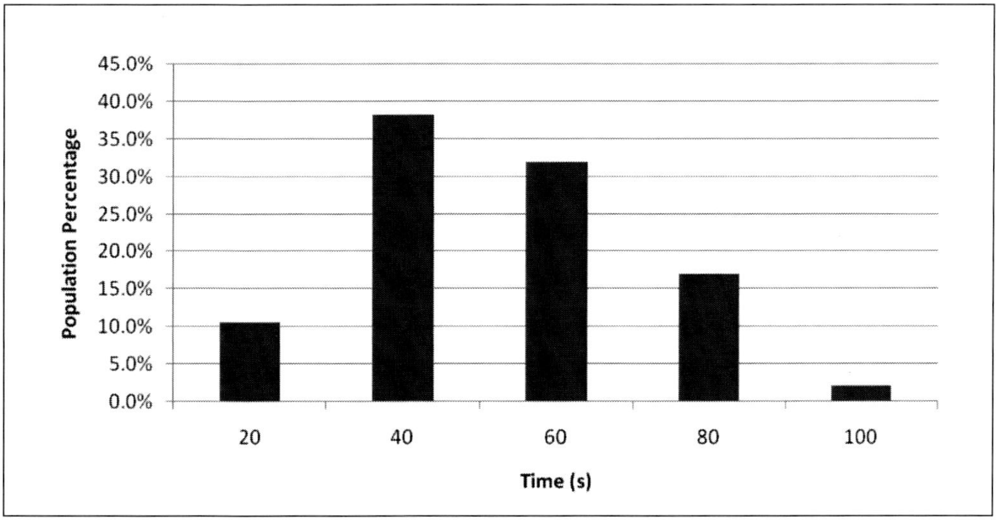

Fig. 7.10: Response time distribution for population notified by staff intervention (Pop1) Czech Library

For Pop2, as there were four different alarm sequences at t = 0 sec; 54 sec; 113 sec and 386 sec; it is possible to determine four different sets of response times, based on each individual notification cue. If we take the response time as being determined from the start of the first notification cue, i.e. the start of the first alarm, we find that the response times are considerably longer than that for the population that responded to staff intervention. The shortest response time is 150 sec while the longest response time is less than 490 sec. The shortest response times for this population are longer than the longest response times for Pop1. Furthermore, we note that it is not until the third alarm sequence has sounded do people end their Response Phase and begin their Evacuation Movement Phase. Indeed, the first people to start their Evacuation Movement Phase do so 39 sec after the third alarm sequence has sounded.

This extended response time may be the result of the nature of the alarm messages. The second alarm sequence (first voice message) informs the population that there is no need to evacuate at this point in time. It simply informs the population to prepare to evacuate. It is only at the sounding of the third alarm sequence (second live voice message) that the population is instructed to evacuate. It is also worth noting that 75% (51/68) of the student population that completed the questionnaire stated that they had received some form of fire safety training prior to the trial. However, only 2 (3%) of the respondents claimed that they had experienced an alarm previously in the building (a 1st year and a 4th year student); and 44% (30/68) of those who completed the questionnaire stated that they had received

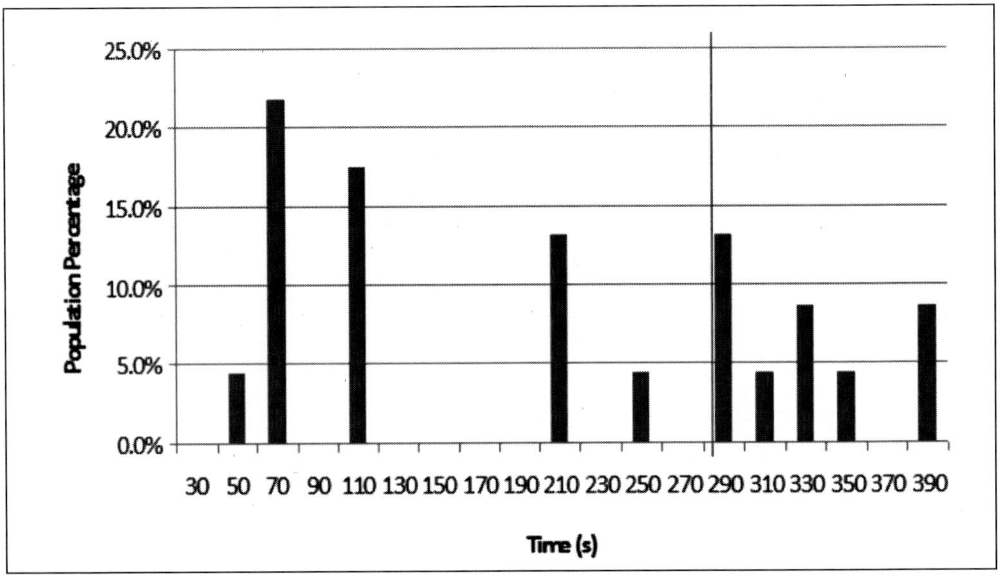

Fig. 7.11: Response time distribution for population notified by alarm system (Pop2) measured from the third alarm sequence (red line indicates sounding of the fourth alarm sequence) Czech Library

specific instructions or training concerning evacuation procedures for the library. Based on these statistics we may expect some 56% of the population did not know what to expect from the alarm system.

Presented in Fig. 7.11 are the response times as measured from the third alarm sequence. It is a similar distribution to that which is determined from the sounding of the first alarm sequence, but shifted 120 sec to the left. Also shown in Fig. 7.11 is an indication of when the fourth alarm sequence was sounded (vertical red line). As can be seen from Fig. 7.11, the response time distribution has an approximate log-normal like profile. Even though the fourth alarm occurs some 273 sec after the start of the third alarm, 39% (9) of the population respond only after the fourth alarm. In comparison to the population responding to staff notification, 34.8% (8) of the population responding to the alarm respond within 100 sec of the third alarm sequence.

The average response time for Pop1 is 43.3 sec while the average response time for Pop2 (measured from alarm 3) is 193.7 sec (measured from alarm 1, the average response time is 306.7 sec) and the average response time for the entire building population is 92.7 sec. Clearly the population responding to staff notification respond significantly faster (4.5 times faster) than the population responding to the alarm sequence only.

Presented in Fig. 7.12 is the response time distribution for the entire library. This comprises response times for Pop1, measured from the point of staff intervention and Pop2 measured from the sounding of the third alarm sequence. The long tail of

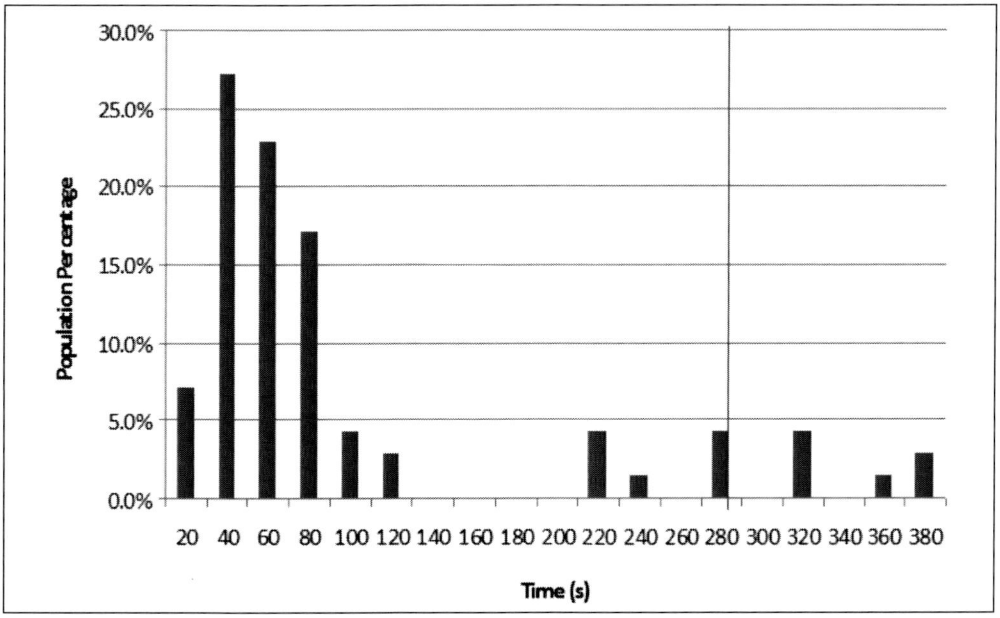

Fig. 7.12: Response time for entire library population (Czech)

this distribution is a result of the population responding to only the alarm sequence, with 100% (13/13) of the population with a response time greater than 120 sec being notified by the alarm sequence only while 84% (47/56) of the population responding in under 100 sec being notified by staff intervention only.

Fitting log-normal curves to the distributions for the overall population, the population reacting to the alarm (population 2) and the population reacting only to staff intervention produces the curves shown in Fig. 7.13 to Fig. 7.15. respectively. The equations describing these log-normal curves are:

$$y = \frac{1}{\sqrt{2\pi} * 0.91 * x} \exp(-\frac{(\ln x - 4.10)^2}{2 * 0.91^2}) \qquad -1-$$

$$y = \frac{1}{\sqrt{2\pi} * 0.73 * x} \exp(-\frac{(\ln x - 5.04)^2}{2 * 0.73^2}) \qquad -2-$$

The log-normal curve shown in Fig. 7.13 and equation 1 has a log mean of 4.1 s and a log standard deviation of 0.91 sec; for Fig. 7.14 and equation 2, the log mean is 5.04 and the log standard deviation is 0.73 sec while for Fig. 7.15 the log mean is 3.64 and the log standard deviation is 0.58 sec.

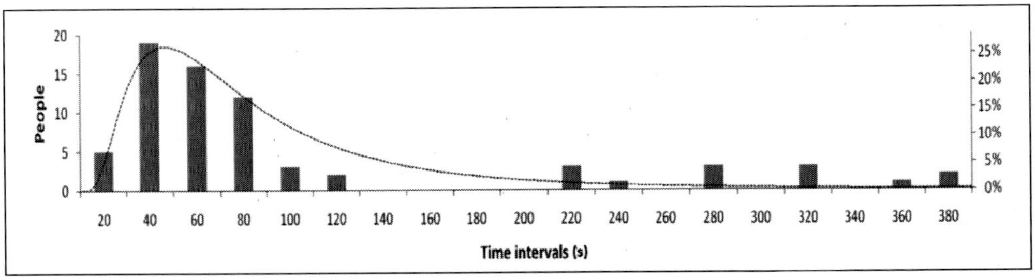

Fig. 7.13: Log-normal fit to the data for the entire Czech library population

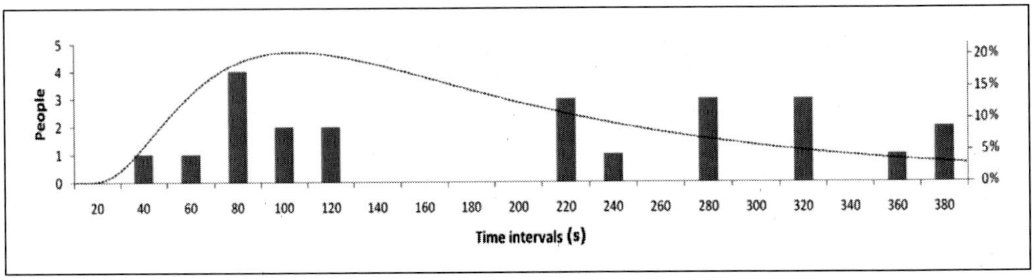

Fig. 7.14: Log-normal fit to the data for the Czech population reacting only to the alarm (Pop2)

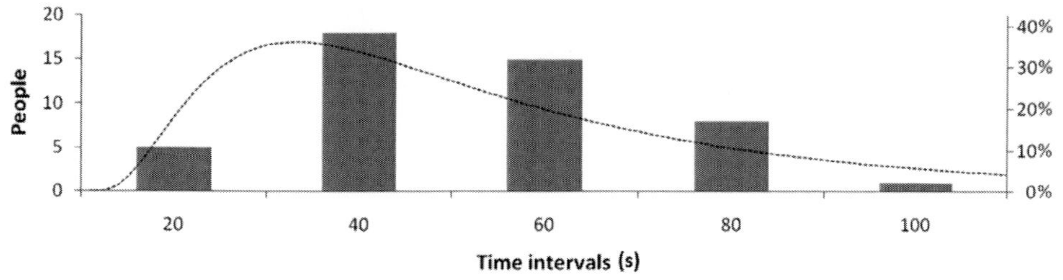

Fig. 7.15: Log-normal fit to the data for the Czech population reacting only to staff intervention (Pop1)

Response phase behaviour

Simply considering the overall response time does not provide insight into the nature of the Response Phase behaviours. To gain a better understanding of the factors contributing to the observed response time distributions it is necessary to decompose the Response Phase into the constitute stages as described in Section 7.4.2.

(a) Notification Stage:

If we consider the duration of the Notification stage for Pop1, we note that 63.8% (30) of the population have completed the Notification stage and disengaged from their pre-notification activities within 5 sec of the start of the notification cues. The longest Notification stage for Pop1 was 45 sec, achieved by 8.5% (4) of the population while the average duration of the Notification stage for Population 1 is 7.2 sec.

In contrast, the Notification stage for Pop2 was considerably longer. During alarm sequence 1 (0–54 sec), only 1 person disengaged from their pre-notification activities and this was after 14.2 sec, during alarm sequence 2 (54–113 sec) 10 persons disengaged after an average of 17.1 sec, during alarm sequence 3 (113–386 sec) 7 persons disengaged after an average of 224.1 sec and after alarm sequence 4 (386–466 sec) 2 persons disengaged after an average of 9.4 sec. Due to the complex nature of the alarm sequence it is difficult to determine a representative time to disengage from pre-notification activities for Population 2 however, the average duration of the Notification stage for Population 2 is 88.6 sec. Clearly, occupants exposed to just alarm notification cues take considerably longer to disengage from their pre-notification activities (12.3 times longer) than occupants exposed to staff intervention. The average duration of the Notification stage for the entire population is 31.5 sec.

The longer duration Notification stage for the population exposed to the alarm will tend to prolong the response time for these occupants compared to those exposed to staff intervention.

(b) Activity Stage:

The nature of the personal behaviours exhibited during the Activity stage can also be analyzed in detail. Presented in Fig. 7.16 is a distribution of the Action, Information and total number of tasks undertaken by the entire building population during the Activity stage. As can be seen, the number of Action, Information and total number of tasks each follow a log-normal distribution. This is an interesting observation and suggests that these distributions are significant in determining the response time distribution.

A total of 268 individual Action Tasks and 235 Information Tasks were identified during the Response Phase for the entire building population. The average number of Action Tasks undertaken is 4.3 while the average number of Information Tasks is 3.7. On average a person undertakes more Action than Information tasks and undertakes a total of 8.0 tasks prior to commencing the Evacuation Movement Phase.

For Pop1 (staff intervention) we find that the average number of Action Tasks is 3.6 while the average number of Information Tasks is 2.0, producing an average of 5.6 tasks performed prior to commencing the Evacuation Movement Phase. Furthermore, the maximum number of tasks performed was 9 Action Tasks, 6 Information Tasks and the maximum total number of tasks was 14. The most common combination of tasks was 3 Action and 2 Information and this combination

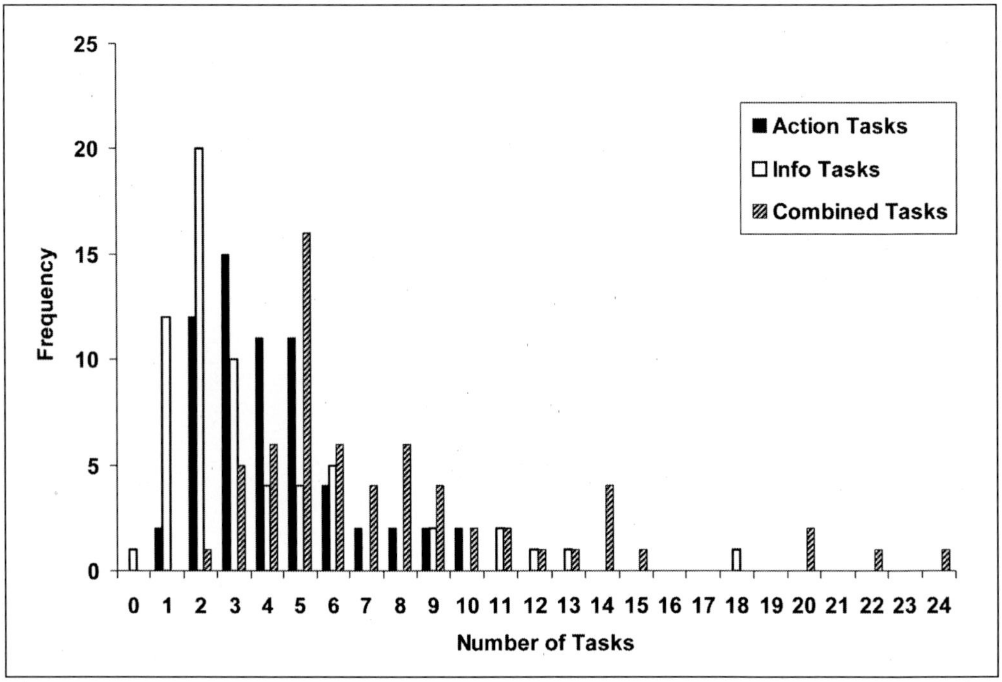

Fig. 7.16: Number of Tasks undertaken for entire population in the Czech library

was completed by 10 people. The most common number of Action Tasks was 3 performed by 13 people and the most common number of Information Tasks was 2 performed by 17 people. In addition, the most common Information Tasks, as a percentage of the total number of Information Tasks were, "Acquire information from the environment (looking, listening)" 81% and "Engage in information exchange" 16.8%. The most common Action tasks, as a percentage of the total number of Action tasks were "Collect Belongings" 23% of the Action tasks; "Shut down computer" 17.4%; "Work at computer" 16.8% and "Collect clothing" 15.5%.

For Pop2 (alarm) we find that the average number of Action Tasks is 5.7 while the average number of Information Tasks is 7.4, producing an average of 13.1 tasks performed prior to commencing the Evacuation Movement Phase. Furthermore, the maximum number of tasks performed was 10 Action Tasks, 18 Information Tasks and the maximum total number of tasks was 24. The most common combination of tasks was 8 Action and 6 Information and this combination was completed by 2 people. The most common number of Action Tasks was 4 and 5 performed by 4 people each and the most common number of Information Tasks was 4 performed by 3 people. In addition, the most common Information Tasks were, "Acquire information from the environment (looking, listening)" 64% and "Engage in information exchange" 34%. The most common Action Tasks were; "Pickup bag" 34%, "Collect Belongings" 24.5%; "Collect clothing" 11.3% and "Shut down computer" 10.4%.

Once a person is notified of the need to evacuate by a member of staff, they undertake an average of 5.6 tasks prior to commencing their evacuation movement phase, compared to an average of 13.1 tasks for a person notified by the alarm system. Here we see that someone notified by the alarm undertakes more than twice as many tasks prior to starting to evacuate compared to someone who is notified by a member of staff. The greater number of tasks performed by the population exposed to the alarm will tend to prolong the response time for these occupants compared to those exposed to staff intervention. Furthermore, the maximum number of tasks undertaken by someone reacting to the alarm was 24 tasks while the maximum number of tasks for someone reacting to staff intervention is 14. Thus we note that not only will the average time for those reacting to the alarm be longer than the average time for those reacting to staff intervention, the maximum response times for those reacting to the alarm will be significantly longer than that for those reacting to staff intervention.

If we further consider the type of tasks that are being undertaken, we again see a significant difference between the two populations. For those reacting to staff intervention, the average number of Action Tasks is 3.6 while the average number of Information Tasks is 2.0. For the group reacting to the alarm, the average number of Action Tasks is 5.7 and the average number of Information Tasks is 7.4. Thus, those reacting to the alarm undertake 3.7 times as many Information Tasks and 1.6 times as many Action Tasks as those reacting to staff intervention. Those reacting to staff intervention spend less time seeking confirmation or clarification information; i.e. undertake less Information Tasks than those who have been notified by the alarm system. This is further supported by noting that significantly fewer Information Exchange tasks were performed by the population reacting to staff intervention compared with the population reacting to the alarm. In addition, those reacting to staff intervention also undertake less Action tasks (such as packing up belongings) than those reacting to the alarm system.

Finally, we note that those reacting to staff intervention undertake fewer Information Tasks than Action Tasks while those reacting to the alarm undertake more Information Tasks than Action Tasks. Furthermore, those responding to the alarm undertake proportionally more Information tasks (3.7x) than Action tasks (1.6x) compared to those reacting to staff intervention.

The time to undertake each individual task can be determined from the video footage. However, it is difficult to reliably measure short duration activities when there is uncertainty in the start and end points of the activity. To increase the reliability of the measurement, the duration of only multiple tasks of the same type were measured. Thus, measurements were made for sequences of tasks in which at least two tasks of the same type were undertaken consecutively. Using this approach the duration for a total of 89 Action Tasks and 114 Information Tasks were measured.

The average duration of a single Action Task was determined to be 6.4 sec while the average duration of an Information Task was determined to be 9.7 sec. Thus, on average, an Information Task takes 1.5 times as long as an Action Task. This is a significant result as it indicates that undertaking many Information Tasks during the Response Phase can severely prolong the response time.

The average duration of Action and Information Tasks can be further broken down to compare the average time for the different populations. For Pop1, the average time for an Action Task (based on 27 tasks) was 6.5 sec while the average time for an Information Task was 6.7 sec (based on 8 tasks). This compares with 6.4 sec (based on 62 tasks) for an Action Task and 9.9 sec (based on 106 tasks) for an Information Task for Pop2. While the average duration of an Action Task is virtually identical for both populations, there is a considerable difference in the average time to complete an Information Task. For the population alerted by the alarm, not only is it necessary to perform more Information Tasks, the duration of these tasks is also longer compared with the population alerted through staff intervention.

(c) Discussion:

For the population as a whole, 92% were engaged in a work related activity at the time of the alarm with 71% engaged in computer activities. 94% of the population had never heard the alarm in the building or evacuated from the building prior to this evacuation trial. On hearing the alarm, 100% of the population thought they were in no risk or low risk of serious injury.

From the questionnaire, on hearing the alarm, 36% (14/39) thought the alarm was a false alarm, 54% (21/39) thought it was a drill and 3% (1/39) thought it was a real fire. As 90% of the participants thought that the alarm was either false or a drill may explain why the perception of risk did not increase when the alarm sounded (see Table 7.1). The population suggested that the cue that caused them to start to evacuate was; seeing others evacuating 31% (23/75), the alarm 19% (14/75) and seeing fire wardens 18% (13/75). The low number responding to the alarm may be due to the majority of the population (i.e. Pop1) not hearing the alarm.

When asked in the questionnaire what was the first thing that they did on realizing that they had to evacuate, 28% (19/68) of the population noted that they did nothing or re-engaged in their previous activities and 21% (14/68) waited for instructions. As almost half the population (49%) did nothing or re-engaged in their previous activities or waited for instructions, this may partially explain the long response times noted for this population (at least for Pop2). Furthermore, the high percentage of people waiting for instructions may be a result of the nature of the alarm (alarm sequence 2). The relatively small number of participants who reported that they started packing their belongings 27% (18/68) in preparation to evacuate and the small number who started to evacuate immediately, 13% (9/68) also contribute to the long response time, at least for Pop2.

Due to the alarm system malfunction, two separate populations were noted in the Czech library evacuation trial, a population responding to staff intervention only (Pop1) and a population responding to a voice alarm system (Pop2). This provides an opportunity to contrast the effectiveness of these two different notification methods. It is noted that the average response time for Pop1 was 43 sec while the average response time for the Pop2 was 194 sec. using the Response Phase Behavioural framework (see Section 7.4.2) the differences in the behaviour of the two populations can be further characterized.

Average Notification Time:
- Pop1 – 7.2 sec; Pop2 – 88.6 sec
- Clearly, occupants exposed to just alarm notification cues take considerably longer to disengage from their pre-notification activities (12.3 times longer) than occupants exposed to staff intervention. This tends to prolong the response time for those exposed to the alarm only cues, while ensuring that those exposed to staff intervention will react relatively quickly.

Average Total Number of Tasks:
- Pop1 – 5.6; Pop2 – 13.1
- Occupants exposed to just the alarm notification undertake more than twice as many tasks prior to starting to evacuate compared to someone who is notified by a member of staff. The greater number of tasks performed by the population exposed to the alarm will tend to prolong the response time for these occupants compared to those exposed to staff intervention.

Average Number of Action and Info Tasks:
- Pop1: 3.6 and 2.0; Pop2: 5.7 and 7.4

- Occupants exposed to just the alarm notification undertake more Action Tasks (1.6x) and more Information Tasks (3.7x) than those exposed to staff intervention. Furthermore, the "alarm only population" undertakes more Information than Action Tasks, while the "staff notification only population" undertakes more Action than Information Tasks. The population exposed just to the alarm requires further confirmation from their environment and peers prior to commencing their evacuation process.

Average Duration of Action and Info Tasks:

- Pop1: 6.4 and 6.7 sec; Pop2: 6.4 and 9.9 sec
- Occupants exposed to just the alarm notification take longer in information exchange (1.5x) and the same amount of time to undertake an action. Not only does the alarm only population undertake more Information Tasks than the staff intervention population, they take longer to undertake the information exchange.

Thus compared to the staff intervention population, the alarm only population take; longer to disengage from their pre-alarm activities (12.3x), undertake more tasks (2.3x), undertake significantly more Information Tasks (3.7x) and take longer in information exchange (1.5x). All of this explains why the alarm only population has an average response time 4.5x greater than the staff intervention population.

The results for the Czech population confirm the commonly held belief that relative response times for populations exposed to staff intervention will be shorter than those exposed to an alarm only. However, it must be noted that the response times reported here do not include the time required for the staff member to respond to the alarm and travel to the population location. If these times are taken into consideration, the absolute response time for the population exposed to staff intervention may be greater than that for the population exposed only to the alarm. However, it is still valid that staff intervention may greater reduce the response time of a population compared to a population reacting simply to an alarm.

Predictive response time model

Using the Ostrava trial information and the Response Phase Framework, it is possible to postulate an empirical predictive model for the average response time. The average response time for a population can be predicted using the following equation.

$$RT = [NT + (NAT * ATT) + (NIT * ITT)] - [W * X * FOL_{max} * ATT] + [Y * Z * TNT * (ATT + ITT)/2] \quad -3-$$

Where: RT = Average Response Time (sec); NT = Average Notification Time (sec); NAT = Average Number of Action Tasks; NIT = Average Number of Information Tasks; TNT = Average Total number of tasks; ATT = Average Action Task time (sec); ITT = Average Information Task time (sec); FOL_{max} = Maximum number of overlapping tasks; W, X, Y and Z are constants.

As the Notification and Activity stages occur sequentially, as a first approximation, the average response time is simply the sum of the average notification time and the average time to undertake the average number of Information and Action Tasks; i.e. the first three terms in equation 3.

The fourth and fifth terms are factors that correct for the simplistic assumption of the strictly additive nature of these terms. The fourth term is a correction factor that takes into consideration that a proportion of Action Tasks can be performed simultaneously with Information Tasks thereby reducing the predicting average response time. The maximum number of overlapping tasks is dependent on the relative number of Action and Information Tasks and is given by:

$$FOL_{max} = NIT \text{ if } NAT \geq NIT$$
$$FOL_{max} = NAT \text{ if } NAT < NIT \quad -4-$$

In equation 3, the constant W is a measure of the likelihood of overlapping tasks occurring. It is difficult to estimate a value for this constant, but from observation of the Czech library video footage it is estimated to be 25% (W = 0.25); i.e. 25% of the Action tasks overlap with Information tasks. The duration of overlap is dependent on the length of time of the Action task (ATT) and the degree of overlap (X%, where X represents the percentage of overlap between the Action and Information Tasks). For the current situation, video observation suggests that the most appropriate degree of overlap is 100% (X = 1.0); i.e. that the Action task totally overlaps the Information task.

The fifth term is another correction factor that takes into account brief periods during the Activity stage where no task is undertaken. This is assumed to be when the occupant is considering their next course of action and so represents a brief Cognitive stage or cognition pause. In this case the Cognitive stage does not occur in parallel to the Activity stage but in sequence to it. To compensate for this a small portion of time, representing the cognition pause, is added to the total response time. Cognition pauses can occur following each of the TNT tasks. However, they are observed to occur significantly less frequently than this, and the proportion of tasks that are followed by a cognition pause is represented by a constant Y. From analysis of the Czech library video footage, it is suggested that cognition pauses occur approximately 25% of the time (Y = 0.25). The duration of the cognition pause is also difficult to estimate as it is variable and context specific. In most cases the cognition pause is a very brief period of time, while in some cases it can be relatively long. Here it is assumed to be a multiple Z of the average time for Action and Information Tasks and we take an overall representative value of Z to be 20% (Z = 0.2).

It should be noted that the constants W, X, Y and Z may be dependent on the nature of the notification process; e.g. staff intervention and the type of structure e.g. library. It is possible that there is also a cultural component to each of these constants. Using the assumed values for these constants, equation 3 simplifies to:

$$RT = [NT + (NAT * ATT) + (NIT * ITT)] - [0.25 * FOL_{max} * ATT] + [0.05 * TNT * (ATT + ITT)/2] \quad -5-$$

It must be emphasized that while equation 3 is quite general, equation 5 is considered specific to library structures, and possibly just to the Czech library, as the constants have been derived from data from the Czech library evacuation.

Predictive response time model applied to Czech library

Using equation 5 it is possible to estimate the response time for the two populations in the Czech library evacuation trial.

For Population 1 (staff intervention), we have the following average values for each parameter:

$NT_S = 7.2$ sec, $NAT_S = 3.6$, $NIT_S = 2.0$, $ATT_S = 6.5$ sec, $ITT_S = 6.7$ sec.

While for Population 2 (alarm intervention), we have the following average values for each parameter:

$NT_A = 88.8$ sec, $NAT_A = 5.7$, $NIT_A = 7.4$, $ATT_A = 6.4$ sec, $ITT_A = 9.9$ sec.

Using the above values in equation 5 we determine the average response times as follows:

$RT_S = 42.6$ sec and $RT_A = 194.8$ sec.

Taking the library as a whole, we have the following average values for each parameter:

NT = 31.5 sec, NAT = 4.3, NIT = 3.7, ATT = 6.4 sec, ITT = 9.7 sec.

Using the above values in equation 5 we determine the average response times as follows:

RT = 92.2 sec.

Using equation 5 the average response time for Population 1 is under-predicted by 1.6% while the average response time for Population 2 is over-predicted by 0.6%. The measured average response time for Population 2 was 4.6 times as large as the measured average response time for Population 1. Based on the predictive model, the average response time for Population 2 is also 4.5 times as large as that for Population 1. The average response time for the entire population is under-predicted by 0.5%.

As can be seen, this approach provides a very good estimation of the average response times for both populations and the overall population. However, more important than this, it provides us with insight into the behavioural factors driving the response time. Thus it is possible to estimate the impact of introducing technical or procedural measures to address various behavioural determinants of response time such as the duration of the average information task, or the number of information tasks. For example, if the population could be trained so that when notified of the need to evacuate, the population undertook no Action Tasks (NAT = 0, ATT = 0 sec), the average response time for Population 1 (staff notification) could be reduced by 50%. In contrast, if an emergency information system was developed that could efficiently convey the urgency of the need to evacuate to the population and if the population was well trained to respond to the alarm message, this may remove the need to undertake any Information Tasks (NIT = 0, ITT = 0 sec). This would result in at least a 34% reduction in the average response time for the overall population. Corrective measures may also have an impact on more than one of the determinants, for example training the population to react appropriately to the alarm may not only reduce the number of Action and Information Tasks undertaken, but may also reduce the Notification time.

7.6.2 Turkey: Izmir Institute of Technology

Alarm sequence

Unlike in the Czech evacuation trial, the alarm functioned as expected. In addition, there was no staff interaction with the students and so the students only reacted to the alarm. As a result there is only one group of response behaviours to be considered.

Population characteristics

A total of 111 questionnaires were given out and 87 were returned and of these 73 respondents were identified as students. From the questionnaire, 55% (40) of the student population was male, 45% (33) were female and 97% (71) were in the age range 18–24 and 3% (2) were in the age range 25-34. Furthermore, 44% (32) were in the first year of study at the University; 21% (15) were in the second year; 4% (3) were in the third year; 32% (23) were in the fourth or more year of study at the University.

From those who provided an indication of their location at the time of the alarm, 43 were located on the ground floor and 15 on the first floor. According to the video analysis, there were 120 people in the library, including library staff, cleaners and students. In total there were 106 students within the library, 56 on the ground floor, 30 on the first floor and 20 students for which their initial location is unknown. Of the 106 students, it was possible to determine response time and response behaviours for 51 students, 35 on the ground floor and 16 on the first floor.

Concerning evacuation experience, 93% (68) stated that they had not experienced an evacuation exercise in the past 12 months and had never experienced an alarm in the library. Furthermore, 94% (67/71) had stated that they had never received specific instructions or training concerning evacuation procedures for the library. The library had only one exit to the outside, the emergency exit being locked. Furthermore, there were several exits leading to the internal courtyard, but these exits did not lead to a place of safety outside the building. It is noted that 80% of the population (51/64) of the participants made regular use of one exit. It is assumed that the population had good familiarity of the structure, but it is unknown how many people knew of the emergency exit, as the exit was not used as an emergency exit.

The participants were asked to rate their perceived risk of serious injury due to fire at several times during the evacuation process; when normally using the library, when they heard the alarm, when they decided to evacuate, during the evacuation process and when they exited the building. The perceived risk varied as shown in Table 7.2. Normally, 35% of the population consider themselves to be at no risk due to fire when in the library. Surprisingly, this increased by 26% during the evacuation process and reached 43% on exiting the library. Normally, the population considers the library to be a safe environment as 82% of the population considers that there is no (35%) or low risk (47%) of serious injury due to fire. Only 18% of the population consider themselves to be normally at Moderate (17%) or High (1%) risk of serious injury due to fire. During the evacuation process, the perception of risk of serious injury due to fire decreased.

Based on the video analysis at the time of the alarm, 49% of the entire population was working at a computer, 18% were engaged in other social activities, 12% were sitting and 8% were walking and 8% were engaged in other work related activities. Thus 57% of the population was engaged in a work related activity at the time of the alarm with 49% engaged in computer activities.

Table 7.2: Risk perception during the Turkish library evacuat

	No Risk	Low Risk	Moderate Risk	High Risk	Number of people
Normally	35%	47%	17%	1%	71
Heard Alarm	37%	46%	16%	2%	68
Decided to Evacuate	40%	45%	15%	0%	65
During Evacuation	44%	44%	13%	0%	64
On Exit	43%	43%	14%	0%	56

Response times

The response time is determined from the start of the alarm (first cue and start of the Notification Stage), to the point where the person began purposive movement towards an exit (end of Activity Stage and start of Evacuation Movement Phase). The response time distribution for the population is presented in Fig. 7.17. As can be seen from Fig. 7.17, the response time distribution approximately follows a log-normal profile, with 49% of the population responding within 40 sec, 90% of the population responding within 100 sec and 92% of the population responding within 150 sec.

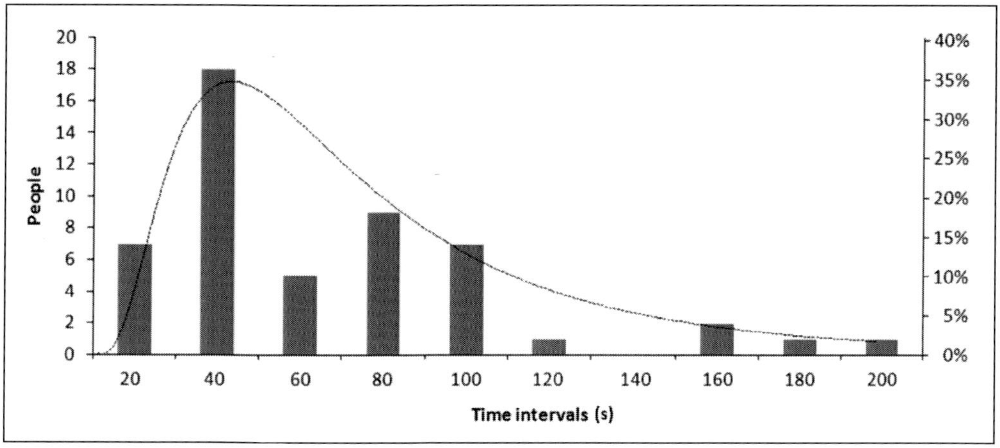

Fig. 7.17: Response time distribution for student population

The average response time extracted from the 51 analyzed people was 56.1 sec, and ranged from 11 sec to 181 sec. The log-normal curve shown in Fig. 7.17 has a log mean of 3.78 and a log standard deviation of 0.72.

Response phase behaviour

Simply considering the overall response time does not provide insight into the nature of the Response Phase behaviours. To gain a better understanding of the factors contributing to the observed response time distributions it is necessary to decompose the Response Phase into the constitute stages as described in Section 7.4.2.

(a) Notification Stage:

If we consider the duration of the Notification stage we note that 61.2% (30 people) of the population have completed the Notification stage and disengaged from their pre-notification activities within 5 sec of the start of the notification cues. The longest Notification stage was 56.2 sec, achieved by 2% (1 person) of the population while the average duration of the Notification stage is 10.0 sec.

We note from the questionnaire that 96% (70/73) noted that they heard the alarm at the start of the evacuation and 82% (56/68) reported that they understood what the alarm signified. The high recognition of the alarm may have resulted in the short average Notification time for the population. The average Notification time is only marginally longer than that for the staff notification population in the Czech trial and the percentage of the population reacting within 5 sec is comparable to that of the Czech trail.

(b) Activity Stage:

The nature of the personal behaviours exhibited during the Activity stage can also be analyzed in detail. Presented in Fig. 7.19 is a distribution of the Action, Information and total number of tasks undertaken by the entire building population during the Activity stage. As can be seen, as with the results from the Czech trial (see Fig. 7.19) the number of Action, Information and Total number of tasks each follow a log-normal distribution.

A total of 429 tasks were identified during the Response Phase for the entire building population, 174 individual Action Tasks (AT) and 255 Information Tasks (IT). The average number of AT undertaken is 3.5 while the average number of IT is 5.1. On average a person undertakes more IT than AT and undertakes a total of 8.6 tasks prior to commencing the Evacuation Movement Phase.

The most common combination of tasks was 3 ATs and 3 ITs and this combination was completed by four people. The most common number of ATs was 1 and 4 performed by 10 people and the most common number of ITs was 3 performed by 10 people. The maximum number of tasks performed by a single person was 23 tasks (made from a combination of ATs and ITs), while the maximum number of ATs performed by a single person was 13 and the maximum number of ITs performed by a single person was 12. In addition, the most common ITs, expressed as a percentage of the total number of ITs were; "Acquire information from the environment (looking, listening)" 63%, and "Engage in information exchange" 27%. The most common ATs, expressed as a percentage of the total number of ATs were "Collect Belongings" 29%, "Pick up bag" 24%, "Shut down computer" 9% and "Work at computer" 6%.

The time to undertake each individual type of task can be determined from the video footage. In order to reduce the error associated with this measurement, it is based on the duration of multiple tasks of the same type were measured. Thus, measurements were made for sequences of tasks in which at least two tasks of the same type were undertaken consecutively and which followed on immediately from the previous task. Using this approach the duration of 92 ATs and 170 ITs were measured. The average duration of a single AT was determined to be 5.2 sec while the average duration of an IT was determined to be 4.7 sec. Thus, on average, for this population ATs take approximately 10% longer than ITs.

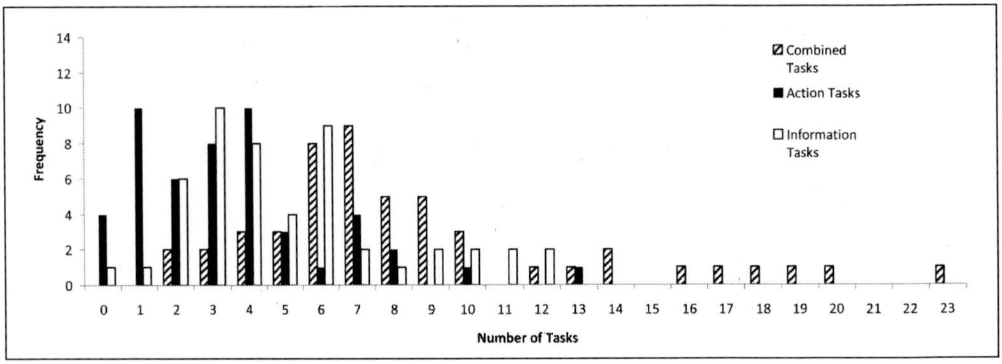

Fig. 7.18: Number and type of tasks undertaken by the library population (Turkey)

(c) Discussion:

For the population as a whole, 57% were engaged in a work related activity at the time of the alarm with 49% engaged in computer activities. 93% of the population had never heard the alarm in the building or evacuated from the building prior to this evacuation trial. On hearing the alarm, 83% of the population thought they were in no risk or low risk of serious injury.

From the questionnaire, on hearing the alarm, 24% (16/68) thought the alarm was a false alarm, 66% (45/68) thought it was a drill and 10% (7/68) thought it was a real fire. As 90% of the participants thought that the alarm was either false or a drill may explain why the perception of risk did not increase when the alarm sounded. On hearing the alarm, 60% (56/94) claimed that the alarm caused them to start to evacuate, while 17% (16/94) claimed that seeing others evacuating caused them to start to evacuate. On realizing that they had to evacuate, the first action that people did was to, collect belongings 46% (32/69), immediately started to leave 19% (13/69), do nothing 9% (6/69) and look for friends 7% (5/69). The relatively small number of Action Tasks undertaken by the population and the relatively small average response time for the Turkish population may be explained by the relatively low number of people who started collecting their belongings in preparation to evacuate and the relatively high number of people who left immediately.

When first alerted by the alarm about half the population (53% or 36/68) were in groups of friends, 34% (23/68) were alone and 13% (9/68) were in groups of strangers. About half the population (52% (35/68)) evacuated as individuals, with 44% (30/68) in groups of friends and only a small number evacuating in groups of strangers 4% (3/68). Of those who started the evacuation in a group, 55% (18/33) exited the building with the group intact.

Of those that were alone prior to the alarm, 91% (21/23) evacuated alone, of those who started in groups of friends, 19% (7/36) evacuated alone while those who started in groups of strangers, 78% (7/9) evacuated alone. Furthermore, if you were in a group of friends during the evacuation, you did not exit the building alone (0% (0/30)), and you were 97% (29/30) likely to exit with all (57% (17/30)) or some (40% (12/30)) of your group members. There was a small chance that you exited with more people in our group, 3% (1/30). Thus if you were in a group of friends prior to the alarm, it was likely that you evacuated in a group and that you exited in a group whereas if you were in a group of strangers, it is likely that you separated from the group and evacuated alone. Thus the bond between groups of friends is seen to be much stronger than the group bond between strangers during the evacuation. Furthermore, if you were alone prior to the alarm, you were very likely to evacuate alone.

Predictive response time model applied to the data from the Izmir Institute of Technology library

Using equation 3 it is possible to estimate the response time for the Izmir library evacuation trial. The constants W, X, Y and Z in equation 3 were determined from analysis of the video footage derived from the Czech Republic evacuation trial. The same values for the constants are used in this analysis. It should be noted that the constants W, X, Y and Z may be dependent on the nature of the notification process; e.g. voice alarm and the type of environment e.g. library. It is also noted that it may be possible that there is a cultural component to each of these constants.

In this assessment, we will investigate if the constant values derived from one library evacuation can be applied to an evacuation in a different library. Using equation 5, it is possible to estimate the response time for the population. Based on the data derived from Turkish evacuation trial, we have the following average values for each parameter.

NT = 9.98 sec, NAT = 3.48, NIT = 5.10, TNT = 8.58, ATT = 5.18 sec, ITT = 4.74 sec, FOL_{max} = NAT

Using equation 5 and the above values for the various parameters, the average response time for the population is RT = 49.8 sec.

The measured average response time for the population was 56.1 sec. Thus using the empirical response time model, the average response time is under-predicted by 11.3%. As can be seen, the empirical response time model provides a good estimation of the average response time for the population. From the earlier analysis of the evacuation trial in the Czech Republic, the empirical response time model produced average response times which were within 1.6% of the measured average response time for that population. Thus the constants used in the empirical response time model appear to be reasonably robust, providing a good level of agreement for two evacuation trials conducted in two different libraries in two different countries.

7.6.3 Poland: University of Warsaw Library

Alarm sequence

Unlike in the Czech evacuation trial, the alarm functioned as expected. In addition, there was no staff interaction with the students during the response phase and so the students only reacted to the alarm. As a result there is only one group of response behaviours to be considered.

Population characteristics

A total of 360 questionnaires were given out and 238 were returned and of these 131 respondents were identified as students. From the questionnaire, 66% (87) of the student population was male, 34% (44) were female and 89% (117) were in the age range 18-24 and 10% (13) were in the age range 25-34. Furthermore, 23% (30) were in the first year of study at the University; 26% (34) were in the second year; 22% (29) were in the third year; 29% (38) were in the fourth or more year of study at the University.

According to the video analysis, there were 710 people in the library, including library staff and students. Of the 710 people in the library, it was possible to determine response time and response behaviours for 192 students, 89 males and 103 females. These students were located as follows: 2 on the entrance stairs, 63 on Level 1 (ground floor), 124 on Level 2 and 3 on Level 3.

Concerning evacuation experience, 94% (123) stated that they had not experienced an evacuation exercise in the past 12 months and 94% (118/124) had never experienced an alarm in the library. Furthermore, 71% (89/125) had stated that they had never received specific instructions or training concerning evacuation procedures for the library, of those that had, 68% (26/38) stated that this consisted of a lecture at the start of their course. The library had only one main exit and six emergency exits accessible to the students.

The participants were asked to rate their perceived risk of serious injury due to fire at several times during the evacuation process; when normally using the library, when they heard the alarm, when they decided to evacuate, during the evacuation process and when they exited the building. The perceived risk varied as shown in Table 7.3. Normally, 17% of the population consider themselves to be at no risk due to fire when in the library. Surprisingly, this increased by 153% during the evacuation process and reached 65% on exiting the library. Normally, the population considers the library to be a reasonably safe environment as 61% of the population considers that there is no (17%) or low risk (44%) of serious injury due to fire. However, a significant 41% of the population consider themselves to be normally at Moderate (30%) or High (11%) risk of serious injury due to fire. During the evacuation process, the perception of risk of serious injury due to fire decreased.

Based on the video analysis at the time of the alarm, 26% of the entire population was working at a computer and 64% were engaged in other work related activities. The remainder of the population was engaged in a variety of activities such as sitting, walking, sleeping, etc. Thus 90% of the population was engaged in a work related activity at the time of the alarm with 26% engaged in computer activities.

Table 7.3: Risk perception during the Polish library evacua

	No Risk	**Low Risk**	**Moderate Risk**	**High Risk**	**Number of people**
Normally	17%	44%	30%	11%	116
Heard Alarm	33%	55%	10%	2%	107
Decided to Evacuate	35%	48%	14%	3%	122
During Evacuation	43%	42%	13%	3%	119
On Exit	65%	25%	9%	1%	110

Response times

The response time is determined from the start of the alarm (first cue and start of the Notification Stage), to the point where the person began purposive movement towards an exit (end of Activity Stage and start of Evacuation Movement Phase). The response time distribution for the population is presented in Fig. 7.19. As can be seen from Fig. 7.19, the response time distribution approximately follows a log-normal profile, with 21% of the population responding within 40 sec, 83% of the population responding within 100 sec and 96% of the population responding within 150 sec.

The average response time extracted from the 192 analyzed people was 69.9 sec, and ranged from 0.1 sec to 177.6 sec. The log-normal curve shown in Fig. 7.19 has a log mean of 4.06 and a log standard deviation of 0.77.

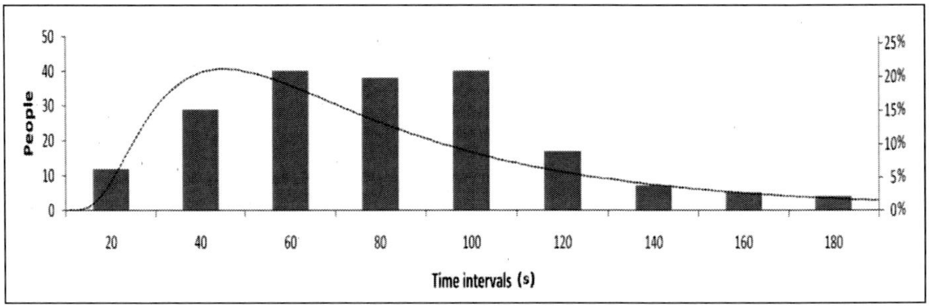

Fig. 7.19: Response time distribution for Polish library evacuation

Response phase behaviour

Simply considering the overall response time does not provide insight into the nature of the Response Phase behaviours. To gain a better understanding of the factors contributing to the observed response time distributions it is necessary to decompose the Response Phase into the constitute stages as described in Section 7.4.2.

(a) Notification Stage:

If we consider the duration of the Notification stage we note that 39% (74 people) of the population have completed the Notification stage and disengaged from their pre-notification activities within 5 sec of the start of the notification cues while 71.9% (138 people) disengaged within 10 sec. The longest Notification stage was 82.5 sec, achieved by 0.5% (1 person) of the population while the average duration of the Notification stage is 8.3 sec.

We note from the questionnaire that 83% (105/126) noted that they heard the alarm at the start of the evacuation and 85% (91/107) reported that they understood what the alarm signified. The high recognition of the alarm may have resulted in the short average Notification time for the population. The average Notification time is only marginally longer than that for the staff notification population in the Czech trial and the percentage of the population reacting within 5 sec is comparable to that of the Czech trail.

(b) Activity Stage:

The nature of the personal behaviours exhibited during the Activity stage can also be analyzed in detail. Presented in Fig. 7.20 is a distribution of the Action, Information and total number of tasks undertaken by the entire building population during the Activity stage. As can be seen, the number of Information Tasks follows a broadly log-normal distribution. The number of Action tasks appear to follow more of a standard normal distribution while the distribution of the combined tasks is less clear, perhaps that of a shallow normal distribution.

A total of 1906 tasks were identified during the Response Phase for the entire building population, 1167 individual Action Tasks (AT) and 739 Information Tasks (IT). The average number of AT undertaken is 6.1 while the average number of IT is 3.8. On average a person undertakes more AT than IT and undertakes a total of 9.9 tasks prior to commencing the Evacuation Movement Phase.

The most common combination of tasks was 4 ATs and 2 ITs and this combination was completed by 12 people. The most common number of ATs was 4 performed by 25 people and the most common number of ITs was 2 performed by 34 people. The maximum number of tasks performed by a single person was 20 tasks (made up from a combination of ATs and ITs), while the maximum number of ATs performed by a single person was 13 and the maximum number of ITs performed by a single person was 10. In addition, the most common ITs, expressed as a percentage of the total number of ITs were; "Acquire information from the environment (looking, listening)" 76%, and "Engage in information exchange" 22%. The most common ATs, expressed as a percentage of the total number of ATs

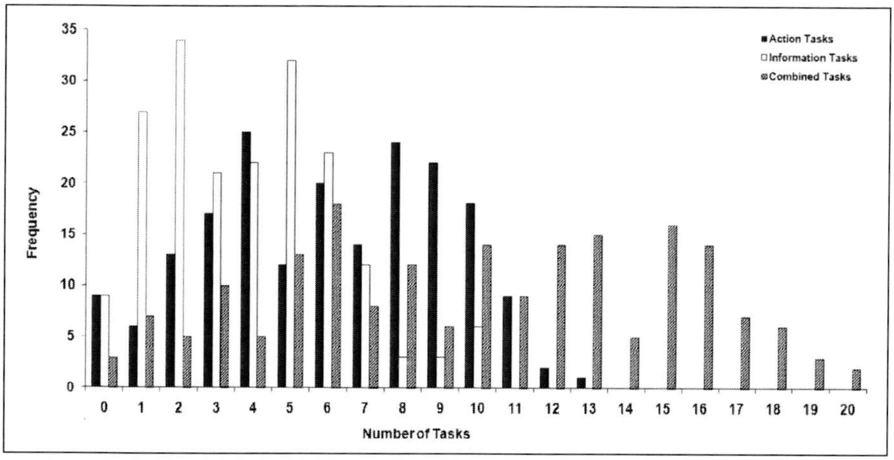

Fig. 7.20: Number and type of tasks undertaken by the library population (Poland)

were "Collect Belongings" 48%, "Pick up bag" 23%, "Pickup, throw away rubbish, tidy area" 7% and "Work at computer" 5%.

The time to undertake each individual task can be determined from the video footage. In order to reduce the error associated with this measurement, it is based on the duration of multiple tasks of the same type were measured.

Thus, measurements were made for sequences of tasks in which at least two tasks of the same type were undertaken consecutively and which followed on immediately from the previous task. Using this approach the duration of 834 ATs and 149 ITs were measured. The average duration of a single AT was determined to be 6.4 sec while the average duration of an IT was determined to be 6.1 sec. Thus, on average, for this population ATs take approximately 5% longer than ITs. This result spans 279 AT sequences and 57 IT sequences).

(c) Discussion:

For the population as a whole, 90% were engaged in a work related activity at the time of the alarm with 26% engaged in computer activities. 94% of the population had never heard the alarm in the building or evacuated from the building prior to this evacuation trial. On hearing the alarm, 88% of the population thought they were in no risk or low risk of serious injury.

From the questionnaire, on hearing the alarm, 6% (7/109) thought the alarm was a false alarm, 62% (67/109) thought it was a drill and 28% (31/109) thought it was a real fire. As 41% of the library population consider themselves to normally be at moderate or high risk of serious injury in the library, this may explain why over a quarter of the library population (28%) thought that the alarm signified a real fire.

On hearing the alarm, 63% (94/149) claimed that the alarm caused them to start to evacuate, while 18% (27/149) claimed that seeing others evacuating caused them to start to evacuate. On realizing that they had to evacuate, the first action that people did was to, collect belongings 73% (89/122), immediately started to leave 16% (19/122) and do nothing 5% (6/122). The relatively large number of Action Tasks undertaken by the population may be explained by the relatively large number of people who started collecting their belongings in preparation to evacuate. Furthermore, the relatively high number of people who left immediately may have contributed to the relatively small average response time for the Polish population.

When first alerted by the alarm almost half the population (47% or 58/123) was alone, 32% (39/123) were in groups of friends and 21% (26/123) were in groups of strangers. Almost half the population (46% [55/120]) evacuated as individuals, with 30% (36/120) in groups of friends and 24% (29/120) in groups of strangers. Of those who started the evacuation in a group (friends or strangers), 29% (19/65) exited the building with the group intact, 31% (20/65) with a smaller group, 35% (23/65) with a larger group and 5% (3/65) alone. There is a complex group dynamic occurring during the evacuation. Approximately half the population in the library prior to the alarm was alone and half was in groups. About half the population evacuated as individuals and half in groups however, just under a third (29%) of those who started the evacuation in a group exited the library with the group intact. This does not mean to say that the groups completely dissolved. Indeed only 5% of those who evacuated in a group exited the building alone with just under a third (31%) evacuating in smaller groups and just over a third (35%) in larger groups. Thus it is unlikely that those in groups before and during the evacuation will exit alone.

Of those that were alone prior to the alarm, 66% (38/58) evacuated alone, of those who started in groups of friends, 10% (4/39) evacuated alone while those who started in groups of strangers, 39% (10/26) evacuated alone. Furthermore, if you were in a group of friends during the evacuation, you did not exit the building alone (0% [0/35]), and you were 89% (31/35) likely to exit with all (40% [14/35]) or some (49% [17/35]) of your group members. There was an 11% (4/35) chance that you exited with more people in your group. Thus if you were in a group of friends prior to the alarm, it was likely that you evacuated in a group and that you exited in a group whereas if you were in a group of strangers, it is more likely that you separated from the group and evacuated alone. Thus the bond between groups of friends is seen to be much stronger than the group bond between strangers during the evacuation. Furthermore, if you were alone prior to the alarm, you were very likely to evacuate alone.

Predictive response time model applied to the data from the Warsaw University Library

Using equation 3 it is possible to estimate the response time for the Warsaw library evacuation trial. The constants W, X, Y and Z in equation 3 were determined from analysis of the video footage derived from the Czech Republic evacuation trial. The same values for the constants are used in this analysis. It should be noted that the constants W, X, Y and Z may be dependent on the nature of the notification process; e.g. voice alarm and the type of environment e.g. library. It is also noted that it may be possible that there is a cultural component to each of these constants.

In this assessment, we will investigate if the constant values derived from one library evacuation can be applied to an evacuation in a different library. Using equation 5, it is possible to estimate the response time for the population. Based on the data derived from Warsaw evacuation trial, we have the following average values for each parameter.

$$NT = 8.3 \text{ sec}, NAT = 6.1, NIT = 3.8, TNT = 9.9, ATT = 6.4 \text{ sec}, ITT = 6.1 \text{ sec}, FOL_{max} = NIT$$

Using equation 5 and the above values for the various parameters, the average response time for the population is RT = 67.8 sec.

The measured average response time for the population was 69.9 sec. Thus using the empirical response time model, the average response time is under-predicted by 3.0%. As can be seen once again, the empirical response time model provides a good estimation of the average response time for the population. From the earlier analysis of the evacuation trial in the Czech Republic, the empirical response time model produced average response times which were within 1.6% of the measured average response time for that population while Turkey was within 11.3%. Thus the constants used in the empirical response time model appear to be reasonably robust, providing a good level of agreement for two evacuation trials conducted in two different libraries in two different countries.

7.6.4 UK: The University of Greenwich Dreadnought Library

Alarm sequence

Unlike the other three libraries the alarm in the Dreadnought library was a simple tone alarm. In addition, there was staff interaction with the students during the response phase and so in some cases, students were subjected to two notification cues, the alarm and staff intervention. As a result there were two population groups, those that reacted just to the alarm, and those that reacted to alarm and staff intervention.

Population characteristics

It is noted that this evacuation trial was not undertaken as part of project BeSeCu but was undertaken by FSEG in 2007. The data was collected by CCTV cameras and was reanalyzed using the protocols presented in Section 0 as part of project BeSeCu. While a questionnaire was used in this trial, it was significantly different to the BeSeCu questionnaire and so a direct comparison with the BeSeCu questionnaire trial results cannot be made.

At the time of the alarm there were 453 people in the library based on an exit count. From the video analysis, the response phase behaviour of 104 students could be analyzed, of which 53 were males and 51 were females. From the results of the exit questionnaire, 55% of the population had never heard the alarm in the building or evacuated from the building prior to this evacuation trial.

There were two populations in the library, those who responded just to the sound of the alarm, Pop1, which consisted of 63 people and those that responded to both the alarm and staff intervention, Pop2, which consisted of 41 people.

Based on the video analysis at the time of the alarm, 53% of the entire population was working at a computer, 36% were engaged in other work related activities and 9% were involved in social engagement. The remainders of the population were engaged in a variety of activities such as sitting, walking, sleeping, etc. Thus 89% of the population was engaged in a work related activity at the time of the alarm with 53% engaged in computer activities.

Response times

The response time is determined from the start of the alarm (first cue and start of the Notification Stage), to the point where the person began purposive movement towards an exit (end of Activity Stage and start of Evacuation Movement Phase). The response time distribution for the population is presented in Fig. 7.21. As can be seen from Fig. 7.21, the response time distribution approximately follows a log-normal profile, with 12% of the population responding within 40 sec, 59% of the population responding within 100 sec and 84% of the population responding within 150 sec. The average response time extracted from the 104 analyzed people was 98.3 sec, and ranged from 22.0 sec to 287.8 sec. The log-normal curve shown in Fig. 7.21 has a log mean of 4.40 and a log standard deviation of 0.57.

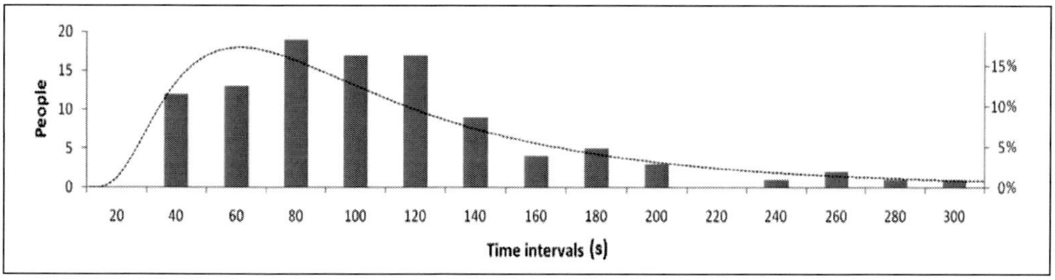

Fig. 7.21: Response time distribution for entire student population (UK)

As already noted the overall population is made up of two groups, those that reacted only to the alarm, Pop1 comprising of 61% of the overall population and those that reacted to the alarm and staff intervention, Pop2 (39% of the population). Here we consider the response times of both populations separately. The response time distribution for Pop1 is presented in Fig. 7.22. As can be seen from Fig. 7.22, the response time distribution approximately follows a broadly log-normal profile, with 19% of the population responding within 40 sec, 63% of the population responding within 100 sec and 87% of the population responding within 150 sec. The average response time extracted from the 63 analyzed people was 91.8 sec, and

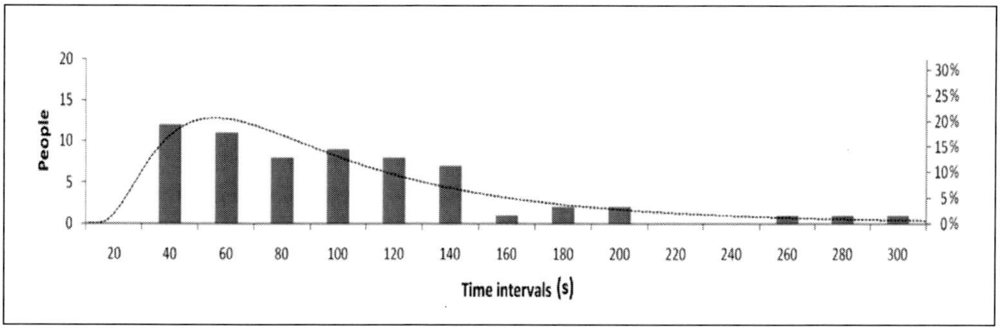

Fig. 7.22: Response time distribution for population reacting only to alarm, Pop1 (UK)

ranged from 22.0 sec to 287.8 sec. The log-normal curve shown in Fig. 7.22 has a log mean of 4.32 and a log standard deviation of 0.64.

The response time distribution for Pop2 is presented in Fig. 7.23. As can be seen from Fig. 7.23, the response time distribution approximately follows a log-normal profile, with 0% of the population responding within 40 sec, 51% of the population responding within 100 sec and 80% of the population responding within 150 sec. The average response time extracted from the 41 analyzed people was 108.1 sec, and ranged from 45.0 sec to 240.2 sec. The log-normal curve shown in Fig. 7.23 has a log mean of 4.60 and a log standard deviation of 0.39.

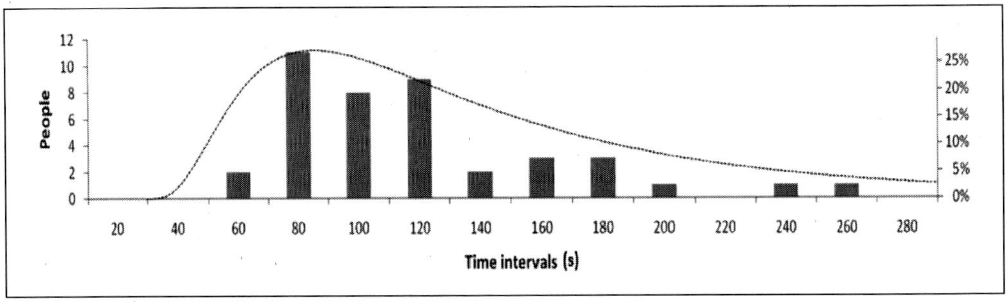

Fig. 7.23: Response time distribution for population reacting to alarm and staff intervention, Pop2 (UK)

It is noted that there are no fast responders in Pop2; i.e. no one responding in under 40 sec, resulting in the log-normal curve being shifted to the right relative to that for Pop1. This indicates that Pop2 tended to be slower in responding to the alarm. This is further confirmed by noting that 63% of Pop1 responded in 100 sec while only 51% of Pop2 responded in 100 sec. However, it is also noted that, due to three students (with response times; 241.7 sec, 276.8 and 287.8 sec), the tail of Pop1 extends to 288 sec. Clearly, these three students would have benefited from a staff intervention but were missed by the staff because they were in an area not patrolled by staff. Furthermore, there are two students in the tail of the staff intervention group with response times of 227.2 sec and 240.2 sec. These two students extend the tail of the staff intervention distribution. Clearly, these students did not respond well to the staff intervention, or the staff intervention occurred late in their response phase.

Response phase behaviour

Simply considering the overall response time does not provide insight into the nature of the Response Phase behaviours. To gain a better understanding of the factors contributing to the observed response time distributions it is necessary to decompose the Response Phase into the constitute stages as described in Section 7.4.2.

(a) Notification Stage:

If we consider the duration of the Notification stage for the entire population, we note that 65.4% (68 people) of the population have completed the Notification stage and disengaged from their pre-notification activities within 5 sec of the start of the notification cues while 70.2% (73 people) disengaged within 10 sec. The longest Notification stage was 231.8 sec, achieved by 1.0% (1 person) of the population while the average duration of the Notification stage is 20.9 sec.

Considering the Notification stage for the population reacting only to the alarm (Pop1) we note that 73.0% (46 people) of the population have completed the Notification stage and disengaged from their pre-notification activities within 5 sec of the start of the notification cues while 77.8% (49 people) disengaged within 10 sec. The longest Notification stage was 231.8 sec, achieved by 1.0% (1 person) of the population while the average duration of the Notification stage is 17.8 sec.

The three people with long response times in Pop1 were located together in a large computer room. There were a number of people in the room but the people appeared to be unconnected. The three people, all females, were engaged in computer work prior to the alarm. Two of the three have extremely long Notification times, the person with the longest response time, 287.8 sec has the second longest Notification time of 193.2 sec and the person with the second longest response time has the longest Notification time of 231.8 sec. The person with the third longest response time of 241.7 sec has a very short notification time of only 2.5 sec. Clearly, the two students with the very long Notification times were engaged in what they considered to be extremely important computer work which is why two of them have extremely long notification times leading to the very long response times. If these two Notification times are removed from the list, the average Notification time for Pop1 decreases from 17.8 sec to 11.5 sec.

Considering the Notification stage for the population reacting to the alarm and staff intervention (Pop2), we note that 53.7% (22 people) of the population have completed the Notification stage and disengaged from their pre-notification activities within 5 sec of the start of the notification cues while 58.5% (24 people) disengaged within 10 sec. The longest Notification stage was 164.6 sec, achieved by 1 person while the average duration of the Notification stage is 25.6 sec.

The two people, both males, with long response times in Pop2 were located together in a private study room. There were a number of people in the room and the two students with long response time appear to be in a group of two. Both are working on their lap top computers when the alarm sounded. Both have extremely long Notification times, the person with the longest response time, 240.2 sec, has the second longest Notification time of 158.6 sec and the person with the second longest response time, 227.2 sec, has the longest Notification time of 164.6 sec. There was a staff intervention at 57.5 sec which apparently had no effect on these two students as they continued with their pre-alarm activities. Clearly, these two students were engaged in what they considered to be extremely important computer work which is why they have extremely long notification times leading to the very long response times. A second staff intervention occurred after 222.2

sec after which the person with the longest response time completed the Response Phase in 18.0 sec and the other person completed after 5.0 sec. If these two Notification times are removed from the list, the average Notification time for Pop2 decreases from 25.6 sec to 1With these four individuals removed from the Notification time distribution, the average Notification time for the entire population decreases from 20.9 sec to 14.3 sec.

(b) Activity Stage:

The nature of the personal behaviours exhibited during the Activity stage can also be analyzed in detail. Presented in Fig. 7.24 is a distribution of the Action, Information and total number of tasks undertaken by the entire building population during the Activity stage. As can be seen the number of Information Tasks follow a broadly log-normal distribution. The number of Action tasks appear to follow more of a standard normal distribution while the distribution of the combined tasks is less clear, perhaps that of a shallow normal distribution.

A total of 957 tasks were identified during the Response Phase for the entire building population, 515 individual Action Tasks (AT) and 442 Information Tasks (IT). The average number of AT undertaken is 5.0 while the average number of IT is 4.3. On average a person undertakes more AT than IT and undertakes a total of 9.2 tasks prior to commencing the Evacuation Movement Phase.

The most common combination of tasks was 5 ATs and 2 ITs and this combination was completed by 7 people. The most common number of ATs was 5

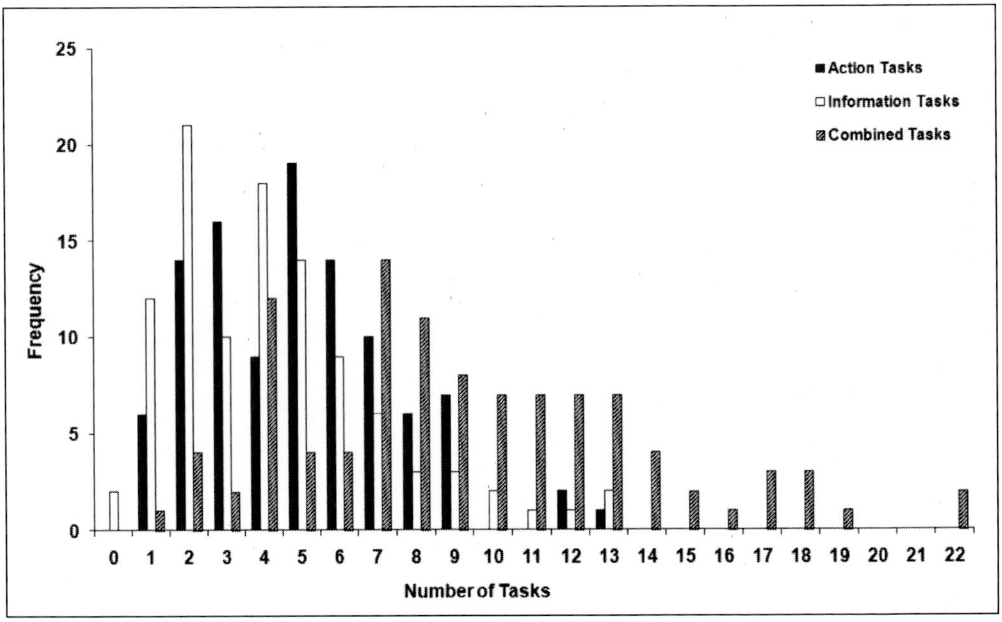

Fig. 7.24: Number and type of tasks undertaken by the overall library population (UK)

performed by 19 people and the most common number of ITs was 2 performed by 21 people. The maximum number of tasks performed by a single person was 22 tasks (made from a combination of ATs and ITs), while the maximum number of ATs performed by a single person was 13 and the maximum number of ITs performed by a single person was 13. In addition, the most common ITs, expressed as a percentage of the total number of ITs were; "Acquire information from the environment (looking, listening)" 71%, and "Engage in information exchange" 24%. The most common ATs, expressed as a percentage of the total number of ATs were "Collect Belongings" 36%, "Pick up bag" 23%, "Collect clothing" 16% and "Secure computer" 6%.

The time to undertake each individual task can be determined from the video footage. In order to reduce the error associated with this measurement, it is based on the duration of multiple tasks of the same type were measured. Thus, measurements were made for sequences of tasks in which at least two tasks of the same type were undertaken consecutively and which followed on immediately from the previous task. Using this approach the duration of 320 ATs and 181 ITs were measured. The average duration of a single AT was determined to be 8.3 sec while the average duration of an IT was determined to be 10.3 sec. Thus, on average, for this population ITs take approximately 24% longer than ATs. This result spans 116 AT sequences and 57 IT sequences).

A similar analysis can be undertaken for Pop1 and Pop2. For Pop1, the distribution of tasks is shown in Fig. 7.25. As can be seen, the number of Information

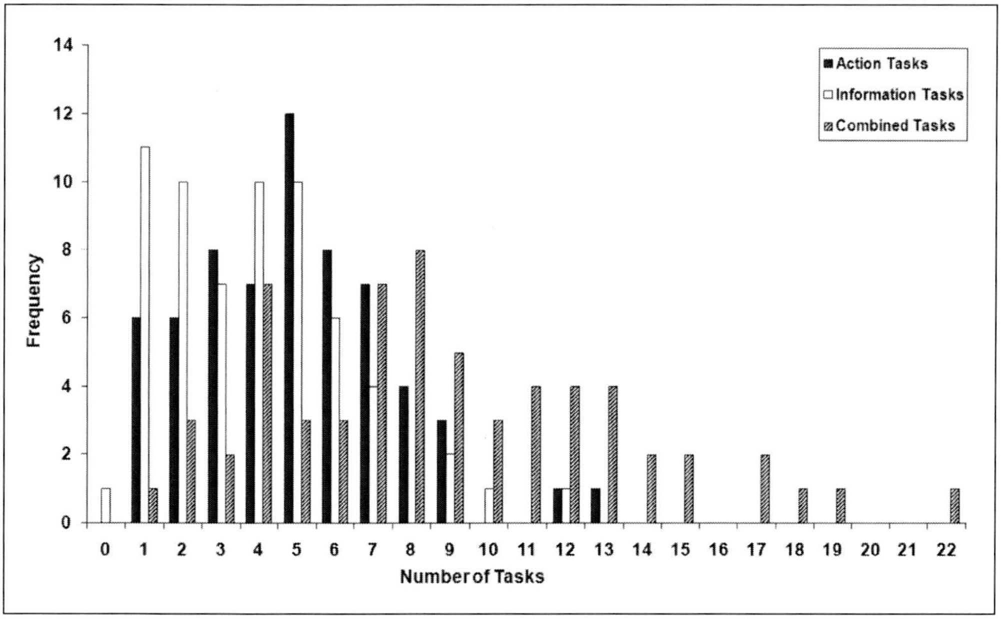

Fig. 7.25: Number and type of tasks undertaken by the alarm (Pop1) population (UK)

Tasks follows a broadly log-normal distribution. The number of Action Tasks appear to follow more of a standard normal distribution while the distribution of the combined tasks is less clear, perhaps that of a shallow normal distribution. A total of 557 tasks were identified during the Response Phase for the entire building population, 311 individual Action tasks (AT) and 246 Information tasks (IT). The average number of AT undertaken is 4.9 while the average number of IT is 3.9. On average a person undertakes more AT than IT and undertakes a total of 8.8 tasks prior to commencing the Evacuation Movement Phase.

The most common combination of tasks was both 5 ATs and 2 ITs and also 3 ATs and 1 IT, these combinations being completed by 4 people each. The most common number of ATs was 5 performed by 12 people and the most common number of ITs was 1 performed by 11 people. The maximum number of tasks performed by a single person was 22 tasks (made from a combination of ATs and ITs), while the maximum number of ATs performed by a single person was 13 and the maximum number of ITs performed by a single person was 12. In addition, the most common ITs, expressed as a percentage of the total number of ITs were; "Acquire information from the environment (looking, listening)" 74%, and "Engage in information exchange" 23%. The most common ATs, expressed as a percentage of the total number of ATs were "Collect Belongings" 33%, "Pick up bag" 24%, "Collect clothing" 15% and both "Secure computer" and "Work at computer", 6% each.

The time to undertake each individual task can be determined from the video footage. Using the approach outlined for the entire population, the duration of 197 ATs and 91 ITs were measured. The average duration of a single AT was determined to be 7.6 sec while the average duration of an IT was determined to be 11.2 sec. Thus, on average, for this population ITs take approximately 47% longer than ITs. This result spans 72 AT sequences and 31 IT sequences).

Presented in Fig. 7.26 is a distribution of the Action, Information and total number of tasks undertaken by the alarm and staff intervention population (Pop2) during the Activity stage. As can be seen, the number of Information tasks follows a broadly log-normal distribution. The number of Action tasks also appear to follow a log-normal distribution while the distribution of the combined tasks is less clear, perhaps that of a shallow normal distribution. A total of 400 tasks were identified during the Response Phase for the entire building population, 204 individual Action tasks (AT) and 196 Information tasks (IT). The average number of AT undertaken is 5.0 while the average number of IT is 4.8. On average a person undertakes more AT than IT and undertakes a total of 9.8 tasks prior to commencing the Evacuation Movement Phase.

The most common combination of tasks was 2 ATs and 2 ITs and this combination was completed by 4 people. The most common number of ATs was 2 and 3 both performed by 8 people and the most common number of ITs was 2 performed by 11 people. The maximum number of tasks performed by a single person was 22 tasks (made from a combination of ATs and ITs), while the maximum number of ATs performed by a single person was 12 and the maximum number of

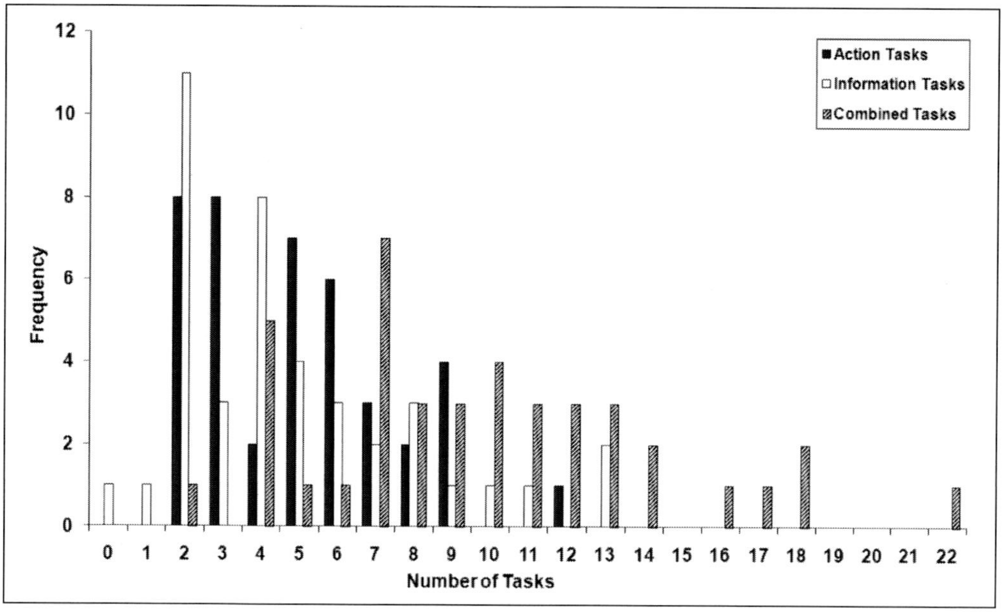

Fig. 7.26: Number and type of tasks undertaken by the alarm and intervention (Pop2) population (UK)

ITs performed by a single person was 13. In addition, the most common ITs, expressed as a percentage of the total number of ITs were; "Acquire information from the environment (looking, listening)" 67%, and "Engage in information exchange" 26%. The most common ATs, expressed as a percentage of the total number of ATs were "Collect Belongings" 41%, "Pick up bag" 22%, "Collect clothing" 17% and "Secure computer" 5%.

The time to undertake each individual task can be determined from the video footage. Using the approach outlined for the entire population, the duration of 123 ATs and 90 ITs were measured. The average duration of a single AT was determined to be 9.2 sec while the average duration of an IT was determined to be 9.4 sec. Thus, on average, for this population ITs take approximately 2% longer than ATs. This result spans 44 AT sequences and 26 IT sequences.

The population that reacted to the alarm and staff intervention (41) can be further sub-divided into a population that effectively ignored the alarm and ended their Notification stage only after staff intervention (Pop2a), comprising of 13 people (32%); and those who commenced their Activity stage prior to staff intervention (Pop2b), comprising of 28 people (68%). For Pop2, staff intervention was not required to commence the Activity stage, but may have speeded up this stage of the Response Phase.

For Pop2a, 100% of the population was involved in work related activities prior to the alarm and 46% of Pop2a experienced two staff interventions and 8% experienced three staff interventions prior to completing their Response Phase. The average staff intervention time (first intervention) was 45.3 sec and this population had an average notification time of 69.8 sec. This population did not disengage from their pre-alarm activities for another 25 sec following the first staff intervention. The average response time for Pop2a measured from the alarm was 133 sec and from the first intervention 87 sec. Pop2a undertook an average of 7.7 tasks in total, made up of 4.7 AT and 3.0 IT.

For Pop2b, 79% of the population was involved in work related activities prior to the alarm and the entire population experienced only one staff intervention. The average staff intervention time was 50.8 sec and this population had an average notification time of 5.1 sec. Clearly this population had started the Activity stage well before the staff intervention. The average response time for Pop2b measured from the alarm was 97 sec and from the first intervention 46 sec. Pop2b undertook an average of 10.7 tasks, 5.0 tasks prior to staff intervention, made up of 3.1 AT and 1.9 IT and 5.7 tasks after staff intervention, made up of 2.0 AT and 3.7 IT.

(c) Discussion:

For the population as a whole, 89% were engaged in a work related activity at the time of the alarm with 53% engaged in computer activities. 55% of the population had never heard the alarm in the building or evacuated from the building prior to this evacuation trial.

Two separate populations were noted in the UK library evacuation trial, a population responding to the alarm only (Pop1 – 63) and a population responding to a combination of both alarm and staff intervention (Pop2 – 41). Pop2 can be further subdivided into two sub-populations, those that started their Activity stage AFTER staff intervention, Pop2a (13 or 32%); and those that started the Activity stage prior to staff intervention, Pop2b (28 or 68%). Using the Response Phase Behavioural framework the differences in the behaviour of the two populations can be further characterized.

Average Response Times:

- Total – 98 sec; Pop1 – 92 sec; Pop2 – 108 sec; Pop2a – 133 sec; Pop2b – 97 sec.
- Total: 12% in 40 sec; 59% in 100 sec; 84% in 150 sec.
- Pop1: 19% in 40 sec; 63% in 100 sec; 87% in 150 sec.
- Pop2: 0% in 40 sec; 51% in 100 sec; 80% in 150 sec.
- The average response time for the entire population is quite long. This may be a result of the use of a tone alarm or that 45% of the population had experienced an alarm previously in the library. Furthermore, a significant proportion of the population was engaged in a work related activity (89%) prior to the alarm, with 55% engaged in computer based work. This may also explain why the population had a long response time. While the average response time for Pop1, the population that did not involve a staff intervention, was similar to that of Pop2, the population with staff intervention, Pop1 had a higher proportion of rapid responders.

Average Notification Time:
- Total – 20.9 sec; Pop1 – 17.8 sec; Pop2 – 25.6 sec; Pop2a – 69.8 sec; Pop2b – 5.1 sec
- Total: 65% in 5.0 sec; 70% in 10 sec.
- Pop1: 73% in 5.0 sec; 78% in 10 sec.
- Pop2: 54% in 5.0 sec; 59% in 10 sec.
- Pop2a: 0% in 5.0 sec; 0% in 10 sec.
- Pop2b: 79% in 5.0 sec; 86% in 10 sec.
- While the average Notification time for Pop1 is quite long, a significant proportion of the population (78%) have notification times of less than 10 sec. Two members of the Pop1 have extremely long notification times (193 sec and 231 sec). These two were involved in computer work prior to the alarm. If these two times are excluded, the average Notification time for Pop1 drops to 11.5 sec.
- Pop2 has a very long average Notification time, and a significant proportion of Pop2 (41%) have Notification times longer than 10 sec. Pop2 is made up of two sub-populations with long Notification times (Pop2a) and short Notification times (Pop2b).
- Pop2a – comprising 32% of Pop2 – started their Activity stage only after staff intervention. The average notification time for this sub-population was 69.8 sec with an average staff intervention time of 45.3 sec. For this sub-population, staff intervention was required to encourage the participants to disengage from their pre-alarm activities – 100% of which was work related. On average, Pop2a disengaged from their pre-alarm activities 24.5 sec after the staff intervention. It is noted that this time is longer than the Notification time for Pop1 (17.8 sec). This produces an average response time measured from (the first) staff intervention of 87 sec. It is possible that without staff intervention, Pop2a would have incurred even longer Notification times. The average response time for Pop2a measured from the first staff intervention is comparable to the average response time for Pop1, but is some 45% longer than Pop1 if measured from the alarm.
- Pop2b – comprising 68% of Pop2 – started their Activity stage prior to staff intervention which occurred on average at 50.5 sec after the alarm. The average Notification time for this sub-population was 5.1 sec, so for this sub-population staff intervention was not required to disengage from their pre-alarm activities. The average response time for this sub-population was 97 sec or 46 sec measured from the staff intervention. The average response time for Pop2b measured from the alarm is comparable to that of Pop1, thus with the staff intervention, Pop2b achieved an average response time only marginally longer than the average response time for Pop1.
- Thus for Pop2b, staff intervention had no impact on Notification time while for Pop2a it may have prevented the population from incurring even longer Notification times.

Average Total Number of Tasks:
- Total – 9.2; Pop1 – 8.8; Pop2 – 9.8; Pop2a – 7.7; Pop2b – 10.7

- On average the population reacting only to the alarm (Pop1) undertook fewer tasks than the population subjected to the alarm and staff intervention (Pop2). This supports the observation that Pop1 had a shorter average response time. However, the two alarm and intervention sub-populations behaved significantly differently to each other.
- For sub-population Pop2a, staff intervention did slightly reduce the number of tasks undertaken compared to the alarm only group (Pop1). While Pop2a undertook the least number of tasks, they still completed a significant number of tasks on average, suggesting that the Activity stage was not significantly reduced to compensate for the extremely long Notification stage. The fewer number of tasks completed in the Activity stage would suggest that the Activity stage for Pop2a was shorter than that for Pop1.
- Sub-population Pop2b undertook significantly more tasks than Pop2a and more tasks than Pop1. Thus rather than undertaking fewer tasks during the Activity stage as maybe expected through staff intervention, this sub-population has undertaken more tasks compared to the alarm only group (Pop1). The large number of tasks undertaken by Pop2b contributed to the long response time. However, it is possible that the staff intervention may have prevented this sub-population from undertaking even more tasks which would have led to an even longer response time.
- Thus for Pop2a, staff intervention may have slightly reduced the number of tasks undertaken during the Activity stage and shortened the duration of the Activity stage. For Pop2b, staff intervention appears to have had no impact on the number of tasks undertaken during the Activity stage, but may have prevented even more tasks from being undertaken.

Average Number of Action and Info Tasks:

- Total: 5.0 and 4.3; Pop1: 4.9 and 3.9; Pop2: 5.0 and 4.8;
- Pop2a: 4.7 and 3.0; Pop2b: 5.1 and 5.6
- For the total population, Pop1 and Pop2, more Action Tasks than Information Tasks were undertaken. Overall, the total population undertakes 16% more Action than Information Tasks. The population exposed to just the alarm (Pop1) undertake 26% more Action than Information Tasks while the population exposed to the alarm and staff intervention (Pop2) undertake only 4% more Action than Information tasks. However, the two alarm and intervention sub-populations behaved significantly differently to each other.
- Sub-population Pop2a undertakes 57% more Action than Information Tasks. Pop2a undertakes significantly less Information Tasks than Pop1. The fewer Information tasks undertaken by this sub-population may be the result of not needing to receive confirmation or transfer information following the staff intervention – which for this group was repeated up to three times. However, the number of Action Tasks undertaken is similar to that of Pop1, suggesting that a minimum number of Action tasks are required to be completed prior to commencing the movement phase.

- Sub-population Pop2b undertakes 10% more Information than Action Tasks. This is a complete reversal of the trends for the other population groups. While the number of Action Tasks is similar to the other population groups, the number of Information tasks is 44% greater than that of Pop1. This is the result of four individuals, who were engaged in social engagement activities prior to the alarm, each undertaking more than 10 Information Tasks. If these four individuals are excluded from the analysis, the number of tasks undertaken by Pop2b becomes 4.5 and 3.9, which follows the trends of more Action than Information tasks.
- Overall the population undertakes more 16% Action than Information Tasks. For Pop2a, staff intervention has not reduced the number of Action Tasks but has reduced the number of Information Tasks. The (repeated) presence of the staff member reducing the need for information exchanges between the sub-population. For Pop2b, staff intervention has not reduced the number of Action Tasks; however, the number of Information Tasks has increased. This is the result of four members of the population engaging in social exchanges prior to the alarm and during the alarm.

Average Duration of Action and Info Tasks:

- Total: 8.3 and 10.3 sec; Pop1: 7.6 and 11.2 sec; Pop2: 9.2 and 9.4 sec
- Information Tasks take longer than Action Tasks for all populations.
- Overall, the population takes 24% longer to undertake an Information Task than an Action Task.
- For Pop1 (the population exposed just to the alarm) Information Tasks take 47% longer than Action Tasks.
- For Pop2 (the population exposed to alarm and staff intervention), Information Tasks take only 2% longer than Action Tasks.
- An Information Task is 19% longer for Pop1 (alarm only) compared to Pop2 (alarm and intervention). This is thought to be due to occupants exposed to a staff intervention being provided with additional information not available to those exposed to the simple tone.

Staff intervention is intended to shorten the response phase of individuals, in particular those individuals that may take excessive time responding. The staff intervention process achieves this by reducing the targeted occupants Notification stage or Activity stage or both stages of the Response Phase.

In the UK evacuation trial the staff intervention population consisted of two distinct groups. The first group (Pop2a) had exceptionally long Notification times. For this group the average Notification time (69.8 sec) exceeded the average notification time for the alarm only population (17.8 sec) and the average staff intervention time (45.3 sec). On average this population disengaged from their pre-alarm activities 24.5 sec after the staff intervention – a longer notification time than that for the alarm only population. Clearly, this sub-population was intent on completing their pre-alarm activities. However, without staff intervention, these individuals may have incurred even longer Notification times. So staff intervention may have resulted in these individuals completing the Notification stage sooner than would otherwise have occurred. Furthermore, these individuals undertook fewer tasks in total (7.7) during the Activity stage than the alarm only group (8.8). This resulted in a shorter Activity stage compared to the alarm only group. The response time for this group (133 sec) was significantly longer than that for the alarm only group (92 sec), but may have been even longer without the staff intervention. For this group, staff intervention potentially reduced what are exceptionally long Notification times from being even longer and reduced the duration of the Activity stage.

The second group (Pop2b) had completed the Notification stage (5.2 sec) and commenced the Activity stage well before any staff members appeared (50.8 sec). For this group the Notification time was extremely short and was not influenced by the staff intervention. However, this group undertook more tasks during the Activity stage (10.7 on average) than the alarm only group (88. on average) (Pop1). It is possible that the staff intervention prevented even more tasks from being undertaken during the Activity Stage, preventing the Activity stage from taking even longer. The response time for this group (97 sec) was marginally longer than that for the alarm only group (92 sec). For this group, staff intervention potentially reduced the duration of the Activity stage.

Predictive response time model applied to the data from the University of Greenwich Dreadnought Library

Using equation 3 it is possible to estimate the response time for the Greenwich library evacuation trial. The constants W, X, Y and Z in equation 3 were determined from analysis of the video footage derived from the Czech Republic evacuation trial. The same values for the constants are used in this analysis. It should be noted that the constants W, X, Y and Z may be dependent on the nature of the notification process; e.g. voice alarm and the type of environment e.g. library. It is also noted that it may be possible that there is a cultural component to each of these constants.

In this assessment, we will investigate if the constant values derived from one library evacuation can be applied to an evacuation in a different library. Using equation 5, it is possible to estimate the response time for the population. Based on the data derived from Greenwich evacuation trial we have the following:

For the overall population, we have the following average values for each parameter:

$$NT = 20.9\text{ sec},\ NAT = 5.0,\ NIT = 4.3,\ TNT = 9.2,\ ATT = 8.3\text{ sec},\ ITT = 10.3\text{ sec},\ FOL_{max} = NIT$$

Using equation 5 and the above values for the various parameters, the average response time for the overall population is RT = 102.0 sec. The measured average response time for the entire population was 98.3 sec. Thus in this case using the empirical response time model, the average response time is over-predicted by 3.8%.

While for Pop1 (alarm intervention), we have the following average values for each parameter;

NT = 17.8 sec, NAT = 4.9, NIT = 3.9, TNT = 8.8, ATT = 7.6 sec, ITT = 11.2 sec, FOL_{max} = NIT

Using equation 5 and the above values for the various parameters, the average response time for the overall population is RT = 95.4 sec. The measured average response time for Pop1 was 91.8 sec. Thus in this case using the empirical response time model, the average response time is over-predicted by 3.9%.

Finally, for Pop2 (alarm and staff intervention), we have the following average values for each parameter;

NT = 25.6 sec, NAT = 5.0, NIT = 4.8, TNT = 9.8, ATT = 9.2 sec, ITT = 9.4 sec, FOL_{max} = NIT

Using equation 5 and the above values for the various parameters, the average response time for the overall population is RT = 110.2 sec. The measured average response time for Pop1 was 108.1 sec. Thus in this case using the empirical response time model, the average response time is over-predicted by 1.9%.

Using equation 5 the average response time for the UK library population is over-predicted by between 1.9% and 3.9%.

As can be seen once again, the empirical response time model provides a good estimation of the average response time for the population. Thus for four different evacuations in four different countries the predictive response time model was able to predict the average response time within: 1.6% in the Czech Republic evacuation trial, 11.3% in the Turkey evacuation trial, 3.0% in the Poland evacuation trial and 3.9% within the UK evacuation trial. The average error across all four trials is 5.0%. Thus the constants used in the empirical response time model appear to be reasonably robust, providing a good level of agreement for four evacuation trials conducted in four different libraries in four different countries.

7.7 Cross cultural comparison of response phase behaviours

Ed Galea, Lazaros Filippidis, Steven J. Deere, Gary Sharp & Markus Sauter

The Response Phase Behaviours derived from each of the four trials are compared. First the population characteristics are compared to ensure that the core population parameters across each of the four libraries are compatible. Once this is established, Response Phase parameters are compared. This includes response time distributions, Notification time, number of Action and Information Tasks, duration of Action and Information Tasks, etc. In addition, the differences in fire culture observed during the four trials are described.

7.7.1 Population characteristics

The core population characteristics were determined from a combination of the responses to the questionnaire and from video analysis. As the UK population did not complete the questionnaire much of this data is missing for this population.

The first set of characteristics concerns the population demographics (see Table 7.4) derived from both video data and the questionnaires. This consists of the number of people for which response time data could be collected and their gender, both determined from the video footage, the population gender and age distribution, the last two determined from the questionnaire data. As can be seen from Table 7.4 the size of the response time data set varies considerably, with the smallest being 51 and the largest being 192. In total response phase data was collected for 417 people. The percentage of females in the questionnaire population varied significantly from a maximum of 45% in Turkey population to a minimum of 22% in the Czech population. However, this is based on questionnaires returned and is not necessarily reflective of the population. The gender distribution based on the analyzed Response Phase behaviours is more uniform, with three of the four libraries having a range of female subjects varying from 49% to 54%. The Czech Republic stands out with having only 13% female subjects. The age characteristics are very similar for the three BeSeCu libraries, with over 89% of the population being in the range 18-24 years of age. The UK age range data was extracted from the video analysis and was reported to be 100% in the range 18 to 39 years of ages.

Table 7.4: Population demographics

Country	# Response Time Data	Male Video	Female Video	Male	Female	Age 18-24	Age 25-34	Age 35-44
Czech Rep.	70	87%	13%	78%	22%	93%	6%	1%
Turkey	51	49%	51%	55%	45%	97%	3%	0%
Poland	192	46%	54%	66%	34%	89%	10%	1%
UK	104	51%	49%	–	–	–	–	–

The age distribution is similar for all three BeSeCu libraries and the gender mix for three of the four libraries is similar, with the Czech Republic standing out as having on 13% females.

The second set of data concerns the population evacuation experience (see Table 7.5) derived from questionnaires. For the three BeSeCu libraries it is clear that the vast majority of the participants (94%) had no prior evacuation experience associated with the library. However, there is varied experience of evacuation training, varying from 6% in Turkey to 71% in the Czech Republic. In the UK, 55% of the population had no evacuation experience and 0% had evacuation training.

Table 7.5: Population evacuation experience and knowledge

Country	No Prior Evac Exp	Training	Consider library safe	On hearing alarm, felt safe
Czech Rep	94%	71%	85%	100%
Turkey	93%	6%	82%	83%
Poland	94%	29%	61%	88%
UK	55%	0%	–	–

What is consistent across all four libraries is that over half the population in each case had not experienced an evacuation from the library prior to the trial. The majority of participants felt that they were normally at no or little risk from serious injury from fire in the library, and this only increased when hearing the alarm.

The three BeSeCu library populations have a similar evacuation experience base with over 90% of each population not experiencing an evacuation in the library. Of the four populations, the UK population had the greatest proportion of experienced participants (45%) and the Polish population normally felt least safe in the library.

The third set of data concerns the activities that the population was engaged in prior to the alarm (see Table 7.6) derived from the video footage. In all four cases more than half the population was engaged in work related activities. However, the vast majority of the populations in the Czech Republic, Poland and UK were engaged in work related activities, with at least 90% of these populations engaged in work. Furthermore, the UK, Czech Republic and Turkey had half or more of the population engaged in computer based work activities.

Table 7.6: Activities prior to alarm

Country	Computer Work	Other Work	Sitting	Social Activity	Other
Czech Rep (alarm)	57%	30%	0%	13%	0%
Turkey	49%	8%	12%	18%	13%
Poland	26%	64%	2%	5%	3%
UK (alarm)	57%	33%	2%	5%	3%

The Turkish population had only 57% of the population engaged in work related activities at the time of the alarm while the other three had over almost 90%. Furthermore, Turkey, Czech Republic and the UK have similar numbers engaged in computer based work.

Every effort has been made to ensure that the initial conditions for each evacuation were as similar as possible. This is essential to ensure that as far as possible the main variables that may influence the evacuation are social cultural. As these trials were full-scale and unannounced, as opposed to laboratory based trials, it is virtually impossible to ensure that initial conditions are exactly identical in each trial.

To summarize the similarities and differences and the potential impact this may have on the cultural analysis:

- The age distribution is similar for all three BeSeCu libraries.
- The gender mix for three of the four libraries is similar, with the Czech Republic standing out as having only 13% females. The predominance of males in the Czech Republic trial may have an influence on the outcome of the trial, but this may also be a social cultural influence associated with gender.
- The three BeSeCu library populations have a similar evacuation experience base with over 90% of each population not experiencing an evacuation. Of the four populations, the UK population had the greatest proportion of experienced participants (45%). However, as with the other three populations, the majority of the population in the UK library had no experience of an evacuation in the library.
- In each of the three BeSeCu library populations, the majority of participants (over 60%) felt that they were normally at no or little risk from serious injury from fire in the library. The Polish population normally felt least safe in the library.
- Three of the four libraries had almost 90% of their populations involved in work related activities immediately prior to the alarm; however, the Turkish population had only 57%. Furthermore, Turkey, Czech Republic and the UK had about half the population involved in computer based work while Poland had about a quarter. Being engaged in a work activity, in particular a computer based activity, may make the participant more reluctant to disengage and engage in evacuation activities. Unfortunately, this variable is beyond our control.

7.7.2 Response time distributions

A statistical analysis was performed on the response time distributions to determine the significance of the differences between the curves. The response time distributions that were used in the analysis are: Turkey, Poland, Czech Republic (alarm only) and UK (alarm only). The Czech Republic data set was restricted to the alarm only respondents as the occupants who responded to staff intervention did not hear the alarm at all due to the malfunction of the system. As the notification cues and likely response associated with staff intervention and voice alarm are considered to be significantly different, it was considered justified to exclude the staff intervention sub-population from this analysis. Similarly, the UK data set was restricted to alarm only. In this case, the two populations were alarm and alarm plus staff intervention. The group exposed to alarm and alarm plus staff intervention were subjected to multiple cues and again it was considered inappropriate to consider this group in the comparison data set. The response time curves for these four populations are displayed in Fig. 7.27. While all four curves are log-normal in appearance they appear to be significantly different to each other.

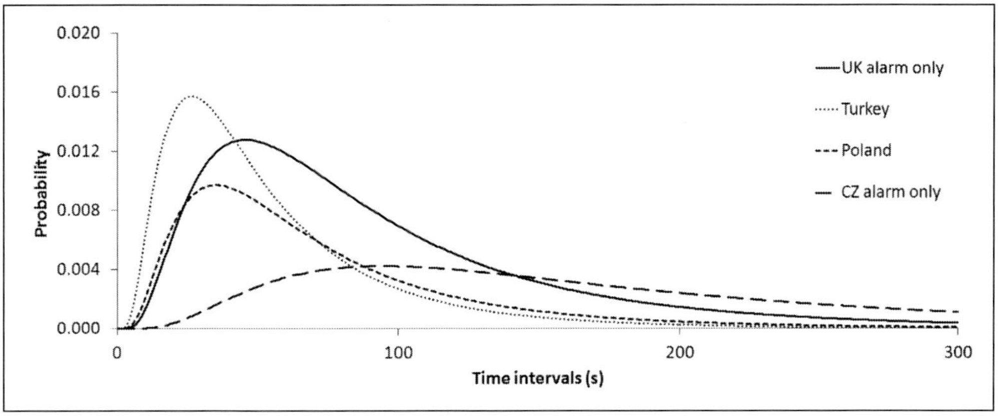

Fig. 7.27: Response time distributions for the four library evacuations

In order to determine whether or not the differences between the curves are statistically significant, non-parametric testing was performed on the response time distributions from the four libraries. It is initially necessary to determine whether the data sets are normally distributed. If the data is not normally distributed the types of statistical comparison possible are restricted to non-parametric tests.

If the data sets are not normally distributed two non-parametric tests that can be used are the Kruskall-Wallis test and the Mann-Whitney test (Field, 2009). The Mann-Whitney test ranks two datasets in ascending numerical order, and compares the sum of the ranks of each data set in order to determine whether they originate from the same distribution. The Kruskall-Wallis test uses the same basic idea of ranking the data sets in ascending numerical order and then comparing ranks of the data to see if the medians of the ranks are equal. The advantage of the Kruskall-Wallis test is that it can be applied across multiple datasets rather than being restricted to just two. All the statistical analysis was completed using the SPSS software (SPSS: PASW Statistics 18, Release 18.0.0, 2009).

Normality testing (Kolmogorov-Smirnov) was applied to all six (Poland, Turkey, Czech Republic [alarm only], Czech Republic [alarm and intervention], UK [alarm only] and UK [alarm and alarm plus staff intervention]) data sets. This showed, with the exception of the Poland data set, that the data sets are likely to be NOT normally distributed within the 5% confidence level ($p < 0.05$ and so the hypothesis that the data set is normally distributed is rejected). As all but one of the data sets are likely to not be normally distributed it is acceptable to compare the data sets using non-parametric methods.

The Kruskall-Wallis analysis (with three degrees of freedom) was applied to the four data sets (Poland, Turkey, Czech Republic [alarm only], and UK [alarm only]) and the result is significant at the $p = 0.01$ level [$H(3)$ $p = 0.000$, $p < 0.01$] indicating that there is a significant difference between the four data sets. The

Mann-Whitney test is then performed on pairs of data sets to identify where significant differences between the data sets lie. The results for this analysis can be summarised as follows:

- UK (alarm only) v. Czech Rep. (alarm only), $p = 0.000$, $p < 0.05$
- UK (alarm only) v. Turkey, $p = 0.000$, $p < 0.05$
- UK (alarm only) v. Poland, $p = 0.018$, $p < 0.05$
- Czech Rep. (alarm only) v. Poland, $p = 0.000$, $p < 0.05$
- Czech Rep. (alarm only) v. Turkey, $p = 0.000$, $p < 0.05$
- Poland v. Turkey, $p = 0.003$, $p < 0.05$

Thus there is a significant difference between each pair of response time distributions at the 5% significance level. It is noted that the above tests were repeated using the UK (alarm and staff intervention) data set in place of the UK (alarm only) data set with the same conclusion.

The UK (alarm only) response time data is:

- Quicker on average than the Czech Rep (alarm only) response time data.
- Slower on average than the Poland response time data.
- Slower on average than the Turkey response time data.

The Poland response time data is:

- Quicker on average than the Czech Rep (alarm only) response time data.
- Slower on average than the Turkey response time data.

The Turkey response time data is:

- quicker on average than the Czech Rep (alarm only) response time data.

7.7.3 Response phase parameters

The response time distributions for the four different national library evacuations have been shown to be statistically significantly different. Here the Response Phase parameters are considered. Presented in Table 7.7 is a summary of the Response Phase parameters for all the distributions along with an average for the Poland, Turkey, Czech (alarm only) and UK (alarm only). If cultural influences Response Phase behaviour and response time, then it can be expected that culture would also influence the Response Phase parameters of NAT, NIT, ATT, ITT and NT. Comparisons between the four national sets are made by comparing relative trends between parameters and also comparing parameter values with cross national average values. In Table 7.7 individual parameters which are greater than the national averages are coloured red while those which are less than the national average are coloured blue.

From Table 7.7 it is possible to identify trends in the average number and average duration of Response Phase tasks (NAT, NIT, ATT and ITT) for the national average and the individual national groups.

- The national average population:
  Undertakes more Action than Information Tasks; the average duration of an Information Task is greater than the average duration of an Action Task.

These trends can be compared with the trends observed in each of the national groups to determine whether the national groups display similar or different trends.

- The UK (alarm only) population:
  Undertakes more Action than Information Tasks and
  The average duration of an Information Task is greater than the average duration of an Action Task.

- The Polish population:
  Undertakes more Action than Information Tasks and
  The average duration of an Action Task is greater than the average duration of an Information Task.

Table 7.7: Summary of response phase parameter

	Poland	**Turkey**	**Czech Alarm**	**UK Alarm**	**Aver-age**	**UK Alarm + Int**	**UK**	**Czech Int**	**Czech**
People	192	51 (50)	20	63	326	41	104	43	70 (63)
NT (sec)	*8.3*	*10.0*	**88.6**	**17.8**	10.4	25.6	20.9	7.2	31.5
NIT	*3.8*	**5.1**	**7.4**	*3.9*	4.2	4.8	4.3	2.0	3.7
NAT	**6.1**	*3.5*	**5.7**	*4.9*	5.4	5.0	5.0	3.6	4.3
TNT	**9.9**	*8.6*	**13.1**	*8.8*	9.7	9.8	9.2	5.6	8.0
ITT (sec)	*6.1*	*4.7*	**9.9**	**11.2**	7.1	9.4	10.3	6.7	9.7
ATT (sec)	6.4	*5.2*	6.4	**7.6**	6.4	9.2	8.3	6.5	6.4
Average Response Time	*69.9*	*56.1*	**193.7**	**91.8**	79.6	108.1	98.3	43.3	92.7
Predicted response time	67.8	49.8	194.8	95.4	71.3	110.2	102.0	42.6	92.2

- The Czech (alarm only) population:
  Undertakes more Information than Action Tasks and
  The average duration of an Information Task is greater than the average duration of an Action Task.

- The Turkish population:
  Undertakes more Information than Action Tasks and
  The average duration of an Action Task is greater than the average duration of an Information Task.

The UK (alarm only) population is the only one of the four national groups whose trends in Response Phase characteristics match that of the trends of the average population. The Polish and Czech (alarm only) populations match different aspects of the average trend, with the Polish population matching trends in the number of tasks, while the Czech (alarm only) population matches trends in the average duration of the tasks. The Turkish population behaves in a way which is opposite to the national average trends. Thus trends in the number and duration of Response Phase tasks differ between the national groups.

In addition to comparing trends in Response Phase parameters, it is also possible to compare how the values of these parameters compare with the national average values.

Virtually all the Response Phase parameters for the Czech (alarm only) group are greater than or significantly greater than the group averages, indicating that this group will take considerably longer in the Response Phase than the national average, and is likely to have the longest response time. It is also worth noting that the sub-population reacting to staff intervention behaved significantly differently to the sub-population reacting to the alarm only. For this group, all the Response Phase parameters were smaller than the parameters for Czech alarm group and the national average parameters. This indicates that the Czech staff intervention group reacted significantly quicker than the Czech alarm group and the national average. One possible explanation for why there is such a significant difference between the two Czech sub-populations is that the population has little regard for a disembodied authority – such as a voice over a public address system, but has significantly more respect for a personalized authority figure.

For the UK (alarm only) group, the NT is significantly greater than the national average. While the number of Action and Information Tasks undertaken are less than the national averages, the average duration of both Action and Information Tasks are greater than or significantly greater than the national group averages. This suggests that the UK (alarm only) group will take longer in the Response Phase than the national average.

For the Polish group, the NT is smaller than the national average. While the number of Action Tasks is greater than the national average and the number of Information Tasks is less than the national average, the average duration of Action Tasks is the same as the national average and the duration of Information Tasks is less than the national average. This suggests that the Polish population is likely to have a shorter Response Phase than the national average.

For the Turkish group, the NT is smaller than the national average. While the number of Action Tasks is less than the national average and the number of Information Tasks is greater than the national average, the average duration of both Action and Information Tasks is less than the national group averages. This suggests that the Turkish population is likely to have a shorter Response Phase than the national average, and is likely to have the shortest Response Phase. It is interesting to note that a number of people in the Turkish library evacuation left all of their belongings behind them when they evacuated the library. This includes personal computers, bags and books. This behaviour was not noted in any of the other library evacuations. This may explain why the average number of Action Tasks for the Turkey library is less than that for the other four libraries.

In terms of average notification times, the UK (alarm only) and Czech (alarm only) are 71% and 752% greater than the national average respectively, while the Turkish and Polish are 4% and 20% less than the national averages respectively. In terms of average response times, the UK (alarm only) and Czech (alarm only) are 15% and 143% greater than the national average respectively, while the Polish and Turkish are 12% and 30% less than the national averages respectively.

Given that the parameters that influence Response Phase behaviour and performance (e.g. population: level of familiarity and training, age distribution and gender mix and type of structure) were reasonably controlled, it is possible that the observed significant differences in response time distributions and the differences in Response Phase parameters are the result of cultural influences on Response Phase behaviour.

7.7.4 Other factors which may have Influenced response times and response phase behaviours

Several factors complicate the nature of the cross national comparisons undertaken in this assessment. These concern, the level of repeatability of each trial, the nature of the alarm in the UK building, the nature of the alarm in the Czech building, the nature of the pre-alarm activities and the initial perception of the alarm. Each of these will now be examined in turn.

Level of repeatability

Only a single evacuation trial was conducted in each of the three BeSeCu libraries and only a single trial was conducted in the UK library. Thus the question arises as to how representative is the response time distribution and Response Phase behaviours measured in these trials. If the trials were repeated, would we get similar results? Ideally, the trials would have been repeated, at least once, using different representative populations. Unfortunately, undertaking such trials was beyond the scope of the project and would have been prohibitively expensive, both in terms of financial resources and time. However, it is argued that given the number of people involved in the trials and given that one of the key parameters is the response time distribution that it may not be necessary to undertake repeat trials. It is suggested that response time distributions generated from identical structures, with identical notification systems and similar populations will be very similar. Detailed evidence to support this view is limited as such repeat evacuation trials are seldom undertaken. However, FSEG have undertaken such a repeat series of trials as part of the EU FP7 project SAFEGUARD (Galea, Brown, Filippidis & Deere, 2010).

As part of project SAFEGUARD two semi-unannounced evacuation trials were conducted on the RO-PAX ferry Superspeed1 (SS1). SS1 is operated by ColorLine and can carry approximately 2000 passengers and crew and over 700 vehicles. The route taken by the vessel during these trials is from Kristiansand in Norway to Hirtshals in Denmark, a trip of 3 hours and 15 minutes. The ship contains a mixture of spaces spread over three decks including; business and traveler class seating areas (airline style seating), large retail and restaurant/catering areas, bar areas, in-door and out-door general seating areas and general circulation spaces. The evacuation drills conducted on SS1 took place on 4 Sept, 2010 at 08:20 and on 5 Sept, 2010 at 08:19 approximately 30 minutes after the vessel departed from Kristiansand. A total of 1,431 and 1,349 passengers were on board SS1 for the first and second trials (different passengers each day). By semi-unannounced we mean that the passengers were aware that there would be an assembly drill on their crossing, but they did not know when this would take place. For these trials, the nature of the structure was identical and complex, with a variety of different types of spaces. The nature of the population on both days was very similar, with a similar gender and age mix and nationality mix (predominately Norwegian and German). The data collection and analysis methodology was similar to that presented in this document however, only response time data was collected. For the first trial 533 response times were collected and for the second trial 470 response times were collected (see Fig. 7.28).

Presented in Fig. 7.28 are the two fitted log-normal curves for the response time distributions for the two trials. As can be seen they appear to be very similar. The curves were subjected to a similar statistical analysis to that conducted for the BeSeCu response time curves (see Section 7.7.2).

Normality testing (Kolmogorov-Smirnov) was applied to the two data sets (Superspeed1 day1 and Superspeed1 day2) data sets. This showed that the data sets are likely to be NOT normally distributed within the 5% confidence level ($p < 0.05$ and so the hypothesis that the data set is normally distributed is rejected). As the data sets are likely to not be normally distributed it is acceptable to compare the data sets using non-parametric methods.

The Mann-Whitney test was performed on the pair of data sets to identify whether there was a significant difference between the data sets. The results for this analysis can be summarized as follows:

- Superspeed Day1 v. Superspeed Day2, $p = 0.08$, $p > 0.05$

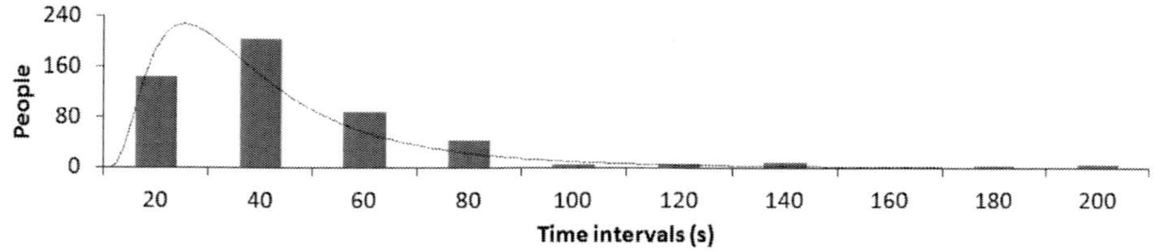

(a) Day 1 response time distribution

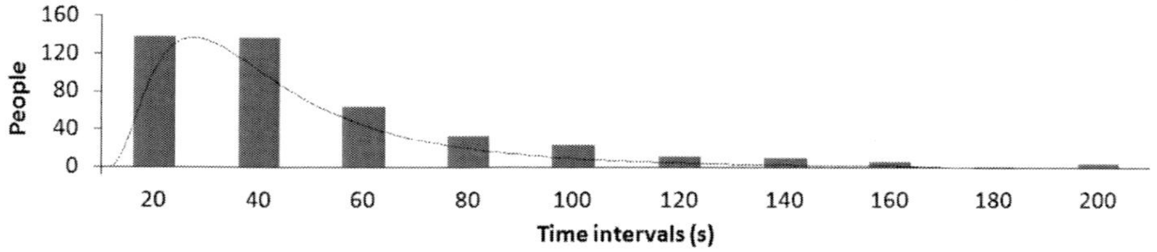

(b) Day 2 response time distribution

Fig. 7.28: Comparison of the two Superspeed response time distributions

Thus there is not a significant difference between each pair of response time distributions at the 5% significance level.

This result supports the view that we may expect repeat evacuation trials in the same structure with a different population but with the same characteristics to produce similar response time distributions. As the response time distribution is a statistical construct – unlike the evacuation exit curve – it is more likely to be invariant with respect to repeat trials. Thus not undertaking repeat evacuation trials may not significantly impact the conclusions derived from these trials.

Nature of the alarm in the UK building

The nature of the notification system is known to have an impact on response time. Therefore in an attempt to control the influence of this parameter it was essential that the populations in all three BeSeCu trials were subjected to the same type of alarm. This was achieved in each of the three BeSeCu buildings in which a voice alarm system was used. However in the UK building, a traditional alarm bell was used. A simple conventional tone alarm is known not to be as efficient as a voice alarm in motivating the population to respond to the call to evacuate. Thus we may reasonably expect that had a voice alarm system been used in the UK building that a shorter average response time may have been produced.

It is thus difficult to isolate culture as the only distinct variable in the UK data set. However, if the UK distribution is removed from the cross comparisons, there are still significant differences between the three BeSeCu response time distributions and Response Phase behaviours.

Nature of the alarm in the Czech building

As has already been mentioned the alarm in the Czech library failed to work as planned. However, part of the library did here the alarm message. Unfortunately, the alarm message was not as originally planned and was overly long and complex being in four parts. This may have had an impact on the response times of the population who could hear the alarm. To address this, the response times and Response Phase behaviours are measured from the third alarm sequence. This should reduce the influence of the lengthy alarm messages and the early messages which simply alerted the population that there was a potential emergency developing in their building. If anything, one may have expected that warning the population that there may be a need to evacuate would elicit a better response if/when the population is notified that they do have to evacuate, not a longer response.

Nature of the pre-alarm activities

The nature of the pre-alarm activities may influence how rapidly the population responds to the alarm. In an attempt to control this variable, the same type of building was used in all four trials. By using the same building it was hoped that the nature of the activities that the population were involved in would be broadly similar. With a library environment it was anticipated that the majority of the population in each case would be involved in study/work related activities. This is indeed the case with 57% or more of the population in each library being involved in study/ work related activities. However, there was a difference between the libraries, with only 57% of the Turkish population engaged in work activities while the Czech Republic, Poland and the UK had 87%, 90% and 90% respectively. The large difference in the number of people actually engaged in study/work at the time of the alarm in the Turkey library compared to the other libraries may explain why this produced the shortest average evacuation time.

However, a closer look at the data suggests that the differences in the number of people at work in the libraries may not be as great as first suggested. Those categorized as "Sitting" (see Table7.8) were at a workstation at the time of the alarm, but did not appear to actually be engaged in a work related activity just at the time of the alarm. However, as they were at a workstation it can be assumed that they were engaged in a work related activity, if not when the alarm was activated, at some time just prior to the alarm being activated. If we include these in the "at work" category then we have the following distribution of "at work" at the time of the alarm, Turkey, 69%; Czech Rep, 87%; Poland, 92% and UK, 92%. While Turkey still has the least involved in work, the difference has decreased significantly.

Perhaps of more significance are the number engaged in computer related work activities. It is suggested that disengaging from computer based activities may incur a longer delay than disengaging from other work activities. Hence being engaged in computer activities may lead to longer notification times and hence longer response times (see Table 7.8). From Table 7.8 we note that the notification times for those engaged in computer related work are between 14% and 175%

longer than those involved in other work related activities. With the exception of Turkey, the response times are also longer. The inconsistency in the response times for the Turkey population could be due to the small size of the Turkey data set not involved in other work.

Table 7.8: Comparison of response and notification times for those at the computer and those involved in other wor

	At Work at Computer			Other Work		
	RT(s)	NT(s)	#	RT(s)	NT(s)	#
Turkey	53.8	6.7	25	86.6	5.9	4
UK (alarm only)	102.0	25.5	36	83.0	9.3	21
Poland	81.8	9.2	51	70.4	7.5	122
Czech (alarm only)	327.9	212.4	11	258.8	123.0	6

It is also noted that the Czech Republic, Turkey and UK have about half their populations involved in computer work related activities while Poland has only about a quarter. While this may account for Poland having the shortest average notification time (see Table 7.9), Turkey has the shortest average response time (and the second shortest notification time). Furthermore, we note that 79% of the Czech staff intervention population were engaged in computer work related activities when notified of the need to evacuate, compared with 57% of the Czech alarm population. Even with such a high proportion of the population engaged in computer activities the notification time for the Czech staff intervention population was the shortest of all the populations. However, this may also have been influenced by the nature of the notification process, with staff intervention being more effective than alarms.

The difference in the proportion of the various populations involved in work related activities prior to the alarm is not considered to have greatly contributed to the observed significant differences in the response time distributions and Response Phase behaviours. However, the relatively small proportion of the Polish population involved in computer work related activities at the time of the alarm compared to the other populations may have had some impact on the notification time distribution with some effect on the response time distribution.

Initial perception of the alarm

It is possible that the difference in response behaviour may be attributed to the initial perception of the alarm. Information relating to the occupants initial perception of the alarm is available from the questionnaire for the three BeSeCu library populations (see Table 7.9). In all three BeSeCu libraries, 68% or more of the populations thought that the alarm was a false alarm or a drill, with this increasing to 90% for the Czech and Turkish populations. However, a significant proportion of the Polish population (28%) thought that the alarm signified a real fire which may have contributed to Poland producing the shortest average notification time.

The three BeSeCu libraries are similar in that over 60% of each population thought that the alarm was a false alarm or a drill. Furthermore, the library in the Czech Republic, which produced the longest average response time, and the library in Turkey, which produced the shortest average response time, 90% of the population considered the alarm to be either a false alarm or a drill. This suggests that initial perception of the alarm is not sufficient to explain the variation in average response times.

Table 7.9: Perception of alarm

Country	False Alarm	Drill	Real Fire
Czech Rep	36%	54%	3%
Turkey	24%	66%	10%
Poland	6%	62%	28%
UK	–	–	–

7.7.5 Summary

Statistically significant differences (at the 5% level) have been observed in the response time distributions for the four library evacuations. Differences have also been noted in the relative trends between Response Phase parameters (NAT, NIT, ATT, ITT and NT) which determine response times.

Every effort was made to ensure that the conditions for each evacuation were as similar as possible. This is essential to ensure that as far as possible the main variables that may influence the evacuation are social cultural. As these trials were full-scale and unannounced, as opposed to laboratory based trials, it is virtually impossible to ensure that conditions are exactly identical in each trial. However, the age, gender and evacuation experience of the population was very similar.

The building type across all three trials was also identical (a library) so as to ensure that the population were involved in similar activities. To a certain extent this was achieved with the majority of people (over 69%) in each library involved in work related activities. However in one case (Polish library), a relatively small proportion of the population (a quarter) was involved in computer work related activities at the time of the alarm compared to the other populations (which had about a half). This may have had some impact on the notification time distribution with some effect on the response time distribution. Furthermore, the fact that only a single trial was undertaken in each library is not considered to be a significant problem as there is some evidence to suggest that response time distributions derived from one trial can be expected to be fairly representative of the scenario being considered. However, of more significance is the fact that a different notification system (alarm) was used it the UK trial compared to the other three trials. As the nature of the alarm system is expected to have a significant impact on the response time distribution, it can be argued that the UK data set should be excluded from the cross-cultural comparison.

Given that the parameters that influence Response Phase behaviour and performance (e.g. population: level of familiarity and training, age distribution and gender mix and type of structure) were reasonably controlled, it is possible that the observed significant differences in response time distributions and the differences in Response Phase parameters are the result of cultural influences on Response Phase behaviour. This conclusion is valid for the three BeSeCu libraries (Turkey, Czech Republic and Poland) and may also be valid for the fourth library (UK).

7.7.6 The Impact of fire culture on evacuation behaviour

The impact of fire culture on the outcome of Response Phase behaviour was controlled, for the most part, by the intervention of the FSEG research team. The intervention consisted of ensuring that some procedure was in place to facilitate the evacuation and that the alarm system would operate (following the Czech Republic experience). Situations in which emergency exits were locked were noted and on the whole not acted upon (with the exception of the Turkish trial) prior to the evacuation trial. Here we highlight some of the issues that were noted in the various libraries.

UK

The fire culture in the UK is such that, the fire alarms are tested each week, there are three unannounced fire drills each year and there are procedures set down for staff to follow in the event of an emergency. Furthermore, all the emergency exits have panic bars allowing them to be utilized in the event of an emergency evacuation.

Czech Republic

Several fire culture issues were encountered during the evacuation trial in the Czech Republic. The first and possibly most serious was the failure of the alarm system to function correctly on the day it was required. It was indeed fortunate that this fault was discovered as part of the evacuation trial as it is unlikely to have been uncovered apart from during an actual emergency. The fact that regular testing of the alarm system is not mandatory in the Czech Republic is the reason that the failure in the alarm system was not detected prior to the trial. In the UK for example, alarms are tested on a weekly basis. The reason that the alarm had failed was that some time prior to the trials major reconstruction work had been undertaken in the library. That the alarm system may have been affected by these works is not surprising, but that the alarm system was not checked when the building was brought back into service is surprising. The nature of the alarm message

(a) Main exit (b) Emergency exit

Fig. 7.29: Exits chained shut in the Czech library building

is also an example of poor fire culture. The messaging that was used on the day was far too long and complex to be effective. The messaging displayed a lack of understanding of good fire safety practice. When the alarm failed there was no backup plan. The staff members were not expected to play a role in the effective management of the evacuation process. Complete confidence was placed in the proper functioning of the alarm system. Finally, a number of exits in the library were chained shut. These included part of the main exit and also emergency exits (see Fig. 7.29). In the event of an emergency, security staff members are expected to find the required keys and unlock the doors. Clearly this is an unsafe practice and not one that would normally be allowed. The fire culture in the Czech Republic is clearly very different to that in the UK. In the event of a real emergency, these differences in fire culture can be expected to contribute to significantly different evacuation performance between the two countries.

Turkey

The library building in Turkey was relatively new, having been opened in October 2007. The building was a modern design and built to modern standards. However, since its opening there had never been an evacuation drill and there were no formal procedures set down for staff in the event of a fire. The fire alarm had never been tested in the library. The staff knew that they had a modern voice alarm system installed, but they had never heard the message and didn't know how to test it or change the messaging. Indeed, when the alarm was finally tested the message was found to be in English rather than the native language (Turkish). It is thus likely that the majority of people in the library would not have understood the messaging in the event of an emergency. When the alarm was tested, it was noted that the elevators/lifts (which were not fire lifts) continued to operate normally during the alarm. Finally, the emergency side exit was locked (see Fig. 7.30 a) and the

(a) Locked emergency exit. (b) Emergency exit sign pointing away from emergency.

Fig. 7.30: Locked emergency exit and modified emergency exit sign in Turkish library

emergency exit sign that pointed to the emergency exit was turned around so that it pointed away from the emergency exit (see Fig. 7.30 b). With the emergency exit locked, there was only one exit from the building.

The fire culture in Turkey is clearly very different to that in the UK. In the event of a real emergency, these differences in fire culture can be expected to contribute to significantly different evacuation performance between the two countries.

Poland

The library building in Poland was a landmark structure. It was of modern design and construction. The building has a modern fire alarm and modern fire safety measures such as smoke screens which descend to compartmentalize the building and prevent rapid smoke spread. In Poland the fire alarms are checked (not as frequently as in the UK) and drills are held on a regular basis (again not as frequently as in the UK). None of the emergency exits were locked in such a manner that could not be opened in the event of an emergency. However, there were a few problems with the layout of the building and the procedures. As is common, the majority of people (67%) utilized the main exit to leave the building. The main

Fig. 7.31: Size of main stair and main exit in Polish library

(a) An emergency exit. (b) Path leading from the emergency exit.

Fig. 7.32: Emergency exit in the Polish library

exit was not dimensioned to accommodate such a large volume of people and so considerable congestion occurred just ahead of the final exit (see Fig. 7.31). In addition, while the emergency exits were well designed and positioned around the library, the immediate access area just outside some of the emergency exits were not appropriate.

Depicted in Fig. 7.32a is an emergency exit in the Polish library. The swing of the door would make staying on the narrow path (see Fig. 7.32b) difficult if not impossible. If you could get around the open door, staying on the narrow path as you walked to a place of safety would be difficult. If large numbers of people attempted to use this exit, their escape would be hampered by the nature of the path.

The fire culture in Poland is similar to that in the UK. In the event of a real emergency, these similarities in fire culture can be expected to contribute to similar evacuation performance between the two countries.

7.7.7 Conclusions drawn from the BeSeCu evacuation trials

The aim of the experimental component of project BeSeCu was to study how people react in an emergency, and to determine whether social culture impacts emergency behaviour. As part of project BeSeCu, three unannounced library evacuations were conducted in the Czech Republic, Turkey and Poland. In addition, the data from these trials was compared with data generated from a similar evacuation conducted previously in the UK. The main purpose of these trials was to examine if social culture influences the manner in which people respond to the call to evacuate. Thus the experimental component of BeSeCu focused on the Response Phase of the evacuation process.

The three evacuations that were conducted as part of this project generated detailed Response Phase behaviours for 373 individuals. Combined with the data analyzed from the UK evacuation, the Response Phase data set studied in BeSeCu comprised of 477 individuals, 192 from Poland, 51 from Turkey, 70 from the Czech Republic and 104 from the UK. In addition, two comprehensive evacuation model validation data sets were also developed from the Turkish and Polish evacuation trials (Galea, 2012; Galea, Sauter, Deere & Filippidis, 2011; Galea, Sharp, Sauter, Deere & Filippidis, 2012).The key developments and findings resulting from this work relating to response phase behaviours are set out below.

Response phase descriptive framework

The comparative studies of evacuation behaviour were based not simply on response times but on a framework, developed as part of project BeSeCu, to describe Response Phase behaviours. The framework not only provides a consistent method for describing Response Phase behaviour, but also provides a systematic means for classifying and quantifying the Response Phase other than simply using the overall response time. By understanding and quantifying the factors which influence and ultimately determine the Response Phase we are better able to compare and contrast different evacuation situations.

Based on the Response Phase Behavioural Framework, key parameters that define the Response Phase for each member of the population are:

- Response Time (sec).
- Notification Time (sec).
- Number of Action Tasks undertaken.
- Number of Information Tasks undertaken.
- Action Task duration (sec).
- Information Task duration (sec).

From these individual parameters a parameter set representative of the population as a whole can be determined by taking the average for each individual parameter. In this way the Response Phase for a particular evacuation can be defined by specifying the average duration of the Notification stage (NT), the average number of Action Tasks (AT) undertaken, the average number of Information Tasks (IT) undertaken, the average duration of an Action Task (ATT), the average duration of an Information and Task (ITT) and the average Response Time (RT).

For a common group of buildings and their populations defined by; building type, nature of notification system, population demographics and levels of population structural familiarity and training, the Response Phase parameter set (i.e. NT, AT, IT, ITT and ATT), and hence the response time distribution, can be expected to be similar for different examples within the group. However, if the Response Phase parameter set and hence the response time distribution are also dependent on culture, it is possible that the response time distributions and Response Phase parameter sets will be different even for buildings from the same group located in different countries.

In addition, the Response Phase Behavioural Framework provides an empirical means of predicting population average response time based on average number of Information/Action tasks, average task duration and average notification time.

Differences in response phase behaviours

For the four library evacuations conducted in four different countries, differences were noted in the relative trends between Response Phase parameters (NAT, NIT, ATT, ITT and NT) defining the Response Phase parameter set.

Of the four countries, the UK (alarm only) population was the only one of the four national groups whose trends in Response Phase characteristics match the trends of the national average population. These trends are that the population undertakes more Action than Information tasks and the average duration of an Information Task is greater than the average duration of an Action Task. The Polish and Czech (alarm only) populations match different aspects of the average trend, with the Polish population matching trends in the number of tasks, while the Czech (alarm only) population matches trends in the average duration of the tasks. The Turkish population behaves in a way which is opposite to the national average trends.

Furthermore, trends in the number and duration of Response Phase tasks also differ between the national groups. Consider the country with the longest response times (Czech Republic) and the country with the shortest response times (Turkey). Virtually all the Response Phase parameters for the Czech (alarm only) group are greater than or significantly greater than the national group averages, indicating that this group will take considerably longer in the Response Phase than the national average, and is likely to have the longest response time. For the Turkish group, both the NT and the number of Action Tasks are smaller than the national average and the average duration of both Action and Information Tasks are less than the national group averages. This suggests that the Turkish population is likely to have a shorter Response Phase than the national average, and is likely to have the shortest Response Phase.

Differences in response time distributions

Statistically significant differences (at the 5% level) were observed in the response time distributions for the four library evacuations conducted in four different countries.

The UK (alarm only) response time data is:

- Quicker on average than the Czech Rep (alarm only) response time data.
- Slower on average than the Poland response time data.
- Slower on average than the Turkey response time data.

The Poland response time data is:
- Quicker on average than the Czech Rep (alarm only) response time data.
- Slower on average than the Turkey response time data.

The Turkey response time data is:
- Quicker on average than the Czech Rep (alarm only) response time data.

On average, the populations with the quickest to the slowest response times are: Turkey, Poland, UK and Czech Republic.

Is response phase behaviour dependent on social culture?

The response time distributions for each of the four libraries have been shown to be statistically significantly different. In addition, trends in and values of the Response Phase parameter sets for the four evacuations have been shown to be different. Furthermore, every effort was made to ensure that the conditions for each evacuation were as similar as possible. This is essential to ensure that as far as possible the main variable that may influence evacuation performance is social cultural. As these trials were full-scale and unannounced, as opposed to laboratory based trials, it is virtually impossible to ensure that conditions are exactly identical in each trial. However, the age, gender and evacuation experience of each population was very similar.

The building type across all three trials was also identical (a library) so as to ensure that the population were involved in similar activities. To a certain extent this was achieved with the majority of people (over 69%) in each library involved in work related activities. However in one case (Polish library), a relatively small proportion of the population (a quarter) was involved in computer work related activities at the time of the alarm compared to the other populations (which had about a half). This may explain why the Polish population had the shortest average notification time. However, the Polish population did not have the shortest average response time and so the differences in the number of people engaged in computer work related activities is not considered significant. While only a single evacuation trial was conducted at each library, this is not considered to be significant as there is some evidence to suggest that response time distributions derived from one trial can be expected to be representative of the scenario (defined by building type, notification system and population) being considered. However, of more significance is the fact that a different notification system (alarm) was used it the UK trial compared to the other three trials. As the nature of the alarm system is expected to have a significant impact on the response time distribution, it can be argued that the UK data set should be excluded from the cross-cultural comparison.

Given that the parameters that influence Response Phase behaviour and performance (e.g. population: level of familiarity and training, age distribution and gender mix and type of structure) were reasonably controlled, it is possible that the observed significant differences in response time distributions and the differences in Response Phase parameters are the result of cultural influences on Response

Phase behaviour. This conclusion is valid for the three BeSeCu libraries (Turkey, Czech Republic and Poland) and may also be valid for the fourth library (UK). Further work is required before a definitive link between social culture and evacuation behaviour can be established.

Predictive response time model

An empirical response time model, based on the Response Phase parameter set (NAT, NIT, ATT, ITT and NT) was developed and applied to the evacuation trial data. For four different evacuations in four different countries the predictive response time model was able to predict the measured average response time within: 1.6% in the Czech Republic evacuation trial, 11.3% in the Turkey evacuation trial, 3.0% in the Poland evacuation trial and 3.9% within the UK evacuation trial. The average error across all four trials is 5.0%.

Thus the constants used in the empirical response time model appear to be reasonably robust, providing a good level of agreement for four evacuation trials conducted in four different libraries in four different countries. Of more importance is the insight it provides into the behavioural factors driving the response time. Using this approach it should be possible to estimate the impact of introducing technical or procedural measures to address various behavioural determinants of response time such as the duration of the average Information Task, or the number of Information Tasks that are performed by a population.

Observations relating to the response phase

The detailed analysis of the BeSeCu and related evacuation data allowed a number of important observations to be made concerning evacuation behaviour. These include.

Average response phase behaviours

Taken across all four evacuations, on average university library populations:

- Have an average notification time of 10.4 s.
- Undertakes on average 4.2 Information Tasks.
- Undertakes on average 5.4 Action Tasks.
- Requires on average 6.4 s to complete an Action Task.
- Requires on average 7.1 s to complete an Information Task.
- Has an average response time of 79.6 s.

Impact of pre-alarm activity on notification time

Across all four evacuation trials it was noted that occupants engaged in computer related work activities incur longer delays in disengaging from work related activities on the sounding of the alarm than those engaged in other types of work activities. Hence being engaged in computer activities may lead to longer notification times and hence longer response times. Notification times for those engaged in computer related work are between 14% and 175% longer than those involved in other work related activities.

Alarm vs. staff intervention

In the Czech evacuation part of the population was exposed only to a voice alarm and part only to staff intervention. This provided a good opportunity to compare and contrast the response behaviours of the two populations. Compared to the staff intervention population, the alarm only population:

- Take 12.3x longer to disengage from their pre-alarm activities,
- Undertake 2.3x more tasks,
- Undertake 3.7x more Information Tasks and
- Take 1.5x longer in information exchange.

All of this explains why the alarm only population has an average response time 4.5x greater than the staff intervention population. The results for the Czech population confirm the commonly held belief that relative response times for populations exposed to staff intervention will be shorter than those exposed to an alarm only. However, it must be noted that the response times reported here do not include the time required for the staff member to respond to the alarm and travel to the population location. If these times are taken into consideration, the absolute response time for the population exposed to staff intervention may be greater than that for the population exposed only to the alarm.

Alarm and staff intervention

In the UK evacuation some of the population was exposed to both the alarm and staff intervention. In such cases, staff intervention is intended to shorten the response phase of those individuals that may take excessive time responding. The staff intervention process achieves this by reducing the targeted occupants Notification stage or Activity stage or both stages. Evidence supporting this view was collected from the UK evacuation trial. In this trial the staff intervention population consisted of two distinct sub-groups.

The first sub-group had exceptionally long Notification times, the group effectively ignoring the alarm. However, this sub-group disengaged from their pre-alarm activities shortly after staff intervention. Clearly, this sub-group was intent on completing their pre-alarm activities. However, without staff intervention, these individuals may have incurred even longer Notification times. So staff intervention may have resulted in these individuals completing the Notification stage sooner than would otherwise have occurred. The response time for this sub-group was significantly longer than that for the alarm only group, but may have been even longer without the staff intervention. For this group, staff intervention potentially reduced what are exceptionally long Notification times from being even longer and reduced the duration of the Activity stage. Had the staff intervention occurred earlier, the notification time may have been even shorter.

The second sub-group had completed the Notification stage and commenced the Activity stage well before any staff members appeared. For this group the Notification time was extremely short and was not influenced by the staff intervention. However, this sub-group undertook more tasks during the Activity stage (10.7) than the alarm only population (8.8). It is possible that the staff intervention prevented even more tasks from being undertaken during the Activity Stage, preventing the Activity stage from taking even longer. The response time for this group was marginally longer than that for the alarm only group (92 sec). For this group, staff intervention potentially reduced the duration of the Activity stage.

Group behaviour

From the Turkish and Polish evacuation, the response to the questionnaires suggests that when first alerted by the alarm about half the population were in groups of friends, a third were alone and about a fifth were in groups of strangers. If you were in a group of friends prior to the alarm, it was likely that you evacuated in a group and that you exited in a group whereas if you were in a group of strangers, it is likely that you separated from the group and evacuated alone. Thus the bond between groups of friends is seen to be much stronger than the group bond between strangers during the evacuation. Furthermore, if you were alone prior to the alarm, you were very likely to evacuate alone. Clearly group behaviour is an important aspect of evacuation and requires further research.

How representative is a response time distribution derived from a single trial?

It is conjectured that repeat evacuation trials in a given structure with a different but similar population (i.e. a population that has similar demographics and key characteristics) will produce similar response time distributions. Evidence to support this view was presented from the EF FP7 SAFEGUARD project which involved two evacuation trials on a large passenger ferry involving a range of accommodation including; business and traveller class seating areas (airline style seating), large retail and restaurant/catering areas, bar areas, in-door and out-door general seating areas and general circulation spaces. The trials were conducted on two days with two different but similar populations. The two response time distributions were made up from 533 and 470 individual response times respectively. Mann-Whitney testing performed on the pair of data sets revealed that there is not a significant difference between the pair of response time distributions at the 5% significance level. As the response time distribution is a statistical construct – unlike the evacuation exit curve – it is more likely to be invariant with respect to repeat trials.

Impact of fire culture on evacuation performance

In the BeSeCu evacuation trials, the impact of fire culture on the outcome of Response Phase and evacuation performance was controlled, for the most part, through the intervention of the FSEG research team. However, in the event of a real emergency, the noted deficiencies in fire culture could be expected to adversely contribute to evacuation performance. Noted short comings in fire culture included:

- Failure of the alarm system to operate in the Czech trial. If regular testing was required by regulation and undertaken, this could have been avoided.

- Nature of the alarm message was too long and complex in the Czech trail. Regulatory guidance should be provided regarding the effective use of a voice alarm system.
- Exits were locked and chained shut in the Czech trial. Fire regulations should prevent exits from being unusable and fire safety inspections should detect when this occurs.
- No evacuation drill had ever been conducted in the Turkish library. Fire regulations should make some form of fire drills mandatory.
- The fire alarm had never been tested in the Turkish library. Fire regulations should make it mandatory to have regular tests of the fire alarm system.
- The alarm message was not in the native language of the building users in the Turkish library. Regulatory guidance should be provided regarding the effective use of a voice alarm system.
- There were no evacuation plans for the Turkish library. Fire regulations and safety regulations should make it mandatory for some form of emergency evacuation plans for public buildings.
- The emergency exit was locked and the emergency signage changed in the Turkish library. Fire regulations should prevent emergency exits from being unusable and fire safety inspections should detect when this occurs.
- In the Polish trial, while the emergency exits were well designed and positioned around the library, the immediate access area just outside some of the emergency exits were not appropriate. Building fire regulations should extend to the outside of the building and to the assembly of the occupants and fire safety inspections should enforce these regulations.

References

Brennan, P., *"Timing Human Response in Real Fires"*, Proceedings of the Fifth International Symposium on Fire Safety Science, International Association Fire Safety Science, Melbourne, Australia, pp 807-818, 1997.

Charters, D., Holbourn, P., Townsend, N., *"Analysis of the number of occupants, detection times and pre-movement times"*, 2nd International Symposium on Human Behaviour in Fire, Interscience Communications, UK, ISBN 0953231267, pp 197-207, 2001.

Field, A.P., *"Discovering Statistics Using SPSS"*, 3rd edition, SAGE Publications Ltd, 2009, ISBN 9781847879066.

Galea, E.R., "Evacuation Response Phase Behaviour," *CMS Press 09/IM/147*, London, 2009, pp. 1-30.

Galea, E.R., Brown, R.C., Filippidis. L. & Deere. S., "Collection of Evacuation Data for Large Passenger Vessels at Sea", *Pedestrian and Evacuation Dynamics 2010. 5th International Conference. Proceedings.* March 8-10, 2010, Springer, New York, NY, Peacock, R.D., Kuligowski, E.D., and Averill, J.D., Editor(s), pp 163-172, DOI 10.1007/978-1-4419-9725-8_15, 2011.

Galea, E.R., Deere, S., Sharp, G., Filippidis, L., Lawrence, P., Gwynne, S., "Recommendations on the Nature of the Passenger Response Time Distribution to be used in the MSC 1033 Assembly Time Analysis Based on Data Derived from Sea Trials", *International Journal of Maritime Engineering, Vol 149, Part A1,* ISSN 1479-8751, pp. 15-29, 2007.

Galea, E.R., Filippidis, L., Deere, S.J., Sharp, G. & Sauter, M., *"Investigating the Impact of Culture on Evacuation Response Phase Behaviour – The Project BeSeCu Evacuation Experiments",* CMS Press 12/IM/160, ISBN 978-1-904521-78-5, London, 2012, pp. 1-283.

Galea, E.R., Hulse, L., Day, R., Siddiqui, A., Sharp, G., Shields, J., Boyce, K., Summerfield, L., Canter, D., Marselle, M., Greenall, P.V., "The UK WTC9/11 Evacuation Study: An Overview of the Methodologies Employed and some Preliminary Analysis", *Proceedings Pedestrian and Evacuation Dynamics 2008,* ED: W.W.F.Kligsch et al, Springer-Verlag Berlin Heidelberg, ISBN 978-3-642-04503-5, http://dx.doi.org/10.1007/978-3-642-04504-2_1, pp3-24, 2010.

Galea, E.R., Sauter, M., Deere, S.J., Filippidis, L. "Investigating the Impact of Culture on Evacuation Behaviour – A Turkish Data-Set". *Proceedings of the Tenth International Symposium on Fire Safety Science*, University of Maryland, 19-24 June 2011, pp. 709-722.

Galea, E.R., Sharp, G., Lawrence, P., Dixon, A., "Investigating the Impact of Occupant Response Time on Computer Simulations of the WTC North Tower Evacuation", *Proceedings of the 11th International Fire Science & Engineering Conference, Interflam 2007,* 3rd-5th September 2007, Royal Holloway College, University of London, UK, Volume 2, pp. 1435-1442. ISBN 978 0 9541216-9-3, 2007.

Galea, E.R, Sharp, G., Lawrence, P.J., Holden, R., "Approximating the Evacuation of the World Trade Center North Tower using Computer Simulation", *Journal of Fire Protection Engineering, Vol 18 (2),* 85-115, 2008. doi: http://dx.doi.org/10.1177/1042391507079343.

Galea, E.R., Sharp, G. & Lawrence, P., "Investigating the Representation of Merging Behavior at the Floor – Stair Interface in Computer Simulations of Multi-Floor Building Evacuations", *Journal of Fire Protection Engineering, Vol. 18, No. 4,* 291-316, 2008 http://dx.doi.org/10.1177/1042391508095092.

Galea, E.R., Sharp, G., Sauter, M., Deere, S.J., Filippidis, L. "Investigating the Impact of Culture on Evacuation Behaviour – A Polish Data-Set". To appear in the *Proceedings of the Fifth International Symposium on Human Behaviour in Fire,* Cambridge University, 19-21 September 2012, Interscience Communications Ltd, 2012.

Galea, E.R., Shields, J., Canter, D., Boyce, K., Day, R., Hulse, L., Siddiqui, A., Summerfield, L., Marselle, M., Greenall, P., "Methodologies employed in the Collection, Retrieval and Storage of Human Factors Information Derived from First Hand Accounts of Survivors of the WTC Disaster of 11 September 2001", *Journal of Applied Fire Science. Vol 15, Number 4,* 253-276, http://dx.doi.org/10.2190/AF.15.4.b, 2006.

Gwynne, S., *"Notification Effectiveness for Large Groups",* Report prepared for The Fire Protection Research Foundation, Quincy, MA, USA, June 2007.

Gwynne, S., Galea, E.R. & Lawrence, P.J., "The Introduction of social adaptation within evacuation modelling", *Fire and Materials, Vol 30, No 4,* pp 285-309, 2006. DOI:10.1002/fam.913.

Gwynne, S., Galea, E.R., Parke, J, Hickson, J., *"The Collection and Analysis of Pre-Evacuation Times from Evacuation Trials and their Application to Evacuation Modelling",* Fire Technology, Kluwer Associates, US, pp 173-195, vol 39, number 2, 2003.

Gwynne, S., Galea, E.R., Parke, J., Hickson, J., "The Collection of Pre-Evacuation Times from Evacuation Trials Involving a Hospital Outpatient Area and a University Library Facility", *Proceedings of 7th IAFS Symposium WPI,* USA, ISBN 0954534808, pp 877-888, 2003.

Proulx, G., "Evacuation time and movement in apartment buildings", *Fire Safety Journal 24:* pp 229-246, 1995.

Proulx, G., *„Time Delay To Start Evacuating Upon Hearing The Fire Alarm,"* Human Factors And Ergonomics Society 38th Annual Meeting, Ergonomics Society, 1994, pp. 811-815.

Proulx, G. & Sime, J. (1991) To Prevent "Panic" In: An Underground Emergency: Why Not Tell People The Truth? *Fire Safety Science 3:* 843-852, http://dx.doi.org/10.3801/IAFSS.FSS.3-843.

Proulx, G., Fahy, R., "The Time Delay to Start Evacuation: Review of Five Case Studies", *Proceedings of the Fifth International Symposium on Fire Safety Science,* Melbourne, Australia, International Association of Fire Safety Science, pp 783-794, 1997.

Purser, D.A., "Quantification of behaviour of engineering design standards and escape time calculations", *Proc First Int. Symp. Human Behaviour in Fire.* University of Ulster, Belfast, 497-508, 1998.

Shields, T.J., Boyce, K.E., "A Study of Evacuation from Large Retail Stores", *Fire Safety Journal 35:* pp. 25-49, 2000.

Sime, J., *„Escape Behavior In Fires And Evacuations,"* Fires And Human Behavior, Fulton, London, 1990, pp. 56-87.

Sime, J., *„Human Behavior In Fires Summary Report",* CFBAC Rept No.450, Portsmouth, 1992, pp. 1-20.

SPSS: *PASW Statistics 18,* Release 18.0.0 (Jul 30, 2009)

Tavares, R.M., Gwynne, S. & Galea, E.R., "Collection and Analysis of Pre-Evacuation time data collected from evacuation trials conducted in library facilities in Brazil", *Applied Fire Science, Vol 15 (1),* 23-40, 2006.

8 Recommendations for different types of end-users

Lena Kecklund, Kristin Andrée, Sara Petterson, Jerzy Wolanin, Dorota Kokoszka, Ed Galea & Silke Schmidt

8.1 Recommendations for design engineers and regulators

Based on response time data for library buildings in Turkey, Poland, Czech Republic and UK and directed towards End-Users such as Design engineers and Regulators, as a core recommendation or application, it can be stated that the data collected for Turkey, Poland and the Czech Republic is the first of its kind. This data will be of great use to design engineers who have up until this time had to make assumptions for response time data for use in this type of structures. Response time data of any kind, for Turkey and Czech Republic has never been published prior to this work.

As concerns the cultural component to evacuation behaviour, it can be forwarded to End-Users such as Design Engineers, Regulators, Model Developers, Evacuation Behaviour and the Research Community. Results from the four evacuation trials suggest that the response phase behaviour may be strongly culturally dependent. This has important implications to the Design Engineers and Regulators in so far as it suggests that evacuation data used to define evacuation scenarios might not be universally applicable i.e. data derived from trials in one country may not be strictly relevant for another country. This is also of importance to model developers who must be careful how they specify default data within their models. It is also of importance to the evacuation research community as it opens a new area of research and suggests that it is important to collect data from other countries.

Based on the evacuation model validation data based on Turkey and Poland evacuation trials, it was forwarded to end-users such as Design engineers, Regulators and evacuation model developers. As a core recommendation detailed evacuation model validation data was collected for the first time that provides precise information for model validation, detailing starting position, exits used and response times and exit time histories (Turkey data set) and detailed crowd densities and exit time histories (Poland data set). This data is unique and provides an excellent basis to perform detailed validation of evacuation models. This will be of great benefit to model developers who can assess their models for the first time, Regulators who will be able to assess the capability and accuracy of evacuation models and Design Engineers who will be able to better select appropriate evacuation models for their design applications.

Based on an empirically based response time predictive model, it was directed towards End-Users such as Design Engineers, Evacuation Behaviour and the Research community. As a core application an empirical model has been developed which can be used to predict mean response times. The model is based on key parameters which define a particular evacuation such as the average number and duration of likely Action and Information tasks undertaken by the participants. This model allows likely response times to be predicted and has been tested against results generated from the 4 evacuation trials. This is particularly useful for Design Engineers who can use the approach to produce meaningful estimates of likely response times for evacuation analysis. This is also useful for the human behaviour research community as it indicates key influencing factors which determine the response phase behaviour within an evacuation.

8.2 Recommendations for emergency communication and information

In order to be able to improve emergency procedures, evacuation procedures and procedures for the rescue services, an understanding of human behaviour and needs is essential. To further investigate the area of communication and information is important to improve this understanding. Answers to questions like "what kind of information do people need?", "who is expected to communicate this information?", and "is previous knowledge important?" would increase the knowledge on human behaviour in emergency situations and be helpful in the work on improving emergency procedures.

From fire safety literature (e.g. Gwynne, 2007; Proulx, 2000; Tong & Canter, 1985) it is clear that prompting occupants to respond to an emergency generally involves two main steps: (i) capturing occupants' attention (i.e. getting them to disengage from their current activities and recognize that there is a real and imminent threat); and (ii) informing them of the situation (i.e. telling them what and where the threat is and what they need to do in response to it). However, there are several issues and obstacles associated with each step.

8.2.1 Capturing attention

Occupants' attention is usually captured through some form of sensory alarm appliance, most often an auditory alarm (e.g. bell, siren, horn). The first issue for safety managers is to ensure that occupants can actually receive the alarm. This requires alarm appliances to be regularly maintained and tested and located in the most appropriate areas. The BeSeCu evacuation trials illustrated the problems that can occur when such steps are not taken. At the other end is occupant ability to hear the alarm. Even if occupants have no hearing impairments, and are not being inattentive, the acoustics of the environment can distort, disguise or mute sounds. For example, in large open spaces such as in airport terminals or train stations the noise made by the high volume of people speaking and moving around, by service announcements, by mechanical equipment operating, and so forth, may all affect the likelihood of hearing things. In recognition of the fact that auditory alarms may not always be heard, other sensory alarm types are available either on their own or combined with auditory alarms, such as visual alarms (e.g. strobes, LED displays) and even tactile alarms in domestic scenarios (e.g. vibrating devices). Again, however, physical, individual, and environmental factors would all need to be taken into account when considering the effectiveness of these alarms (Gwynne, 2007).

While sensory alarm appliances circumvent language problems, it should not automatically be assumed that they will be universally effective. As well as receiving the alarm, it is important for occupants to recognize what the alarm represents, i.e. an emergency, and that the alarm is genuine, not a false alarm (Gwynne, 2007; Tong & Canter, 1985). In different cultures or countries particular sounds and visuals might be associated with different things, thus an emergency alarm may not always be recognized as such. In fact, it is questionable whether people within a single culture or country associate particular sounds and visuals uniformly. For example, a Canadian study by Proulx, Laroche, Jaspers-Fayer and Lavallée (2001) revealed half or fewer of participants tested were able to recognize emergency alarms among the sounds heard. Indeed, the T-3 signal – an emergency alarm pattern considered to be the standardized evacuation alarm signal – was correctly recognized by as few as 6% of participants, mistaken by others for such things as the engaged tone on a phone, a vehicle reverse alarm, and an alarm clock. It should be noted that participants were hearing the sounds without supporting context, and this may have reduced their ability to correctly identify them. Furthermore, the study was conducted approximately five to six years after Canada adopted the international standard (ISO 8201, 1987) regarding the T-3. Thus, participants might not yet have had great exposure to that sound pattern. Nevertheless, this study underlines that certain sounds are not universally recognized, at least not without a period of learning and familiarization first, and that until such education occurs globally, there is still the likelihood that people from various cultures and countries will respond in a non-uniform manner to an emergency alarm. Of course, over-familiarization with alarm sounds may also be problematic. If alarms are heard repeatedly, outwith real emergency situations (e.g. during overly-frequent building evacuation drills or through hoax/mistaken/malfunctioning alarms), this could be counterproductive and slow occupant responses to alarms in the future (Gwynne, 2007; Tong & Canter, 1985). As fire safety regulations and legislation vary from country to country – again, highlighted in the BeSeCu evacuation trials – there is reason to believe that some cultures might be more exposed to false alarms than others and therefore likely to behave in a different manner upon hearing an alarm.

8.2.2 Informing occupants

While alarms can capture attention and alert occupants to the fact there is a threat, this in itself may not be sufficient. Evidence suggests that occupant responses to emergencies and disasters can be improved with the provision of information (Tong

& Canter, 1985). The information should reinforce or clarify the warning provided by the alarm but, in addition, inform occupants about such things as the nature or location of the threat and what form of response is appropriate (Proulx, 2000). There have been fears over providing occupants with such information lest "panic' break out. However, the idea that people will react in such a way when told they are facing an emergency seems to be more a product of media representations of disasters rather than of real-life cases. Research, including the BeSeCu field study, has shown that "panic' occurs only very rarely, and in very specific circumstances, and thus should not preclude safety managers from providing occupants with information about the situation (Mileti & Sorensen, 1990; Sime, 1980).

Information may be best communicated "live'. The advantages of live communication of information includes flexibility in the content of the message imparted (Proulx, 2000). While pre-recorded messages and visual displays have some benefits (e.g. less financial and personnel resources required), they might not be able to cope with all possible permutations of a rapidly and dynamically unfolding event, as the Düsseldorf Airport fire in 1996 fatally demonstrated (NFPA, 1998). Furthermore, issuing information live allows flexibility in the manner the information is delivered (Proulx, 2000). For example, if there is an urgent need to evacuate, a person can indicate this through the tone of voice used. The need to stay calm can also be communicated through controlled use of one's voice. In addition, a live communication will likely increase occupants' beliefs that someone really is aware of the situation and is attending to it. This should reinforce the idea that the situation is genuine (Proulx, 2000) but also reassure occupants that help is on its way. One major complaint from terrorist attack survivors interviewed in the BeSeCu field study was the lack of information, not just about what the nature of the problem was, but also about whether anyone was actually aware of their problem and was dealing with it.

A further benefit of communicating information live is that the message can be tailored to its known (different) audience(s) on a given day, which in turn should increase the sense that the communication is actually directed at the individuals listening to it, that they are at risk and need to respond; occupants should be less likely to ignore warnings if they are "personalized' (Mileti & Sorensen, 1990). However, even if different messages are announced to different groups of occupants, each message should be repeated, not just because some people might not hear it or be able to process it all at first, but also because repeating the warning message should act as confirmation of the warning, and confirmation is believed to be an essential part in the process of prompting occupants into action (Mileti & Sorensen, 1990). Without confirmation, occupants will often seek further information from other social (e.g. family, friends) or physical (i.e. the environment) sources (Mileti & Sorensen, 1990), which may delay them from taking protective action. However, there is a threshold after which repetition becomes tedious and thus communicators should be aware of and try to avoid such an outcome (Lindell & Perry, 2004).

Information may be communicated live via a voice system and/or direct from someone physically present at the scene. In fact, if the former is unavailable, the latter may cope quite well in its absence, for the physical presence of an authority Figure who is well trained, knowledgeable, assertive and respected has been described as "the most effective means of informing an individual of an incident" (Gwynne, 2007, p.25), and there were indications in the BeSeCu evacuation trials that this was indeed the case. Of course, putting people to the scene raises resource implications. It also could mean a delay in the message being delivered (Gwynne, 2007). However, one major advantage of someone being physically present to communicate information is that they can use visual means in addition to auditory means to impart information to occupants. Their actual physical appearance (both in the sense of turning up and in the sense of what they are wearing, e.g. a fire warden uniform) can convey much about the genuineness of the warning (Gwynne, personal communication). Although not explicitly discussed in the fire safety literature, their body language would also conceivably assist in informing occupants and in improving occupant responses to such information. For example, eye gaze or pointing with hands could be used to increase the sense of the warning being personal as well as to direct occupants to exits, or at least to exit signs. As this form of communication is non-verbal, it is possible it would be helpful for occupants whose first language is not the one used in the voice system communications. However, it should not automatically be assumed that non-verbal gestures will be universally understood. Consequently, the BeSeCu study has included an initial investigation into cross-cultural comprehension of non-verbal emergency communications and the results will follow.

In summary then, to initiate an emergency response from occupants, safety managers need to not only capture occupants' attention and alert them to a threat but also inform them of the situation. The combined use of different forms of sensory alarms and live communications should improve responses and, in turn, safety by overcoming the various obstacles (e.g. to hearing, seeing, understanding, etc.) that each type of emergency notification faces. As a final note, it should be pointed out that, as survivors highlighted during interviews for BeSeCu, occupants may encounter other things during emergencies which alert or inform them of how to respond. For example, cues from the threat itself, such as flames or smoke, will capture attention in many cases, as will the sudden cessation of normal activity, e.g. electrical equipment shutting down/cutting out. Moreover, social cues such as everyone else leaving the room or everyone continuing on with their conversations or work will impact occupant responses (Lindell & Perry, 2004). However, these cues are less predictable in terms of their presence and the nature of their influence on occupants. Thus, safety managers might be better focusing their efforts first on the more controllable measures of notifying occupants discussed in this review.

8.3 Recommendations for developing standards in emergency communication

Presently, there are a few standards available on emergency communication systems, e.g. NFPA 72 (National Fire Alarm and Signalling Code) and British Standard BS 5839 (Fire Detection and Fire Alarm Systems for Buildings, Part 8). These standards contain technical requirements on fire alarms and fire detection systems, e.g. installation, service and message dissemination, but they contain little guidance on the specifics of emergency messages.

The following research questions were studied concerning people's perceptions, feelings, behaviours and communications in emergencies and disasters:

Previous knowledge

Level and type of previous knowledge

- Does previous knowledge have an impact on people's behaviour during the emergency situation?
- Is there a relationship between previous knowledge and emotions?
- Is there a relationship between previous knowledge and perceived control?
- Is there a relationship between previous knowledge and active search for information during the emergency situation?

Prior experience of incidents

- To what extent do the participants have prior experience of emergency situations?
- Does prior experience have an effect on people's behaviour during the emergency?
- Does prior experience of emergencies influence emotions in a new emergency situation?
- Does prior experience of emergencies affect the need for more information during a new emergency situation?

Information and communication during the emergency

- How do people become aware of the danger?
- Do people realize what is happening?
- Do people engage in communication/information activities?
- What is the first thing people do when they understand that something is happening/an emergency is evolving
- Do people engage in information seeking activities during the emergency?
- Do people evacuate? What guides people out?
- Would people need more information to help them respond?
- What kind of information do people need?
- From whom do people need more information?
- Degree of trust in information from different actors
- Communication with emergency services

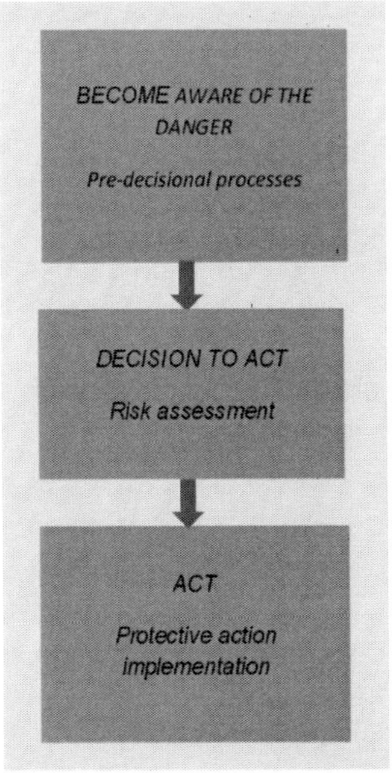

Fig. 8.1: Model of human behaviour in emergency situations, based on the Protective Action Decision Model (Lindell & Perry, 2004, Kuligowski, 2011).

Questionnaire data was collected in eight European countries; Czech Republic, Germany, Italy Poland, Spain, Sweden, Turkey and UK.

The data in this report are presented mainly as frequencies. Some correlations and regression analyses were made, and significance tests (significance level $p < 0.05$) were done.

The results presented in this document concern survivors of domestic fires. The results are presented for the domestic fire group across all countries. In several cases comparisons between the countries are made in order to further explore similarities and differences between countries.

To be able to act safely in an emergency situation those involved firstly has to become aware of the danger (pre-decisional processes). The next steps are to assess and evaluate the situation and the potential risks, evaluate if there is a need to act, consider possible actions, and finally make a decision about how to act (risk assessment, see Fig. 8.1).

Available information and communication possibilities for people involved in an emergency influence people's ability to become aware of the danger make decisions and will also influence behaviour in the emergency situation.

Emergency communication can be defined as the information people have and the communication that people engage in during an emergency which affect people's ability to assess risks and to manage the risk situation. Emergency communication could consequently be given a wide definition and include in addition to information and communication during the emergency situation, also previous knowledge, prior experience of emergency situations, as well as environmental factors.

Emergency communication includes accordingly by our definition verbal and non-verbal information and communication during the emergency, previous knowledge, e.g. education, training, drills, prior experience of emergency situations and environmental factors, e.g. building design, signs, messages etc.

The three issues previous knowledge, experiences and information and communication during the emergency are investigated in this project. Environmental factors are not studied in depth.

A model describing communication and information in an emergency situation could thus be presented as in Fig. 8.2.

The total number of participants in the entire questionnaire study (including participants who had experienced domestic fires, fires in public buildings, floods, terrorist attacks and earthquakes) was 1130 from all eight countries.

About half of the participants had been involved in a domestic fire, in total 592 participants. The results presented in this report concern only the group of partici-

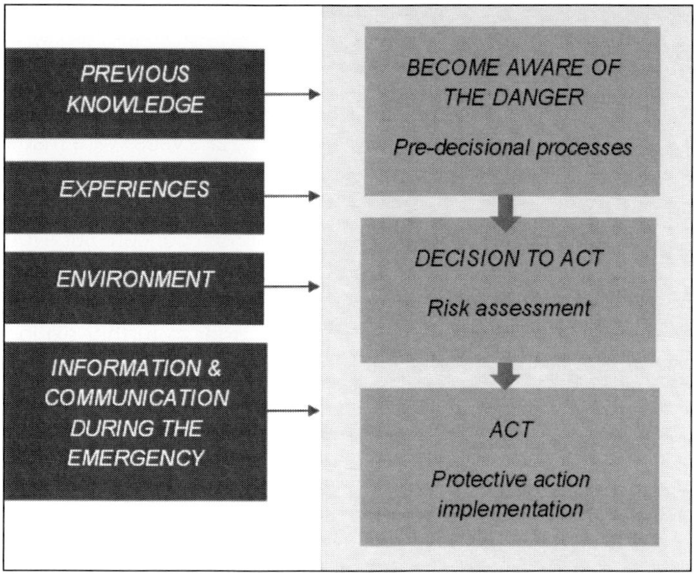

Fig. 8.2: A model for communication in emergency situations

pants who had experienced a domestic fire. The valid number of responses for each question will be presented in relation to each question.

The number of domestic fire participants varies between the countries. Many participants are from Germany (130) and Poland (118), and only 21 participants are from UK as presented in Fig. 8.3.

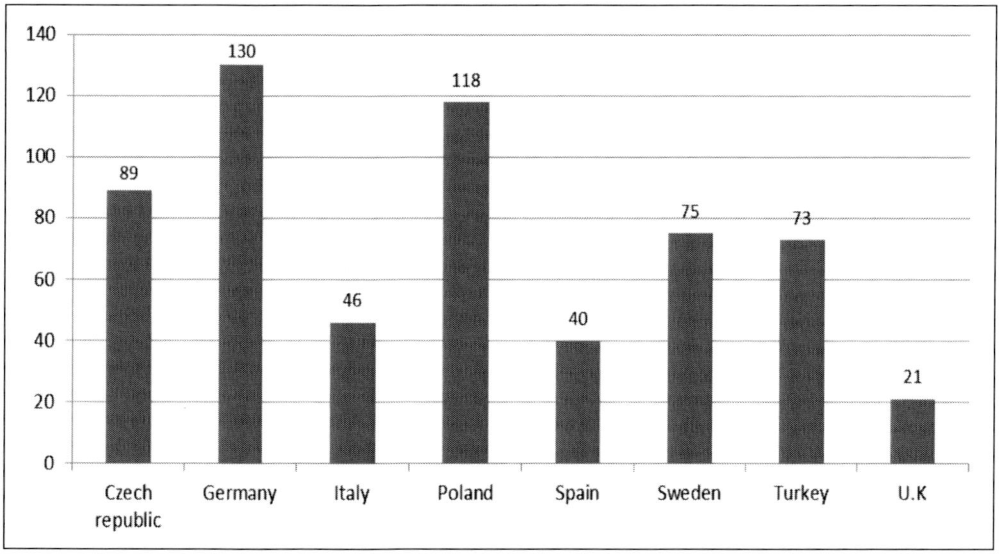

Fig. 8.3: Number of participants from different countries (N = 592)

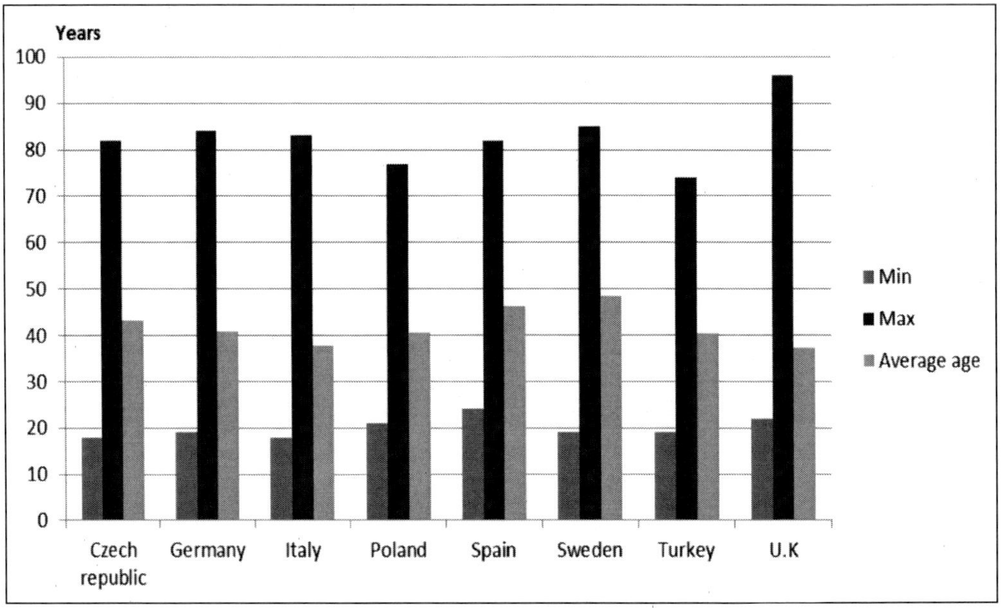

Fig. 8.4: Age distribution within the eight countries (N = 588)

Mean age of all domestic fire participants is 42 years. The age variation is from 18 to 96 years. The mean age variation between the countries is from 37 years in UK and Italy to 48 years in Sweden. The age distribution is presented in Fig. 8.4.

55% of the domestic fire participants were females and 45% were males. See Fig. 8.5 for distribution according to gender within the countries.

The participants were asked about their previous knowledge regarding emergency situations which they had before the incident happened and that would be of use in an emergency. They were asked to rate their knowledge level regarding several types of knowledge on a scale from "not at all" (1) to "extremely" (5).

From these ratings a knowledge index was created as a sum of all scores on the questions (types of knowledge) divided by the number of questions.

The highest rated knowledge types are first aid knowledge, having read safety notices or evacuation plans and having taken part in drills at school, see Fig. 8.6.

More than 30% of the participants had never taken part in fire drills at school, 40% had never taken part in fire drills at work, and almost 30% had no first aid knowledge (Fig. 8.7).

The mean value of all knowledge types presented by country, shows that the participants from Turkey estimated the highest level of knowledge, followed by Sweden, UK and Germany. Italy estimated the lowest level of previous knowledge, see Fig. 8.8.

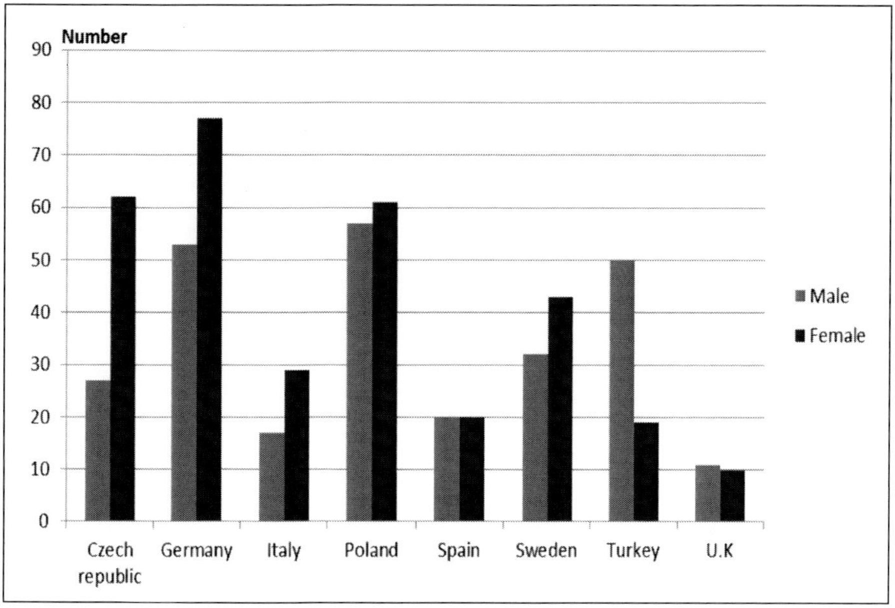

Fig. 8.5: Distribution according to gender within the eight countries (N = 588)

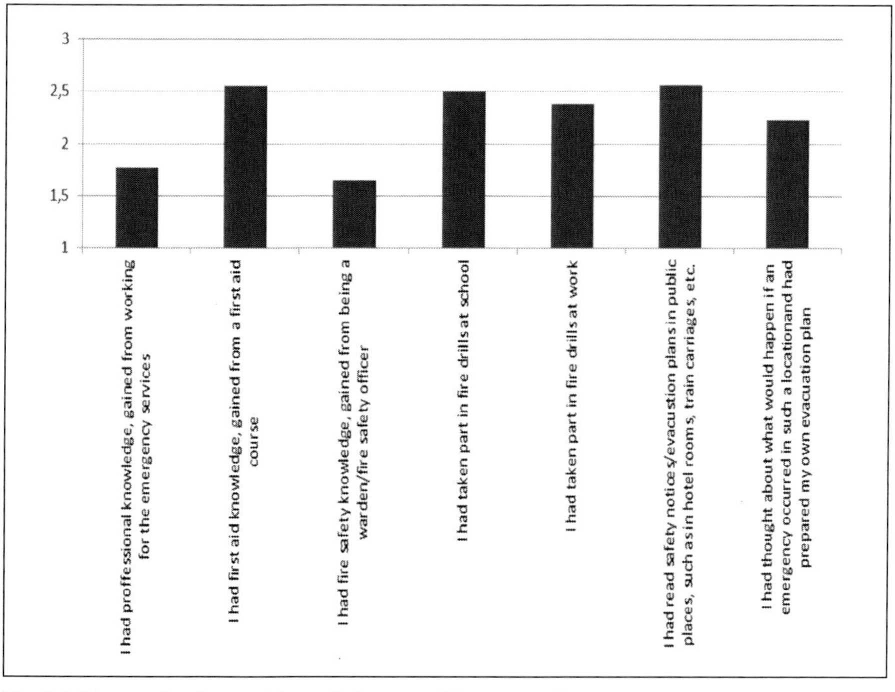

Fig. 8.6: Mean value for each knowledge type (N = 568-578)

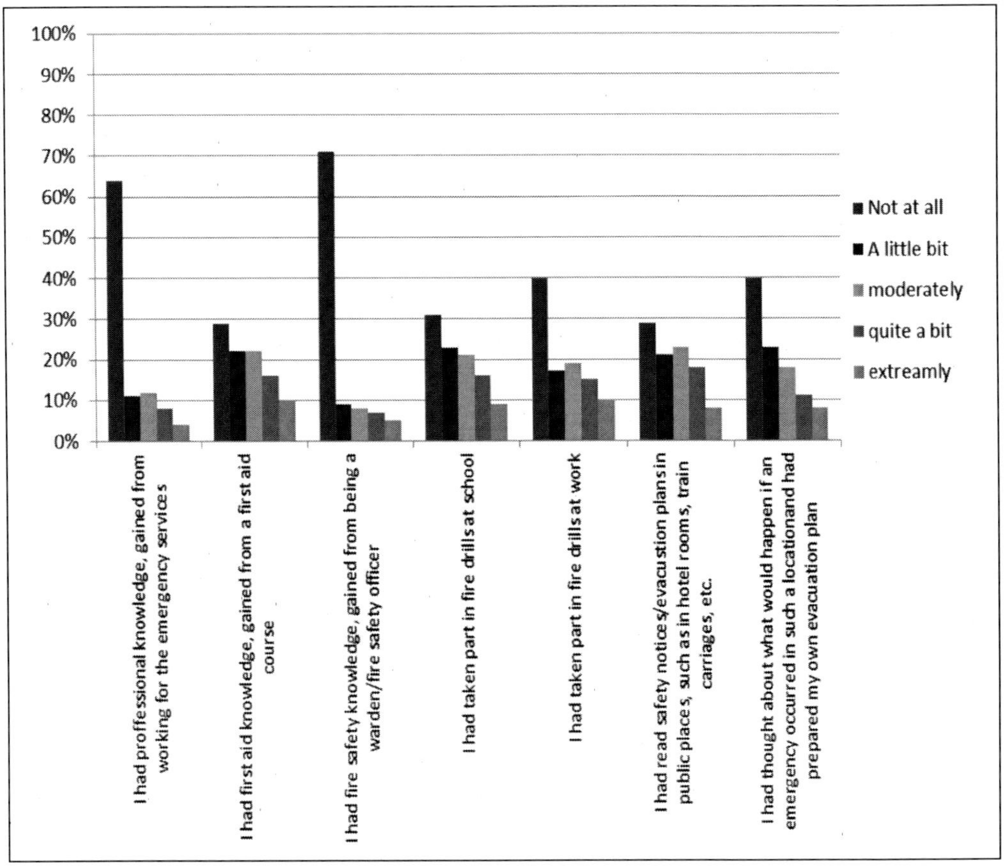

Fig. 8.7: Distribution of knowledge level for several types of knowledge (N = 568-578)

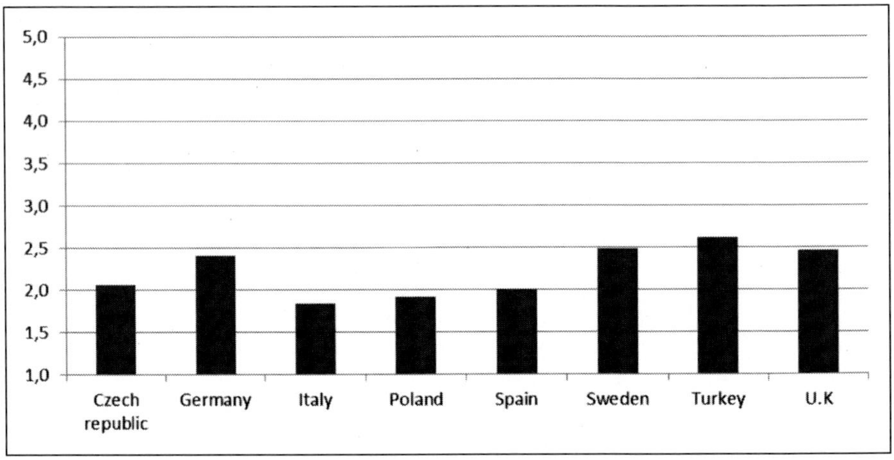

Fig. 8.8: Mean value of all knowledge types for each country (N = 568-578)

8.3.1 Is there a relationship between previous knowledge and emotions?

The participants were asked to estimate their emotions (nervous, scared, upset, stress) on a scale from "not at all" (1) to "extremely" (5) at the time when they realized that they were in an emergency situation.

An emotion index was created as a sum of all scores on the questions (types of feelings) divided by the number of questions. This emotion index was compared to the knowledge index.

An analysis was made to see if the participants' level of previous knowledge of emergency situations affects their level of emotions during the emergency situation. A significant relationship was found between these two variables. This indicates that a higher level of previous knowledge leads to less strong negative feelings.

8.3.2 Is there a relationship between previous knowledge and perceived control of the situation?

The participants were also asked if they thought that they were able to deal with the situation when they realized that they were in an emergency situation. The participants made this estimation on a scale from "not at all" to "extremely".

This question was compared to the participants' knowledge level. A significant positive correlation was found between the participants' previous knowledge of emergency situations and their perceived control in the emergency situation. This indicates that the participants who had more previous knowledge regarding emergency situations experienced a higher level of control in the emergency situation.

A comparison was also done between the questions on perceived emotional level and perceived control. A significant negative correlation between the participant's emotions and their perceived control was found. This indicates that the participants who reported having more control were calmer, or that participants with a lower level of negative emotions (nervous, scared, upset, stress) reported a higher level of control.

To what extent did the participants have prior experience of emergency situations?

The participants were asked about their prior experience of certain types of incidents (fire in a home, fire in a public building, earthquake, flood, terrorist attack, and building evacuation that turned out to be a false alarm).

24% of the participants had experienced a fire in a home before, 8% experienced a fire in a public building before and 20% experienced a building evacuation that turned out to be a false alarm. 43% had never experienced any of these incidents or a false alarm before (Fig. 8.9).

A study of differences between the countries shows that the percentage of people that had experienced one incident before is high in the Czech, Italian and

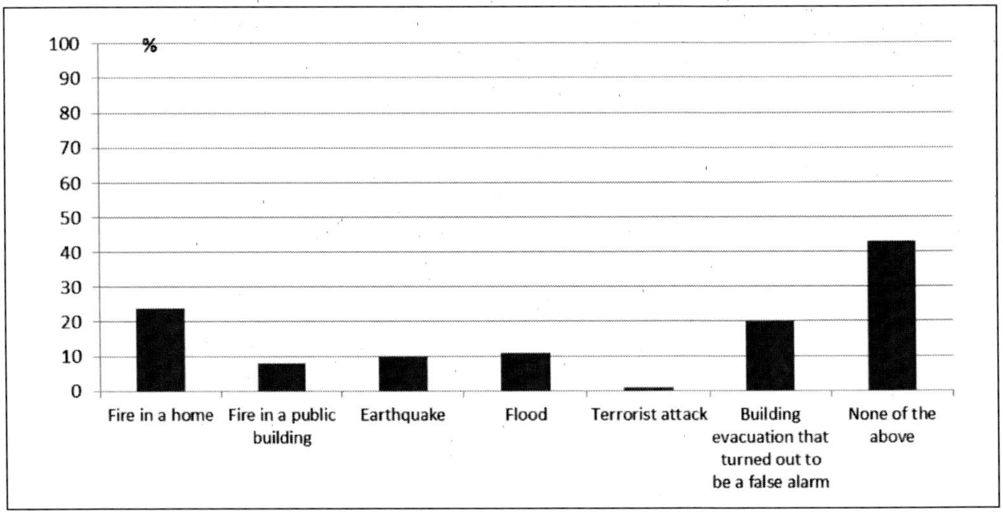

Fig. 8.9: Percentage of the participants that experienced different incidents and false alarms before (N = 592)

Turkey samples. The percentage of participants that had experienced more than one incident before is highest in Turkey. "Building evacuation that turned out to be a false alarm" is treated in the "no incident" group (see Fig. 8.10).

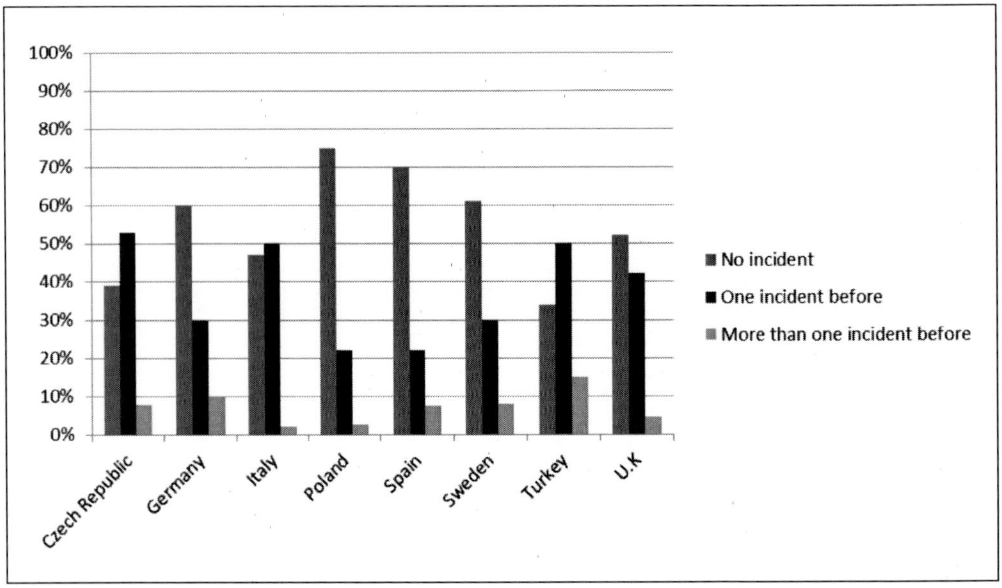

Fig. 8.10: Prior experience of incidents, by country (N = 592)

8.3.3 Does prior experience of emergencies influence emotions in a new emergency situation?

A comparison was made to examine if there was a relationship between prior experience of emergencies and emotions in a new emergency situation. The participants' prior experience was compared to the participants' estimated emotional level at the point where they realized that they were in an emergency situation.

A new experience variable was created where the experience question was recoded into 0-5 depending on whether the participants had experienced zero, one, two, three, four or five different kinds of emergencies before. A regression analysis was made with this experience variable and the emotion index.

A significant relationship was found which indicates that more prior experience can lead to less strong negative feelings (nervous, scared, upset, stress) in an emergency situation.

The participants were asked about whom or what initially alerted them to the fact that something was happening Fig. 8.11). About 90% were alerted by sensing environmental cues. About 70% were alerted by noticing others' reactions, and about 65% were specifically informed about the incident.

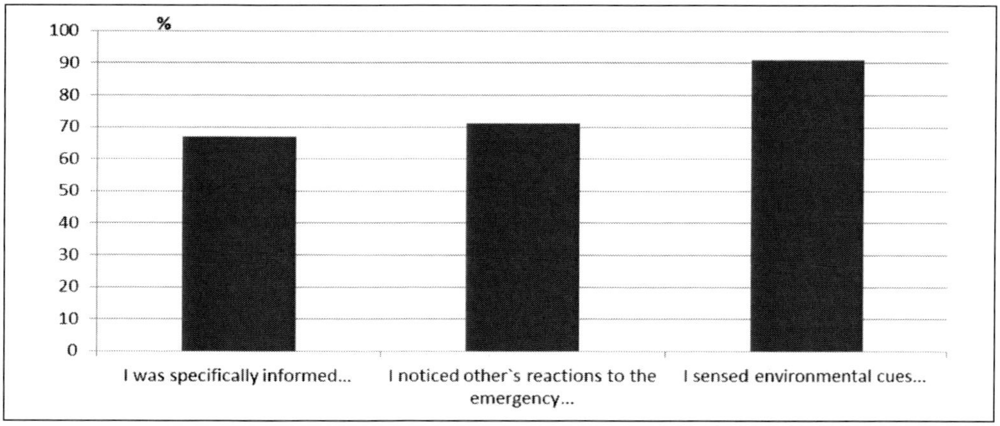

Fig. 8.11: Who or what initially alerted people to the fact that something was happening (N = 580- 590)

The most common way to be specifically informed was by family, friends and neighbours. More than 30% was not specifically informed at all (see Fig. 8.12).

The most common reactions of others that alerted people were commotion and shouting and signs that the emergency services were arriving (see Fig. 8.13).

The most common environmental cues that alerted people were smoke, flames or fire, and unusual smell (see Fig. 8.14).

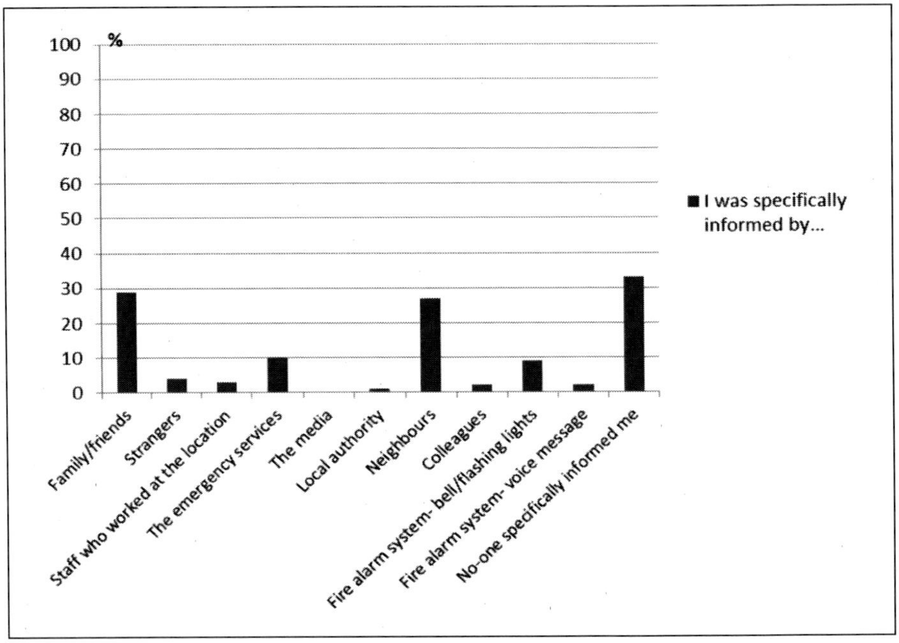

Fig. 8.12: Sources of information (N = 590)

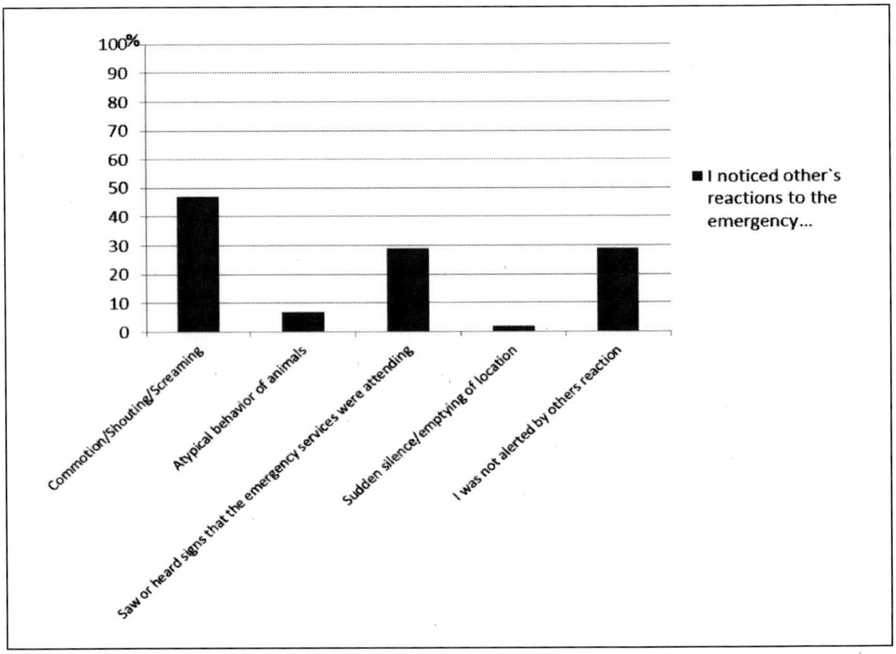

Fig. 8.13: Reactions from others that alerted people (N = 580)

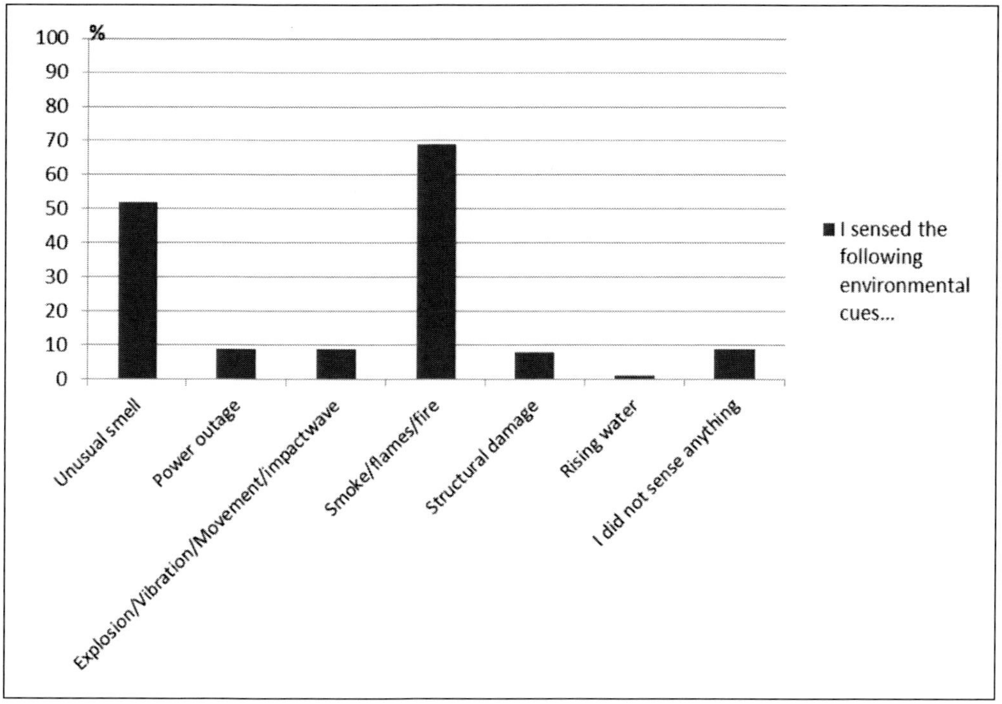

Fig. 8.14: Environmental cues that alerted people (N = 582)

8.3.4 Did people realize what was happening?

The participants were asked if they thought that it was a fire at the point when they were initially alerted. More than 80% answered that they thought that it was a fire (see Fig. 8.15 and Fig. 8.16).

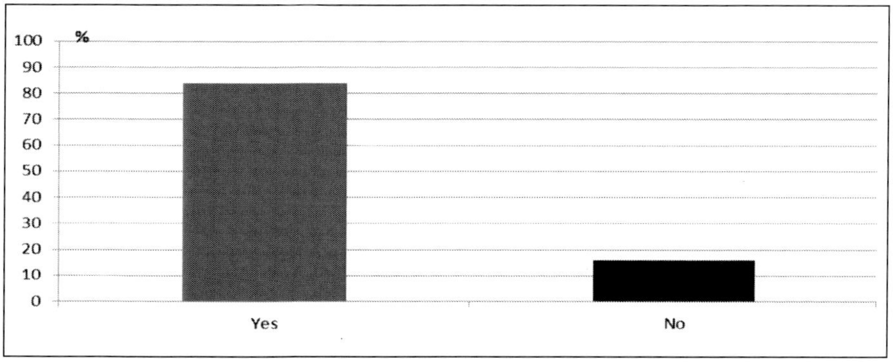

Fig. 8.15: Percentage that realized that it was a fire when they were initially alerted (N = 584)

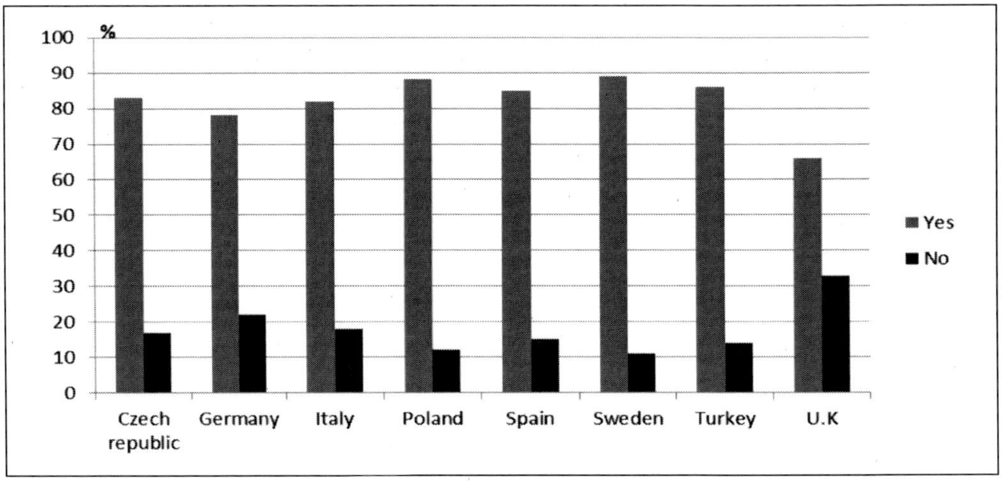

Fig. 8.16: The distribution within each country that thought that it was a fire when they were initially alerted (N = 584)

8.3.5 What was the first thing people did when they understood that something was happening?

The participants were asked about the first thing they did when they understood that something was happening. The most commonly reported first things to do were communication activities, e.g. trying to alert others (26%) and seeking help from emergency services (18%). 10% actively sought further information as the first thing to do (see Fig. 8.17).

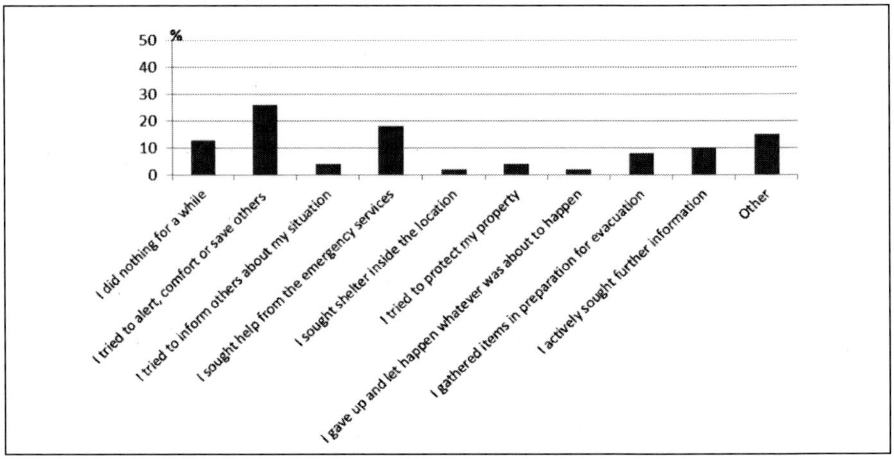

Fig. 8.17: The most common first things to do (N = 532)

There are differences between the countries in the percentage of the participants who actively sought further information as their first activity. About a third of the Swedish and a fourth of the British participants responded that they actively sought information as their first action. The other countries had a considerably lower percentage reporting that information seeking was the first activity. Though, the number of participants in each country is rather small (see Fig. 8.18).

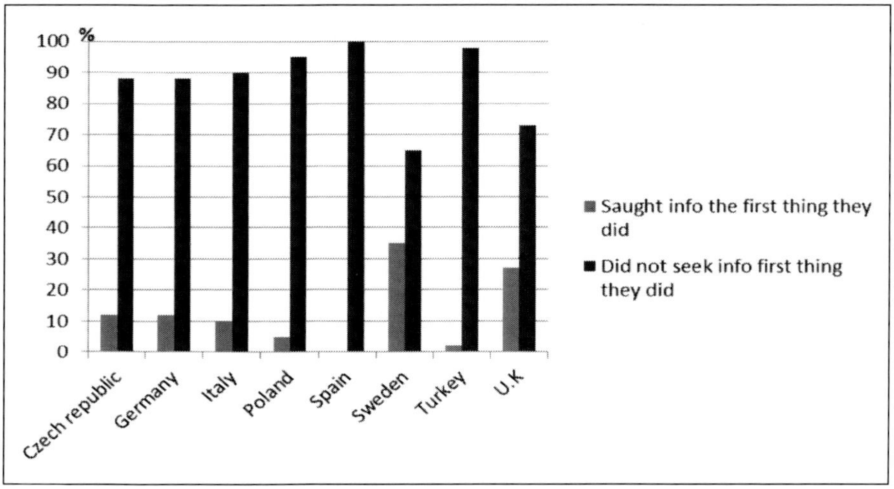

Fig. 8.18: Percentage that actively sought further information, by country (N = 532)

8.3.6 Did people engage in information seeking activities during the emergency?

The participants were asked not only about what was the first thing they did but also what else they did when they understood that something was happening. In all 20% of the participants engaged in actively seeking further information.

8.3.7 Did people evacuate? What guided people out?

62% of the participants evacuated during the emergency. 7% were rescued by others, and 31% did not evacuate (see Fig. 8.19).

The participants who evacuated or were rescued were asked to specify what guided them out during the evacuation. The most common answer (almost 60%) was that they went out the same way as they usually used, thus it was a habit (see Fig. 8.20).

Would people have needed more information to help them respond to what was happening?

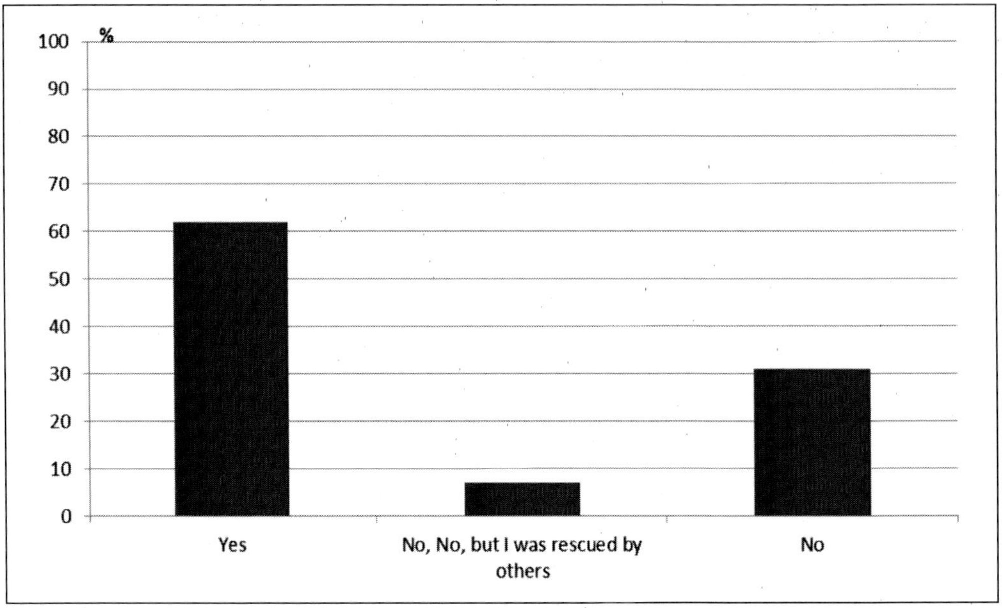

Fig. 8.19: Evacuated during the emergency situation (N = 583)

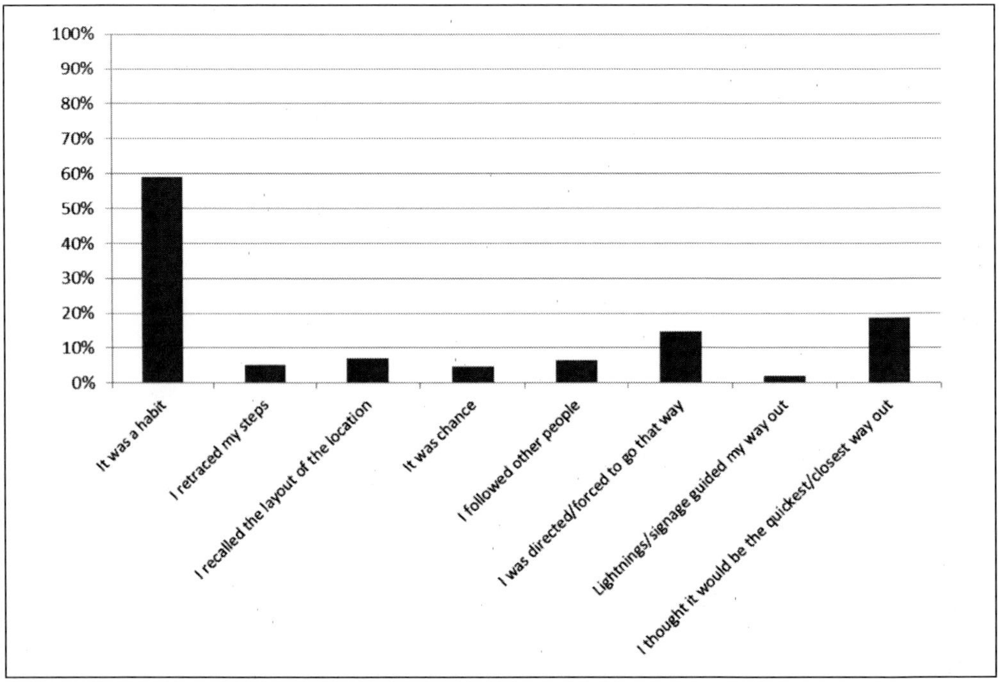

Fig. 8.20: What guided people out during the evacuation (N = 383)

The participants were also asked if they, in retrospect, think that they needed more information during the incident to help them respond to what was happening. 37% of the participants answered that they did need more information (see Fig. 8.21).

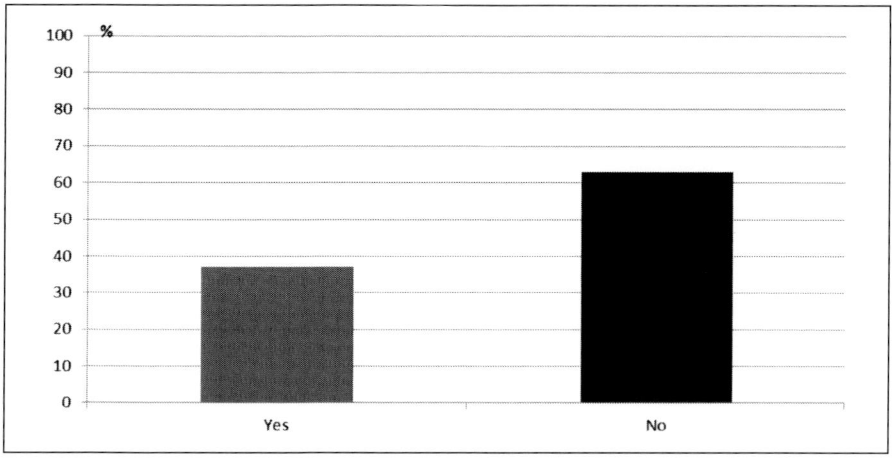

Fig. 8.21: Percentage of people that needed more information during the incident to help them respond to what was happening (N = 570)

There are quite big differences between the countries. In Spain 67% needed more information, and in Turkey 55%. In Italy only 22% needed more information, see Fig. 8.22.

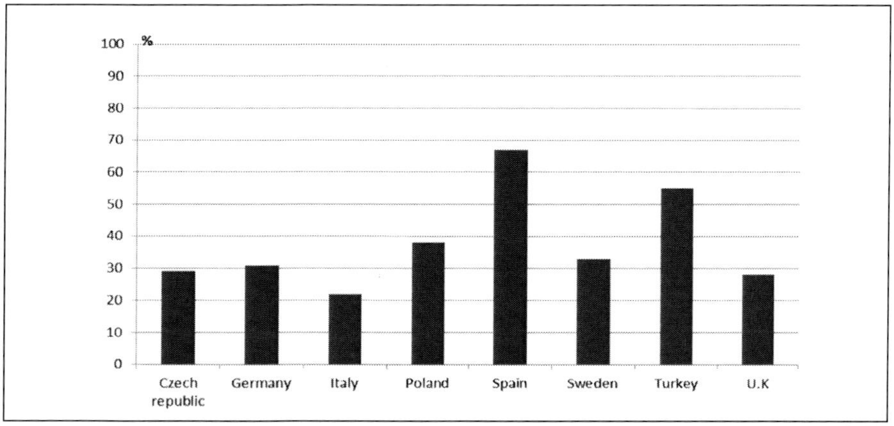

Fig. 8.22: Percentage of people in each country that needed more information to help them respond to what was happening (N = 570)

8.3.8 What kind of information would people have needed?

The participants who answered that they needed more information during the incident to help them respond to what was happening, were asked to specify what kind of information they think would have been useful, see Fig. 8.23. The kind of information the most people needed was information about what they should do (64%), about the nature of the incident (56%) and the type of threat that the incident posed (52%).

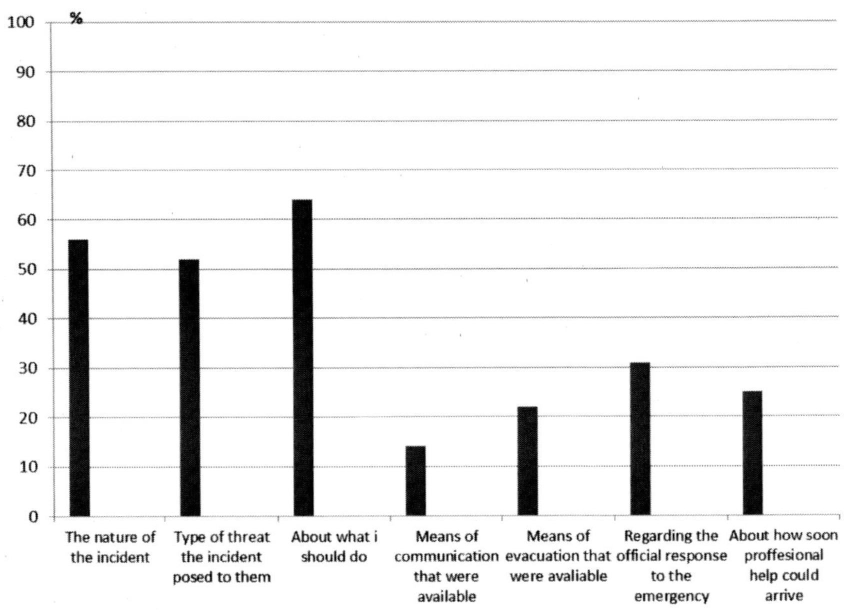

Fig. 8.23: The kind of information that the participants needed during the incident to help them respond to what was happening (N = 205)

There are differences between the countries, see Fig. 8.24, please note that only about 33% of the participants answered this question.

8.3.9 From whom did people need more information?

The participants that answered that they needed more information during the incident to help them respond to what was happening were also asked from whom they needed this information. Almost 70% of those people answered that they would have needed the information from the emergency services, see Fig. 8.25.

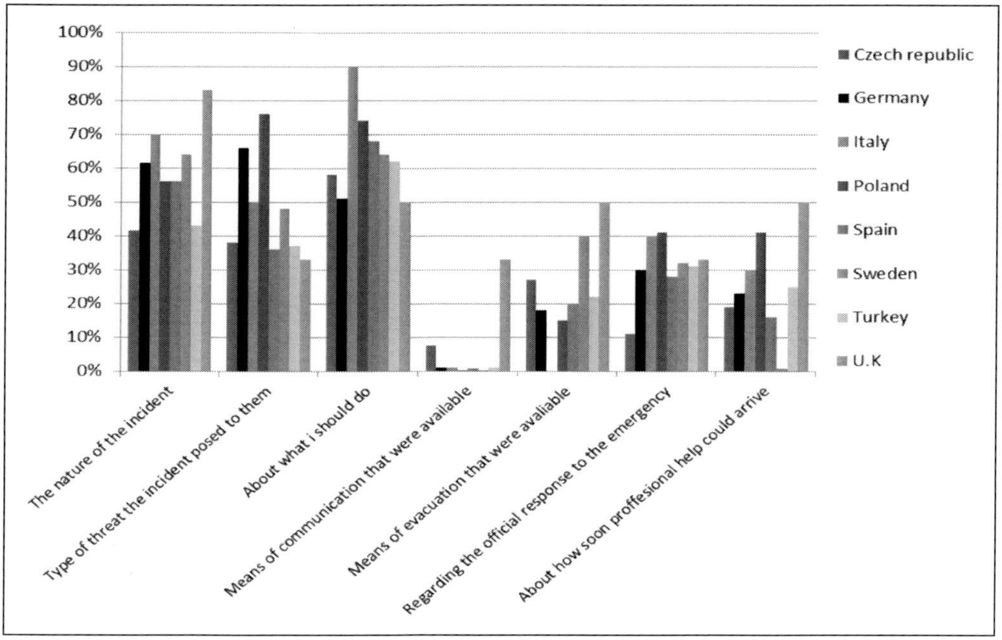

Fig. 8.24: Kind of information needed, by country (N Czech = 26, N Germany = 39, N Italy = 10, N Poland = 39, N Spain = 25, N Sweden = 25, N Turkey = 35, N UK = 6)

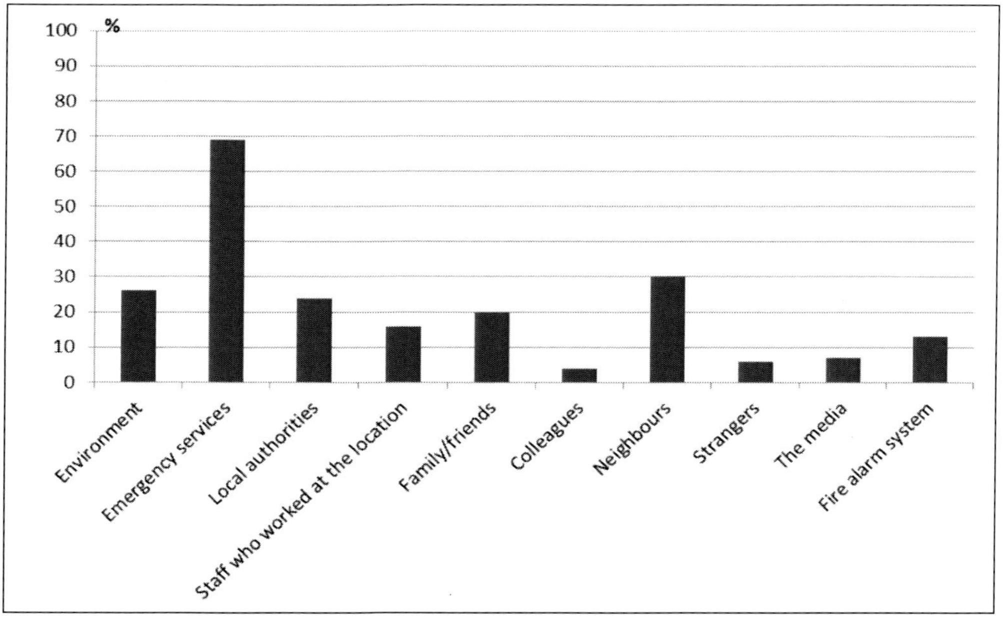

Fig. 8.25: From whom or what people needed information (N = 201)

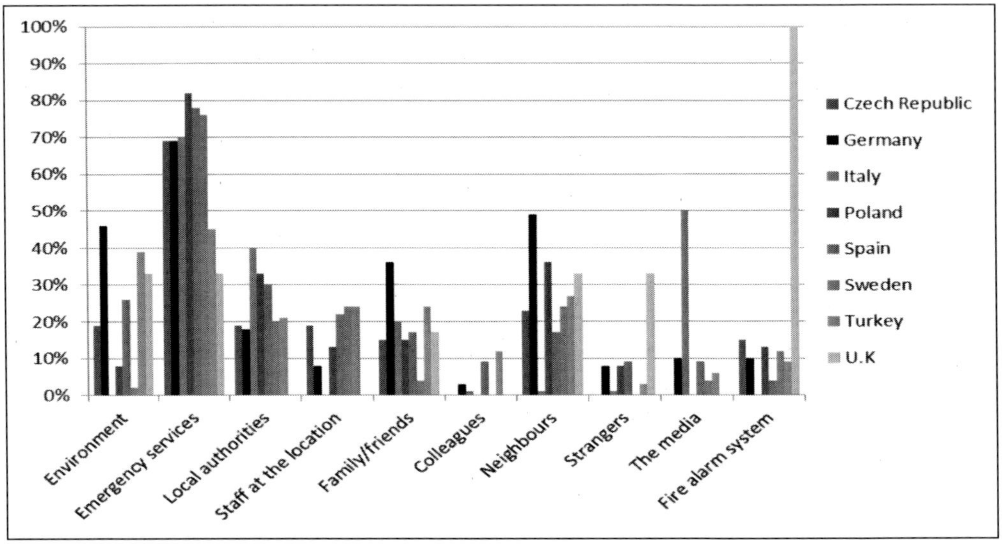

Fig. 8.26: From whom or what people needed information, by country (N Czech = 26, N Germany = 39, N Italy = 10,N Poland = 39, N Spain = 23, N Sweden = 25, N Turkey = 33, N UK = 6)

Fig. 8.26 shows differences between countries. The participants were asked to estimate to what extent they believe they could rely on different people to assist them in an emergency, before the incident occurred as well as at the time when they answered the questionnaire. The estimation was made on a scale from "not at all" (1) to "extremely" (5).

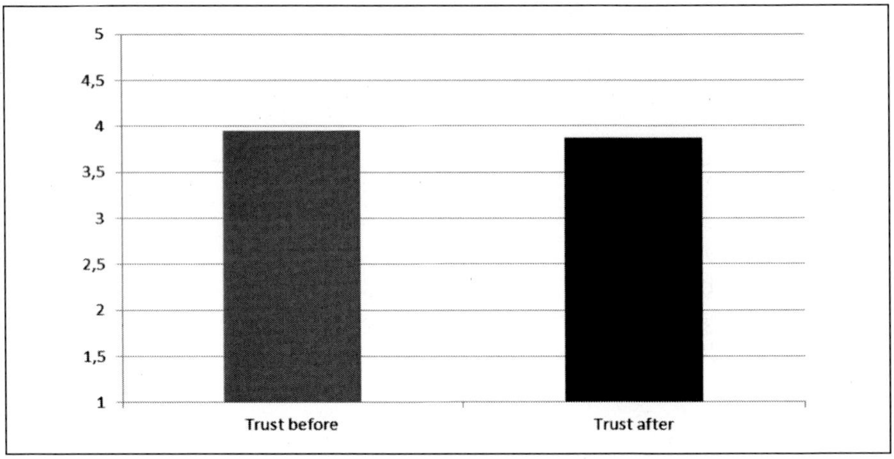

Fig. 8.27: Trust before and after the incident for medical service/police/fire service (N before = 536, N after = 525)

A trust score was created as a sum of all scores on the questions (medical service, police, and fire service) divided by the number of questions. An analysis was made to see whether there was a difference in trust for medical services/police/fire services before and after the incident occurred.

The analysis showed that there was a small statistically significant difference. The mean trust score before reduced from 3.95 before to 3.87 after the incident (see Fig. 8.27).

Fig. 8.28 shows the trust for medical service/police/fire service before and after, by country. Sweden has the highest trust score, and UK and Italy the lowest.

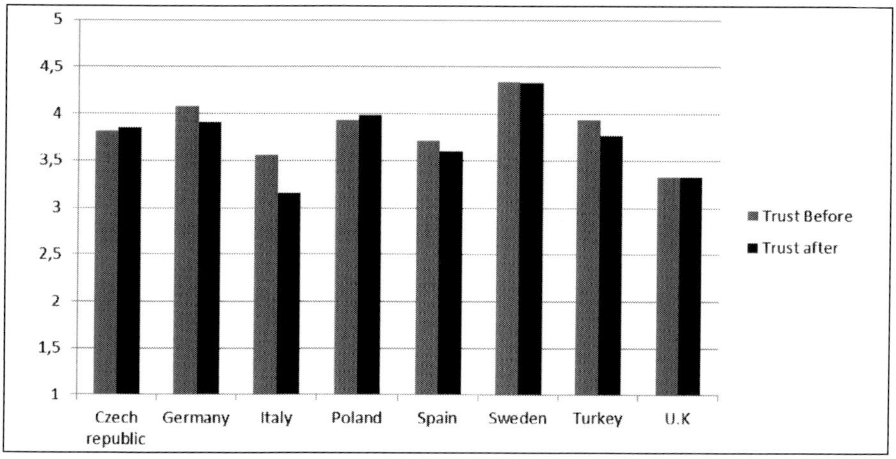

Fig. 8.28: Trust score before and after, by country, for medical service/police/fire service) (N before = 536, N after = 525)

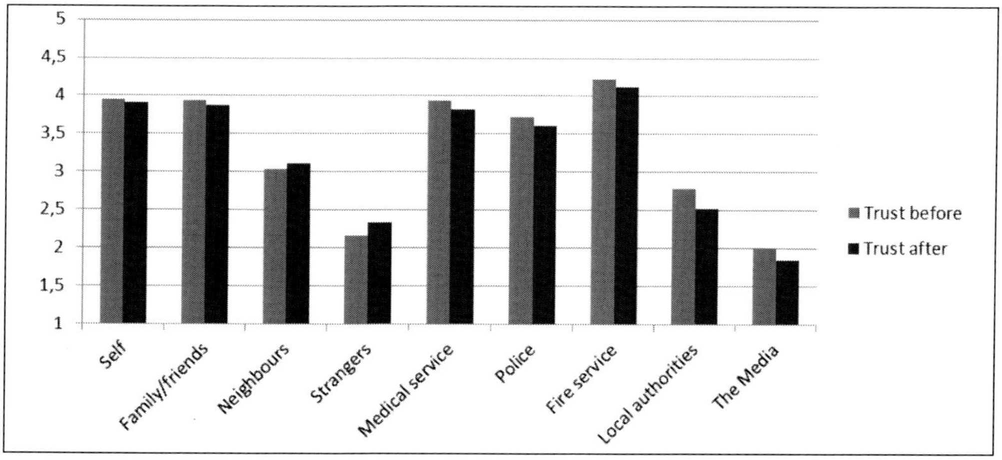

Fig. 8.29: Trust score before and after the incident for different actors (N = 523-562)

The trust is a bit lower or the same after the incident in most of the countries. In Czech Republic and Poland trust is a bit higher after the incident.

Fig. 8.29 shows trust scores for several types of actors before and after the incident.

71% of the participants communicated with the emergency services during the incident. Czech Republic, followed by Sweden, Germany and Poland had the highest percentage of people who communicated with the emergency services. Turkey had the lowest percentage (see Fig. 8.30).

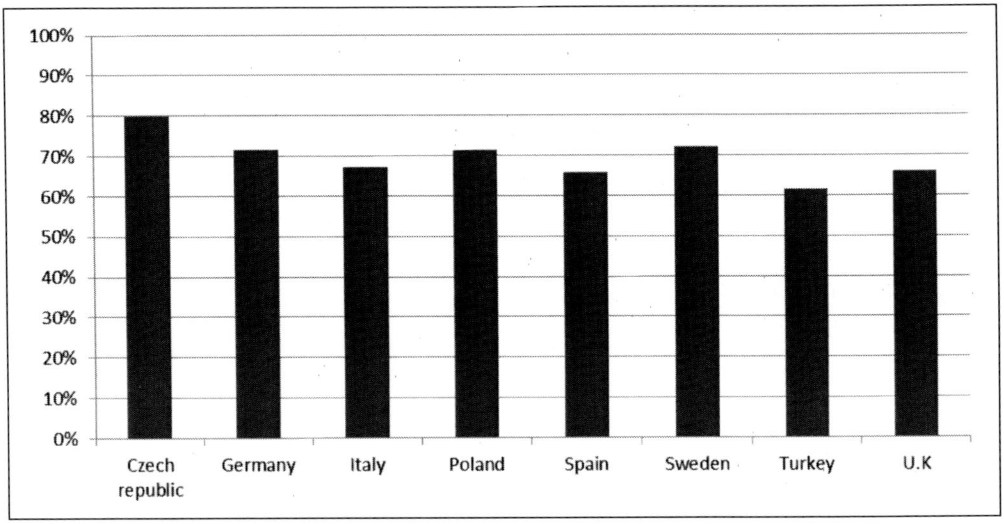

Fig. 8.30: Percentage of people who communicated with the emergency services during the incident, by country (N = 582)

A very large majority (97%) of these people communicated verbally with the emergency services. Only very few (8%) communicated non-verbally (see Fig. 8.31).

The total number of participants in this study is 592 and the number of participants from the eight different countries varies from 21 to 130. Due to the variation in the size of the samples in the different countries conclusions based on comparisons between countries should therefore be interpreted carefully. Differences between countries could also be related to differences in recruitment of participants and due to differences in the severity of the incidents that the participants experienced.

The following conclusions could be drawn from this study based on the results across all countries:

The knowledge level of the participants is not very high in general. The mean knowledge level regarding first aid knowledge and taking part in fire drills is esti-

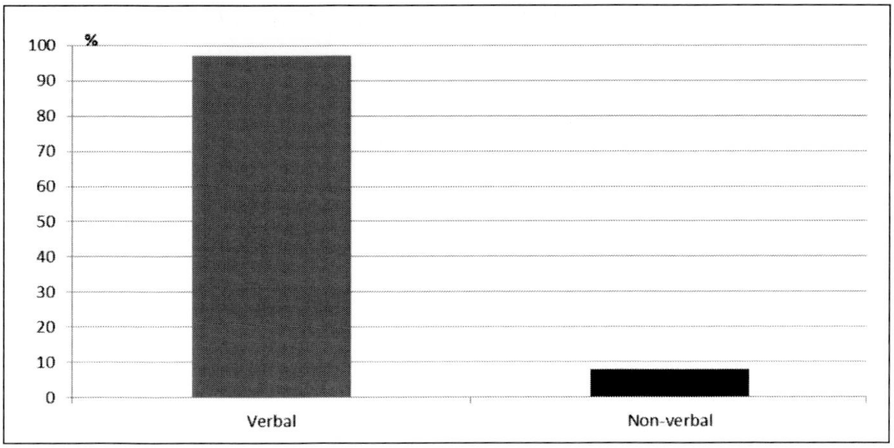

Fig. 8.31: How did you communicate with the emergency services? (N = 390)

mated around 2-2,5 on a scale from 1 (not at all) to 5 (extremely). About 30% had never participated in fire drills at school, and about 40% had never participated in fire drills at work.

The results indicate that a higher level of previous knowledge, as well as a higher level of prior experience, leads to less strong negative feelings (nervous, scared, upset, stressed) in an emergency situation. The results also indicate that people who have a higher level of previous knowledge regarding emergency situations experience a higher level of control in the emergency situation. These results show that knowledge as well as practical experience seems to help people stay calm and in control in an emergency situation.

The most common way to become aware of a domestic fire seems to be sensing environmental cues (such as smell and smoke), which alerted 90% of the people who experienced a domestic fire. Noticing others reactions and being specifically informed by someone (most often family, friends or neighbours) alerted 70% and 65% respectively. These results mean that more than 30% was not specifically informed about the incident by anyone.

However the majority, more that 80%, of the participants understood immediately that it was a fire. This is probably due to the fact that fire causes smoke and smell which in a normal situation can be perceived by most people.

About one fifth of the participants actively sought information when they understood that something was happening.

Quite a large percentage, 37%, of the people experiencing a domestic fire would have needed more information to help them respond, though there were quite large differences between the countries. Most people needed information about what they should do, the nature of the incident, or the type of threat the incident posed to them. A majority would have needed this information from the emergency services.

A majority of the participants in this study, more than 70%, communicated with the emergency services during the incident, and this communication is most often verbal.

The trust for medical service, police and fire service was a little lower after the incident than before, for the sample as a whole. However, there were variations between the countries. The reason for the difference in trust before and after the incident is not clear. The difference found in this study is however small.

According to the results from this study the following recommendations could be given:

People should be given education, theoretical as well as practical (drills), on how to manage an emergency situation. Training programs, e.g. held by emergency services, should be given in schools, pre-schools and workplaces.

People should be given the available information during an emergency. People have a need to know about what they are expected do, about the nature of the incident, and about the type of threat the incident pose to them.

9 Educational modules for professionals in crisis situations

Jordi Sans, Olga Jubany, Malin Roiha, Carles Cervera & Lola Vallès

The objective of a training module for First Responders should be to provide the tools and knowledge necessary to enable them to act appropriately in both emergency situations and dealing with victims. It should enable the FR to get a greater understanding of what social and cultural factors may influence the behaviour of victims and partners. Exercises were developed to help FR gaining experience in something that can rarely be found in real life (many victims, victims of multiple countries, victims in special situations, etc.). Furthermore situations were detected that can cause problems or unwanted effects on the psychology of the FR and learn coping techniques. Besides it is important to ensure the safety and psychological health of FR, so knowledge needs to be imparted how to manage stress and lead teams to avoid FR traumatic situations.

Regarding this a 22 hours course was designed (see Fig. 9.1), divided into 14 hours of theory lessons and 8 hours of practical sessions. The structure is set from the necessary content taught in the firefighters general training course, only in those issues regarded by the scope of the BeSeCu project. However, to complete

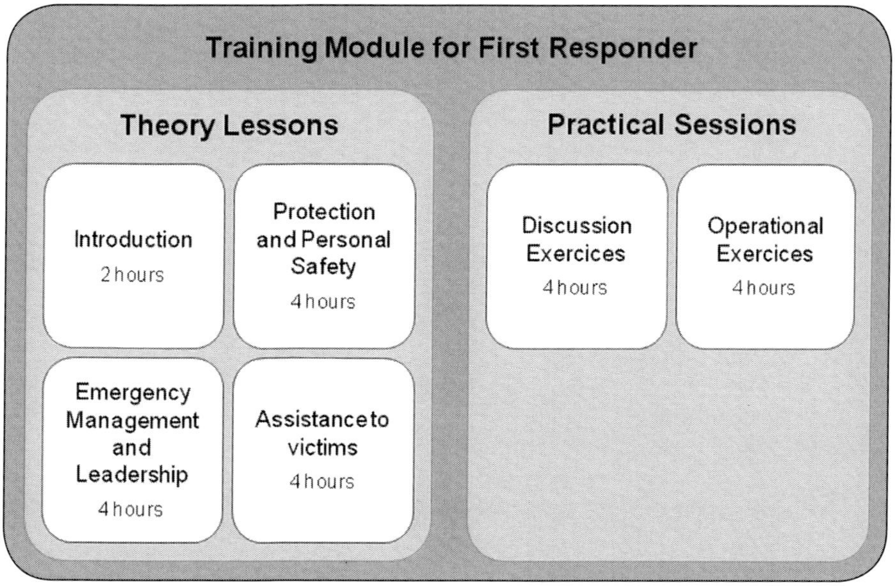

Fig. 9.1: Structure of the educational module

and provide consistence to the course, some of the parts don't have a direct reference to the project's results, although it is necessary to include them.

Depending on the type of FR it is necessary to adapt certain contents, however, it can also be done in a generic way so that different emergency services can participate at the same time.

The module is structured as follows: The theoretical part contains 14 hours of theoretical lessons, divided into 2 hours of introduction to the BeSeCu project and a 12 hours theoretical basis. The theoretical basis is divided into three lessons, four hours each, about protection and personal safety, emergency management and leadership and assistance to victims.

The practical training of eight hours aims to incorporate gradually all the knowledge and skills to be achieved at the end of the course using exercises that get more complex. Discussing exercises and an operational exercise are conducted (four hours each). The practical training should be performed after the theoretical part.

The two hours of introduction to the BeSeCu project in the beginning explain the project, its motivation, objectives, working methodology, and hypothesis. The participants and partners are presented. Findings „in general" with respect to cultural and behavioural differences among participating countries are explained, on the one hand aspects that vary considerably from one country to another and on the other hand aspects that do not vary. The aim is to explain that the different results found have been incorporated to the aspects of the syllabus which needed real and contrasted data. The lesson about protection and personal safety aims to communicate psychological risks such as the effects of stress, burn out and psychological disorders. Concerning the personality factor and discontinuity inaction-stress are highlighted. Which extreme situations do FR (RB) encounter? Which was the risk for its own life perceived by firefighters (RB)? What changes in the life of a FR (RB) can result from an extreme situation? Techniques to prevent and deal with psychological risks are discussed: How is stress usually faced (RB)? Which are the best ways to address it? Who helps FR usually (RB)? The entity about emergency management and leadership focuses on the human factor. Communication and information between performers as well as decision making, conflict resolution, leadership and emotional intelligence, team management and the psychosocial framework of an emergency are thematised. Stress management and post-traumatic stress prevention concerning team management are important points here. How good is the communication with other responders (RB)? What information sources are perceived with greater confidence? What factors influence the decisions of the FR (RB)? The third theoretical part about assistance to victims contains various units about the emergency effects on the victims, information about the psychological shock and interaction with the victims. How can victims with special need be identified? Which is the best way to interact with the victim? What factors influence the behaviour of the victims? How is the FR supposed to act? How does the victim perceive information? The practical training aims to incorporate gradually all the knowledge and skills to be achieved at the end of the course using exercises that get more complex. Practical exercises evolve in complexity and should be performed after the theoretical sessions, there should also be a final phase using specially prepared extras (performers). There are two parts: discussion exercises and operational exercises.

Discussion exercise are table top exercises to discuss coping strategies for different scenarios in a group, with a moderator and assessed by observers. And role playing between the participants exchanging the role of victim and FR. This is a conducted exercise, in group 2 times in order to exchange roles. The emergency is simulated only at the theoretical level and the performance is focused on the psychological aspect.

The operational exercise should be a realistic setting so it is possible to recreate the emergency effects. Actors are trained to simulate people's behaviour in an emergency situation using the results of the victims BeSeCu questionnaire. There ought to be observers for the evaluation afterwards. During the exercise each FR acts in accordance with the duties of his rank and organisation.

10 Conclusions

Silke Schmidt & Ed Galea

Background

Whilst witnessing in recent years a range of emergencies and disasters in Europe the following questions about human behaviour in such events gain importance: How do people react in an emergency or a disaster, and does culture have an impact on behaviour during such events? More significantly, could a better understanding of cultural responses to such events assist in developing better procedures to increase people's safety?

The project

BeSeCu (Behaviour, Security and Culture) was an investigation of cross-cultural differences of human behaviour in emergencies and disasters in order to better tailor security-related communications, instructions and procedures. The BeSeCu consortium includes researchers and SMEs, as well as first responder organisations from eight different countries. The BeSeCu group's approach to analyzing human responses is unique concerning its cross-culture scope as well as the inclusion of different emergencies and disasters.

Methods

As part of the largest, multi-stage simultaneous field study on human responses to emergencies and disasters and evacuations, expert and survivor focus groups and a cross-cultural field study with 1,130 survivors and 3,011 first responders were conducted in eight European countries with diverse cultural backgrounds. In addition, as part of the experimental component of project BeSeCu, three unannounced building evacuations were conducted in the Czech Republic, Turkey and Poland resulting in the generation of response phase data from 70, 51 and 192 people from the respective countries. This data was then compared with data from 104 individuals generated from a similar evacuation conducted previously in the UK.

Results

1. Study data enable analysis of whether culturally appropriate evacuation processes and security-related communication are required.
2. Study showed where information about occupants is necessary.
3. Information about the situation itself is crucial for occupants in order to initiate a response.
4. The study produced scientifically sound and cross-culturally validated instruments to assess survivors' behaviour in security-relevant events, i.e. emergencies and disasters (BeSeCu-S).
5. The study produced scientifically sound and cross-culturally validated instruments to assess attitudes and reactions of first responders concerning individual communication with survivors (BeSeCu-FR).
6. Two comprehensive evacuation model validation data sets were developed from the Turkish and Polish evacuation trials.
7. A set of behaviours and cognitions which are unique or differ across cultures was identified; indices for cross-cultural differences were identified, e.g. in prevention knowledge and safety culture habits.
8. The results from the experimental programme demonstrate that there are significant differences in response time distributions and differences in Response Phase parameters between all four populations.
9. BeSeCu has gathered first evidence on non-verbal communication by first responders.

Conclusions

The significant findings from BeSeCu will inform future research and developments that aim to improve communications and evacuations. The results from the BeSeCu evacuation trials suggest that the observed differences in human behaviour are the result of cultural influences on Response Phase behaviour. However, further work is required before a definitive link between social culture and evacuation behaviour can be established. The research also underlines that we have to capture the magnitude and scope of physical impact and social disruption at the community, regional, or societal level and the social significance attached to these effects on human populations. BeSeCu has also shown that individual significance is a function of past experience with and future expectations of these effects.

BeSeCu executive summary

Background

Whilst witnessing in recent years a range of emergencies and disasters in Europe (including terrorist-inspired incidents such as the Madrid train bombings in 2004, the London Underground and bus bombings in 2005, floods such as those in 2002 in Germany and the Czech Republic or earthquakes such as the Marmara earthquakes in Turkey in 1999), the following questions about human behaviour in such events gain importance: Did culture play a role in determining how people in these events responded? More significantly, could a better understanding of cultural responses to emergencies and disasters assist in developing better procedures to increase people's safety?

The project

BeSeCu (Behaviour, Security and Culture) was a cross-cultural investigation of human behaviour in emergencies and disasters in order to better tailor security-related communications, instructions and procedures and was funded by the 7th framework programme of the European Commission. The BeSeCu consortium existed of an international group of nine partners and combines the work of researchers and end-users from eight different countries.

Methods

Interviews, focus groups and a cross-cultural field study with 1,130 survivors and 3,011 first responders were conducted in eight European countries with diverse cultural backgrounds. In addition, experimental trials were carried out in countries simulating real-time evacuation scenarios in standardized settings including objective measures (e.g. response time) as outcomes as well as video-tape analysis.

Results

1. Development of a standardized international instrument to assess survivors' behaviour in security-relevant events, i.e. emergencies and disasters (BeSeCu-S)
2. Development of a standardized international instrument to assess attitudes and reactions of first responders concerning individual communication with survivors (BeSeCu-FR).
3. Informing occupants of the situation is crucial in order to initiate a response.
4. Study data enable analysis of whether culturally appropriate evacuation processes and security-related communication are required.

11 Publications from the project

Freitag, S., Grimm, A. & Schmidt, S. (2011). Talking about traumatic events: A cross-cultural investigation. *Europe's Journal of Psychology, 7 (1),* 40-61.

Galea, E.R., Deere, S.J.,Sharp, G., Filippidis, L. & Hulse, L. (2010). Investigating the Impact of Culture on Evacuation Behavior. *Proceedings of the 12th International Fire Science & Engineering Conference, Interflam 2010,* 879-892.

Galea, E.R., Sauter, M., Deere, S.J. & Filippidis, L. (2011). Investigating the Impact of Culture on Evacuation Behavior – A Turkish Data-Set. *International Association of Fire Safety Science 2011, 10,* 709-722.

Galea, E.R., Sharp, G., Sauter, M., Deere, S. & Filippidis, L. (2012). Investigating the impact of culture on evacuation behaviour – A Polish data-set. In: *Proceedings of the 5th International Symposium on Human Behaviour in Fire 2012* (pp. 62-73). London: Interscience Communications. ISBN 978-0-9556548-8-6

Grimm, A., Hulse, L., Preiss, M. Schmidt, S. (2012). Behavioural, emotional and cognitive responses in European disasters: Results of survivor interviews. Disasters: *The Journal of Disaster Studies, Policy and Management.* Accepted for publication.

Grimm, A., Hulse, L., Preiss, M. Schmidt, S. (2012) Post- and peritraumatic stress in disaster survivors: An explorative study about the influence of individual and event characteristics across different types of disasters. *European Journal of Psychotraumatology, 3,* 7382

Grimm, A., Hulse, L. & Schmidt, S. (2012) Cross-cultural pilot study on peritraumatic emotional and cognitive responses in disasters. *Europe's Journal of Psychology.*

Grimm, A., Schmidt, S. & Hulse, L. (2009). Risk perception and psychological reactions in public crisis situations using the example of terror attacks. *Bundesgesundheitsblatt – Gesundheitsforschung – Gesundheitsschutz, 52,* 1129-1140.

Hulse, L.M. & Galea, E.R. (2012). The UK BeSeCu firefighter study: A study of UK firefighters' emotional, cognitive and behavioural reactions to emergencies. In: *Proceedings of the 5th International Symposium on Human Behaviour in Fire 2012* (pp. 86-97). London: Interscience Communications. ISBN 978-0-9556548-8-6.

Kecklund, L., Petterson, S., Gabrielsson, M. (2012). Human Behaviour In Crisis Situations: A Cross-Cultural Investigation in Order to Tailor Security-Related Communication, poster. In: *Proceedings of the 5th International Symposium on Human Behaviour in Fire 2012* (p. 593). London: Interscience Communications. ISBN 978-0-9556548-8-6.

Kepka, P. (2011). *Non-verbal evacuation – to provide efficient evacuation of people. Emergency Evacuation Behavior of people from buildings* (pp. 309-316).

Knuth, D., Kehl, D., Hulse, L. & Schmidt, S. (2013). Perievent distress during fires – The impact of perceived emergency knowledge. *Journal of Environmental Psychology, 34,* 10-17.

Prati, G., Pietrantoni, L., Dabrowa, R., Wolanin, J., Kepka, P., Beltowski, G., Dobrodziej, C., Kulesza, D., Kokoszka, D., Czakis, M. & Krzeminska, A. (2012). The Semantic Specificity of Gestures in Cases in Which Verbal Communication Is Not Possible: the Case of Emergency Evacuation. *International Journal of Psychology.* Advance online publication. doi: 10.1080/00207594.2012.701750.

Prati, G., Pietrantoni, L., Saccinto, E., Kehl, D., Knuth, D. & Schmidt, S. (2012). Risk perception of different emergency situations in a sample of European firefighters. *WORK: A Journal of Prevention, Assessment, and Rehabilitation.* Advance online publication. doi: 10.3233/WOR-121543.

Preiss, M., Sotolárová, M. & Holubová, M. (2011). Trauma and Stress in 6 Years After Floods in 2002 – Experiences From the Focus Groups. *Psychiatrie, 15 (2),* 65-77.

Saccinto, E., Prati, G., Pietrantoni, L. & Pérez-Testor, C. (2013). Posttraumatic stress symptoms and posttraumatic growth among Italian survivors of emergency situations. *Journal of Loss & Trauma, 18 (3),* 210-226. DOI:10.1080/15325024.2012.687321

Schmidt, S., Knuth, D. & Kehl, D. (2011). Human behavior in crisis situations: A field study of fire fighters and survivors across different types of disaster situations. In: W. Jaskolowski & P. Kepka (Eds.), *Emergency evacuation of people from buildings.* Warszawa: BEL Studio Sp. z o.o.

Vallés, L. & Roiha, M. (2012). Revista Catalana de Seguridad Pública. *Journal of the ISPC, 25.*

Planned publications

Cervera, C. & Vallés, L. (2012). Book Collection of the ISPC *"Segments de Seguretat".*

Feuerherd, M., Knuth, D., Mühlan, H. & Schmidt, S. *Differential Item Functioning (DIF). Analyses of the Impact of Event Scale Revised (IES-R).* Manuscript is submitted for publication.

Galea, E.R. *Evacuation model validation data sets derived from the BeSeCu evacuation trials.* Manuscript is going to be submitted for publication.

Galea, E.R. *Evacuation response phase behavior.* Manuscript is going to be submitted for publication.

Galea, E.R. *Investigating the impact of culture on evacuation behavior (cross-cultural comparison).* Manuscript is going to be submitted for publication.

Hulse, L. & Galea, E. *An analysis of UK firefighters' reactions to emergencies.* Manuscript is going to be submitted for publication.

Hulse, L. & Galea, E. *An overview of a UK survey of firefighters' and survivors' responses to emergencies.* Manuscript is going to be submitted for publication.

Hulse, L. Galea, E., Vallés, L., Roiha, M. & Cervera, C. *A comparison of survivor experiences from the 7/7 London and 11-M Madrid train bombings.* Manuscript is going to be submitted for publication.

Hulse, L. & Grimm, A. *An interpretative phenomenological analysis of survivors' experiences in the 7/7 London bombings.* Manuscript is going to be submitted for publication.

Kehl, D., Knuth, D. & BeSeCu-Team. *Advancing disaster relief: Development of a self-report questionnaire for firefighters.* Manuscript is submitted for publication.

Knuth, D., Kehl, D. & BeSeCu-Team. *BeSeCu-S – A self-report instrument for emergency survivors.* Manuscript is submitted for publication.

Kehl, D., Knuth, D., Hulse, L. & Schmidt, S. *Postraumatic reactions among firefighters after critical incidents – cross-national data.* Manuscript is submitted for publication

Kehl, D., Knuth, D., Hulse, L. & Schmidt, S. *Predictors of symptomatic stress symptoms and posttraumatic growth among firefighters after work-related emergencies – a cross-national study.* Manuscript is submitted for publication.

Kehl, D., Knuth, D., Holubova, M. & Schmidt, S. *Relationship between firefighters' posttraumatic growth and PTSD symptoms at different times post trauma.* Manuscript is submitted for publication.

Knuth, D., Kehl, D., Galea, E., Hulse, L., Schmidt, S. *Safety knowledge and Preparedness in Europe – A comparison between different nationalities.* Manuscript is going to be submitted for publication.

Knuth, D., Kehl, D., Hulse, L., Schmidt, S. *Risk perception, real risk and experience: A cross national study with European emergency survivors.* Manuscript is submitted for publication.

Knuth, D., Kehl, D., Preiss, M., Holubova M., Bełtowski, G., Wolanin, J., Schmidt, S. *Posttraumatic growth in flood survivors – A cross-national comparison.* Manuscript is going to be submitted for publication.

Knuth, D., Kehl, D., Spangenberg, L., Hulse, L., Brähler, E. & Schmidt, S. *Risk perception and disaster experience: comparing a representative German sample with German disaster survivors.* Manuscript is submitted for publication.

Preiss, M., Knuth, D., Kehl, D. & Schmidt, S. *Survivors of domestic fires – influence of demographical, cultural and situational characteristics on later traumatic symptoms – cross-cultural study.* Manuscript is submitted for publication.

Schmidt, S. *A cross-cultural analysis of survivors' behaviour in domestic fires.* Manuscript is going to be submitted for publication.

Vallés, L. & Roiha, M. (2012). Posttraumatic stress in emergency situations. *Psychology International.*

12 Affiliation of authors

Ernst-Moritz-Arndt-Universität Greifswald (EMAUG) –
Coordinating Centre
since January 1st, 2009

Prof. Dr. Silke Schmidt
Project Coordinator
Department Health and Prevention
Robert-Blum-Str. 13
17487 Greifswald
Germany
Phone +49 3834 863800
Fax +49 3834 863801
silke.schmidt@uni-greifswald.de

Daniela Knuth, Psychologist
project manager, researcher survivor
Doris Kehl/Charlotte Auer,
Psychologist
researcher first responder
Dieter Rhode, Psychologist
project management assistant
Pinar Kücükbalaban, Psychologist
research assistant
Tim Rostalski, Psychologist
research assistant statistics
Katrin Stegemann
administrative staff

Student assistance for transcription, statistics and project management:
Katja Kallies, Nicole Schlundt, Michael Feuerherd

University of Greenwich (UoG)

Prof. Ed Galea, Principal Investigator
School of Computing and
Mathematical Sciences
University of Greenwich
Old Royal Naval College
30 Park Row
Greenwich SE10 9LS
London UK
Phone +44 20 8331 8730
Fax +44 20 8331 8925
e.r.galea@gre.ac.uk

Dr. Lynn Hulse
Gary Sharp

SZKOLA GLOWNA SLUZBY POZARNICZEJ, Warsaw, Poland
MAIN SCHOOL OF FIRE SERVICE (SGSP)

Prof. Jerzy Wolanin
Pro-Rector for Science, Education
and Students' Affairs, Deputy
The Main School of Fire Service (SGSP)
Faculty of Fire Safety Engineering
Slowackiego 52/54
01-629 Warsaw
Poland
Phone +48 22 5617777
Fax +48 22 5617777
jerzy.wolanin@sgsp.edu.pl

Gen. Ryszard Dabrowa
Rector-Commandant of SGSP –
Legal authority
Grzegorz Beltowski
Coordinator of the project at SGSP

Cezary Dobrodziej,
Psychologist, field study
Dorota Kokoszka,
Psychologist, field study
PhD. Pawel Kepka,
Coordinator of non-verbal communication
Adriana Krzeminska,
administrative staff
Agnieszka Chotomska,
assisting personnel
Ewa Szostak,
assisting personnel
Marcin Cisek,
involved in non-verbal communication
Financial department representatives

Ambulance and Emergency Physicians Association (AAHD)

Dr. M. Turhan Sofuoglu MD
Association of Emergency Ambulance Physicians
Hurriyet Bulvari 1
35210 Izmir
Turkey
Phone +90 505 5645565
turhans112@yahoo.com

Zeynep Baskaya Sofuoglu MD
Yucel H Koyukan MD
R. Tolga Olcucu MD
Hakan Keskin MD
Atalay Kabakcıoglu MD
Ismail Umit Bal MD
Halil Nadas Financial Advisor

Psychiatricke Centrum Praha (PPC)

Dr. Marek Preiss
(Principal investigator)
Prague Psychiatric Centre
University of Prague
Ustavni 91
18103 Prague
Czech Republic
Phone +42 266 003 338
Fax +42 266 003 337
preiss@pcp.lf3.cuni.cz

Marie Sotolářová
Markéta Holubová
Karolína Řípová
Alexandr Borovička, Economist, PPC

MTO SÄKERHET/MTO SAFETY (MTO)

Lena Kecklund, Ph.D. – project leader
Man-Technology-Organisation (MTO) Psychology
Hornsbruksgatan 28
11734 Stockholm
Sweden
Phone +46 8 53525950
lena.kecklund@mto.se

Sara Petterson B.Sc., researcher
Kristin Andrée B.Sc., researcher
Marcus Arvidsson Ph.D., researcher
Maria Gabrielsson,
statistics specialist

Landesfeuerwehrschule Hamburg
Hamburg Fire and Emergency Service Academy (HFESA)

Frank Seidler
(coordinator and contact person of HFESA and the fire department Hamburg)
Feuerwehrakademie Hamburg
Bredowstraße 4
22113 Hamburg
Germany
Phone +49 40 428514511
Fax +49 40 428514518
frank.seidler@feuerwehr-hamburg.de

Wolfgang Lindner, Principal of HFESA
Eberhard Diebe, advisor for specific questions regarding to fire and rescue service
Several employees of the Hamburg Fire Department

Institut de Seguretat Pública de Catalunya (ISPC)

Jordi Sans (Fire engineer),
Project coordinator
Institute of Public Safety of Catalonia
Crta. C-17 km13,5
08100 Mollet del Vallès
Spain
Phone +34 93 5675079
josans@gencat.net

Lola Vallès, Social Anthropologist main investigator
Gloria Morera,
official/research assistant
Isabel Serra,
official/managing assistant
Malin Roiha, Research staff
Carles Cervera, Research staff

Alma Mater Studiorum Universita Di Bologna (UNIBO)

Prof. Luca Pietrantoni
(Associate Professor)
Department of Education
„Giovanni Maria Bertin"
Via Filippo Re, 6
40126 Bologna
Italy
Phone +39 051 2091610
Fax +39 051 2091489
luca.pietrantoni@unibo.it

Dr. Gabriele Prati,
Researcher and Psychologist
Elisa Saccinto, Psychologist
Alice Papi, Master Student